MODERNIST IDEALISM

Modernist Idealism

Ambivalent Legacies of German Philosophy in Italian Literature

MICHAEL J. SUBIALKA

UNIVERSITY OF TORONTO PRESS
Toronto Buffalo London

Toronto Buffalo London
utorontopress.com

ISBN 978-1-4875-2865-2 (cloth)
ISBN 978-1-4875-2868-3 (EPUB)
ISBN 978-1-4875-2867-6 (PDF)

Toronto Italian Studies

Library and Archives Canada Cataloguing in Publication

Title: Modernist idealism : ambivalent legacies of German philosophy in Italian literature / Michael J. Subialka.
Names: Subialka, Michael, author.
Series: Toronto Italian studies.
Description: Series statement: Toronto Italian studies | Includes bibliographical references and index.
Identifiers: Canadiana (print) 20210228229 | Canadiana (ebook) 20210228482 | ISBN 9781487528652 (cloth) | ISBN 9781487528683 (EPUB) | ISBN 9781487528676 (PDF)
Subjects: LCSH: Italian literature – 19th century – History and criticism. | LCSH: Italian literature – 20th century – History and criticism. | LCSH: Italian literature – German influences. | LCSH: Philosophy, German – 19th century. | LCSH: Idealism, German – Italy. | LCSH: Literature – Philosophy. | LCSH: Modernism (Literature) – Italy. | LCSH: Italy – Intellectual life.
Classification: LCC PQ4033 .S83 2022 | DDC 850.9/007 – dc23

This book is freely available in an open access edition thanks to TOME (Toward an Open Monograph Ecosystem) – a collaboration of the Association of American Universities, the Association of University Presses, and the Association of Research Libraries – and the generous support of University of California, Davis. Learn more at the TOME website, available at: openmonographs.org.

University of Toronto Press acknowledges the financial assistance to its publishing program of the Canada Council for the Arts and the Ontario Arts Council, an agency of the Government of Ontario.

Canada Council for the Arts
Conseil des Arts du Canada

Funded by the Government of Canada
Financé par le gouvernement du Canada

To my parents, Carol and Joe, who have encouraged me in all my intellectual endeavors, even the most extravagant ones, with unconditional love.

Contents

Acknowledgments

Modernist Idealism is the product of what feels like almost too many years of thinking and rethinking, writing and rewriting. While it takes as its point of departure the work published in my dissertation, *The Aesthetics of Ambivalence: Pirandello, Schopenhauer, and the Transformation of the European Social Imaginary*, which was supported by the Dolores Liebmann Fellowship, my book was shaped by subsequent years of travel and research in Asia, Europe, and now back in the United States. As I expanded the scope of my project, I also accumulated a great debt to many interlocutors who have helped me develop my perspective. I can hardly do them all justice here, and I fear that many generous colleagues, students, and friends who provided stimulating feedback at various conferences, seminars, roundtables, and even some very good dinners will go unnamed. All the same, I would be remiss not to thank them (even if only as a whole). And of course, among these unnamed interlocutors pride of place goes to the generous and thoughtful feedback I received from the three anonymous reviewers who read and commented on my manuscript.

Guides and companions have offered sage advice and support all along the way. My passion for literature and philosophy was ignited by wonderful mentors at the University of Notre Dame, especially Ed Manier, Christian Moevs, Colleen Ryan, Kristin Shrader-Frechette, and John Welle. Likewise, I will always remain tremendously grateful for the inspiration and gentle direction of Thomas Pavel, Rebecca West, Armando Maggi, and David Wellbery at the University of Chicago; likewise, to Justin Steinberg's friendly and reliable advice I owe much. Agnes Malinowska helped me cultivate my passion for literature and philosophy. To Hannah Mosher, who has been there every step of the way, I can only say I really don't think I would have survived six years without your friendship, support, and introduction to occult retro-Victorian cloning conspiracies; likewise, my knowledge of the inner truths of idealism would be incomplete without your frightening insight into philosophical vampirism.

During my fleeting moment in Turkey, I was fortunate to meet many engaging colleagues at Bilkent University, and positively blessed to discover my star-crossed academic partner in (MPE) crime whose feats of poetic boating I shall never match – though at least we'll always have an Ocean Winner, I assume. Jennifer Reimer, you taught me everything I know about keşke.

At St Hugh's College, I was very fortunate to benefit from the support of the Powys Roberts Research Fellowship in modern languages, and without the time and space it provided this project would never have developed as it did. To Giuseppe Stellardi, in particular, I am most grateful, as I am to the many fellows in the College who provided intellectual companionship – and especially Matt, Nadja, Dora, Bruce, Damian, and surprise Pirandello fanboy, Tom. My colleagues from across Oxford were magnificent sources of inspiration, collegial support, and vibrant new connections and directions: to all of them, and especially to Ela Tandello and Nicola Gardini, thank you. Alberica Bazzoni has been a brilliant collaborator. Clare Hills-Nova, as insightful as she is fashionable, and Oren Margolis, as scholarly as he is witty, will no doubt be disappointed in the lack of sartorial textuality here – I am sorry. Ziyaad Bhorat, who played the role of ringmaster provocateur extraordinaire for days-long discussions in a house of Rhodes Scholars, knows what he's done.

At my new academic home in UC Davis I have been no less fortunate in terms of the intellectual companionship and support that I have received from countless colleagues and friends. Margherita Heyer-Caput has been an ideal interlocutor, and I have learned much from her work on modernism as well as from her passion for everything that she does. Brenda Schildgen, your warm welcome and generous mentorship have been essential. Julia Simon, Jeff Fort, and Joshua Clover have all been valuable mentors and guides. My research assistant, Jiyuan Ren, provided important help sifting through Japanese titles and tracing down connections. And a thank you to all of my students, particularly those from my Literature, Philosophy, and the Arts seminar who read an earlier translation of De Sanctis's dialogue. Last but certainly not least, Diana Aramburu, whose friendship is invaluable, whose feedback is pointed and smart, and whose collaboration in all things has meant the world – thank you.

Along the way I have also benefited from the support and generosity of colleagues across the world, from Dina Saponaro and Lucia Torsello who kindly guided me through the archives at the Istituto di Studi Pirandelliani in Rome, to the generous and insightful scholars who read versions of chapters or suffered through them as presentations and still kindly provided feedback and ideas: Alessio Baldini, Tom Harrison, Lucia Re, Elisa Segnini, Gigliola Sulis, Kelly Walsh, John Welle, Laura Wittman, and so many more. Lisa Sarti has been a source of great inspiration and collaboration, and without her help co-editing the journal of the Pirandello Society of America it would have been difficult to find the time to finish this book. And I am tremendously grateful for the support and know-how of Mark Thompson and Robin Studniberg at the University of Toronto Press; the brilliant editorial work of Matthew Kudelka, who has done much to improve the manuscript; and the support of Michael Ladisch and UC Davis Library's TOME Open Access fund, which is making this volume possible.

Last and most important, I am deeply thankful for the love and support of my family and friends who have provided input essential not so much for the content of the book as for the character of its author. Carol and Joe, Terri and Rick, Kathy and Jeff, Karen and Adam, and everyone else (you know who you are): thank you for helping raise me to be a curious thinker. Teresa and Kelly have earned their weight in gold for not just their love but their patience. Carlos, of course, gets pride of place for reminding me not to dwell in the clouds of the ideal too long, but understanding me all the same when I do (often enough). After all, what is the ideal without love? And you are the love of my life.

MODERNIST IDEALISM

Introduction: Modernist Idealism Revitalizing Italy

We spoke of Italy, the painful one, we spoke of our sacrifice, our blood, of the desperate days and our undefeated hope. Do you remember? I suddenly saw two vivid teardrops flowing from your stranger's eyes. And then I recognized you as a brother; and my heart opened.

– Gabriele d'Annunzio to Shimoi Harukichi, *La guerra italiana* (1919)[1]

The "brotherhood" evoked in this poetic pronouncement spans what appear to be two profoundly different cultures, removed from each other not least of all by half the distance of the globe. It is a striking assertion made by the Italian poet-warrior of the First World War, Gabriele d'Annunzio, to his foreign "brother"-in-arms, the Japanese literary and cultural figure Harukichi Shimoi, who had moved to Naples in 1915 to become a lecturer in Japanese at the Royal Oriental Institute (then called the Regio Istituto Orientale, now the Università degli Studi di Napoli "L'Orientale"). Shimoi reproduced the letter as a preface to his 1919 memoirs of the Great War, *The Italian War* (*La guerra italiana*), authorizing his text with an homage from the nation's most famous war hero. More than an authorizing gesture, though, this document is also a window into the unexpected literary-political transnationalism of a fervently nationalist moment, not only in Italy but also in Japan. It raises questions that cut to the heart of how we understand modernity and modernism as a perhaps conflicting confluence of artistic and political ideals.

Shimoi's (1883–1954) participation in the Great War, and his subsequent encounter with D'Annunzio (1863–1938), were motivated by his idea that to foster national renewal in a modernizing Japan it was necessary to mobilize the youth around a spiritual ideal of the nation. He thus pursued literary and artistic means of inculcating that national spirit. He saw Italy as a model in this regard, believing that Italian nationalism and the popular embrace of war had been spurred by the cultural politics of artists like the Futurists and D'Annunzio. His goal in writing *La guerra italiana* was to become part of the literary-artistic action spurring national renewal in a way that would bring together Japan and Italy, forging a bond based in what he perceived as their shared trajectory leading from a relatively "late" experience of modernization to a national spiritual reinvigoration that could compensate for that lateness.[2]

This international bond and reception highlights a set of key dynamics at the heart of my study: modernization entails a political push to renew the nation, one that seeks to use political action to realize what is seen as a spiritual ideal; at the same time, this political ambition is tethered to a complex artistic stance on life that is resonant with decadent aestheticism yet simultaneously embodies the vitalist impulse of avant-garde artistic production. What we see, in other words, is a complex set of relations holding various modernist forces in orbit around a shared commitment to the project to redefine art and the world in terms of a new notion of the ideal. Literature and philosophy, politics and art, all come together in an effort to revitalize and reshape actual reality by infusing it with a spirit that will transform modern life.

D'Annunzio and Shimoi, Italy and Japan: A Case of Modernist Idealism

The relationship between Italy and Japan crystallized in the complex interactions of D'Annunzio and Shimoi is an ideal starting place to articulate these dynamics. Indeed, D'Annunzio was a well-suited spiritual "brother," given Shimoi's interests. A national war hero, D'Annunzio had gone so far as to lead his own military expedition after the end of the Great War, capturing the city of Fiume (now known by its Croatian name of Rijeka) and declaring an Italian regency that linked national revitalization with his modernist aesthetics (la Reggenza Italiana del Carnaro, 12 September 1919–12 November 1920). His brash defiance of the Treaty of Versailles only further solidified his status as a nationalist hero; as John Woodhouse has nicely observed, D'Annunzio's invasion and regency had a staged and almost literary aesthetic quality to them.[3] Shimoi participated in that expedition personally and reported on the new city-state under the warrior-poet's rule, recognizing in it a model for the fusion between aesthetic principles and the political will to reshape and revitalize the nation.[4]

Shimoi played a significant role in the popularization of D'Annunzio in Japan, but he also benefited from a broader surge of interest in the Italian writer. In fact, from the early twentieth century on, D'Annunzio's literary work was received as a part of the new fascination with the art of European decadence that Japanese modernization and Westernization stimulated. D'Annunzio's reception in Japan thus serves as a window into the paradoxically transnational dimension of the confluence of artistic culture and politics that became a part of burgeoning Japanese nationalism. The Japanese interest in European *décadence* and Italian *decadentismo* took off in the early 1900s, and starting as early as 1901, D'Annunzio's works were beginning to circulate in Japanese translations, particularly by two pupils of Natsume Sōseki: Morita Sōhei and Ikuta Chōkō. In 1909, Ishikawa Gian published a translation of the third of D'Annunzio's trilogy of decadent novels, *Triumph of Death* (*Trionfo della morte*, 1894; translated as *Shi no shōri*), in the journal *Subaru*, which was at the forefront of the Europeanization of Japanese literature.[5] So even before Shimoi left home for Naples, D'Annunzio's literary fame was on the rise. And Shimoi was hardly the only person to see D'Annunzio as a model for aesthetic fascism; a much more prominent writer, Yukio Mishima (1925–1970), admired D'Annunzio greatly and helped popularize him by adapting some of his theatrical works in his own plays.[6] Thus while the initial reception in the early 1900s was focused on his decadent literary style, D'Annunzio became famous especially as a persona, a poet-warrior whose bold action and fierce nationalism represented a confluence of aesthetic and political aims that aligned with the fascist outlook of figures like Mishima and with the project of Japanese modernization in the years leading up to the Second World War.[7] Both a poetic inspiration and a fascist-nationalist hero, D'Annunzio appealed to the fusion of aesthetic and political aims integral to the modernist project.[8]

The Japanese interest in D'Annunzio and in decadence is only one part of a much broader turn toward Europe that constituted a driving force in the Meiji push to modernize. The Meiji modernization project redesigned Japanese education, modelling the study of specific subject areas directly on the education systems of particular Western powers. The reception of D'Annunzio's decadence coincided with a broad turn in Japan toward German idealist philosophy: German professors were imported to teach it (in German, which students were required to learn); the best Japanese students were then sent to Germany to complete their studies so that they could return and teach their compatriots.[9] Japan had determined that to forge a modern nation, it would be necessary to borrow and replicate European systems and ideas. The growing prominence of German idealist thought thus coincided with a nation-building effort in a way that was paradoxically both transnational and nationalist.

I highlight this transnational nationalism because, as I will argue throughout this book, that same dynamic is likewise a hallmark of the Italian reception of German idealist thought, one that similarly spanned aesthetics and politics. In both Italy and Japan, foreign models were received and domesticated so as to bring them into wider circulation and to mobilize them as part of nation-building efforts; those same models also established a narrative meant to situate these relatively young and marginal nations as part of the intellectual trajectory of the modernized West. However, the transnational formation of a modernist sensibility in Italy and Japan was not solely one-way; in fact, the process was bidirectional and spoke to an interactive systems model of exchange. After the fabled "opening of Japan" by Commodore Perry's fleet of Black Ships, which arrived in Edo Bay in 1853, not only Italy but all of Europe and America were swept by an artistic and commercial fascination with Japanese goods. In the artistic sphere, this developed into *Japonisme* and *Japonaiserie,* a fetishized interest in Japanese art (especially woodcut prints but also textiles and artefacts of all types) and Orientalized images of an exotic, alternative world.[10] While Dutch traders had previously given Europe access to some Japanese artefacts, after the finalization of trade treaties in 1858 there was a new permeation of this "alternative" to what were increasingly seen as stagnating aesthetic forms in the traditional (academic) European visual arts. Artists responded to the influx of Japanese models in a variety of ways that aligned with the avant-garde reimagining of artistic representation, including by adopting strategies of "asymmetry, broad areas of color and pattern, expressive stylized lines, abstraction, and emphasis on the flatness of the picture plane."[11] This movement to renovate Western art through contact with the Orientalized other swept across Europe between the 1850s and World War I, with at least seventeen major exhibitions in cities ranging from London, Paris, Vienna, and Amsterdam to Nuremberg and Glasgow, not to mention American cities including Philadelphia, Chicago, St. Louis, Seattle, and San Francisco.[12] From Monet and Manet to Van Gogh – and far beyond – *Japonisme* offered a way of renovating artistic production.[13] The same force was likewise felt in literature: the decadent writers reacted to the new stylization of *Japonisme* by integrating it into their "imaginary museum" of anti-traditionalism in a process that Pamela Genova has termed the "aesthetic translation" of this visual impulse into a written one.[14] And while Genova focuses on the French case, I would add that D'Annunzio likewise partook in that aesthetic translation, first engaging the refined aestheticism of *Japonisme* in his journalistic and decadent works and then turning toward a model of Japan as a modernizing military nation in his later writings.[15] As Christopher Reed has brilliantly argued, the veritable cult of interest in Japan served not only to enlarge and transform the visual and literary imagination but also to combat what we might now call the mentality of toxic masculinity in the mainstream European social imaginary: Japan offered a way of rewriting masculinity, just as *Japonisme* promised to upend traditional models in the arts.[16]

The Europe–Japan and D'Annunzio–Japan relationships are thus both bi-directional, pairing aesthetic with social and political aims. Meiji artists of the period were influenced by Western models just as their contemporaries in Europe were altering their art thanks to *Japonisme,* and this "mutual influence" can be read in the production of "surprising and unique 'hybrid' artefacts."[17] Likewise, the Japanese fascination with D'Annunzio, both aesthetic and political, is mirrored in D'Annunzio's dual-faceted aesthetic and military-political interest in Japan. What holds both of these relationships together, I contend, is a shared effort to generate an aesthetics of spiritual renewal that can pair with the modernizing push toward national renewal. Though these two "poles" may not always align, it is clear that at both an artistic and political level these artists were responding to the perceived limits of traditional forms as well as to the stultifying forces of what they conceived as modern materialism – whether of a crass capitalist sort or of a revolutionary Marxian sort. In the view of transformative figures like D'Annunzio and Shimoi, modernization requires an accompanying intellectual, artistic, and spiritual push to reshape the nation around an organizing ideal – a revitalization of the spirit.

If Italy and Japan shared the status of marginal and developing modernities in contrast to the already industrialized Continent, this perhaps helps us understand the special brotherhood that D'Annunzio suggested in his letter to Shimoi. Both artist-revolutionaries sought to reshape their modernizing nations and to craft a national spirit through aesthetic means. Both, in other words, were modernists. Modernism as a philosophical-literary-political project thus represents an effort not just to modernize but to offer another source or foundation for the modernizing impulse, to reground modernization in the realm of the ideal as opposed to the material. It is this sort of modernism that will be the subject of my study, and opening with the example of an unexpected exchange between a Japanese poet-translator-educator and Italy's most famous war hero and poet is thus doubly fitting: on the one hand, it indicates the paradoxical transnational nationalism of this modernist moment, an aspect of the Italian case that I will argue is paradigmatic of a broader trend; simultaneously, it highlights how seemingly separate aesthetic and political commitments in fact have a common grounding in the project of what I will term modernist idealism.[18]

Modernism, Idealism, and Modernist Idealism

The Japanese interest in D'Annunzio calls our attention to several key questions that have faced scholars in recent years – questions at the core of my analysis in this book. The new global direction in modernist studies has led to shifts in how we understand modernism and to a renewed debate about how best to approach its comparative study. One way of approaching that global comparative study is through the lens of reception and historical networks or nodes connecting various figures from different contexts; another is to think of modernism conceptually and to build a theoretical lexicon allowing us to see family resemblances in writers, artists, and thinkers from various contexts. Both approaches have been used fruitfully, and both are active components of what I undertake here.

Italian modernism, I contend, offers an excellent case for studying the ways in which a series of conflicting impulses overlap and find expression in the outlook and form of modernist production: at once nationalist and simultaneously cosmopolitan, transnational, and global, the modernist texts I examine here help us understand not only Italy's place in the sphere of global modernism but also how the dynamics of the transnational and the national play out against each other in the modernist imagination. At the same time, modernist writers and thinkers embrace conflicting approaches to fostering national and cultural renewal, as a function of how they blend political action and artistic transformation. What unifies these seemingly diverse approaches is ultimately the foundational role of an idealist philosophical stance.

The Meaning of Modernism

It is a feature of our current scholarship that any study employing the term modernism will take as its unavoidable point of departure a consideration of how to understand that slippery key term. One prominent framework views modernism as a historical "period" exhibiting particular styles or defined by networks of relationships among modernist authors and texts; this framework has a long presence in the critical tradition, beginning in the modernist era itself.[19] The modernists, in this view, were a group of authors and artists who responded to the changed conditions – artistic, social, economic, political – of a specific historical modernity through experimental shifts in the forms of representation that challenged earlier traditions. The idea of modernism as an anti-traditional heresy, a rejection of coherence and continuity, an engagement with purposeful difficulty, or a shift in aesthetic paradigms away from realist representation toward abstraction or self-reflective materiality are all versions of this view, which focuses on the historical emergence of a paradigm shared by some group of writers, artists, and thinkers responding to modernity's challenges.[20]

This type of historical framework for modernism developed largely out of the study of English literature and has long retained something of a penchant for anglophone writing, even as its scope has widened beyond Britain and her empire. In recent years, however, the advent of the new modernist studies has challenged these constraints, calling for a shift toward a more global outlook. Even if the focus is still predominantly on anglophone production – likely a result of contingent factors, including the location of most modernist studies faculty in English departments – the widened scope of the new modernist studies has forced a reckoning with many of the assumptions built into a historically periodizing approach to the notion of modernism. The spatial expansion of modernist studies as it has become global in scope has likewise entailed a temporal expansion rooted in the recognition that modernity is not singular but plural: there are multiple modernities in different places and times.[21]

The challenge arising from this double expansion has been how to articulate a more historically flexible understanding of modernism, one that responds to that multiplicity of experiences of modernity. Scholars have pursued various strategies in this regard. One has been to build comparative compendiums of various modernist moments, thus reflecting (to some extent) Wittgenstein's notion of a family resemblance holding together different but in some ways overlapping modernist figures from across historical moments and geographical locations. Recent volumes of this sort, which have assembled a truly global collection of scholarship on modernism, include the *Oxford Handbook of Global Modernisms* (2012) and *The Cambridge History of Modernism* (2016), both of which aim for global representation and the articulation of shared or overlapping paradigms of modernist form through the juxtaposition of these global instances of the term. The editors of the *Oxford Handbook* go so far as to insist that the global turn in criticism requires a rethinking of disciplinary approaches, a shift away from the model of national literatures toward that of comparative literature.[22] A whole host of publications in the new modernist studies attest to similar efforts to broaden the scope of modernism to a global or planetary scale, examining not only direct exchange (influence, networks, etc.) but also conceptual or family resemblances through a comparative look at modernity in its varied forms.[23]

It thus makes sense that a related approach has emerged from the new modernist studies, one that aims less at encompassing and juxtaposing the full geographical extent of modernism and more at drawing on instances in order to articulate a conceptual vocabulary of various forms, strategies, and issues that recur and, together, fill out an always incomplete notion of what modernism is. Perhaps the most notable of these interventions is Eric Hayot and Rebecca Walkowitz's volume, *A New Vocabulary for Global Modernism*, which understands modernism as singular despite the multiplicity of global sites that interface with specific local histories. They write:

> Weakly defined, fluid, internally differentiated, this modernism is nonetheless singular, we claim, insofar as it corresponds to a set of historical circumstances that have not happened exactly this way before and that have carried in their wake a variety of social changes (capitalism, secularization, modernity) that, for now, seem to define a period and a state of affairs. We imagine modernism to be a reaction to the various points of intersection between that state of affairs and the local conditions of its production.[24]

Here the notion of modernism as a period is maintained even while it is made multiple by the different trajectories leading specific localities to interface with the conditions of modernity – forces such as capitalism and secularization. The entries in their vocabulary thus speak to a multiplicity of such interactions, delineating what they suggest is a first set of key concepts that will invite the development of further terms that need to become a part of the lexicon with which we approach global modernism.[25] The concept of modernist idealism that I develop in this book takes up that invitation, adding a key notion that emerges both in particular localities – as in my case study of Italy's relation to a specific German philosophical tradition – and in a way that links localities together not only across Europe but also beyond, as evidenced by the Japanese interest in D'Annunzio.

My study engages Hayot and Walkowitz's method, which is to fuse a periodized understanding of modernity with a conceptual vocabulary highlighting commonalities that unite the diverse locations of modernist responses to the conditions of modernity. Like theirs, my examination of modernist idealism locates modernism in the historical moment of a particular form of modernity. At the same time, though, it articulates a conceptual response to that moment that has the potential to speak more broadly, thus locating a way in which philosophical thought and literary form support each other in an attempt to reconfigure the experience of modern loss and to revitalize an experience of modern deadness. In this respect, my project draws on the approach recently articulated by Vincent Sherry, for whom modernism is not a specific form or network but rather "the expression of a sensibility, the practice of an attitude, and ... a particular (if diversely manifested) state of artistic and cultural mind."[26] This notion of a cultural mind aligns with the artistic/cultural side of what Charles Taylor has called a "social imaginary," and I would contend that it points us in the direction of investigating how concepts (philosophical ideas) take on artistic form and are thus realized – brought into actuality as elements of a functioning social imaginary.[27] The specificity of that particular cultural mind as Sherry understands it is rooted in modernism being a response to crisis time: modernism, in his view, is the self-aware aesthetic response to the experience of loss and newness that characterizes the temporal moment of rupture that delineates a modern "now" from a receding past against which that "now" is defined.[28] While he focuses on the moment of late nineteenth- and early twentieth-century artistic production, implicit in Sherry's logic here is the sense that these temporal dynamics may find related responses in other moments.[29]

My notion of modernist idealism engages a similar dynamic: the specific authors and texts that I examine fit into the historical moment of nineteenth- and early twentieth-century modernization; nevertheless, just as Sherry's definition of modernism theoretically extends beyond that specific historical period to any moment of crisis defined by the experience of temporality he outlines, so too can this concept of modernist idealism be extended to other moments in the elaboration of an idealist outlook that responds to such ruptures. What I trace are ultimately the contours of a particular form of cultural mind or social imaginary that has practical actuality as the artistic or aesthetic realization of an idealist philosophical world view.

The Meaning of Idealism

The moment of perceived historical crisis at the opening of the twentieth century in Italy reverberated with calls to restore (or create) a governing ideal that could shape and animate a supposedly degenerate nation, one whose historical promise had never been realized. Indeed, during the Risorgimento itself there was already a strong sense that pushing the political project of unification required some form of idealism. Thinkers in the Hegelian tradition, such as Bertrando Spaventa (1817–1883) and Francesco De Sanctis (1817–1883), combined philosophical idealism with a political project of revolution and renewal. This Hegelian impact on modern Italian nation-building continues to be a major focus for scholarship, with a special issue of the *Journal of Modern Italian Studies* dedicated to it in 2019: "Hegel in Italy: Risorgimento Political Thought in Transnational Perspective" (vol. 24, no. 2, 2019). Meanwhile, Italian political idealists could themselves take on world-historical importance, as indicated by a political hero like Giuseppe Mazzini (1805–1872), the lynchpin of the liberal side of the Risorgimento movement. Mazzini sought to establish a new political idealism to both reinvigorate and reground the Italian project.[30] This vision of Mazzini as propagator of an idealist national project even became the topic of an anthropological study by an American scholar writing in 1900, who concluded that "Mazzini was … an idealist who was at the same time a man of action."[31]

As this assertion indicates, and as my brief overview of the "idealist" project of unification suggests, the span of the word "idealist" can indeed be quite wide. It entails a specific reception of idealist philosophy and political theory as well as a broader stance and outlook seeking to structure lived life and the actual world by means of a governing idea, or to see actuality as itself constituting the idea in some form.[32] It can span from Mazzini's unifying liberalism, defined by a "religion" of altruism against the prevailing (base) forces of individualism,[33] to a proto-fascist vision of the strong state that offers a higher ideal than the "animality" of individualist materialism that limits national unity – a view advocated by Alfredo Oriani in his *The Ideal Revolt* (*La rivolta ideale*, 1908).[34] And while the most studied node of idealist thought in the Italian context has surely been the reception of Hegel, we must widen our conception of the idealist legacy if we want to understand the complexity of a phenomenon like Italian modernism – or modernist idealism more generally.

Before examining the specifics of the Italian case, then, it is necessary to map the conceptual terrain in much broader strokes. My aim here is not to offer a complete account or to delve into the many complex particularities of how specific idealist thinkers relate to one another. In fact, an important component of my claim here is that idealism can be understood both as a general stance and in terms of a particular historical constellation of philosophical thought that gained traction in the nineteenth and twentieth centuries, one that can be traced in great detail through the intellectual history of the period. I will be using both the wider and more restricted senses of the term throughout this book, so it is valuable to pause here and delineate both meanings, seeking not completeness but rather a point of departure.[35]

In its broadest sense, idealism refers to an outlook that understands what is true, absolute, or really real as existing outside the realm of material reality and the actual world of our sense experiences.[36] Reality, in such a view, exists in the mind, as an idea or as some other form of non-material entity. This can be taken in both an epistemological sense and in an ontological sense: epistemologically, an idealist stance holds that we cannot know anything except through our mind and thus that even if there are existing things "out there" in the actual world, our access to them is limited by the forms of our mental experience; taken ontologically, the claim goes further by insisting that the world itself is really an immaterial thing and that the mental (the ideal – pertaining to an idea) is the foundation of the world and its existence. Such outlooks have found powerful voices throughout the history of philosophical thought – from Western traditions going back at least to Plato's notion that Ideas or Forms are the fundamental reality of which all else is mere reflection, to the Indian tradition of the Vedas and other texts that include a notion of Maya, the magic or power by which human beings are made to believe in an illusory world of things when in fact reality is other. And as this last example makes evident, the broad idealist stance is by no means limited to academic philosophy: indeed, religious systems often assume an idealist outlook, grounding the material world in a pre-existing or conceptually prior ideal reality, whether that be called "God" or something else. Contemporary academic philosophy is sometimes sceptical of the notion that "idealism" can refer beyond the more specific set of concepts developed in European modernity and thus doubts that there is such a thing as ancient idealism, for instance.[37] In a more historically specific, and philosophy-specific, context, there may indeed be reasons to think of ancient sources as prefiguring but not coinciding with modern philosophical idealism. My point here, however, is that idealism not only *denotes* a precise set of philosophical claims/views but also *connotes* a wider field of outlooks that reject the primacy of material reality and posit some other source of what is really real, true, or absolute, which can ultimately have the power of grounding values or meaning more broadly. Thus, even if the word "idealism" only entered the English lexicon in the eighteenth century as a derivation of French and German philosophical terms (later taking on more general shades of meaning, including "aspiration after or pursuit of an ideal"), the outlook to which it points – its broader connotation, as

I am calling it here – is much older and encompasses not only philosophy but also religion, myth, and all manner of spiritual or magical beliefs that a contemporary (analytic) philosopher might want to hold at a distance.[38]

Two important facets of this broad notion of idealism have particular resonance for my purposes here: first, an idealist stance creates a problem for the notion of what constitutes reality; and second, an idealist stance is in some sense oppositional, as the ideal reality to which it gestures is often (but not always) defined in negative terms as the *im*material and not through a set of positive ascriptions. By insisting that what appears to be real is actually illusory or secondary in some way, idealist outlooks create difficulty for the word and concept "real" and its cognate forms. While there is sometimes a tendency to speak of the ideal as being opposed to the real, in fact idealism asserts that what we take to be real is not really real at all. For this reason I will frequently use the word "actual" to refer to what we perceive in the material world available to our sense perception.[39] But it bears noting that many of the authors I discuss will use versions of the word "real" to refer to the actual world in ways that create confusion, often deliberately. Numerous authors who assume an idealist stance in some form highlight the problem that results from challenging the reality of the real. This is true not only for Italian authors like Luigi Pirandello (1867–1936) and Italo Svevo (Aron Ettore Schmitz, 1861–1928), whom I discuss throughout my study, but also more broadly – it is enough to think of Jorge Luis Borges's love of collapsing layers of reality with paradoxical self-reference in stories like "The Circular Ruins" and "The Garden of Forking Paths."[40]

Before further articulating the stance of modernist idealism, however, it is necessary to account for the more precise and historically delimited meaning that idealism took on in the eighteenth and especially nineteenth centuries in Europe. While there were a host of idealist thinkers in modern Europe – figures ranging from Descartes to Leibniz to Berkeley – the most prominent direction in idealist thought was the version emerging from and responding to Immanuel Kant's (1724–1804) transcendental idealism. To offer a highly simplified summary, Kant argued that our knowledge of the world is only possible through the forms of human understanding – space, time, causation – that are themselves *a priori* forms of the human mind and not, then, properties inherent in the objects we perceive; thus what we know is always a mental construction in some important sense because the categories through which we represent objects are categories of our mind, and we have no access to a state of affairs outside of those categories, what he famously terms the thing in itself. Importantly, then, Kant's view did not negate the reality of a world outside of our mind or necessitate ontological idealism.[41] At base, Kant's transcendental idealism maintains that while there is some kind of reality that is the source of our mental representations (there are things in themselves), there is no way for us to access that reality outside of those representations.[42] In other words, we can have no knowledge at all as to the nature of things in themselves.[43]

While Kant was careful to insist, repeatedly, that his epistemological claims did not necessitate ontological ones, the legacy of his idealism is often less interested in such a distinction; indeed, it tends to take for granted that what Kant has really demonstrated, perhaps despite his own protestations, is that the world – whatever that means – is a product of consciousness or mind in some essential way: the world is ideal. A host of important thinkers took up this fundamental view, particularly in early- and mid-nineteenth century Germany, and it is these thinkers who now constitute the loose grouping of German idealism, which has itself become more or less synonymous with "idealism" in much philosophical discourse.[44] Fichte, Schelling, Schlegel, Schiller, Hölderlin, and Novalis can all be considered figures who worked in this legacy – although each of them took up different aspects of Kant's outlook and developed them in different ways that are beyond the scope of my investigation here.[45] Indeed, the many and varied distinctions among these figures and their views have been the subject of much critical attention.[46] I mention them here not to address how or to what extent they embraced epistemological and/or ontological forms of idealism but rather because an essential component of the philosophical development of post-Kantian thought has been its close connection to the emergence of German romanticism as a literary and artistic movement.[47] Even the more philosophically delimited notion of idealism that emerged in the wake of Kant's "Copernican Revolution" was immediately connected to the elaboration of idealist thought through artistic form. While this is not a book about German romanticism, I take it as indicative that a deep relation between philosophy and literary or artistic creation was already flourishing in that period, as reflected in the re-elaboration of idealist thought, with notions such as romantic irony at the core of that conjunction.[48]

While the German reception of and engagement with idealist philosophy constitutes a rich moment of literary-philosophical dialogue, my focus is on the development of that dialogue in the transnational reception of idealist thought. For this reason, I focus not on the complex moment of debate among German idealists themselves but rather on two key models that emerge as what we might call forking paths in the response to Kant. One of these fork prongs moves idealism toward a complicated view according to which consciousness emerges in and through world history and comes to the point of self-reflection in stages of self-awareness characterized by a dialectical movement. The other shifts idealism in a very different direction, focusing on the epistemological starting point of Kant's transcendental idealism to insist that the world as we know it is an illusion but that we can intuit a glimmering sliver of what constitutes the true reality beneath that illusion, a surging force of irrational will that pushes all of the world we experience into (temporary) being. The former is the absolute idealism developed by Georg Wilhelm Friedrich Hegel (1770–1831); the latter is the metaphysics of will expounded by Hegel's greatest detractor, the man who saw himself as the true heir of Kant's system, Arthur Schopenhauer (1788–1860). These two were hardly the only thinkers to revise and give new and different life to Kant's thought in the nineteenth century; they do, however, represent the two key strands of post-Kantian thought that I will trace into my elaboration of modernist idealism, in part because of the strong contrast between them and in part because of the rich, overlapping, and conflicting reception histories for both thinkers in the context of modern Italy. They serve, ultimately, as "types" characterizing two idealist outlooks and thus as conceptual lenses for examining how those outlooks operate and realize themselves in modernist production.

Hegel's philosophical system has been the subject of extensive commentary and debate for nearly two centuries; any summary of it will inevitably prove insufficient relative to the complexity of his thought. Still, it is possible to sketch out some key features of this strand of post-Kantian idealism, which played a major role in the formation of modern Italy's national political consciousness.[49] In the reading I adopt here, Hegel's system articulates a notion of "absolute idealism," contending that thinking and being are ultimately the same and thus that all objects are in some way conceptually informed.[50] One result of this view is a particular philosophy of history that came to be one of the most important legacies of Hegel's thought: for Hegel, history is the progressive unfolding of a universal concept or, put differently, the coming into self-consciousness of what is really real – spirit. His teleological vision of historical self-becoming in turn informs both his philosophy of art and his political thought. In his aesthetics, Hegel articulates a general view in which the work of art is an object purposefully made such that human spirit sees itself reflected in the sensuous form of the object; art thus provides a materially organized complement to the purely conceptual self-reflection of spirit in philosophy and the metaphorical representation of that self-reflection in religion. He then organizes the various arts in terms of both form (sculpture, painting, music, etc.) and historical moment, differentiating among "symbolic," "classical," and "romantic" representations, which find their respective ideal forms in architecture, sculpture, and painting/music/poetry.[51] On a parallel track, his philosophy of history offers a teleological account of how self-consciousness emerges in the actual forms of societies and their organizing principles and corresponding actions; for Hegel, the "successive steps" of world history unfold progressively in such a way that "world history as a whole is the expression of the spirit in time, just as nature is the expression of the Idea in space."[52] Both Hegel's aesthetics and his philosophy of history thus offer teleological accounts of the objective forms through which spirit achieves its self-reflective end, ultimately depicting the Idea as a self-unfolding rational organization of the world that plays out over time and space.[53]

In contrast to this rationally structured notion of the ideal that animates Hegel's encyclopedic project, Schopenhauer offers a very different rearticulation of Kant's idealism. Schopenhauer elaborates his system in a single principal text, which he revised and expanded several times during his life, *The World as Will and Representation* (1818, 1844, 1859), and which he complemented with a series of related essays, *Parerga and Paralipomena* (1851), along with other, shorter studies.[54] What unites all of these works is a basic metaphysical view rooted in a reinterpretation of Kant's epistemological idealism: the world that we know is only ever a representation of something that is beneath it but impossible to perceive or understand through our senses and our reason. With the exception, that is, of one crucial caveat, which Schopenhauer locates in our immediate intuitive experience of will (the experience of willing something to happen, such as lifting our arm, say). This experience of will is, for Schopenhauer, a fleeting glimpse beyond the phenomenal world of representation into what Kant called the unknowable noumenon. Thus while all the world we think we see and know is an illusion, a mere representation, what is at the root of that representation is will – this is its inner reality, though it cannot be known or thought in any conceptual terms. The most notorious feature of Schopenhauer's metaphysics of will is its profoundly pessimistic outlook: will is an irrational, blind surge of desire, and it structures the world in such a way that desire is endless and impossible to satisfy. On the one hand, the satisfaction of any one individual desire involves doing damage to some other being with conflicting desires; on the other, the satisfaction of an individual desire only gives rise to new desires. Will's self-expression in the objective world is thus destructive or, if seen from the perspective of the whole, self-cannibalizing. Ultimately, the world is will, and will is suffering.

Schopenhauer's pessimistic account of life gives rise to two responses within his system, one aesthetic, the other ethical. Both are attempts to contend with the suffering that characterizes his pessimistic version of an irrational ideal reality. The aesthetic response argues that in the experience of beauty the subject is removed from its relation to will and desire and thus temporarily escapes from suffering; simultaneously, artworks themselves give us glimpses of what Plato called Ideas or Forms and what Schopenhauer characterizes as the most adequate representation of some fundamental aspect of will's nature, the type of one of its (infinite) forms. Aesthetic experience thus involves both a negative pleasure (the absence of suffering) and a positive content that offers another way of glimpsing will's nature. But this experience is necessarily transitory, as well as insufficient for actually escaping will altogether, and for that reason Schopenhauer's system culminates not in aesthetic escape but in the ethics of renunciation. He depicts a new (old) ideal drawn from both Eastern and Western religious systems: the ascetic saint who freely renounces himself and his desires. For Schopenhauer, it is only in this supreme (and supremely difficult) act of self-abnegation that will is definitively quieted; indeed, the ascetic saint represents the culminating point of will's movement from blind forms through self-awareness (in humanity) to the point of self-extinguishing, where the rationality of the human mind is able to perceive will for what it is and thus can choose to turn will against itself through renunciation. Yet few are capable of treading this saintly path, so a fleeting immersion in beauty remains the most accessible response to will's suffering. And indeed, it was precisely in the field of artistic production and aesthetic thought that Schopenhauer's system would find its most prominent proponents and most lasting legacy.[55]

These brief summaries of Hegel and Schopenhauer are not designed to be comprehensive, nor do they aim at contributing to the history of philosophy; rather, the purpose of my summary, like my book, is to draw on interpretations of these two post-Kantian thinkers to establish a dual-pronged trajectory in modern thought that engages in elements of both of these (deeply opposed) systems. Naturally, Kantian thought itself is important for this understanding – it is, indeed, the underpinning of both directions; all the same, it is in the Kantian aftermath that idealism develops toward the modernist positions that come to special fruition in the cultural production I examine here. Hegel's philosophy of history and his progressive view of the rational unfolding of world history were key elements in the philosophical reception of his thought by Italian idealists and Neo-Idealists in the nineteenth and twentieth centuries: for these thinkers, Hegel's philosophy of history had concrete political implications in the moment of Risorgimento nationalism and the effort to craft a new national consciousness in the newly unified state. At the same time, Schopenhauer's pessimistic, irrational approach to idealism influenced a whole strand of artistic production and critical interpretation, elevating beauty as an end in itself and underpinning a starkly ascetic aestheticism. These political and aesthetic elements came together in a series of strange configurations in the literary and artistic/cultural projects of modernism's response to the deadening conditions of modernity. The ambivalence of this mixture is constitutive of the problematic set of outlooks and works that can be grouped under the rubric of modernist idealism.

Modernist Idealism

If being an "idealist" can thus mean many, potentially conflicting, things, the nature of modernist idealism is itself ambivalent. While the contradictions in idealist thought tend to appear in clashes among different thinkers – an example being the fierce intellectual animosity between Schopenhauer and Hegel – in the context of modernist idealism those clashes are frequently internalized and play out within the works of a single figure or movement, or within a single work itself. Just as D'Annunzio's modernist writing is at once nationalist and cosmopolitan, politically engaged (even if problematically so) and aesthetically distanced or idealizing, so too do other modernist writers combine elements of the Hegelian and Schopenhauerian idealist alternatives within their outlooks. The aesthetic realization of idealist thought unfolds these internalized contradictions and gives them the power to effect change in the actual world through their presence in the social imagination.

What holds these divergent positions together despite their conflicts is their fundamental rejection of a reductive cultural logic rooted in what they see as material baseness – the capitalist obsession with material gain in the form of profit, which becomes a bourgeois ideology driving social and political decisions, say; or scientific empiricism that seeks to reduce all things to observable material causes; or the logic of a philosophical positivism that insists on the coherent logical explication of all things. And of course, in a moment of intensely felt transformation in religious belief, the most traditional source of an idealist outlook was being displaced within the modern social imaginary – the Church, and faith in God, could no longer be taken for granted as once they were.

Thus, as Charles Taylor has convincingly argued, modernity does not mean the end of faith per se but rather a shift in faith's hegemonic status in the social imaginary; this shift results in a split frame of reference for modern subjects, who inhabit the outlook of their own view (or set of beliefs) even while seeing that view from outside, as a perspective that has been assumed rather than as a direct (naive) fact.[56] In the midst of these multiple transformations that decentre modern life, human experience undergoes a crisis of what Taylor characterizes as "fullness," a crisis that can lead to a nostalgic sense of loss at the same time that it seems to reject the very things that are lost.[57]

Modernist idealism responds to this sense of loss with the conviction that the decadent aspect of modernity is a problem introduced by changes that reduce life to less than what it really is.[58] Modernist idealists thus seek to revitalize the world by reintroducing the spiritual or ideal element – some connection to the fullness of transcendence that has otherwise been displaced. In this sense, modernist idealism seeks to recentre modern life after the loss of an orienting axis, or set of orienting axes, that had structured the traditional world – even if, in some extreme cases, that reorientation could even seem to entail the totalization of relative flux and change.[59] We can see here a useful parallel to what Jonathan Lear describes in his account of radical hope as a response to the devastating decentring of the Crow Nation's world after the onslaught of white American hegemony – the vulnerability of a society or culture to the possibility of collapse requires, in some form, a dream or spark of hope that can reorient it, "projecting [it] into an enigmatic future."[60]

Unlike the case Lear examines, where the Crow Nation aligned around a dream-vision articulated by a key chief, Plenty Coups, the writers and thinkers of modernist idealism hardly agree in terms of what the alternative, reorienting axis of values is. This is precisely why it is necessary to examine these authors in light of a genealogical unearthing of the philosophical outlooks that underpin their (overdetermined) ideals. Doing so provides a framework that helps us think about both the historical philosophical influences to which modernists respond and also the conceptual impetus of their work – its drive toward new or renewed models of artistic, cultural, social, political, individual, and even material vitality. Thus, the reception of Hegel's philosophy of history by figures at the centre of Italy's ongoing political renewal – from Risorgimento thinkers and revolutionaries like Francesco De Sanctis and Bertrando Spaventa to twentieth-century philosophers and political figures in the liberal period and at the birth of fascism like Benedetto Croce (1866–1952) and Giovanni Gentile (1875–1944) – created a model for an idealism that sought to reinvigorate national sentiment through the transnational reception and domestication of German sources. At the same time, the artistic and aesthetic reception of Schopenhauer's pessimistic metaphysics and its aesthetic and ethical outlooks inflected generations of artists with an elevated sense of the revelatory and vital powers of artistic production, along with a notion of the darkly irrational or mystically unknowable truths it unearths. While these German thinkers and their philosophical followers are generally adamant about maintaining the opposition between those two strands of post-Kantian thought, the artists and cultural figures who receive them are not so meticulous, and these outlooks' varying and often opposed facets overlap in the work of various figures, from the decadent D'Annunzio and the avant-garde Futurists to modernist authors including Svevo, Pirandello, Grazia Deledda (1871–1936), Eugenio Montale (1896–1981), and a great many others.

What this brief overview of some complex groupings of modernist idealists already indicates is that this concept not only provides a new entry into the growing lexicon of global modernism but also offers insight into the ongoing discussion about the relationships among three interrelated categories of artistic production: decadence, avant-gardism, and modernism.[61] My intervention is to recognize that these terms, while pointing to significant differences related to their stances on the political efficacy and orientation of artistic production (along with other questions, such as how to relate to modern temporality), nonetheless align in their idealist response against the conditions of modernity. Even if decadence is the attachment to loss and avant-gardism is the attachment to or encouragement of the new, both are components of the broader modernist response against modernity's progress, constituting different strategies that share an underlying idealist framework. Decadentism aestheticizes loss (or crisis) so as to transfigure and preserve it, using an idealist framework to reconfigure material reality as an aesthetic object. Avant-gardism seeks to mobilize artistic production and aesthetic ideality to intervene in matter, revitalizing or respiritualizing the material realm itself so that it can unfold and develop in line with some spiritual (national, or irrational) ideal. Modernism mixes the two ambivalently, enmeshing political and aesthetic aims, reconfiguring materiality and revitalizing it, offering a renewed spirituality to reorient modern life.

The Artistic Fruition of Idealism: Vitalism, Spiritualism, and the New Materialism

As this outline of my notion of modernist idealism should make clear, the conceptual history that I am tracing here intersects with several evolving discussions in recent criticism. The idealist push toward the revitalization of the material world speaks to the powerful presence of vitalist philosophies and outlooks in the modernist imaginary, on the one hand, and thus to the contemporary critical discourse of the new materialist studies, on the other. At the same time, modernist idealism's shift toward various models positing the interpenetration of the ideal and material actuality dovetails with recent work to unearth the complex dynamics of modern spiritualism and the ways in which it intersects not only with literary and artistic culture but also with empirical science. While the chapters that follow will articulate these connections much more fully, here I want to pause to outline some key conversations into which my study intervenes.

A burst of interest in the vitalist philosophies that reshaped nineteenth- and early twentieth-century science has motivated significant recent research. The picture that has emerged shows a century pervaded by efforts to complicate and re-envision the limits of a reductive materialism and to challenge traditional notions of logic, order, and knowledge.[62] This upsurge of vitalist thought reshaped the literary and artistic imagination of the period, informing experimental ideas about artistic form in avant-garde projects like the Futurist "reconstruction" of the world as well as reconfiguring central components of literature's content, such as its use of, and notion of, character. As Omri Moses has convincingly argued, vitalist notions of an emergent world in flux – decentred and refusing to conform to a reductive logic – informed the ways in which key modernist figures like Henry James, Gertrude Stein, and T.S. Eliot rewrote traditional visions of character: instead of a foundational model of the centred individual subject, these modernists envision the character as in flux, overdetermined, and responding to relational feelings and situational inputs.[63] What Moses describes with a focus on anglophone literary production can, and indeed must, be expanded into the broader context of transnational modernism. That geographical and linguistic expansion is one of the tasks of my book (and a specific topic of chapter 4).

Expanding the discussion in this way, I likewise seek to complicate it, showing how schools of vitalist thought such as *Lebensphilosophie* and a related resurgence in the discourses of spiritualism – from occult religious philosophies and practices to a newly scientific interest in the paranormal – are implicated in conflicting modernist alternatives. I thus contribute a new dimension to the work of scholars like Jason Josephson-Storm, for whom the resurgence of spiritualism was a defining element of nineteenth-century thought not only in popular culture but also in scientific realms: my account of the ways in which modernist vitalism and spiritualism aim to revivify the material world positions his focus on magic and science in terms of the literary-artistic reception of idealism, offering a new matrix for conceiving such projects.[64] Likewise, I participate in the growing shift in scholarly narratives about the alleged decline of religious belief in the nineteenth century; just as J. Jeffrey Franklin has recently shown that the confrontation between modern materialist paradigms and Christian orthodoxy led not to disenchantment and secularization but rather to the "proliferation of alternative religions,"[65] I contend that modernist idealism is eager to engage various alternative religious or spiritual systems – including occult beliefs infused with vitalist assumptions – as components of the effort to find a juncture between the ideal and the actual (the topic of chapter 5). This adds a new dimension to the sense in which Jean-Michel Rabaté identifies the "ghostly" presence of previous systems in modernism's confrontation with the lost or disappearing past.[66]

This multifaceted discourse on vitalism and its centrality to the project of modernist idealism could be seen as a subset of the recent critical turn toward the theorization of "new materialism." The need for a new materialism is positioned as a response against the perceived inadequacies of a prior move against traditional materialist approaches (Marxian historical materialism, for example) by privileging "language, discourse, culture, and values."[67] By rethinking what materialism means, and expanding the concept of matter itself, theorists working under this rubric aim to generate new avenues for political and cultural critique and action. For instance, as the political theorist Jane Bennett argues in *Vibrant Matter*, our notions of individual agency can be challenged by new ways of thinking that seek to locate a vital force within things themselves. She thus positions her theory as part of a long line of vitalist philosophical arguments that align in key ways with the description of nineteenth-century vitalism I have outlined above.[68] These approaches to materialism suggest the need to move beyond a reductive picture of materiality and thereby move beyond the dualism that seems to be implied in many idealist stances that separate the ideal (the immaterial) from the actual, material world.[69]

However, as Elizabeth Grosz has argued in her recent intervention, the new materialism may overly limit our conceptual horizons, so "it is perhaps necessary to simultaneously call into being a new idealism, no longer Platonic, Cartesian, or Hegelian in its structure, that refuses to separate materiality from or subordinate it to ideality, resisting any reduction of the qualities and attributes of each to the operations of the other."[70] This she terms the "*new* new materialism," one that understands the world as being "material-ideal."[71] Her aim is to incorporate both body and mind, the corporeal and the incorporeal, without reverting to dualistic models or "mystifying" either term or their relations. The ambition of such a project speaks to the importance of recuperating a positive sense of the ideal as not just the immaterial but part of materiality itself. But in fact, as I shall argue here, that project of recuperating the ideal has a long literary-philosophical history and is already at the core of the outlook I am calling modernist idealism: the idealist stance of modernist writers and thinkers is not a mere rejection of modernity's preference for materialism; it is also an effort to reinvigorate materiality itself by recourse to a new idealism that engages matter even as it transfigures it or reanimates it.

Because the writers and thinkers of modernist idealism embrace that same effort to channel the ideal into and through the actual, material world, aiming to expand our concept of materiality, they offer not only texts that can be read in light of new materialism but also texts that importantly prefigure it. Insofar as this is true, we might be justified in suggesting that the new materialisms are not really so new, and that despite their protestations they can be placed in continuity with the logic of idealism itself.[72] They are all ways of understanding the actual, sensible world as organized or animated by some vital principle that is not reducible to matter *qua* inert material – they seek to redefine the status of materiality. But what this reveals is that there is nothing inherently progressive or politically radical about the effort to expand the horizons of matter – and it is no doubt for this reason that new materialist critics like Bennett have been so adamant about trying to take their distance from the earlier positions that fall within the scope of modernist idealism.[73]

In fact, there is no inherent connection between a vibrant picture of the material world and a progressive political agenda: as the ambivalence of the texts and authors I examine here shows, the project to bridge immanence and transcendence, the actual and the ideal, is overdetermined and thus politically flexible. More than this, however, my argument shows how important it is to consider not only the conceptual articulation of theories – of vitalism, of spiritualism, of idealism – but also, and especially, how those theories enter into the actual world and become a part of how people think and behave. Ideas become present and thus take on affective charge, I contend, through their realization, a realization that occurs both in artistic form (as literature, visual art, film, theatre, music …) and in political praxis.[74] The kinds of ideas that lend themselves to a practical political realization and those that lend themselves to artistic realization vary based on the philosophical outlook those ideas imply. Hegel's philosophy of history, for instance, charts a view in which the ideal is realized in world historical becoming, and it is thus a natural fit for political philosophers and political activists like Spaventa, De Sanctis, Croce, and Gentile, all of whom sought to use political tools to reshape actual reality so that it aligned with their understanding of the ideal. In contrast, Schopenhauer's philosophy renounces any interest in reshaping political actuality, which it does not value; instead Schopenhauer emphasizes the importance of artistic insight and practices of self-abnegation. As Sophia Vasalou has convincingly shown, his system valorizes these not through rigorous logical argumentation but rather by presenting a world view, developing an "aesthetic standpoint" from which life is evaluated and its nature (as will, as suffering) emerges with the force of something perceived rather than something demonstrated.[75] Schopenhauer, in other words, constructs his system through the depiction of a world view: as David Wellbery has neatly put it, his work "elicits conviction primarily through the force of aesthetic presentation."[76] For this reason, in order to be fully compelling, Schopenhauer's system *requires* aesthetic realization. If Hegel's idealist philosophy of history makes itself real, so to speak, through political action, Schopenhauer's idealist metaphysics (and thus aesthetics and ethics) requires artistic form to become fully real. The production of modernist idealists is thus not simply the dissemination of Schopenhauer's ideas – it is integral to the full articulation of his world view itself.[77]

Viewing modernist idealism as the aesthetic and political realization of these conflicting elements of an idealist outlook allows deeper insight into what it means to think of philosophical vitalism or spiritualism in relation to modernist artistic creation. In their quest to revivify the deadened world of modern materialism, modernist thinkers and creators engage a host of ideas about how the transcendent and the immanent can be united, about how the ideal can be channelled into the actual world and thus reshape and reanimate reality. Modernist idealism takes that quest to the next level, not simply theorizing but enacting that union, and in the process unleashing a host of conflicting and problematic forces through their art, their politics, and the idealist world views realized in both.

Italian Modernity and Modernist Idealism: A Transnational Paradigm

The anxiety over the political and ethical dimensions of idealism's long history understandably gives rise to the desire for a theoretical alternative such as those sought through the new materialism. Idealist thought has a troubled political legacy, to be sure. Troubled, but hardly single-faceted. Much like the other dimensions of modernist idealism, its political history is ambivalent, and nowhere is this clearer than in the Italian context. As the scholarly discourse on Italian modernism has developed over the last two decades, the complexity of its political dimensions has become increasingly evident. Efforts to understand this complexity have involved elaborating new canons of Italian modernism, delving into intellectual history to unearth loci of exchange, and articulating the theoretical stances implied by the modernist response to crisis. One of the primary interventions of my book is to elucidate a different way of conceiving Italian modernism, one defined not by stylistic/formal categorizations, nor by a limited or precise canon of modernist authors, nor by an effort at political critique that requires us to characterize modernism in an overly negative form. Instead, by excavating the shared philosophical framework underpinning a host of stylistically, socially, and politically diverse figures, I point to a new way forward that draws on frameworks from the anglophone new modernist studies to rethink debates about the Italian case.

The Italian Modernism Debate

To clarify this intervention, it will be necessary to consider the different key directions of recent scholarship in more detail. For most of the twentieth century the word "modernism" was generally applied not to the writers I examine here but rather to the movement within the Catholic Church to modernize or reinterpret Church doctrine in light of the changed frameworks of modernity.[78] Instead of being called "modernists," many of these writers were grouped under the (negative) rubric of decadentism or *decadentismo* – not just Gabriele d'Annunzio but also the Futurists and other avant-garde or modernist innovators of the early twentieth century. Just over a decade ago, a number of critics launched themselves into this debate with the aim of showing how Italian writers and artists clearly belong to the broader discourse on modernism, a position that has since been firmly established.[79] Mario Moroni and Luca Somigli's essential volume, *Italian Modernism* (2004), served as a watershed moment in this regard by demonstrating quite clearly not only that there *was* an Italian modernism but also that it was complex and nuanced and that it encompassed a wide array of writers, artists, thinkers, and specific projects and styles, spanning from decadence to Futurism – in addition to a considerable variety of political valences. Their volume sought to trace a series of "thematic itineraries" across a diverse set of figures and issues.[80] Since then, in the Italian-language debate, significant work has been done to dig into specific figures, many of whom were already central to Somigli and Moroni's volume; special focus has tended to fall on major writers like Carlo Emilio Gadda (1893–1973), Montale, Pirandello, Svevo, and Federigo Tozzi (1883–1920), but it extends to many others.[81] The volume edited by Romano Luperini and Massimiliano Tortora, *Sul modernismo italiano* (2012), worked to construct a new canon of Italian modernists to add to the global canon of modernism on the basis that the usual critical association of these writers with "decadence" had led to an overly negative view of their production, one driven by critics' ideological frameworks. They argued instead that modernism should be viewed as separate from both decadence and historical avant-gardes like Futurism. The scholarly discussion has led on the one hand to panoramic studies like that of Moroni and Somigli and on the other to specific examinations digging through a single figure or set of figures for the purpose of characterizing the particularities of Italian modernism.

Most recently, the debate has shifted again with the development of an approach rooted in cultural history and critique. This direction, which offers intellectual histories of modernism to elucidate its political valence in Italy, is represented by two important voices: Walter L. Adamson (particularly *Avant-Garde Florence* and *Embattled Avant-Gardes*) and Mimmo Cangiano (*La nascita del modernismo italiano*). Studies like theirs articulate a set of conceptual positions through a biographical, intellectual-historical reading of key figures in the early years of the 1900s. Adamson focuses on elaborating modernism as a configuration of cultural politics that emerged in response to the crisis of commodity culture. He arrives at a utopian or positive appraisal of the political ambitions of the movement in its "avant-garde" phase – a conclusion that dovetails with Marjorie Perloff's analysis of the "futurist moment" of avant-garde culture in Italy.[82] In contrast, Cangiano sees modernism as an ideology that actually supported the bourgeois system and order despite appearing to be situated as a response against that system. Following in the footsteps of thinkers like Norberto Bobbio and Giorgio Agamben (though the latter is never named), Cangiano characterizes modernism as essentially nihilistic, as reconfiguring the old system of certain values to form a new system that absolutizes or totalizes uncertainty. He thus suggests how the utopian assault on the institutions of art manifested in avant-garde modernism might seem to be belied by other elements of the modernist outlook.

An important feature of Cangiano's intervention into this debate is his recognition of a fundamental similarity between what he sees as nihilist modernism and the pathway of a neo-Kantian or Catholic modernism that seeks to reestablish the lost (moral) horizon through arguments that are informed by but do not totalize the uncertainty and relativity of the modernist outlook.[83] This complicates the idea that modernism is forward-facing, seeking to respond to crisis without turning back.[84] The new moral universalism of some key modernists is in fact rooted in an alternative to actual modernity, be it the peasant traditions of Piero Jahier's idealized Italian alpine communities or the effort to establish a new ethical grounding of absolute values pursued by figures like Giovanni Amendola and Scipio Slataper. As Cangiano argues, these efforts do nothing to revolutionize the conditions giving rise to the crisis they are positioned against; they may *seem* diametrically opposed to the "nihilistic" outlook of modernists like Pirandello, yet they all end up leaving intact the essentially static character of a totalized view. For Cangiano, this is the key critical point to understand about modernism's false appearance as a cultural revolution.

My approach in this book owes much to the intellectual histories of Adamson and Cangiano as well as to the way in which their interventions have pointed attention squarely at the essential way in which modernism positioned itself as a response against materialism, as an effort to respiritualize or to recapture the ideal. However, as will emerge in the following pages, my examination of Italian modernism also takes a different approach, not only in the sense that I place greater emphasis on the literary and artistic production of modernism than on the intellectual debates themselves, but especially insofar as I offer a more ambivalent picture of the political and philosophical stance implied by modernist idealism. The modernist idealism I describe counters the allegedly "nihilistic" character assumed in accounts like Cangiano's – an assumption, I would offer, that may be at least partly rooted in the belief that modernism is *expressing* the force of modern crisis rather than responding to it with an active alternative.[85] But while taking seriously the possibility that aesthetic production can act and not just express, I complicate the close alliance that Adamson wants to draw between the avant-garde and modernism, showing that the utopian principle rejecting (aesthetic) decadence is in fact only one aspect of a shared outlook that also embraces decadence in other respects. The aesthetic religion of art not only lives on in a "later" phase of avant-garde modernism; indeed, the two are mutually imbricated from the start. As Thomas Harrison has shown, the fight to overcome aestheticism actually conceals an ongoing *continuity* with aestheticism, and what is really rejected by modernist artists and authors is not so much decadence as it is the pretension to completeness represented by the decadent-aesthetic outlook in its own supposedly heroic production.[86] For Harrison, then, modernism marks a turn toward "essayism" as the embrace of an incomplete, fragmentary venture toward some truth that can never be fully grasped.[87] In this sense, I would contend, Harrison's analysis clarifies for us how both Cangiano and Adamson provide only partial views. Essentially ambivalent, modernist idealism both elevates art and seeks to enter into world history; it rejects the *hoi polloi* while also engaging in cultural politics; and it grasps for a fleeting ideal that is both realized in aesthetic form and understood as essentially unreachable.

At the core of this ambivalence is the multifaceted reception of post-Kantian idealist thought in the Italian context, a reception that draws together seemingly incompatible outlooks such as those espoused by Hegel and Schopenhauer. In one respect, the reception of Hegel's thought through Risorgimento thinkers like De Sanctis and Spaventa was integral to inspiring revolution and to the liberal project of forming a new nation and establishing a parliamentary order; this idealist trajectory would seem to align nicely with the positive, utopian ideal of an avant-garde modernism. At the same time, though, Neo-Idealists working with the legacy of Hegel's philosophy of history, most notably Giovanni Gentile, were central to remaking the government in the 1920s, helping usher in and sustain the ideology of Italian Fascism – and these thinkers drew on a transformed version of some of the same concepts and legacies, as is evident in the way Gentile and Mussolini himself "reclaimed" Alfredo Oriani as a proto-fascist theorist of the authoritarian state.[88] Our picture of this political ambivalence becomes even more complicated when we consider more marginal or unusual figures in the Italian reception of German idealist thought, like the fascist-occultist avant-garde artist and theorist Julius Evola (1898–1974), whose idealism was an unusual mix of Hegelian history and Schopenhauer's irrationalism, inflected with the mystical turn common to other Schopenhauerian and vitalist thinkers who drew on exoticized Eastern religious traditions and occult beliefs and practices.[89]

Evola's name – long obscured and marginal – has suddenly emerged from the shadows thanks to his dubious honour as one of the "traditionalist" thinkers lionized by the current phase of American white nationalism, a testament to the ways in which marginal and discredited modes of thought can unexpectedly shape or reshape (elements of) the popular imagination.[90] Evola and his version of modernist idealism can thus be fruitfully understood in terms of Jonathan Eburne's notion of "outsider theory."[91] My study engages the renewed critical interest in mainstream Italian philosophy of the period – exemplified by the publication of Massimo Verdicchio's recent introduction to Croce's thought and Brian and Rebecca Copenhaver's fundamental volume examining modern Italian philosophy – but it also follows Eburne's lead, expanding its scope beyond those mainstream figures.[92] I thus build on the work of Cangiano in another sense, as he has recently shown how an "outside" thinker like Carlo Michelstaedter (1887–1910) engaged and transformed the discourses of Marxism in the modernist period painting a vast, detailed picture of the rich and multifaceted array of philosophical ideas that circulated in the modernist moment.[93] Eburne has argued that we must understand such outsider views and reconstruct their intellectual histories to better grapple with how they have entered and affected the mainstream; I argue, similarly, that developing a broad concept of modernist idealism and tracing its conflicting political and aesthetic impulses will help clarify how seemingly opposed figures and movements were responses to the same quest for renewal, drawing on similar or overlapping philosophical outlooks. This approach may provide us with traction on the question of how seemingly discredited or problematic stances are able to gain or recapture cultural currency and thus the power to influence action through a shared social imaginary.

Italian Modernity: Late, Incomplete, Transnational

These multiple directions in modernist idealism are responses to specific historical contingencies. A key framing point is the perception that modern thinkers held of Italy's late and marginal modernity in the period between the Risorgimento and the end of the Second World War, a circumstance I alluded to earlier when comparing Italy and Japan. Italy's political modernity arrived late, given that before 1861 there was no nation of Italy at all (and only in 1870 was Rome added to the unified country); the result was an enduring sense that Italy lacked both a coherent body politic and spirit of nationalism. Moreover, Italy was late to industrialize, and its social progress was uneven: the north of Italy had begun industrializing in key areas in the nineteenth century, yet even after unification southern Italy remained predominantly agricultural in terms of its economy and traditional in terms of its social and political structures. The continuing power of the Catholic Church throughout the country, but especially in the more agricultural south, contributed to this complicated trajectory of modernization. This delayed development has been integral to recent theoretical work by Franco Cassano, which connects Italy to the global South and articulates a version of southern or "meridian" thought that positions itself against the dominant capitalist logic of northern European "Westernization."[94] This perspective on Italian modernity lends further credence to Amano's idea, considered above, that Japanese modernity and Italian modernity shared an element of marginality that contributed to their global modernist exchange.[95] In both contexts, "delayed" economic, social, and political modernization provided fertile ground for a new, modernist nationalism. And it was modernist idealism that provided an intellectual framework for that nationalism.[96]

Why would Italy's late and uneven modernization lend itself to an idealist outlook? The answer – and an essential facet of what motivates the broad modernist interest in idealism – is to be found in the widely held notion that national progress conceived as social and political transformation requires a spiritual renewal that cannot be accomplished by material means alone. This belief was widespread and articulated in many forms, and one of its most famous iterations came in a children's fable that has had profound, and ongoing, global resonance: Carlo Collodi's *The Adventures of Pinocchio* (*Le avventure di Pinocchio: Storia di un burattino*), first published serially in 1881–82, a decade after Rome became part of unified Italy – though the so-called "unredeemed" areas of supposed Italian ethnicity or belonging remained outside the new nation still. In the well-known story, set in Tuscany in the years leading up to Italian unification, a wooden puppet seeks to become a real boy. Scholars have connected this tale to the Risorgimento and the effort to compose not just a new body out of the various, previously separate pieces of Italy, but a unified whole that could operate as a real nation with its own national spirit.[97] Pinocchio's fable reveals what was perceived as the fundamental problem facing the new, "belated" state: the need for a national identity that could create organic coherence and offer a way for Italy to take its seat at the table with the other modern European powers. Idealist outlooks provided a way of reconceiving the modern order; they were appealing because they suggested models of how the state, society, and the individual could all be imbued with more than a reductively material reality and thus, it was hoped, the intellectual grounds for remaking the modern world by remaking the modern social imaginary.

Of course, the ways in which various modernist figures sought to incorporate an idealist outlook into this broad project for renewal are varied: they led not only in different political directions but also to contrasting formal or stylistic developments, ranging from D'Annunzio's florid language of aesthetic refinement to the Futurist destruction of syntax.[98] This, perhaps, is part of what led to the long-standing critical disagreement over whether Italy truly participated in literary and artistic modernism at all. My approach to understanding Italian modernity thus proposes to draw on both the cosmopolitan, comparative frameworks that constellate key modernist moments and the intellectual history that examines local contexts and figures within their networks – approaches like Harrison's (*1910: The Emancipation of Dissonance*) on the one hand and Adamson's and Cangiano's on the other. At the same time, I draw on and join the work of several recent scholars who have examined how specific figures and locations in Italian modernism are transnationally situated. Saskia Elizabeth Ziolkowski has recently offered a complex vision of how the works of Franz Kafka serve as a pivotal intertext for a series of modern Italian authors across genres and decades; in so doing, she has underscored both the powerful insights that can come from a comparative reading of Italian modernism and the fundamental role that German literature and thought has played in the formation of Italian modernism.[99] In a similar vein, Jennifer Scappettone's examination of modernism in the specific context of Venice, *Killing the Moonlight*, shows how that city is situated at the geographical threshold of Italy, Europe, and Asia while being constituted by overlapping layers of history that have created a confused temporal experience resistant to linear notions of modern development. As a result, Venice is an ideal locus for modernist projects of renewal as well as a challenge to such endeavours. Her examination of how foreigners view Venice and how Venice inspires or reshapes not only Italian but also European views of modernity and modernism serves as inspiration for the transnational ambitions of my own study, which zooms out from a specific city to think about Italy's place vis-à-vis European modernity and modernism. I contend that it is within this frame that we can best understand Italy as a paradigmatic case for the complex dynamics of a global modernism, as a place where the reception and rearticulation of idealist outlooks provides a shared conceptual grounding for varied and sometimes contradictory projects of renewal.

If the goal of modernist idealism aligns with the need to animate the body of the new Italian nation with a spirit to unify it as a meaningful whole, we can say that this spirit is itself cosmopolitan. Pinocchio's limbs may be Italian wood, but to endow his form with life is to connect it to a soul spanning cultures and languages. The real boy must become a nation yet be more than merely national. At the same time, the ideas that inform this new life need his body as much as he needs them. For the ideal enters into the actual world in ways suited to its nature, and if some idealist notions find their realization in world-historical action, others require a specifically aesthetic fruition. As such, modernist idealism offers a new, and necessary, entry into the lexicon of global modernism: the encounter with crisis time takes on the specific characteristic of a pressing need to intervene in and renew a deadened world, and idealist philosophy becomes the vehicle for that intervention. But it is not enough for it to be conceived, it must be enacted. And it is to that end that the writers and artists of modernist idealism dedicated themselves to ushering thought into being by giving it a hybrid aesthetic form.

Chapter One

Italy at the Banquet of Nations: Hegel in Politics and Philosophy

Would Hegel be conceivable without the French Revolution and the Napoleonic wars, that is, without the vital and direct experiences of an extremely intense historical period during which all previous beliefs were peremptorily challenged by the realities of the time?

– Antonio Gramsci, *Prison Notebooks*, vol. 2, notebook 4, section 56[1]

Hegel is not just a philosopher who theorizes a revolutionary vision of world history with the potential to reshape the trajectory of modern politics; he is also, fundamentally, a philosopher who is himself responding to revolutionary crisis. Gramsci's historical insight into this dual-faceted aspect of Hegel makes a natural starting point for considering how the reception of Hegelian thought shaped a significant component of the Italian response to modern crisis. For if the importance that Hegel played in the moment spanning the Risorgimento and the Second World War has become relatively well-known to scholars of Italian political and philosophical history, it is a story that still needs to be fully integrated into our understanding of how Italian modernism evolved and how it is situated on the global stage.

Gramsci was already thinking about Hegel's reception as a component of Italian political philosophy and the history of Italian revolution. He goes on in the same entry to draw a distinction between Hegel's contributions to (the history of) history and those of Italian philosophers interested in similar questions, such as the Enlightenment thinker, Giambattista Vico (1668–1744), and the Risorgimento philosopher, Bertrando Spaventa. In Gramsci's analysis, Hegel's position in the moment of the French Revolution and its aftermath in the Napoleonic Wars situates him at the heart of a world history that is notably global:

> What could Vico and Spaventa offer that was similar? (Spaventa, too, for he participated in historic events whose importance was regional and provincial when compared to the events between 1789 and 1818 that shook the whole civil world of the time and compelled everyone to think in "global" terms, events that set the social "totality," the entire conceivable human race, the whole "spirit" in motion. This is why, in Hegel's eyes, Napoleon could appear to be "the world spirit," on horseback!).[2]

Gramsci's contention is that the philosophy of history becomes a philosophy of world history with world-historical implications specifically in the Hegelian moment. My argument here will trace out the transnational dimensions of this specific strand of idealist thought. In the first place, Hegelian philosophy is tied to specific moments (of revolutionary potential) in which Italian nationality takes centre stage, and thus his thought is often integrated into narrowly nationalist discourses. Indeed, nationalism and nationality, as we shall see, take on a complex and multivalenced meaning both in Hegel and in the various phases of Hegelian reception that are relevant to the constitution of Italian modernity and the formation of its modernist idealism. Spanning from a patriotic push to create a unified national state and culture to the development of fascist totalitarianism, nationalism as a concept requires further unpacking. For in the second place, key thinkers both in the Risorgimento and afterwards also utilized Hegelian idealism to combat nationalism in Italian philosophy and politics, aiming instead toward a transnational cosmopolitanism that would re-envision Italy's place at an imaginary "banquet of nations," its place at the table to participate in actively reshaping modern history and culture through an intervention into the modern "spirit."

This way of re-examining the reception of Hegel's philosophy likewise allows an intervention into how we understand modernism as a philosophical project and the philosophical status of modernist responses to the new reality of modernity.[3] As Herbert Marcuse notes in the opening lines of his prominent study on Hegel's influence on modern social theory, German idealism played a foundational role in this response to modern crisis. This is at least in part because German idealism emerged in the wake of what may have been the archetypal shift in modern social and political relations:

> German idealism has been called the theory of the French Revolution. This does not imply that Kant, Fichte, Schelling, and Hegel furnished a theoretical interpretation of the French Revolution, but that they wrote their philosophy largely as a response to the challenge from France to reorganize

> the state and society on a rational basis, so that social and political institutions might accord with the freedom and interest of the individual.[4]

The shape and trajectory of idealist thought were in key respects a response to political exigencies – a reordering of how we understand and theorize the world to match the shifting historical conditions that already implied a reordering of actual relations in the world.[5] The rupture signalled by the French Revolution can be seen as the most concrete historical instance of the broader process of modern transformation to which German idealism responded: Kant's *Critique of Pure Reason*, it has been said, represents the philosophical acknowledgment of the new freedom of thought won for individuals with the modern age's departure from traditional dogmatisms.[6] Responding to the problems presented by the rise of modernity, idealism can be seen from at least one angle as a philosophical system that aims to comprehend and respond to the logic of revolutionary change.[7]

The precise contours of the link between the French Revolution and specifically Hegelian thought is the subject of ongoing debate.[8] Habermas argues that Hegel's response to the French Revolution "elevates the revolution to the primary principle of philosophy for the sake of a philosophy which is to overcome the revolution."[9] In this way, Hegel can be thought of as purging actual political revolution through his absolute idealism. More recently, Rebecca Comay has suggested that Hegel and Kant should be seen not simply as responding to the exigencies of revolution but also as demonstrating the traumatic force of the French Revolution as an absent loss, as an ideal that their notion of reason can only theorize whereas it has been experienced in practice elsewhere. She concludes that Kant and Hegel both attempt to absorb the shock of revolution and redirect its force.[10] The resulting picture relates their philosophical idealism to revolution both as cause and as sublimated effect.[11]

Whether viewed through the narrower lens of the specific historical shock of the French Revolution or seen more broadly as a philosophical confrontation with historical transformation as such, it is clear that German idealism is integrally linked to a narrative of liberation that aims toward a free future.[12] Inspired by the ideas and realities of political crisis and the shift toward romantic poetics in the early Jena period of German romanticism, Hegel reconceived the role of reason in modernity – from a positive or dogmatic vision of reason in the Kantian system to a dialectical image of reason as a continual process of self-relation.[13] In other words, Hegel's thought celebrates the revolution but only once it has been rendered harmless, so to speak, by integrating it into his broader philosophy of world-historical development leading through various moments toward the realization of freedom in the modern state. Robert Pippin's assessment of Hegel's role as the culminating figure in the tradition of German idealism pushes this dialectical picture further. As he argues, the idealists aim toward a practical goal of "working out, articulating, helping to defend and so to realize, the possibility of free self-determination, agency, spontaneity, activity, a self-directed 'purposive life,' eventually (in Hegel) a necessarily collective agency."[14] Both for Habermas and for Pippin, the Hegelian variation on this project of establishing self-determining, free rationality is ultimately intersubjective and must be understood as a facet of social relations. That is to say, freedom for the individual is impossible without a political and social order that enables those relations of freedom and, in some sense, constitutes them. Hegel's philosophy of history thus responds to the crises of modernity's revolutionary transformation of politics by channelling that crisis toward its teleological outcome in the self-determining rationality of the modern state.

With this picture in mind, I would submit the following: Hegelian idealism represents a strand of thought responding to modernity with an optimistic push toward a future that will realize its ideals through the (institutional) reorganization of social and political life. This strand of thought travelled and flourished in precisely that cosmopolitan moment of European change that J.W. Burrow has identified as the "crisis of reason" – when new notions of community, the self, and social evolution coincided with the reverberations of 1848 and the revolutions across Europe.[15] Examining the reception of Hegelian thought in Italy thus provides a case study in how that outlook was integrated into and realized through not only Italian philosophy but also and especially political praxis and the reshaping of a new, modern nation and developing national identity. Idealism, transnational in its formation and also (sometimes) nationalist in its application, becomes a key lens for understanding modernity and responding to it in an effort to renew the spirit of and thus reshape the modern world.[16]

Philosophy, Nationality, and a New Italy: Hegel Comes to Naples

For several decades there was no name that loomed larger over the Italian intellectual scene than that of Benedetto Croce, the renegade thinker who criticized academic philosophy while developing a system that aimed to draw together everything from art and history to philosophy. Late in his career, after the fall of the fascist state that he opposed, Croce wrote a short essay of some twenty pages, "An Unknown Page from the Last Months of the Life of Hegel" ("Una pagina sconosciuta degli ultimi mesi della vita di Hegel," 1948, republished by Laterza as a separate volume in 1950 and translated by Sprigge in Croce 1966). It is an imagined dialogue set "toward the end of the summer of 1831" (thus a few months before Hegel's death in November of that year). In it, a Neapolitan philosopher, an imagined character named Francesco Sanseverino, turns up at Hegel's home in Berlin. Sanseverino is represented as a serious student of Hegel's thought, someone who has spent much time in Germany, first "as an officer in one of the Neapolitan regiments which took part in Napoleon's invasion of Russia and in the subsequent armed clashes on German soil," and then in two subsequent visits that coincided with Hegel's rise to fame alongside the rise of the Prussian state.[17] The imaginary Sanseverino has read Hegel's major works, attended his lectures, talked with his leading students, and even once met with Hegel himself, "telling him of the ardour and zeal with which he was following his work, and of the hope which he cherished of finding *himself* in that pursuit."[18] He is now back for a final visit, in the course of which Sanseverino lays out both his appreciation and criticisms of Hegel's thought, separating what is vital and powerful in it from what seems mistaken or problematic.

In this literary representation, in other words, Croce is setting out and rearticulating his own assessment of Hegel's philosophy through the fictional voice of an imagined Neapolitan forbearer. We will have occasion to reflect in more detail on how Croce adopts and criticizes Hegel's system, but here I want first to consider how Croce's dialogue frames the whole encounter with a series of reflections on the role of nationality in the formation and reception of philosophical thought. What he ultimately underscores, I would suggest, is the transnational character of Italian thought in particular and of philosophical progress more generally. This vignette thus serves as a point of entry into my argument that the reception of Hegel pitted nationalist impulses against a transnational cosmopolitanism, both of which characterized the conflicted Italian response to modernity from the revolutionary moment of the Risorgimento into the twentieth century.

Croce on Hegelian Nationalism

Croce explicitly links Hegel's rise to that of the Prussian state. Likewise, he emphasizes the cosmopolitan nature of his character, Sanseverino, who has travelled far and wide as a part of the world-historical undertaking of the Napoleonic Wars.[19] That event drew him out of Naples and onto the international scene, and as a result he has come into contact with a philosophical system that he hopes will help him understand himself. The set-up in these first pages of the dialogue, before any dialoguing has begun, already highlights the principal theme, the idea that philosophy is a project of self-understanding or self-recognition that is integrally tied to history and historical situation (what we might call the self-unfolding of *Geist* in the form of political history). Philosophy and this self-understanding are constituted by the progress of world history.

Hegel's own thoughts on nationality come up twice in these first pages. First, the narrator (Croce?) refers to Hegel's inaugural lecture at the University of Berlin in 1818, in which he named "the German people as 'God's chosen people in philosophy.'"[20] Then, when Sanseverino finally meets Hegel in 1831, he tells the great philosopher about the studies he has undertaken, "avoiding mention, incidentally, of his participation in the Neapolitan constitutional revolution of 1820–21, for he was aware of Hegel's political attitude and of his opinion that such revolutions and convulsions were a 'weakness of the Latin peoples.'"[21] Hegel's thought is thus being connected to a moment of Prussian nationalism that is eager to establish its own superiority and to reject other groups (the "Latin peoples" here) as inferior. Likewise, before we hear anything about the content of Hegel's philosophical system, we hear of his conservative political stance toward revolution.

The end of their imagined encounter likewise returns to the topic of nationality, only this time focusing not on Hegel and the Prussians but rather on Naples, the city that Croce's character claims is the place "upon which the alert minds of South Italy converge," going on to say:

> Naples has in the past provided almost all the serious philosophers of Italy, and while alive to sublime speculations, is kept on the firm ground of the concrete and historical by an unfailing realism. Herder, Hamann, and even Goethe observed or sensed this robust aptitude of Naples for philosophy. A young King has come to the throne, there is a feeling of fresh air, of hope and confidence, private study circles are springing up, voluntary universities, as it were, outside the official university, formed by eager men of study. Foreign literature passes from hand to hand and reviews of a serious character are appearing with contributions by competent authors. All this draws me back to Naples.[22]

This encomiastic description of Naples focuses on its role as a cosmopolitan centre – a centre of learning and networks of knowledge exchange, but also a political centre and home to the new king (Ferdinand II, who took the crown on 8 November 1830 at the age of twenty). It is thus a centre of both intellectual and world-historical revitalization – the fresh new air invigorates this cosmopolitan space of convergence as it enters into a phase of renewal. This description mirrors the political and philosophical pairing that Croce had established earlier in the dialogue between the rise of Hegel around 1819 and the rise of the Prussian state, both centred in Berlin, where Hegel moved in 1818 to take up the chair in philosophy that had previously belonged to Fichte. Both descriptions underscore the cosmopolitan conditions that help generate philosophical renewal.

On the one hand, then, Croce recognizes the strong tie between political history and philosophical history – the ways in which the history of ideas is permeated and shaped by political forces operating across borders and languages. On the other, he is describing a process in which ideas developed by Hegel in a moment of growth and change in Prussia naturally migrated to a new location where they could undertake the next "steps" in their development: from Berlin to Naples, the development of philosophy is being imagined here as a necessarily transnational endeavour.[23]

Another way of looking at this vignette from Croce's late philosophical writings would be to see it as an indication that in an era of rapid cultural change, Italian thinkers who were eager to re-establish their own national tradition were nonetheless aware of how that national tradition had to be situated beyond its own borders. My contention in this book is that we must follow through on that critical realization, examining how the particular case of Italian modernism underwent a transnational formation and how that formation then translated into a deep conceptual relation linking Italy to other locales across Europe and the globe. Writers, artists, and thinkers from an array of national contexts came into a rich nexus of interrelation, spurred in part by a shared relation to modernist idealism.

To understand Italian modernism will thus require first looking back to what Croce here identifies as the key historical moment in which modern Italy was informed by foreign sources of thought: the revolutionary movements culminating in the Risorgimento. And while it would be difficult to justify looking only at Naples in this context, Croce's choice to focus on the Neapolitan scene can certainly guide us in a fruitful direction. German idealism played a role in fomenting new ideas and an energetic new vision of Italy as a nation and Italians as a people, and the philosophers and institutions of Naples are thus a key stop on the itinerary of a developing instance of modernist idealism.

Hegelian Nationalism and Cosmopolitanism in Risorgimento Politics and Philosophy

So we will take a quick jaunt back to the tumultuous scene of Risorgimento Naples.[24] In a city that had a long and fraught history of political revolution and reactionary repression, the period of Italian unification saw a not unsurprising return of fervent political activity. Naples was, after all, the mainland capital of the Kingdom of the Two Sicilies (Regno delle Due Sicilie) where the Bourbon king, Ferdinando II, ruled from 1830 to 1859, a time span that witnessed multiple revolts. After the violent repression of a Sicilian revolt and demands for a constitution in 1837, 1848 saw the greatest challenge to Bourbon rule: liberal agitators sewed discord starting in September 1847, leading to revolutionary uprisings in numerous cities and finally the king's decision to grant a constitution in January of 1848. However, by spring of 1849 the newly formed parliament had been disbanded and Ferdinando II had reasserted absolute control, using military force to subdue the liberal rebellion. As a part of quashing this rebellion, thousands of suspected revolutionaries were jailed or sent into exile. But the restoration was short-lived – the Risorgimento of 1860–61 brought an end to the Bourbon monarchy and to this independent kingdom that had existed since the mid-1400s. The energy previously channelled into rebellion now took a new course: a surge of Italian nation-building dedicated to forging a new national identity under the rule of Vittorio Emanuele, King of Italy. These dramatic changes played out not only in the realm of geopolitics but also in the sphere of local cultural politics.

The nature of Italian national identity now became a contentious topic at the University of Naples, which had long been a leading seat of learning. The Regno effectively ended in March 1861, and by the beginning of the following academic year in Naples, a loud debate was under way about how to conceive of Italian nationality in this new era of unity. In 1860, Luigi Palmieri (1807–1896), a prominent scientist who believed in the superiority of the Italian people and nation, was awarded a newly established chair as professor of meteorological physics and geophysics (he would go on to become a senator of the newly unified state in 1876). In this role, he gave an opening address on 16 November 1861.[25] In it, he evoked the spirit of Italian nationalism, which during the Risorgimento entailed a political project to forge new national institutions, in addition to cultural and social claims about the nature and character of the Italian people, their shared history, and their special place or even "primacy" in European history. In this way he situated contemporary Italy in the lineage of Italian scientists and proto-scientists, including thinkers like the Renaissance natural philosopher, Bernardino Telesio. His call for a renewed emphasis on the power of Italian "genius" followed the legacy of a then-famous philosophical figure, Vincenzo Gioberti (1801–1852), who in 1838 had published the treatise *On the Moral and Civil Primacy of the Italians* (*Del primato morale e civile degli italiani*).[26] That text called for a reinterpretation of Italian genius through the creation of a genealogy of "Italic" thought leading back to the ancient world, which would then be used to justify forms of philosophical and cultural nationalism aimed at establishing the legitimacy of a specifically Italian contribution to European culture.[27] Gioberti was aiming for the formation of a new, united federation of Italian states ruled by the Pope, and his treatise would continue to resonate for Risorgimento nationalists like Palmieri immediately after the founding of the new Kingdom of Italy. Thus the academic year opened on a nationalist note, one that fused philosophy and politics in a picture of world history developing both out of and toward Italy's own national glory.

All of this may sound like another example of the patriotic rhetoric typical of a moment of political revolution and upheaval, but what is interesting for my purposes is what happened next. The newly appointed chair in philosophy, Bertrando Spaventa (1817–1883), responded by offering his own, contrasting vision of the philosophical underpinnings of Italian nationality in the Risorgimento age, "On Nationality in Philosophy."[28] Spaventa was likewise a patriot – the older brother of Silvio Spaventa (1822–1893), a prominent Risorgimento revolutionary – as well as a fierce proponent of a free, unified Italy.[29] At the same time, his vision for Italian culture was one that insisted on recognizing not the *primacy* of Italic thought but rather what we would today call the transnational character of Italian culture. To establish the significance of Italian thought and culture, he sought first to depict Italy's place in a complex space of ideas, a history of philosophical thought spanning both centuries and countries in a gradual progress in the course of which truth emerged as a collective project and freedom was both the ideal guiding and the outcome resulting from the struggle for philosophical consciousness.

Spaventa's inaugural address reiterated some patriotic elements of Palmieri's earlier speech but then went on to suggest a new question, now that the issue of whether or not to become Italians had been settled:

> But the difficulty now, Gentlemen, lies not in maintaining a national sentiment and the conviction that our genius must reflect itself in every form of our life and thus also in philosophy; the difficulty does not lie in loving our philosophers. We all yearn to be Italians; that is no longer an issue.

> Especially for us, as professors and students, the point is to turn this love into knowledge; for where philosophers are concerned, to love them is to know them. The point is to interpret this sentiment so that it does not degenerate into an empty conceit. Above all, we need to form a clear and distinct account of our genius.[30]

For Spaventa, understanding the nature of "Italian genius" and what it meant to be Italian would require a genealogical account of the Italian people and their place in the broader history of all peoples. In other words, it would require placing Italy in its international context. The history that he traced in outline form in this inaugural address, and then in depth through a series of ten lectures on the history of philosophy, aimed to demonstrate that throughout the centuries Italian philosophy had in key ways prefigured major conceptual advances in philosophy across Europe. But it had also responded to those advances and fed back into the general progress of philosophical thought: neither a secret source nor a hidden destination, it was an integral part of an international endeavour of consciousness coming to light (coming to itself).[31]

This circular relation of Italian and European thought thus represented an ongoing exchange of ideas, but more than that it indicated the fundamentally transnational character of all modern thought:

> And so it happens that in the modern world, in contrast to the ancient world, the lives of all nations move together, unconcealed. Each nation is not only itself but also the other. Indeed, it is not really itself except insofar as it is related to and intimately unified with the others. The natural and characteristic foundation does not disappear but gives way to a new, common, and universal foundation that is no longer something immediate and primitive – as with the original community before separation – but is the result of a long, patient, painful, and common elaboration that emerges from the commingling and battling of peoples and lineages. All in all, it amounts to a new origin, a rebirth. As such, the meaning of nationality is altered. It no longer appears as something that is given naturally and immediately (I will even say blindly) by an inexorable destiny, but rather as an absolutely spiritual product. It is the place that each people occupies on its own – through its own conscious energy – at the splendid banquet of new life. From this point on, nationality no longer entails the exclusion or absorption of other nations, but rather involves the autonomy of a people within the common life of all peoples – just as the individual's personality consists in conserving its own autonomy in the community of the state.[32]

In typically Hegelian fashion, Spaventa was separating the ancient world from the modern by insisting that while the ancients had inhabited a type of nationality that was given blindly as a form of destiny, the moderns had come into self-consciousness and so could understand themselves and create themselves as "an absolutely spiritual product."[33] Modern nationality, then, was a historical achievement whereby the spirit of a people developed itself and came into awareness of itself through the struggle of its own self-constitution.[34] This allowed Spaventa to arrive at a metaphor that captured the cosmopolitan character of his vision: the nations of Europe had become like individuals gathered into a collective – each self-conscious, each autonomous, but each also operating together with and in relation to the others. Seated together at the banquet of nations, the peoples of modern Europe would achieve their individual character through their collective interactions, which we might call mutually self-constituting.[35]

The metaphor of the banquet of nations is worth focusing on because it depicts the idea of a transnational nationalism and simultaneously enacts that vision. Spaventa is not simply describing a Hegelian approach to history; he is also manifesting that history in the way he structures his own history of philosophy. For Hegel, the absolute spirit (or Idea, which is generally the term used in Italian texts) manifests itself and comes into self-consciousness through the operations of history. In other words, Spaventa's articulation of how Italian nationality should be understood is itself filtered through a German world view (and is thus already rejecting in practice the blind nationalism of some Risorgimento thinkers, who sought to expel all foreign influences from their ideal construction of the new Italian nation). In his lectures he would go on to domesticate this foreign influence by connecting it to the thought of Italian philosophers like Giambattista Vico.[36]

This domestication of Hegel was hardly limited to Spaventa's history of philosophy. In fact, as Croce's imagined dialogue suggests, Hegel became a cornerstone of Neapolitan culture and a fixture in its intellectual life. According to Paul Piccone, this broad reception and integration of Hegel set Naples apart from other centres of learning where Hegel was read and discussed: "Unlike the French students of Hegel such as Cousin who never became Hegelians, the Italian Hegelians – especially the Neapolitans – immediately incorporated Hegel and translated his thoughts into their social and political projects of cultural and national rejuvenation."[37] Indeed, following Rocco Rubini's characterization, Bertrando Spaventa "was the leading representative of a group of left-leaning Hegelians who had faced persecution in 1848 when they sought to introduce German idealism to the revolutionary youth of Naples."[38] Others have focused on Augusto Vera (1813–1885) as the leading figure in this circle of Neapolitan Hegelianism, as in the characterization offered by Gerhart Hoffmeister.[39] Whatever the case, however, it is clear that a network of young intellectuals, formed by the revolutionary moment of 1848 and carrying that spirit forward into the Risorgimento, had embraced Hegelian philosophy as a way of fomenting radical political change.[40] The burgeoning theorization of a specifically Italian national character converged with new ideas about the ethical state, thus establishing a liberal phase in the reception of Hegel that would contrast with later developments.[41] In this way, these Risorgimento thinkers made the philosophy of history an exercise in historical praxis; they realized Hegel's idealism in the form of political action culminating in not just the foundation but also the formation of modern Italy.[42]

In these circles, orthodox Hegelianism was made a key part of the Italian political project. However, returning to Croce's literary-philosophical dialogue, we also see an emphasis on the importance of its Italian reception as a mode of providing critical distance for a reinterpretation of Hegelian thought. In his dialogue, the imaginary interlocutor Sanseverino argues against the overly devout repetition of Hegel's ideas and words, a tendency that he sees as all too common among many of Hegel's followers. At the end of the text, after Sanseverino has gone back home and Hegel has died, Croce adds a final paragraph that looks "forward" in time from the death of the philosopher to his reception in modern Italy:

> It was not just in Naples, where Hegel was much studied in the nineteenth century, retaining disciples even in the age of Positivism, but in Italy at large, that the Hegelian crisis matured. From that moment, in Italy, the thought of Hegel the philosopher has recovered potency in a systematization altogether different from that chosen by Hegel himself, in which consequences are drawn which he never intended, while theories which he had taken over from his forerunners, but which could not be retained, have been entirely reshapen. The very name of the systematization has been changed. "Absolute Idealism" no longer fitted the case or underlined the fundamental feature of it: and spontaneously the appropriate term came into being – "Absolute Historicism." Be that as it may, Hegel now belongs to us: he cannot be all in all to us if only because his belonging to us, our possession of him, can only be of value (as the possession of any thought can only be of value) when it incites new life, new thought.[43]

Croce here is referring to himself, obliquely, as the key successor to Hegel's thought, for it is in his own study of Hegel that the term "absolute historicism" comes into play as he reworks Hegel's system, discarding what is "dead" to preserve what is "living."[44] In this way the domestication of Hegel's foreign ideas is doubly complete: in a first step, the Risorgimento Hegelians have domesticated Hegel by fitting him into a historical account in which Italian thinkers like Vico are seen as his predecessors and by using him to help situate the new Italy and its new, transnational vision of nationality.[45] In a second step, Croce himself reshapes Hegel's ideas so that they fit his own conception of history (while, simultaneously, other neo-Idealist thinkers in Italy like Giovanni Gentile are reshaping other elements of Hegel's thought into what will become the philosophical outlook of the authoritarian state). In this second step, Hegel's history becomes actualized as his system is jettisoned in favour of what are perceived to be the kernels of vital philosophical truth underlying it. In both steps, Hegel is envisioned as passing through the conduit of Neapolitan thinkers into the sphere of Italian thought more broadly, so that "Hegel now belongs to us." In this claim we see *in nuce* the conflicted place of modern Italy, a country seeking to establish itself both in itself and in relation to a broader map of modern progress.

Institutionalized Hegelianism: Networks of Reception in Modern Italy

Croce's articulation points us to the way in which Hegel became integral not just to Italian politics and philosophical thought but also to the formation of the institutions that were to structure public and political life in the new Italy. The modernization of the new state was in some key respects influenced by networks organized around the reception of Hegel's thought. My goal here is not to trace out all the routes and networks active in that reception, which would be not only tedious but also, and more importantly, superfluous to understanding that broader picture. Rather, the point I want to illustrate is how Hegelian idealism was received and transmitted through a network of highly connected institutional figures who were integral to the founding of the modern Italian state and who influenced how state power would be used to shape culture, especially through education. Seeing this pattern of transmission will help make sense of my broader contention that modernist idealism has followed a forked path – one trail leading toward political and institutional praxis, the other focused on the transformation of culture (or spirit) through aesthetic rather than political means.

There is a remarkable legacy of institutionalization in the reception of Hegel's thought. By institutionalization, I am referring to the ways in which the reception of Hegel became a point of commonality tying together figures who coalesced into institutions and who in turn led or formed new institutions. This is not of course to imply that Hegelian thought was the only force in those institutions or even the guiding force. But it does point to the ways in which thinkers sharing an interest in his approach to history and its links with the philosophy of the state and nationality created networks that helped establish Hegel's centrality for the Italian project of modernity, not only in theory but also and especially in practice, so as to realize Hegel's own view of the historical actualization of the ideal in political forms.[46]

The ideologically unifying aspect of Hegel's role in Italy was evident in the way that the Neapolitan circle developed in 1860 and 1861. It is no accident that Augusto Vera and Bertrando Spaventa, two of the leading exponents of this philosophy, both found themselves in Naples at the moment of unification.[47] In fact, it was the political and institutional power of Francesco De Sanctis (1817–1883) that brought them together there. After his "exile" in Zurich, where he held a chair teaching at ETH Zurich from 1856 to 1860, De Sanctis was able to return to Italy in 1860. He became an important political figure, was nominated by Garibaldi to be governor of the province of Avellino, and then was charged with the task of restructuring the educational system, first in Naples, where he led an intensive effort from October to November of 1860, and then as the Ministro della Pubblica Istruzione in the cabinets of Cavour and Ricasoli (March 1861–March 1862).[48] De Sanctis's philosophy of political engagement led to a life of political power, and his restructuring of public institutions reflected that philosophy. His political alignment with the moderate left meant that he lost political power in 1865, but by then he had already offered important institutional support to Hegelian thinkers. And his exit from the government was hardly an exit from institutional public life. As the leading figure of post-Risorgimento literary criticism, he was a guiding force in the construction of the new national canon, besides being a public intellectual whose views would continue to shape the direction of the fledgling nation.

Bertrando Spaventa and Augusto Vera, both at the University of Naples under De Sanctis's leadership, then taught a young philosopher who would go on to become a leading exponent of Marxian thought in the second half of the nineteenth century, Antonio Labriola (1843–1904). Labriola enrolled at the University of Naples in 1861, at precisely the fervent moment when De Sanctis's administrative power brought together a school of Hegelian thinkers there. Spaventa not only taught

Labriola but also advocated on his behalf, helping him attain a university education and then a job in the police prefecture in Naples.[49] Labriola did not graduate immediately but nevertheless went on to publish and gain notoriety, eventually obtaining his doctorate and becoming a professor at the University of Rome in 1874. In his first piece of critical writing, Labriola argued against Eduard Zeller, a German professor and neo-Kantian, concluding that it was not Kant but Hegel who provides the essential starting point for understanding the union of empirical and rational sources of knowledge.[50] Over the course of the 1880s, he became increasingly radical, shifting toward Marxism and coming into contact with thinkers like Friedrich Engels (whom he met in 1893), and in fact his first letter to Engels asserted that his socialist political philosophy was a result of his participation in the "reflowering" of Hegelianism in Naples under Spaventa's guidance.[51] Labriola was also deeply involved in the debates over the need for sweeping educational reform to provide public schooling for all young Italians; between 1877 and 1891, he headed an institute aiming to achieve those reforms.[52] From Hegelian idealism to Marxian materialism, his prolific writings and teachings on socialism helped establish him as a leading figure in the foundation of Italian Marxism.[53] He was likewise pivotal in the brief but important phase of Marxian thought that impacted the intellectual trajectory of another giant of Italian educational institutions, Benedetto Croce.

Croce is probably the most famous of the modern Italian philosophers (though likely overshadowed by Gramsci in contemporary scholarship), and his pivotal role as a leading intellectual made him a tremendous force in his time. Croce's political alignment went through shifting phases: he flirted briefly with Marxism under Labriola's guidance and later was temporarily sympathetic to Mussolini's fascism in its early days, until the assassination of Matteoti began to push him away from the regime.[54] Early on, Croce read and rejected Hegel out of hand, and it was only due to the pressure exerted by his long-time friend and interlocutor, Giovanni Gentile, that he returned to Hegel. Croce's return to Hegel thus pushed him closer to Gentile, and even if he was critical of aspects of Hegel's thought, he saw at its core a picture of dialectical reason that would enable him to develop a new philosophy for the twentieth century.[55] Amidst these shifting political and philosophical stances in the early twentieth century, Croce took on a lead role not only as a public intellectual but also in the ongoing process of education reform, thus solidifying a prominence that was both institutional and written into the modern Italian social imaginary.[56]

During the period of his shifting alignments, Croce was for some time a close friend and collaborator with Gentile, another Hegelian idealist who would take on increasingly influential roles in the institutional structure of the Italian state. Unlike all of the thinkers discussed so far, Gentile had no connection to the University of Naples, for though he was born in Sicily he had been educated at the elite Scuola Normale Superiore in Pisa. Yet his professor of philosophy there, Donato Jaja, was a Hegelian who had been trained by none other than Bertrando Spaventa. In this connection we see how the institutional decisions of an administrative figure like De Sanctis, who was able to bring together the Hegelian school in Naples, had reverberations that stretched outward in unexpected trajectories, resembling a form of philosophical cultural politics.

Gentile eventually developed his own derivation of Hegelian idealism, *attualismo* or actual idealism, an approach that was meant to inform the necessary interrelationship of philosophy and cultural life. As the official philosopher of fascism, he saw his institutional power snowball in the years following Mussolini's march on Rome, and he took on numerous positions.[57] As Minister of Public Instruction from 1922 to 1924, he headed a large project to reform the educational system, the "riforma Gentile" of 1923. Later on he rose even higher in the fascist hierarchy, eventually becoming a member of two elite commissions and taking on important roles in major institutions, such as Bocconi University in Milan, where he became the vice-president in 1930. He remained affiliated with the regime to the end, and was assassinated in 1944 by resistance fighters who held him responsible for the Italian Social Republic's execution of five young men in March of that year. Gentile's take on Hegel was certainly not an orthodox Hegelianism; nonetheless, we can see how Hegel's thought had an afterlife well beyond its original Risorgimento manifestations, linked directly to state power and institutional reform.[58] Stretching from the founding of a new Italian nationality to an imperial and totalitarian sense of nationalism – with its ethnic implications – the shadow cast by this Hegelian engagement was not only long but almost Protean in its changing contours.

In Italy, Hegelian thought was institutionalized. And so there it remained central, even after it had lost its force or been diluted in other national contexts. As Brian and Rebecca Copenhaver have aptly put it: "The heart of the Italian anomaly, very briefly, is that idealism of a Hegelian kind thrived in Italy long after it had expired elsewhere, until after 1952, when Croce died and the catastrophe of Fascism and two world wars could finally be addressed from other philosophical perspectives."[59] The tight link between idealist philosophy and the political struggle to forge Italy's national identity thus took on multiple forms, inspiring not only Risorgimento liberals but also a later generation of fascist intellectuals seeking a new spiritual foundation for their floundering young nation. The result is that Hegelian thought became institutionally entrenched, albeit in different ways and different inflections over time. From ministers of education to the most famous intellectual of the fascist period, Hegelian thinkers dominated Italy's progress from separate regional governments to unified nation and from unified nation to centralized and authoritarian state power. From a philosophy with revolutionary implications for self-liberation and actualization to a philosophy of state power that supported fascism, Hegelianism permeated the self-understanding and political refashioning of Italian modernity.[60]

Hegelian Idealism as a Response to Modern Crisis: History, Nationality, and the State

The purpose of tracing these channels of Hegel's impact on the formation of Italian modernity is to enable us to unpack the conceptual nexus implied in this reception. Key concepts that would later become integral to Italy's modernist idealism are visible in the Hegelian project of responding to crisis through world-historical action. Hegel's philosophy was a response to historical transformation and crisis; simultaneously, it offered a model of thought for intervening into that crisis to effect political change aimed at renewing modern life. The real world of material actuality thus became the locus of an ideal transformation that sought to reorganize that life following a rational concept of progressive historical development. Hegelian idealism was in this way an important framework for the broader modernist project of achieving self-awareness of and through modern crisis, and it offered an idealist grounding for projects of national self-becoming realized through political action. Unpacking key conceptual elements in this stance will enable us to understand the ambivalent complexities of modernist idealism more clearly.

In the first place, Hegel offers a new philosophy of history that dovetails with the need to reconceive modernity and the experience of modern crisis so as to redirect these toward a positive futurity. Hegel offers a highly developed philosophy of history that is central to his overall project of articulating the freedom of self-consciousness.[61] From the Risorgimento struggle for Italian autonomy to the national projects to colonize North Africa to the twentieth-century foundation of

Fascism, the creation of a modern Italian state required that a complex notion be developed of how political action could be conceived and justified as part of a broader pattern in world history. Each stage of Italian nation-building unfolded in different circumstances and with different guiding ideals, but throughout, Hegelian thought was present as an idealist inspiration that could be reconfigured to suit those changing circumstances. Thus, Risorgimento thinkers sought to link Hegel to a liberal project of fostering Italian autonomy and unity, while later figures like Alfredo Oriani pushed in an explicitly colonial direction.[62] Tellingly, it was Croce who led the movement to "rediscover" Oriani, whose works were largely met with silence until Croce wrote an essay in which he positioned him as an anti-positivist compatriot working to inject Hegelian idealism into Italian modernity; yet within the span of just over a decade, Mussolini and Gentile were claiming Oriani as the herald of the fascist state and its imperial nationalism.[63] Italian modernity thus constituted itself at least in part through an active intellectual debate over Hegel's idealism. Its historical dimensions created an opening for the reimagining of the Italian community and a concomitant reconfiguration of its place in the world.

Contrary to what one might assume about a system that posits the "idea" or spirit as the locus of what truly exists, Hegelian idealism views the realization of self-consciousness as an achievement that operates through world history and the various objectified forms of spirit (*Geist*). As he puts it in his *Lectures on the Philosophy of World History* (published posthumously in 1857 from notes collected by his students): "History is the process whereby the spirit discovers itself and its own concept."[64] This process, for Hegel, unfolds in stages that can be traced around the globe, telling the story of spirit's self-becoming, the process of awakening into rationality.

In the Hegelian picture, early phases of human development correspond to relatively small and weak states, and peoples (nations) simply assume themselves to constitute a group based on contingent, natural factors that place them together (geography, racial characteristics, etc.). Religions likewise follow something like a tribal alignment, with each people worshipping its own god. Hegel describes world history as having pre-historical roots in societies of this sort – pre-historical, that is, from the perspective of his philosophy, according to which history is constituted by the objective activities through which *Geist* comes into self-knowledge as it rearranges the world in its own image. The path of history then shifts to involve peoples who are subject to a battle over who they are – it enters, in other words, into the contentious space of self-reflection. As the identity of a people emerges from pre-given or "natural" categories and becomes a point of contention – as the tribe gives way to the polis and the polis to the state – the meaning of nationality becomes increasingly complex. This is the teleological aspect of Hegel's history at work. It ultimately grounds a notion of the modern state as the fruition of a process of historical development leading toward rationality's self-realization. In other words, the modern state takes on the role of an endpoint in historical development: it is what allows human beings to operate as fully rational subjects.

There is significant scholarly disagreement about precisely how Hegel's philosophy understands this process. For some, including the philosopher Charles Taylor, Hegel develops a new metaphysics in which the process of world-historical becoming is also the process of spirit coming to know itself precisely as God.[65] For others, Hegel's turn toward history is an affirmation of the Kantian project to make philosophy self-critical, revealing that philosophy itself requires historicization and that its ideas are not eternal truths but rather reflections of concrete truths that emerge historically.[66] It is not my purpose to enter into the wider debate over how best to interpret Hegel's thought. My interest is, rather, in how its reception helped reshape the trajectory of Italian culture from the Risorgimento through the Second World War. It is thus important to note that the metaphysical view of Hegel's system predominated in the late nineteenth and early twentieth centuries, precisely the moment of that reception. Whether this was the best possible reading of Hegel or not, it was certainly a reading that helped Italian thinkers to do two key things: align their political project with an account of world-historical progress that aimed at the achievement of freedom; and align that system with their own tradition, both in terms of Italian political history and in terms of the religious commitments and culture of the Risorgimento period.

We can in fact trace the reception of this philosophy of history through three key moments, each of which demonstrates how the content of Hegel's world view translated into modes of operating in the concrete context of Italian political and institutional history. In the first instance, Hegel's notion of world history became central to the transnational articulation of Italian nationality, as we saw in the previous section. In the second instance, Hegel's philosophy of history was translated into a form of historical vitalism according to which history was still alive in the present. In the third, that vitalism was taken a step further, to the point of making the pure act of the present into an absolute reality, thus drawing together the immanent and the transcendent. All three of these (overlapping) modes of conceiving history vis-à-vis Hegel's philosophy played a key role in the emergence of new conceptions of nationality and the state in the process of Italian modernization.

Risorgimento thinkers drew on Hegel as a way of making sense of their own position in history, as latecomers but participants in the new world of free peoples claiming their rightful place in a general narrative of historical progress. In his excellent study on how Italian thinkers progressively reconceived the notion of the Italian Renaissance through the nineteenth and twentieth centuries, Rocco Rubini argues that Risorgimento-era thinkers saw the political ramifications of the Renaissance as a legacy of weakness and subservience. Italy was fragmented, and its various city-states and regions were subject to foreign rule or influence, minor players in the broader field of European history. As such, Rubini contends that there is an important sense in which the Renaissance era (as a political era) never ended in Italy until the unification movement. Thus the Risorgimento needed a whole new approach to philosophy, a whole new outlook on world history and Italy's place in it.[67] Rubini goes on to show how a line of humanist thinkers, from Vincenzo Cuoco and Vincenzo Gioberti to Bertrando Spaventa and Francesco De Sanctis, dominated the key moment in which Italian national unity was first theorized.[68] Struggling with the legacies of the Renaissance, they sought to establish a new narrative of Italy's rightful place on the international scene.

This reception took off in pre-Risorgimento Naples, and by the Second World War it had spread to become a national phenomenon. Hegel's *Philosophy of History* was first translated into Italian in 1840 by Giovanni Battista Passerini as *Filosofia della storia*, and its effects were particularly felt in connection with the burgeoning move toward a new nation or notion of nationality. Bertrando Spaventa, whose inaugural address at the University of Naples we have already had a moment to consider, was one of the key figures influenced by this reception.[69] He sought to use the history of philosophy as a means to establish not Italian primacy but rather Italian participation in a broad, transnational development in which the idea was successively refined through various historical phases. Using this Hegelian model of history, Spaventa hoped to write what he termed in an earlier inaugural address, one given at the University of Modena in 1859, "the biography of the nation."[70]

This approach to utilizing history as a tool for writing the living story of a people and nation resonated with the reinterpretation of Hegelian history pursued by Croce, who was eager to separate the aspects of Hegel's thought that were still living from the overall system and then use those "living" parts of his thought to intervene in the actual world. For Croce, this living aspect was to be found precisely in Hegel's move to unify philosophy and history by theorizing the Idea as both concrete and universal. As Croce's imaginary interlocutor, Sanseverino, puts it:

> Now once we have grasped the concept of the universal concrete, we can dismiss the distinction between rational and factual truths, finding every rational truth to be at the same time factual. And, something which is of the greatest importance, we may do away with the separation of, nay with the very distinction between history and philosophy. Every historical proposition contains a philosophical affirmation and every philosophical proposition an historical affirmation. History is redeemed from the age-long contempt in which it has been held as a mere collection of facts, and philosophy from the vacuity and uselessness with which it has been and is so often charged.[71]

This approach to history allows it to move from being merely "chronicle" (the dead retelling of events without a practical connection to the construction of actual life in the contemporary world) to being a living history that is active in the construction of the present. Croce makes this point in many of his philosophical writings. In his *Theory and History of Historiography* (*Teoria e storia della storiografia*, 1917), he writes: "Chronicle and history cannot be distinguished as two forms of history that occur at the same time or in which one is subordinate to the other, but they are two different spiritual modes. History is living history; chronicle is dead history. History is contemporary history; chronicle is past history."[72] For Croce, then, Hegel was a source for a new understanding of Italy's emergence into a living present, a source for a philosophy of history dedicated to remaking the world rationally in a time of crisis calling out for spiritual renewal.

Giovanni Gentile's philosophical idea, "actualism," followed this same basic pathway in interpreting Hegel's philosophy of history as pointing to the vitality of the present as the moment for intervening in and reshaping the world. As Claudio Fogu has articulated it, "Gentile posited actualism itself as a reform of Hegelian dialectics aimed at affirming the absolute immanence of theory and practice in the 'pure act,' against all transcendental components of idealist as well as materialist thought."[73] While Gentile's vision of the state embraced fascism, the actualism at the core of his philosophy of history aligned in some key respects with Croce's vision of history, despite the fact that the latter would result in a liberal notion of the state. This consonance should not be surprising, for it was Gentile who convinced Croce to reread Hegel, and Croce attributed much of the way his philosophy developed to his desire to debate Gentile on these issues – a debate that took place especially in a series of articles in *La Voce* in 1913 and 1914.[74] Much could be said about the particularities of their disagreement, but what is interesting for my purposes here is that while the reception of Hegel can pull in radically opposed political directions, at the core of these divergent stances is a drive to merge historical becoming (as consciousness) with actual action.

These divergent political stances range even wider when we consider the pivotal role Hegel played in the work of Marxist philosophers and activists like Labriola and Gramsci. Indeed, for Gramsci, the philosophy of history advocated by Croce and Gentile, whom he grouped together as "reformers" of Hegel, failed to carry Hegelian philosophy further in the way that Marx's rethinking of it does.[75] He saw their thought as rendering Hegel more abstract rather than more historical and thus as failing in their own objectives as well as in contrast to Marx, for whom world history was the manifestation of philosophy in which thought melds with action. Notable here is that even this criticism reveals a solid continuity among their positions: for all of these twentieth-century thinkers, Hegel's approach to history provided an essential conceptual move that was necessary in order to revitalize or renew the Italian spirit, and with it the Italian nation and state. According to this view, history is a meeting point of the immanent and the transcendent, the space in which absolute spirit or consciousness emerges into its concrete realization; in this way, action in and through history becomes a means of responding to modernity and bringing it into self-reflection through praxis. The shape of the state that should result varies based on the interpreter – from the Risorgimento debates over monarchy versus liberal democracy to Croce's liberalism, Gentile's fascism, and Gramsci's Marxism. But for all of these thinkers in the lineage of Hegel, the state furnished a space for the self-constitution of a truly free rationality and thus was situated as a kind of telos for the process of historical self-becoming, echoing Hegel's own position on the importance of Prussia and the world-historical role of the German people.

In Hegel, this account of world history frames a conception of the special character of German nationality. This comes through nowhere more clearly than in his patriotic Inaugural Address at the University of Berlin, which he gave in 1818 in the wake of Napoleon's defeat and the Prussian Restoration. This new era, he declares, is the time for Germany to reclaim the mantle of philosophy: "This need [for truth], by which *spiritual* nature is distinguished from that nature which merely *feels* and *enjoys*, is for that very reason the deepest need of the spirit; – it is an inherently *universal need*, and on the one hand, it has been *stirred more profoundly* by the seriousness of our times, and on the other, it is a characteristic property of the *German* spirit."[76] Both historical circumstance and national character are at work in this key moment when world history has shifted its focus from French notions of individual freedom and their disastrous results to the German alternative Hegel wants to articulate. In a rousing patriotic invocation, Hegel then goes on to assert that only in Germany is it now possible for philosophy to be realized in its proper form: "This science [philosophy] has sought refuge among *the Germans* and survived *only* among *them*; we have been given *custody* of this *sacred light*, and it is our vocation to tend and nurture it, and to ensure that *the highest* [thing] which man can possess, namely *the self-consciousness of his essential being*, is not extinguished and lost."[77]

The idea that nations have characters is of course by no means unique to Hegel; rather, it is part of a broader discourse central to what Habermas refers to as the rationalization of the public sphere. In the moment of the French Revolution, ideals of "national, popular sovereignty" drew on this discourse and reconceived the idea of a nation's will and its character in order to shift power from the monarch into a people; in so doing, it also reshaped modern nationalism.[78] In the Enlightenment articulation of this notion, Montesquieu envisions the spirit of the law in relation to national characters that are influenced by a wide range of factors, from religious beliefs to physical climate: "If it is true that the character of the spirit and the passions of the heart are extremely different in the various climates, *laws* should be relative to the differences in these passions and to the differences in these characters."[79] In Hegel's view, following his reaction to precisely the events of the Revolution, the notion of a people's character is tied to the narrative of spirit's world-historical development that animates his philosophy of history, and as such national character also comes to represent "moments" in the progress of reason toward self-consciousness – the creation of free, self-determining consciousness.

This basic sense that the formation of a nation requires the formation of its people and an active intervention into the character of those people was a fundamental component of the post-Risorgimento push toward the construction of a new Italian identity. This need was expressed in the well-known phrase "fatta l'Italia, bisogna fare gli italiani" (i.e., Italy has been made, but they still need to make Italians). The phrase itself has a complicated history, which Stephanie Hom has traced through its permutations, showing how its Risorgimento origins were transformed when it was reappropriated by D'Annunzio and the fascist state.[80] The idea that a nation requires not only laws and institutions to structure state power but also the formation of a shared national character or people thus serves as another bridge drawing Hegel's philosophy of history and the state together with the modernist political push for renewal. As Pericles Lewis has shown in his compelling study of the modernist novel's connection to nationalism, it was precisely this notion of the state's influence on the individual consciousness and the individual consciousness's role in redeeming the state that generated key elements of modernism's experimental form.[81] The overlap of aesthetic form and political nationalism in projects of renewal constitutes a key element of what scholars have identified as a particular strand of "modernist nationalism,"[82] and indeed, the fascist project was in important ways rooted in modernist cultural politics as a means to reshape not only aesthetic forms but also, through those forms, the character of the nation itself.[83] While that project of cultural politics certainly cannot be reduced to a straightforward extension of Hegel's philosophy of history, my claim here is that the reception of Hegel's thought informed the development of that discourse and that the Hegelian lens allows us to better understand a key dynamic underlying that project: it is, perhaps in ways that are not always obvious, fundamentally an idealist project, one that envisions the people as a conduit of world history and their spirit as both shaped by and shaping that confluence of immanence and the absolute.

Modernity and Spiritual Renewal: Italian Modernism and Hegelian Idealism

Hegel's philosophy proved enduring in Italy, and that endurance may be tied in part to the fact that Italy's political crisis following the immediate post-unification period seemed unshakeable. Crisis and the need to renew, transform, and remake constituted an ongoing narrative not just in the Risorgimento moment but all the way through the Second World War (indeed, long after that). It led to developments ranging from colonial expansion to First World War interventionism. Just as in the moment of Hegel's own philosophical ascendency in Prussia, his reception in Italy can be tied to a period focused on the need for national spiritual renewal.

This ethos of renewal helps us understand how and why Hegelian thought affected the development of Italian modernism in the late nineteenth century and the first few decades of the twentieth. The importance of Hegelian thought for Italian modernism cannot be disentangled from the modernist battle with political and cultural pessimism as well as efforts to establish or reground a culture of vital energy, creation, and renewal – in other words, the two sides of the modernist coin, following Vincent Sherry's convincing articulation of the relationship between decadence and modernism as rooted in the same temporal experience of rupture and transformation, with the former focusing on the experience of loss and pastness receding and the latter turning its attention instead toward the emergent now and its possibilities.[84] In this respect, Hegelian modernism is the modernism that emerges from a profound sense of crisis time but with an optimistic futurity rooted in a complex, idealist stance: the philosophy of history that sees consciousness itself emerging through historical immanence grounds a belief that the world can be rationally refashioned through a form of cultural politics, the remaking of identity. That belief reaches a limit case in the aesthetic refashioning of the people and nation envisioned by the new idealism that seeks to replace religion: the cult of the fascist state. Though the fascist state itself was not structured by these idealist or Gentilian concepts, the ethos animating thus falls in that lineage.

Even after Italy had become a unified nation and the Italian state had begun attempting to construct a national culture, a series of battles were fought over other forms of deadened spiritual existence. These battles spanned wide in the cultural sphere. For one, there was the Church's ongoing war against the loss of religious spirit (secularization and the spread of the profane) and against the proliferation of what were deemed false forms of spirituality (Theosophy and similar "heretical" spiritualisms). At some moments, this battle pitted the Church against the ascendant state in a cultural continuation of Italy's uneasy struggle to integrate Rome into its territory (a struggle that lasted from 1861 to 1870, ending only after the French withdrew their troops from the Eternal City, largely due to events in France).[85] On another front, there were widespread confrontations involving various spiritualist, vitalist, and idealist thinkers who were committed to battling the reductive materialism of positivist culture. It is here that we encounter a key confluence of the philosophical reception of Hegelian thought and the modernist literary and artistic imagination.

As I will argue in chapters 3 and 4 of this book, the uneasy confluence of a nationalist political strand of vitalist thought and a modernist vitalism that often problematized or flat-out rejected nationalism and/or politics is only one example of how difficult it is to distinguish the specific role of Hegelian idealism in the broader cultural sphere. That it had effects is beyond doubt, but how to disentangle those effects from myriad other motivations and outcomes is less clear. Indeed, just as modernism and decadence can be seen as emerging from the same temporal rupture and as feeding off each other and even orienting each other, so too are there two sides to this legacy of idealist thought in the modernist imaginary.

Italian modernism and its response to the perceived spiritual deadening of modern life certainly resonate with aspects of what motivated the eager reception of Hegelian thought. But this reception did not, I maintain, dominate Italian artistic modernism in the way that it seemed to dominate Italian philosophical and political life during the same period. One limiting factor was its ambivalent and even conflicted relation to a cosmopolitan outlook rooting Italian modernity in a world history of spiritual becoming; another was a close-minded nationalism that ultimately sought revitalization through imperial mastery and subjugation and that envisioned the authoritarian state as the ultimate locus of collective action that could realize the spiritual goal of active being. In the modernist production of the avant-garde effort to reshape the world through culture, this Hegelian strand of modernist idealism becomes visible to us. Yet even those Futurists who espoused a Hegelian sense of historical transformation and its relation to consciousness through culture simultaneously inhabited the other side of this ambivalent outlook. Later in this book I will examine those artistic movements and figures in more detail; first, though, we must turn to the other side of that outlook and see how modernist idealism oscillates between two radical alternatives. The institutionally powerful and philosophically privileged legacy of Hegelian idealism needs to be contextualized relative to another idealism that has been much less studied and whose legacy has remained largely hidden, that of Arthur Schopenhauer.

Chapter Two

Italy's Modernist Idealism and the Artistic Reception of Schopenhauer

Were chance, or fortune, or destiny to have it that Schopenhauer were to peek his head out in Italy, he would find Leopardi there, who would attach himself to his feet like a lead ball and impede him from going forward.

– Francesco De Sanctis, "Schopenhauer and Leopardi: A Dialogue between A and D"[1]

Italian modernity unfolded amidst an experience of national crisis that proved to be fertile ground for a Hegelian project of idealist renewal – the forging of a new national consciousness in what I described in the previous chapter as a progressivist vision of active world-historical transformation. But this was only one face of the response to that moment of historical/temporal crisis in Italian culture. Progress has its shadow, and while the hope of rebirth (*risorgimento*) was enough to propel some thinkers toward the model of a progressive philosophy of history rooted in Hegelian idealism, the repeated failures and disappointments of that hope pushed others toward a less optimistic alternative.

This alternative maintained the idealist opposition to the rise of materialist thought in scientific positivism and the increasing reach of modern industrial capitalism that brought its own version of a materialist logic to the fore. It was not in those materialist veins but within idealist thought itself that an alternative formed, one characterized by a pessimistic push to reconceive modernity not as revolution toward progress but rather as a rupture that belied the dark underbelly of progress itself. This notion of the monstrous ideal was visualized early on in the powerful representation that Goya made of Enlightenment's grotesque ambivalence in the aftermath of the French Revolution and its Terror.

In Goya's etching (figure 1), the semantic ambiguity of the text mirrors the visual ambiguity of the figures that surround the sleeping thinker in the foreground. As Goya wrote in a short description that accompanied the publication of the image in his series, *Los Caprichos*: "Abandoned by reason, fantasy produces impossible monsters; united with reason, fantasy is the mother of the arts and origin of the marvelous."[2] Indeed, "el sueño de la razón produce monstrous" could imply that the monsters result from reason's sleep (and thus its lack of vigilance – when reason lets its guard down, so to speak); but it could also suggest that reason dreams up the monsters, that they are the product of reason itself, its shadowy other, its excess. Thus the clearly individuated owls in the foreground, symbols of reason (the owl of Athena, etc.) slowly morph into other shapes and creatures, less defined, darker, looming in their terror. Yet the possible historical reference to the French Revolution morphing into the Terror hardly exhausts the image's meaning.[3] To think more in terms of the broader culture (or cult) of Enlightenment reason, we might say that while reason can imprint the ideal with a rational structure – like the one Hegel develops in his project – reason also unveils its self-contained other, the irrationality of an ideal that brings not ever-better order but nightmares of chaos, dissolution, and decay. The trials of history reveal not only rationalism but also its ideal other, irrationalism.[4]

This bifurcation in the ideal has been integral to Italian responses to modernity, as well; indeed, it is written into the core of the intellectual history that helps us understand the ambivalence of Italian modernism. Alongside the optimism or progressivism of Hegelian idealism, there is a pessimistic outlook that is frequently associated with the aesthetic movements of the late nineteenth century, the *fin de siècle* characterized as a moment of loss, dissolution, and crisis. This moment is dominated not by Hegel's revolutionary potential for realizing modern self-consciousness but rather by the ascetic aestheticism of his great rival (and detractor), Arthur Schopenhauer (1788–1860).[5] For Schopenhauer, what truly exists (as "absolute," in Hegelian language) is not the Idea but rather an irrational surge of vital impulse, will.[6] At the same time, in Schopenhauer's aesthetics, that irrational surge of life manifests itself in ideal forms, what Schopenhauer calls the Platonic Ideas – highly individuated crystallizations of some aspect of will's multiform becoming. A pessimistic vision of the disordered world is thus coupled with an aesthetics that offers a momentary glimpse of order, removing the subject of aesthetic experience from the destructive flux of will's becoming, though only for a brief moment.

Figure 1. *Francisco Goya,* El sueño de la razón produce monstruos (1797–1799).

By examining the impact of Schopenhauer's thought on Italian modernity, I intend to clarify the complex dynamic driving the ambivalence in modernist idealism more generally. While a Hegelian idealism took hold, especially in political and philosophical spheres where his notion of world history could feed into progressivist impulses of modernization and nation-building, another idealism posited a very different solution to the perceived crisis of the modern Italian "spirit." Visible less in the (reductive) history of direct reception and more in the complex interplay of influences constituting a broader cultural and artistic paradigm, this Schopenhauerian world view both refracted modern Italian cultural production and was refracted by it. A closer examination of Schopenhauer's complex, multi-stage reception in the Italian context will serve as a springboard for articulating an ambivalent concept of modernist idealism by unearthing its genealogy.

I begin that task in this chapter by focusing on the philosophical reception – or perhaps rejection – of Schopenhauer's thought, spearheaded by the Italian literary critic and Neapolitan Hegelian Francesco De Sanctis (1817–1883). De Sanctis's reception of Schopenhauer, and his efforts to divert or block that reception to protect the Italian public from what he perceived as the politically dangerous aspects of Schopenhauer's thought, reveal several key insights that will prove pivotal to understanding the historical development of the literary-philosophical outlook I am calling modernist idealism.

De Sanctis appears to "divert" Schopenhauer's reception from the realm of official philosophy to that of literature by pairing Schopenhauer with Leopardi, comparing them to the advantage of the latter, as the quote at the beginning of this chapter suggests. This despite or perhaps in part because of the fact that Leopardi was a deeply philosophical poet, one who wrote a series of philosophically charged dialogues, *Short Moral Works* (*Operette morali*, first published in 1827), along with his capacious collection of philosophical reflections, the *Zibaldone* (published posthumously in 1898). While De Sanctis's dialogue on "Schopenhauer and Leopardi" refers to Leopardi as a poet in contrast to Schopenahuer the philosopher, it can actually be seen as reflecting a key component of Schopenhauer's own method of argumentation: presenting a world view or stance that he renders compelling in large part by means of aesthetic form, by painting a convincing picture, as it were. In this regard, my reading of the Italian reception of Schopenhauer dovetails with and expands on the arguments made by recent scholars of Schopenhauer, especially Sophia Vasalou, David Wellbery, and Sandra Shapshay, who have emphasized this aesthetic element in

Schopenhauer's argumentation and reception.[7] Speaking to this fundamentally artistic reception, Wellbery has summed it up neatly:

> The conspicuous feature of Schopenhauer's legacy is that it has been most fecund not in academic philosophy (for which his contempt was boundless), but in a tradition of literary writing that includes, along with Kafka, other artists of staggering achievement such as Melville, Tolstoy, Hardy, Machado de Assis, Mann, Proust, Pessoa, Borges, Beckett and Cioran. As long as the worlds their works disclose remain compelling, Schopenhauer's philosophical vision will continue to exert its fascination.[8]

This reception speaks to an element central to Schopenhauer's philosophy itself, what Vasalou articulates in saying that "Schopenhauer's philosophical standpoint can be understood as an exercise in vision" that is not outside or after philosophical reflection but rather located "within philosophy itself."[9] Indeed, as Shapshay puts it, Schopenhauer's method fuses aesthetic intuition and philosophical argumentation – both disclosing and analysing what is disclosed – in a way that she labels metonymic, allowing for a "Schopenhauerian symbiosis between what can only be shown and what can be said."[10] This sense of Schopenhauer's fundamentally aesthetic mode of argumentation is not just a recent discovery: in 1875 Friedrich Harms, a professor of philosophy at the University of Berlin, gave a lecture on Schopenhauer, which was translated and published as an article in *The Journal of Speculative Philosophy*. There he identified precisely "form" as a key component of Schopenahauer's thought and its influence.[11] Harms contended that Schopenhauer presents not arguments but rather a "collection of pictures" – in other words, the power of Schopenhauer's thought is rooted in the force of its aesthetic disclosure of a world view and the possibilities for transformative insight that such disclosure affords.[12]

My argument is that the Italian case of Schopenhauer's reception, one of the earliest in Europe outside of Germany (though not one that has been as well documented as his reception in, say, France or England), not only highlights the prominence of this specific aesthetic-argumentative hybridity in Schopenhauer but also in an important sense *enacts* that very same hybridity: when De Sanctis attempts to divert Schopenhauer from the realm of philosophy to the realm of literature, pairing him with the Italian poet Giacomo Leopardi, what he is actually doing, I contend, is assisting in the realization of Schopenhauer's own project. The content and form of Schopenhauer's philosophy require this aesthetic reception in order to be fully realized. This reading of the Italian reception of Schopenhauer thus also provides an essential insight into the nature of modernist idealism. Just as Schopenhauer's philosophy is itself already aesthetic and calls for literary and artistic forms to bring it to fruition, so too is the outlook of modernist production deeply hybrid. Modernist idealism is situated at the juncture of artistic production and philosophical reflection or argumentation, and Schopenhauer's thought is thus formative not only in its content but also in its hybrid form.

Alternative Ideals: From Hegel to Schopenhauer

The World as Will and Representation contains those tendencies that have gained ascendency in contemporary philosophy: anti-intellectualism, voluntarism, and the return to Eastern thought. [Schopenhauer] was among the first to react against the Hegelians' rationalist formalism, one of the first to re-establish the rights of living reality against the grand concepts of the kingdom of the clouds. It was he who intervened into modern thought by establishing the supremacy of feeling, instinct, and will over the pure idea and rational reason. And it was he who demonstrated most eloquently the wisdom and greatness of the great Asiatic religions' asceticism of renunciation and purification. Wagner took inspiration from him for his dramas of fatality and salvation, and Nietzsche took from him the idea of the will to live, exalting it instead of denying it.

– Giovanni Papini, *The Twilight of the Philosophers*
(*Il crepuscolo dei filosofi*, 1906)[13]

Giovanni Papini (1881–1956) was an influential thinker in the early twentieth century not only on account of his own philosophical writings but also as a key node in the networks diffusing avant-garde thought in the period of modernist experimentation. He was the editor of many journals that played an integral role in the development of the cultural moment: first editing *Leonardo* (1903–7, in collaboration with Giuseppe Prezzolini) and then the important literary and cultural periodicals *La Voce* (1908–16, again with Prezzolini) and *Lacerba* (1913–15, with Ardegno Soffici). It is thus telling that in his fervent work of "anti-philosophy," *Il crepuscolo dei filosofi,* he situated Schopenhauer as a key moment in philosophy's progress and dissolution.[14] Schopenhauer brings two models of progressivism to an end, that of idealist rationalism (typified by Hegel) and that of the positivists, whom Schopenhauer both embraces and rejects in Papini's reading. At the same time, however, Schopenhauer is not strong enough to hold to his convictions and ends up positing a mode of redemption even within his pessimistic system – the redemption of renunciation (what Papini groups as an instance of "oriental thought"). He is thus not the figure of reference for Papini's own vitalism, but rather a generative intermediary who gives rise to Wagner and Nietzsche.[15] This view sees Schopenhauer as both the force opposing progressivism and the force generating new responses to pessimism, a turning point between a pessimistic rejection of progress and the development of an alternative in philosophy and the arts.[16] It is a view that resonates with the broader Italian reception of Schopenhauer's thought as an alternative to Hegelian idealism.

The standard narrative has held that there was little interest in Schopenhauer's thought in mainstream Italian philosophy. Certainly, Schopenhauer never achieved the kind of institutional hegemony in Italian philosophy that we have seen in the case of Hegel and his reception. However, in the last few years a number of Italian scholars have begun to challenge that standard narrative by reconstructing the multiple, less prominent ways in which Schopenhauer entered into philosophical discourse in the late nineteenth and early twentieth centuries. As Marco Segala has shown, if we shift our focus away from thinking about the translation and diffusion of Schopenhauer's main work, *The World as Will and Representation*, we see that Schopenhauer's influence was more expansive than imagined – partial translations, short essays, and "salon" ideas circulated throughout Italy and made a significant mark on bourgeois society even when a more "official" academic reception was still lukewarm at best.[17]

Building on these insights, Fabio Ciracì's long and substantial account (weighing in at some 650 pages), *La filosofia italiana di fronte a Schopenhauer: La prima ricezione 1858–1914*, makes a compelling case that there was much more philosophical interest in Schopenhauer than has previously been admitted, even if the major players (Spaventa, De Sanctis, Croce, Gentile) remained hostile to his outlook. Indeed, Ciracì is able to distinguish two distinct phases in the early Italian reception of Schopenhauer's thought, one rooted in his initial popular diffusion and a second in which his thought was utilized as part of a raging debate about the nature of idealism in the moment of Italian Neo-Idealism. In the first phase of this reception, starting in the 1870s and enabled by partial translations and selections focusing on his aphorisms and moral writings, Schopenhauer was seen through two primary lenses: on the one hand, as an epistemological thinker whose philosophy participated in a modern turn against illusion in all its forms (thus fitting into an Enlightenment narrative of philosophy that had ongoing resonance in the age of positivism); on the other, as a romantic thinker whose esoteric spiritualism, Buddhism, and aestheticism (especially his philosophy of music) fit with the irrationalism and vitalism that flowed against the impulses of that positivist moment. In the subsequent, second phase, which Ciracì traces in the early 1900s, these two lenses merged as academic philosophers like Giuseppe Melli and Piero Mertinetti turned to Schopenhauer to help them respond to and refine Kantian ethics in the era of Italian Neo-Idealism.

So there is more to say about Schopenhauer in Italy than has previously been admitted, particularly in the English-language scholarship, which has thus far lagged behind the recent Italian reconstructions. But as both Ciracì and Segala note, ultimately it is less in the realm of academic philosophy than in the realm of popular cultural discourse and artistic creation that Schopenhauer's legacy becomes most significant. Echoing a term coined by Hans Zint in 1938, Ciracì argues that in addition to the deep philosophical impact (Schopenhauer's "effetto in profondità") there is also a broad impact, "un suo *effetto in ampiezza,*" one constituted by "a cultural impact that extends beyond the realm of philosophy and embraces the world of literature and the arts."[18]

Perhaps it was this enduring presence that prevented Papini from following through on the bold proclamations of his 1906 book, in which he aimed to kill off philosophy once and for all through his attack on, among others, Schopenhauer. In fact, four years later, he was back writing about Schopenhauer again, this time in the essay "Schopenhauer in Italia," published in Rome in *La cultura contemporanea* (16 April 1910). There, he argued that the "fortune of Schopenhauer in Italy" was an essential component of "the history of culture" and necessary to a *spiritual* understanding of culture itself.[19] Papini insisted on a spiritual reading as a way of opposing the deadening forces of materialism. Likewise, we see that he recognized the enduring force of Schopenhauer's thought, not just as a philosophy but as a world view – what in his earlier account from *Il crepuscolo dei filosofi* he had described precisely as a "veduta."[20] This vision of the world in its pessimism permeated the modernist moment, and even if he had promised to bury the legacy of philosophers like Schopenhauer, Papini knew he was living in a time when that outlook was inescapable.

Schopenhauer in Italy: De Sanctis as Domesticating Redirection

To inquire into the sources of this deep, permeating presence of Schopenhauer's thought in Italian culture, it will be necessary to overcome the false binary that results from studies that divide up the philosophical and cultural (literary-artistic) reception of Schopenhauer's thought. For whether he meant to or not, in suggesting a differentiation between the "depth" of Schopenhauer's philosophical reception and the "breadth" of his cultural reception (mere diffusion), Ciracì was obscuring the mutual interdependence of these two aspects. From the very beginning of Schopenhauer's reception in Italy, the attempt to forestall his importance for academic philosophy was characterized by arguments pushing Schopenhauer's thought out of the realm of philosophy and into the realm of literature and the arts, with Francesco De Sanctis not only authoring the first Italian study on Schopenhauer but also pairing him with an Italian literary figure, the romantic poet Giacomo Leopardi (himself a hybrid writer working between literature and philosophy). He thus sought to domesticate the foreign, making it more comprehensible, while simultaneously privileging the domestic alternative. In the wake of De Sanctis's intervention, that literary-cultural reception gained further traction even as De Sanctis's philosophical followers continued to reject the importance of Schopenhauer's thought *qua* philosophical system.

It is somewhat ironic that Schopenhauer's presence in Italian culture begins with an essay penned by one of the central proponents of the Hegelian outlook.[21] De Sanctis's interest in Hegel clearly overlapped with the political reception of that philosopher, who was tied to a revolutionary ideology in the period leading up to the revolts of 1848 and eventual Italian unification. De Sanctis was imprisoned between 1850 and 1853 for his role in a secret plot against the Bourbon monarchy in Naples with a group of other revolutionaries, including Luigi Settembrini (1813–1877). During that time, while Settembrini was translating Lucian and authoring a work on Neoplatonism, De Sanctis was translating Hegel's *Logic*.[22] Only three years later, after his release and subsequent exile to Switzerland, he published an imaginary philosophical dialogue with the aim of introducing Schopenhauer to the Italian public via the Torinese journal of letters, the *Rivista contemporanea* (vol. 15, no. 61, December 1858: 369–408). Thus while De Sanctis was committed to the political progressivism that motivated his contemporaries' Hegelian view of world history, he nevertheless was the first to make Schopenhauer's philosophy accessible to an Italian-reading public. This chronological position as the first Italian to write a significant study of Schopenhauer (and among the earliest outside of Germany at all) certainly makes him the obvious point of departure for my considerations here, but there are more important reasons to start with his dialogue. In fact, De Sanctis exemplifies the complex interplay of these two German philosophers in the intellectual history of the Risorgimento, how they are from the start positioned as opposite poles in a political-philosophical battle; at the same time, he also represents the complex interplay of philosophical and literary reception, showing how drawing a sharp distinction between the two offers an overly reductive vision of Schopenhauer's legacy and, more importantly, of how that legacy functions in the Italian cultural system.[23]

What I intend to show through this closer examination is that De Sanctis's dialogue accomplished three interrelated tasks: first, it played an essential historical role in the reception and diffusion of Schopenhauer's thought; second, it offered valuable insights into the political and cultural significance of that reception in a way that predicted major shifts and also contributed to our own contemporary efforts to understand the development of European modernism; and, finally, it amounted to an implicit recognition of what would become Schopenhauer's greatest strength – his aesthetic impact, both in terms of the argumentative power placed on the aesthetic as a mode of philosophical insight in Schopenhauer's own thought, his "aesthetic standpoint," and in relation to the specifically artistic afterlife of his world view. Indeed, De Sanctis's dialogue was an attempt to introduce Schopenhauer in conjunction with Leopardi in such a way as to combat a spiritual decline in Italian culture leading to political exhaustion, and in so doing to reinvigorate the national project of becoming (along somewhat Hegelian lines). But by inaugurating Schopenhauer's reception in this way, he inadvertently contributed to the growing aesthetic interest in Schopenhauer, not stopping but diverting his cultural impact in the Italian sphere. It is for this reason that the next chapter in this book will focus on Schopenhauer's association with the literature and art of decadence.

De Sanctis's Dialogue: The Reception of a Formative Source

Before examining De Sanctis's essay in detail, it is important to explain why this particular text was so significant for Schopenhauer's reception in Italy and so indicative with regard to the ambivalent formation of modernist idealism more generally. His dialogue about Schopenhauer had a complicated reception in Italy. It was first disseminated through a popular journal of letters that De Sanctis had collaborated with for several years by that time.[24] The dialogue was later reprinted in numerous venues, starting with De Sanctis's own collection, *Saggi critici* (1874), and continuing to this day.[25] Benedetto Croce showed a particular interest in De Sanctis's dialogue, authoring a study of it in which he asserted that it was the best work on Schopenhauer's thought to have come out of Italy – that it surpassed the usual treatments by professional philosophers and was unmatched for both its "profundity" and its "pithy brevity."[26] He added that it had been unjustly overlooked precisely because it bridged philosophical and literary criticism, thus managing to alienate both groups of readers: "For those solely concerned with literature that philosophical discussion comes out difficult to understand and assess; scholars of philosophy, on the other hand, wouldn't think to look in a collection of essays on literature for a piece of philosophical importance."[27] The same reasoning makes it an important starting point for my examination of Schopenhauer's influence on modernism.

Following Croce, then, I would contend that there is a double legacy that must be traced when considering De Sanctis's dialogue: on the one hand, it seeks to use a comparison with the Italian poet as a way of activating what I have called a subterranean critique in which the revolutionary outlook of politicized Hegelianism attempts to circumvent the possible threat represented by the new philosophical school appearing in Germany; on the other, its approach to making this comparison crosses the boundary of literature and philosophy and in this way prefigures what will be a predominantly "marginalized" (from the perspective of academic philosophy) and literary-artistic reception of Schopenhauer's thought, in contrast to the more "institutionalized" political-philosophical reception of Hegel that I have outlined in the previous chapter.

This literary-philosophical legacy becomes even richer if we pause for a moment to consider the hypothesis that De Sanctis's dialogue may have been a formal inspiration for Croce's own later essay on Hegel, which he likewise wrote as an imagined dialogue and which I examined in detail in chapter 1. In a footnote at the end of Croce's dialogue between Hegel and the imaginary Neapolitan philosopher Francesco Sanseverino, Croce explains the origins of his essay and justifies its dialogue form. After asserting that it was a "caprice" that "occurred to me during a sleepless night and was put down on paper the morning after," he nevertheless goes on to situate it historically:

> For the rest, it cannot be said that an historical basis for the caprice is entirely lacking. Traces of a constructively critical attitude towards Hegel's philosophy were really to be found in nineteenth-century Naples, if not as early as 1830, at any rate towards the middle of the century. They are to be found, however, not among the orthodox Hegelians, not even in the severest and most thoughtful of them, Bertrando Spaventa, but in the fresh and uninhibited mind of one who without formally professing philosophy had a clearer and more genuine vein of it than the professors – Francesco De Sanctis.[28]

In other words, Croce is acknowledging that his model in addressing Hegel was not a philosopher but a literary critic. While Croce stops short of attributing the formal structure of his dialogue to De Sanctis' model, it certainly seems a likely influence given the explicit debt Croce acknowledges. Setting aside whether De Sanctis's dialogue is the specific model for Croce, however, what is clear is that De Sanctis not only introduced Schopenhauer to Italians but also did so in a way that fertilized the cross-pollination of disciplines both as objects of study and as modes of inquiry.

Croce thought of De Sanctis's essay as overlooked. Its fate in the twentieth century has been less marginal: it was republished in collections of De Sanctis's writings, and it was the title essay of a short book (*tascabile*) that is still in print today: *Schopenhauer e Leopardi, e altri saggi leopardiani* (Como-Pavia: Ibis, 1992, reprinted in six editions, most recently in 2013).[29] Just last year a significant Italian-language study of the dialogue was published in Fabio Ciracì's *La filosofia italiana di fronte a Schopenhauer (1858–1814)*, "Francesco De Sanctis e lo Schopenhauer dell'esilio," indicating the emphasis that Italian scholars have continued to place on De Sanctis's work. The essay's long afterlife in Italy makes it all the more notable that it has never been published in English and so has largely been ignored by English-language criticism.[30] This makes it all the more necessary to examine the dialogue closely and unpack the unique way in which it introduced Schopenhauer's philosophy through a conversation with Leopardi's poetry and poetics. It is also the reason why I have undertaken my own translation, included here as an appendix.

De Sanctis's Dialogue: A Transnational Exchange

When Schopenhauer's philosophy began its rise to prominence in the 1850s, it was often characterized first and foremost as antagonistic to Hegel's. Ciracì has argued that this turn against the then-dominant philosophy of Hegelianism helps us understand how De Sanctis ended up writing his article on Schopenhauer in the first place. He focuses on De Sanctis's growing dissatisfaction with Hegel's limitations and his desire for an alternative, a desire that we see him developing and experimenting with in the lectures on Dante that De Sanctis delivered in Zurich in 1858.[31] But of course, as Ciracì, Heyer-Caput, and others have pointed out, the dialogue on "Schopenhauer and Leopardi" of 1858 is shot through with an irony that makes it difficult to see him as affirming Schopenhauer's philosophy.[32] My suggestion is thus that if De Sanctis was dissatisfied with Hegel, he was nevertheless committed to the political activism and progressivism that the Hegelian school represented – he could not affirm an alternative like the one offered by

Schopenhauer, even if he could appreciate that Schopenhauer's growing prominence signalled a shift in the historical moment that highlighted the need to move beyond a restrictive version of Hegelianism. The reading I offer in this section aims to illustrate how De Sanctis ultimately moves toward Leopardi as a better alternative, using the Italian poet as a way of countering the negative elements that render Schopenhauer's philosophy problematic. At the same time, the kinds of limitations that Hegel imposes and against which De Sanctis militates are precisely the kinds of philosophical-systematic motivations that a literary alternative avoids. It is thus the poet, not the philosopher, the Italian, not the German, who can speak to the pessimism of post-1848 Europe in a way that inspires a renewed drive for spiritual and political growth. A closer look at De Sanctis's dialogue helps us make more sense of how the reception of Schopenhauer's philosophy was diverted from philosophical circles toward artistic re-elaboration as its primary channel for influencing Italian culture as well as modernist idealism more generally.

The relatively long essay – forty-three pages in the 1921 edition of *Saggi critici* – was written during the period of De Sanctis's exile in Switzerland, where he taught at the Eidgenössische Technische Hochschule Zürich from 1856 to 1860. Structured as a dialogue, it presents a conversation between a scholar, named "D" (who quite clearly stands in for De Sanctis), and a traveller, named "A." The two meet by chance on a train to Zurich.[33] A, we learn, was a revolutionary in Naples who was active in the uprisings of 1848 and was caught by the police, who are personified throughout the dialogue by the ominous character of Campagna, a police chief in Naples who recurs in their exchange as a symbol of the repressive power that has quashed revolutionary idealism. Ever since his brush with this state authority, A has drifted away from philosophy, which he sees as dangerous, and toward the positive sciences, which he sees as safe territory. Nevertheless, he cannot help asking D about the books he sees him reading on the train, and this gives rise to the dialogue's long discussion of the new philosophy from Germany, that of Arthur Schopenhauer (frequently referred to as "Arthur," "Arturo," throughout the dialogue).[34]

The self-reflexive aspect of this fictionalized encounter creates some ironic distance from the reader and from actual political reality so that De Sanctis has space in which to criticize not only Schopenhauer but also the repressive Neapolitan police. Using that quasi-fictional, quasi-biographical set-up as a starting point, the dialogue goes on to cover all the key facets of Schopenhauer's thought. But as he expounds his notion of the world as will and his position as a response against post-Kantian idealists like Fichte, Schelling, and Hegel, De Sanctis focuses especially on the political ramifications of Schopenhauer's pessimistic outlook and its asceticism. The essay covers all of the primary areas of Schopenhauer's thought, offering an overview of his metaphysics, ontology, epistemology, and ethics in significant detail. Perhaps surprisingly to a modern reader, De Sanctis focuses strongly on something that is infrequently discussed by critics today – Schopenhauer's political theory, including his justification of monarchic absolutism and his rejection of an ethics of revolutionary idealism.[35] Obviously this is the crux of De Sanctis's concern with Schopenhauer and the reason for his ultimate rejection of him: he views Schopenhauer's transformation of idealism through a political lens, always with an eye on the political consequences of his alternative to Hegel's idealism. At its core, this dialogue is focused not just on the meaning of Schopenhauer's thought but even more on the meaning of a moment ripe for Schopenhauer's thought – a moment that has lost sight of the political ideals attached to the reception of an earlier, revolutionary interpretation of idealism.

This shift of attention to the political corresponds to what would seem to be a surprising lack of attention to Schopenhauer's emphasis on aesthetics and his ideal of aesthetic liberation. De Sanctis very briefly mentions that Schopenhauer sees the will as creating forms outside of space and time that align with Plato's Ideas (in contradistinction to a Hegelian notion of the Idea), but he does not focus on the aesthetic character of this link to Plato, which is perhaps the key point Schopenhauer himself aimed to make.[36] While much present-day scholarship tends to focus on the idea of aesthetic liberation in Schopenhauer, De Sanctis's relative inattention to that aspect is nonetheless in keeping with a great deal of the early reception of Schopenhauer's philosophy, not just in Italy but also elsewhere.[37] At the same time, though, by comparing Schopenhauer to the Italian poet, Giacomo Leopardi, De Sanctis offers a different and unexpected perspective on the aesthetic element of Schopenhauer's thought. It is to this comparison that we now turn to understand how the first major treatment of Schopenhauer in Italy domesticates his philosophy by juxtaposing it with an Italian alternative that is meant to supplant it.

De Sanctis's Dialogue: Combating Cultural Pessimism

De Sanctis presents Schopenhauer as a philosopher opposed to revolutionary ideas who is transforming idealism into a kind of pessimistic spiritualism; the comparison with Leopardi thus functions as a way of combating the effects of that pessimism not by rejecting it straightaway but rather by locating a more suitable pessimist whose writing can be aligned with the nascent Risorgimento political project.

As I have suggested, De Sanctis focuses on Schopenhauer's ethical outlook (renunciation) to criticize the philosopher as a "dangerous" cultural phenomenon whose thought needs to be neutralized. Yet elaborating this pessimistic metaphysics and its ethical consequences is what enables De Sanctis to draw a clear link to Leopardi's poetry: "Leopardi and Schopenhauer are the same thing. At almost the same time the one created the metaphysics of suffering and the other the poetry of suffering."[38] This way of forging the link is not unique to De Sanctis, of course: both Schopenhauer and Leopardi have often been identified with their pessimism. For example, in his recent study of their pessimism as a "problematic" (rather than as a doctrine), Joshua Dienstag focuses on Leopardi and Schopenhauer in succession, showing how for both the problematic of pessimism is at the core of their production – to the point that where Leopardi "comes close" to recommending suicide as a response, Schopenhauer instead offers an ideal of aesthetic and ascetic withdrawal.[39]

Notwithstanding this similarity, however, Dienstag contends that the two operate with different modes of pessimism (Leopardi's being "cultural" and Schopenhauer's "metaphysical," in his terms), and emphasizes the way in which Leopardi, in the end, commends a life of action as a heroic alternative to resignation.[40] In a similar vein, De Sanctis does much more than simply draw the two thinkers together based on their pessimism. In fact, he devotes whole pages of his dialogue to articulating the surprising way in which Leopardi and Schopenhauer operate with different philosophical assumptions yet seem to arrive at similar world views and a similar (almost "religious") ethics of compassion as a result.[41] De Sanctis's D claims that while Leopardi's pessimism is grounded in materialism, Schopenhauer's is actually a form of spiritualism: "For Leopardi, power is eternal matter endowed with one or more mysterious forces, whereas for Schopenhauer power is a single force, the *Wille*, and matter is one of its appearances, the veil of Maya. The one is materialist and the other spiritualist."[42] Thus they begin from seemingly opposed principles but arrive at the same results, which is surprising, given that materialism seems conducive to a pessimistic outlook whereas spiritualism does not. The key distinction, De Sanctis notes, is that for Schopenhauer the spirit is like the Christian soul but with the significant alteration that where traditional Christianity saw the soul as good and the material body as its "bad" prison, Schopenhauer sees the spirit, will, as the source of all suffering and the material body as just one of its manifestations: "That's why Leopardi and Schopenhauer agree in their consequences, placing the same blind, malign power as the principle of the world. It makes little difference that in the one it's a material force and in the other a force that manifests itself under the aspect of matter. The same *ergo* follows."[43]

But the comparison does not end with an examination of how these differing principles can arrive at the same pessimistic conclusion. D also suggests that Schopenhauer and Leopardi might be seen as highlighting a transformed social reality in Europe after the failure of the uprisings of 1848. The rise of Schopenhauer's philosophy corresponds to a culture of disillusionment, not just in the sense of a positivistic rejection of faith but also in the more concrete, political sense of the times. Thus, both pessimistic world views resonate with a changed cultural landscape and with a sense of defeat in the wake of the revolutionary fervour of 1789 and its resurgences in 1830 and 1848. This sense of defeat is registered in the character of A, who has been scared away from philosophy by the repressive police power exercised in the restoration of the Bourbon monarchy:

> My friend, you are tempting me. In the end it is still a philosophy. And I want to suggest an observation to you. All of these modern philosophers quarrel, they make a show of arms, but in substance they agree about certain maxims that stink of the gallows. Robespierre, or whoever else, discovered the secret with his goddess Reason. They made reason into a sort of governor: reason governs the world. This is the bad seed from which sprout the theory of progress, the divinized world, the triumph of the Idea, Doctor Pangloss's everything is the best, the inviolability and dignity of humanity, freedom, and similar such frights. And to think that I believed in all this, and I was practically about to risk my hide. I forgot the theory of sacrifice and how the individual must precisely let himself be killed for the greater glory and prosperity of the species. Squeeze and squeeze and then tell me that this isn't the juice of all modern philosophies.[44]

The course of history seems to have turned against revolutionary optimism in the post-1848 world. What A and D both depict now is a culture of spiritual resignation, one in which ideals (and the Idea) have been abandoned. This places De Sanctis's treatment of Schopenhauer in a broader European context and makes it an early articulation of how Schopenhauer could become a philosopher not just of pessimism (the content of his thought) but also of cultural decadence (the historical context ripe for his message). Indeed, other early treatments of Schopenhauer would offer a similar explanation for the sudden rise in Schopenhauer's popularity after so many years of obscurity. In England, for instance, the earliest review of his philosophy positioned Schopenhauer as a response to the prevailing Hegelianism that expressed a lack of faith in liberal political ideals.[45] De Sanctis's argument seems to make a similar point by describing Schopenhauer and Leopardi in the same context, suggesting that Leopardi (the materialist) roots his cultural pessimism in disenchantment – it is for this reason that he militates against the current order of the world. Both Schopenhauer and Leopardi are thus, in some important sense, thinkers of decline (seen from the perspective of a liberal-Hegelian narrative of progressive liberation). In this way, already in 1858, De Sanctis is articulating a deep fear of the rising culture of what would come to be known as "decadence" in the following decades. I would suggest that this is why De Sanctis places so much emphasis on the political aspects of Schopenhauer's thought: Schopenhauer and Leopardi have become proxies for Italian and European decadence *avant la lettre*.

By pairing Schopenhauer with Leopardi, then, De Sanctis has taken this foreign and unfamiliar thinker and made him accessible not only by explicating his thought but also, more importantly, by depicting his world view in a way that "domesticates" it, showing how it speaks to Italy in the years of fervent patriotism even while speaking to the delusion and despair that led to the Risorgimento.[46] What distinguishes the two figures' responses to this sense of decline or loss is not the content of their respective outlooks (since he asserts that the two agree in this respect) but rather the formal dimensions of how they communicate those outlooks and, as a result, the affective outcomes for the reader/audience who responds to their writing:

> [Leopardi] doesn't think about making an effect; he's too modest, too sober. His gaunt prose reflects the squalour of life that he wants to represent like a mirror; his style is like his world, an unlovable desert where you search for a flower in vain. Schopenhauer, on the other hand, when you cut through his loquacity, can't contain himself: he is copious, florid, lively, happy. He enjoys pronouncing the most bitter truths to you, because beneath it all is the thought: "The discovery is mine." He distracts and is distracted, and when he reasons sometimes you feel like you're in a pleasant conversation where, in between a cup of tea and a glass of champagne, he declaims on the vanity and poverty of life. As such you read Schopenhauer with pleasure, and you esteem Leopardi.[47]

In contrast to the "mirror" of Leopardi's prose, Schopenhauer's writing is defined by what De Sanctis sees as a style that puts him at odds with the content of his world view: he does not recoil in horror from or invite the rejection of the pessimistic world view he articulates, but rather takes a refined, distanced pleasure in it, turning suffering into a spectacle to be observed from a distance (with cup of tea in hand).[48] For De Sanctis, Schopenhauer's pleasant and refined style of writing is precisely what makes it so dangerous – on the one hand, it could seduce a reader into accepting the world he depicts (what De Sanctis would view as a dangerous political outcome), and on the other, it belies Schopenhauer's own character, his ability to be content as he describes the suffering of others. Far from accepting a bad world order, De Sanctis's project is one of amelioration; thus it requires an opposing outlook.

The dialogue thus mobilizes Leopardi's national renown as a way of stunting the spread of Schopenhauer's philosophy among Italian readers. As D says, in the passage I have quoted as an epigraph to this chapter, "were chance, or fortune, or destiny to have it that Schopenhauer were to peek his head out in Italy, he would find Leopardi there, who would attach himself to his feet like a lead ball and impede him from going forward."[49] More than domesticating the German philosopher to establish some form of Italian primacy, De Sanctis is identifying an alternative stylistic model that he believes can be used to confront the cultural danger of growing pessimism. He does this by setting up a comparison between the two in a way that ultimately privileges Leopardi, thereby advancing a patriotic argument in favour of national renewal. The passage is long but bears quoting in full:

> [...] Leopardi produces the opposite effect from what he intends. He doesn't believe in progress, and he makes you desire it. He doesn't believe in freedom, and he makes you love it. He calls love, glory, and virtue illusions, and he lights up an inexhaustible desire for them in your chest. You cannot take your leave of him without feeling better, and you cannot approach him without first trying to compose yourself and purify yourself so that you don't have reason to blush in his presence. He is a sceptic, and he makes you a believer; and while he doesn't believe it is possible to have a less-sad future for our shared fatherland, he awakens a vital love for that fatherland in your breast and inflames you toward noble deeds. He has such a lowly notion of humanity, yet his high soul, gentle and pure, honours and ennobles it. And if destiny had prolonged his life up to '48, you feel that you would have found him beside you, giving comfort and fighting. A pessimist and anti-cosmic thinker, like Schopenhauer, he does not preach the absurd negation of the *Wille*, the unnatural abstention or mortification of the cenobite – that philosophy of idleness that would have reduced Europe to an emasculated Oriental immobility if the

> freedom and activity of thought had not defeated Dominican ferocity and Jesuit cunning. Leopardi is certainly opposed to the passions, but only the wicked ones; and while he calls all of life a shadow and error, without knowing how, you feel yourself holding tighter to everything in life that is noble and great. For Leopardi idleness is an abdication of human dignity, cowardice. Schopenhauer requires activity as a means of preserving good health. And if you'd like to measure the abyss that divides these two souls with a single example, reflect that for Schopenhauer the difference between the slave and the free man is more one in name than in fact, for if the free man is able to go from one place to another, the slave has the advantage of sleeping peacefully and living without thinking, having his master to provide for his needs.[50]

If Schopenhauer's philosophy breaks down ideals and leaves the political spirit unmoored and adrift in an "oriental" torpor, Leopardi's only *appears* to do the same thing. In fact, however, according to De Sanctis's reading, Leopardi inspires the opposite effect of his proclaimed pessimism and reinvigorates the Italian heart – so much so that De Sanctis envisions him as a compatriot fighting alongside him in the uprisings of 1848.[51] It is interesting that a similar reading has been articulated by numerous scholars since De Sanctis, thinkers who have seen in Leopardi a response to and engagement with revolutionary thought.[52] If these analyses are correct, then De Sanctis was a forerunner of a more complicated view of Leopardi and of a deeper understanding of the cultural significance of Schopenhauer's belated rise to prominence after so many decades of critical neglect. What he sees, we might say, borrowing from the terms of recent theories of affect, is that Schopenhauer's dispassionate style means that his ideas are able to sink in as "objective" or distanced truths, whereas Leopardi's lament for lost virtue acts as a prod to kindle the passions and activate readers' affective responses. This affect, of course, is needed to motivate a political activism that seeks to transform (and improve) the world.

De Sanctis's Dialogue: Toward an Aesthetic Reception

Beyond its role in De Sanctis's politicized critique of Schopenhauer, I would suggest that the contrast he draws with Leopardi's affective power can be seen as having the unexpected outcome of highlighting the role of Schopenhauer's aesthetics in how the philosopher is received. Schopenhauer's distanced, charming, detached philosophical style, the source of what De Sanctis portrays as an undesireable outcome that muffles the passions and prevents action, is also an expression of what

Vasalou terms Schopenhauer's aesthetic stance. In fact, in an earlier passage D describes Schopenhauer again as watching from afar with his cup of tea, taking distance from actual historical events so that he is able to look down upon those silly men who got caught up in revolutionary fervour:

> [...] in '48, while everyone ran about like madmen fighting against one another, [Schopenhauer] sat back observing them all through a telescope, laughing under his moustache and saying: "You all can go get yourselves killed, but I'm here contemplating the *Wille*." In effect, if men were to allow themselves to be persuaded that freedom, humanity, nationality, the fatherland, and all the other things for which they feel passion are abstractions and appearances, each one would stay at home in peace and cling to the contemplative life in private and public alike. Then instead of running out into the squares and toiling and tormenting himself and others, he would stretch out on a sofa, smoking with gusto like a Turk, and watch as his individuality evaporated bit by bit among the circles of smoke, and he would feel himself to be pure *Wille*.[53]

So Schopenhauer's contemplative withdrawal from history corresponds to the same "cup of tea" mentality that De Sanctis uses to characterize the philosopher's prose – it is both a distanced approach to life and a refined aesthetic style. Though De Sanctis does not say it in these words, I would argue that what he highlights is thus how Schopenhauer's system enacts in its form (or stylistically) the theory of detachment from will articulated in its content. An element of this world view is an ascetic withdrawal from the passions (the desires that orient action by pointing it toward outcomes). But another element of this is aesthetic, modelling the disinterested observation of the forms (Ideas) of life itself – the world is rendered "objective" or visible not so that we can act on it but rather in a way that encourages a detached vision where the subject experiences but does not act upon the object of representation. Ultimately, then, where it may have at first seemed that De Sanctis neglected the role of Schopenhauer's aesthetics in his system, in fact what he perhaps inadvertently shows is how aesthetic objectivity and the withdrawal of the subject coincide with the self-abnegating drive of Schopenhauer's ascetic ethics. Of course, for De Sanctis, both are negative, a point depicted in Orientalist garb when he characterizes Schopenhauer's distance from the events of 1848 by comparing him to a Turk smoking on his sofa – an Orientalism laden with political undertones in which the Turk is ruled despotically but without concern, just like the German philosopher whose aesthetic standpoint coincides with a conservative defence of monarchy.

De Sanctis thus not only inaugurates the Italian reception of Schopenhauer but also simultaneously diverts it. Still attached to the political progressivism of the Neapolitan Hegelian tradition, even if dissatisfied with Hegel himself, De Sanctis condemns Schopenhauer for political reasons while attempting to block the growth of his pessimistic outlook by using Leopardi as a domesticating foil. But at the same time, by describing Schopenhauer together with Leopardi and by focusing on his style and its affective outcomes, De Sanctis nevertheless helps nudge Italian interest in the new German philosophy in the direction of its aesthetic and artistic reception. These, of course, are precisely the directions that would bear the most fruit in the late nineteenth and early twentieth centuries.

The Other Side of Modernist Idealism

At the beginning of De Sanctis's essay, D reflects ironically on the way in which post-1848 culture has become disillusioned, on the one hand, while simultaneously characterizing Schopenhauer as a philosopher of the future who speaks to an era of disillusionment, on the other. He had no idea how right he would be: even despite the upsurge of Italian nationalism in the Risorgimento and the long shadow of a Hegelian philosophy of history and thus of politics in the new nation, the seeds of Schopenhauer's enduring importance were already being planted. They would sprout both in Italy and abroad less in a mainstream scholarly or philosophical reception and more in the form of a new aesthetic outlook tied to the artistic reappropriation of decadence. And so they would bear fruit in modernist art, constituting a key aspect of the ambivalent stance that modernism takes toward the perceived spiritual crisis of the modern era. One side of this stance leans toward the revitalization of the nation through action and conquest (resonating with a Hegelian interpretation of spiritual progress through and in the state); but the other inclines instead toward the renunciation of practical involvement in life while simultaneously exalting art as a means of escape, not through action but through the aesthetic rendering of that spiritual crisis in all its objective forms.

This shift, from the romantic-era politics of the bourgeoning Italian nation to decadent and modernist responses, perhaps traces out precisely the dynamic that Goya's etching had already suggested. For De Sanctis, the monstrosity of Schopenhauer's irrationalism was its political manifestation as a rejection of revolutionary politics. But for the artistic legacy that would integrate Schopenhauer's thought into its re-envisioning of the world, it would be a source of marvel, an intimation of the other emerging from within reason itself. Modernity's shadow took shape in the space where Schopenhauer's philosophical argumentation met the irrational boundary of its thought. And on monstrous wings, it acquired the aesthetic self-awareness that would issue into a modernist ambivalence both embracing and rejecting the transformations of world history that earlier thinkers had sought to approach from a much more single-minded point of view. The artistic shadow of Schopenhauer's irrational idealism, in other words, far from being repressed by the reassertion of reason or the insistence on a committed, romantic art, inspired a distance from history that uprooted reflection and gave it wings, making way for the aesthetic self-awareness of modernity's crisis that constituted the core of modernist representation. This made Schopenhauer's legacy a lynchpin for the formation of an ambivalent modernist idealism.

Chapter Three

Aesthetic Decadence and Modernist Idealism: Schopenhauer's Literary-Artistic Legacy

Two prongs in the forking path of idealism's reception head in very different directions when it comes to their engagement with politics and the actual world: Hegelian idealism sees the ideal as immanent, and thus it becomes the task of world-historical action to realize that ideal; in contrast, Schopenhauer's irrational idealist stance rejects any such action as futile and ultimately, in a metaphysical sense, illusory. Both paths can be taken as a response to the perceived crisis of modernity, the spectre of a deadened world reduced to mere materiality, but whereas the former leads to the political and historical realization of a revivifying ideal, the latter seeks its realization in the special subjectivity of artistic production. When De Sanctis attempted to reject Schopenhauer by way of a comparison to the poet, Leopardi, what he actually accomplished was to push Schopenhauer's reception farther down the path to which his own world view already led.

In the context of European responses to modern crisis, Schopenhauer's path led directly through the burgeoning discourse on decadence. Experiencing modernity as loss, the artists and thinkers of the decadent moment aimed not to repress or overcome that loss by recourse to political praxis but rather to transfigure it through their highly cultivated aesthetic reflection. The form of this reflection and its implied aesthetic stance along with the content on which it focused – modernity as sickness, deadness, loss – combined the aesthetic and ethical dimensions of Schopenhauer's thought. What better channel for his world view to find not just its most powerful articulations but also its *realization*?

Unpacking the multifaceted role of decadence in the reception of Schopenhauer reveals more than just a historical account of how his thought emerged in the wake of De Sanctis's condemnation of it. In terms of temporality, Vincent Sherry has shown how decadence is always modernist and modernism is always already decadent in some mode: they are both ways of responding to an experience of the new that constitutes modernity, but each emphasizes a different aspect of that temporality, with decadence focused on the loss of what is passing away and modernism focusing on the coming into being of the new itself.[1] My argument builds on Sherry's notion of this paired relationship by showing how these two seemingly opposed lenses on modernity may share an underlying philosophical perspective, an idealist outlook that orients their response not just to temporal rupture but also to the experience of loss associated with modern materialism. The aesthetic outlook of decadence may on the one hand render death and decay into beautiful spectacles for distanced observation, but at the same time it can entail a notion of artistic creation where distanced observation forms or reforms the world through artistic praxis, reframing materiality through art's ideal stance. As such, decadence is ambivalent in a way that is even more complex than the already nuanced view Sherry has articulated.

In subsequent chapters I will examine how the outlooks of decadence and modernism overlapped and fed off of one another in a host of writers and movements in the late nineteenth and early twentieth centuries. But here I look first to the Schopenhauerian aestheticism of the decadent moment of nineteenth-century European culture, arguing that even in this aesthetic obsession with death, decay, and loss we see the ambivalence of modernist idealism at work. The aesthetic self-awareness of modern loss was also a creative act that, from an idealist standpoint, entailed ushering a new world into being. This stance took form not only in the decadents of the *fin de siècle* but also in various modernist afterlives, including as an integral component of the modernist epiphany's notion of aesthetic *Erhebung*.

Aestheticism and the Decadent Imagination: Art as Alternative Source of Value

In an era rife with worry over the supposed decline or decadence of modern, Western societies, the reception of Schopenhauer's thought clearly was charged with cultural and political significance. We have seen this in De Sanctis's effort to forestall that reception, stoked by political fears; it is likewise clear in the anglophone rejection of Schopenhauer as a thinker of decadence.[2] But at the same moment, a counter-current formed among a group of writers and artists who associated themselves positively with the label of decadence, deliberately going against the grain. It is no surprise that these artists served as key nodes in the reception of Schopenhauer's thought – reading it intently, replicating key aspects of its world view in their artistic production, and disseminating it through their own artistic and intellectual networks in what Potolsky has called a cosmopolitan (elite and self-selecting) "community of taste."[3]

My account of that decadent reception in this chapter does not aim for an exhaustive map of these nodes and networks. While such a project might be possible, following the mapping methods of Franco Moretti's distant approach to reading, my argument is focused on the close-up details that such an approach forgoes.[4] When we examine Schopenhauer's decadent legacy, we find a model for artistic production not as a regenerative intervention into political actuality but rather as the construction of an alternative sphere, a retreat from and reconfiguration of the values that have dessicated the spiritual lifeblood of modernity. Spiritual renewal is then rooted in a transformation of materialism that is enacted through aesthetic reflection and distance.

On the one hand, this aestheticism, which is at the core of the decadent project articulated by writers like Joris-Karl Huysmans (1848–1907), Oscar Wilde (1854–1900), and Gabriele d'Annunzio (1863–1938), transforms modern loss and suffering – the decay of decadence – into an object of aesthetic reflection in a self-aware form that fits closely with what Vincent Sherry has seen as the key stance of decadent art. On the other hand, though, the decadent rearticulation of Schopenhauer's world view also involves an element of aesthetic exultation in which the aesthetic object and its creation are transfigured and valued precisely as acts of artistic creation, offering an artistic counterweight to Nietzsche's philosophy of art. Art and aesthetic reflection thus become substitutes for the deadened world of modern life – not reanimating that world in practical, political terms, but offering an alternative in the form of artistic praxis itself. Both of these elements are already present in Schopenhauer's thought and take on new life and power in its reception and rearticulation.

Decadence and Decadentism: Schopenhauer's Reception as a Transnational Aesthetic Paradigm

Tracing Schopenhauer's reception through decadent literature and culture reveals the way in which this outlook developed and emerged in an Italian context that otherwise seems to have opted for the regenerative optimism of political action. Indeed, on the face of it, it may seem that De Sanctis's move to stunt the growth of a Schopenhauerian outlook largely accomplished its goals. In the reception of De Sanctis's dialogue there was in fact a marked tendency to privilege its treatment of Leopardi rather than to see it as being about Schopenhauer.[5] Likewise, De Sanctis's efforts were renewed and taken further by Benedetto Croce in the beginning of the twentieth century, when Croce oversaw an important series of philosophical texts in translation and directly blocked efforts to include Schopenhauer's works in that series, viewing him as what Fabio Ciracì has labelled an "enemy within" – that is, another (albeit undesirable) idealist who shared Croce's, and Italian Neo-Idealism's, enemies: positivism, scientism, and materialism.[6]

Summing up this situation, Marco Segala concludes that the Italian reception of Schopenhauer was characterized by the delayed and partial access that Italian readers had to his works, meaning that it was not in the "academic world" but rather in "social and cultural history" that Schopenhauer's thought diffused in Italy.[7] The social world in question, I would add, was precisely the literary and cultural space of decadence. As Barbara Spackman has compellingly shown, the culture of decadence was a key target of two otherwise intensely opposed groups of Italian thinkers – Croce's camp of Neo-Idealists, and Marxist materialists.[8] Anxiety over decadence and scepticism of Schopenhauer's pessimistic metaphysics went hand-in-hand. It is thus unsurprising, perhaps, that the literary and artistic figures who embraced decadence were likewise the ones to re-elaborate and diffuse Schopenhauer's thought through their creative work.

Decadence has a complex history, both in Europe and Italy. In the Italian context, various figures have been associated with the term *decadentismo,* from the Milanese assortment of Bohemian-style artists grouped in the loose movement of Scapigliatura, to notable writers and poets including Giovanni Pascoli (1855–1912), Antonio Fogazzaro (1842–1911), and D'Annunzio.[9] For some time the Italian critical tradition also identified modernist writers like Pirandello and Svevo with this the term.[10] Thus David Weir notes "whereas [Mario] Praz treats decadence as a species of romanticism, more recent Italian critics associate *il decadentismo* closely with modernism, so closely, in fact, that the two concepts are all but interchangeable."[11] Likewise, Italian decadence, like European decadence, was broadly transnational; Spackman goes so far as to say that "almost all of the bibliography on D'Annunzio could be cited" in reference to the rich intertextuality of decadentismo/decadence, placing D'Annunzio in conversation with not only Baudelaire and Huysmans but also Nietzsche in this regard.[12] At the core, this transnational cultural phenomenon is a threshold concept both in terms of its historical placement (between a moment of romanticism and one of modernism) and in terms of its aesthetic hybridity.[13]

My argument contributes to this conversation by adding a new dimension to the historical articulation of decadence while also intervening into the theorization of the category as an aesthetic modality that results from those historical accounts. On the one hand, the reception of Schopenhauer is an essential, and surprisingly often overlooked, factor in the historical formation of decadentism as an aesthetic outlook.[14] On the other, Schopenhauer's philosophy also provides a conceptual lens through which we can reinterpret the meaning of decadence as an aesthetic category that operates not only in "decadent" works but also in "modernist" ones: the conjunction of aestheticism and ascetic renunciation, which is at the core of Schopenhauer's responses to suffering, becomes a way of transfiguring the material world so that it is not just repeating or celebrating decay but actively transforming it, making this stance both decadent and modernist in the sense that Vincent Sherry articulates for those two different modes of responding to modernity's crisis times.

One key node in Schopenhauer's diffusion is visible in the case of Joris-Karl Huysmans, who illustrates neatly the conjunction of aestheticism and pessimism at the core of the decadent obsession with Schopenhauer, as well as his place in a quasi-religious cult of aesthetic sensation.[15] Just as De Sanctis had paired Schopenhauer with a romantic poet in Leopardi, a similar pairing occurs in Huysmans's linking of Schopenhauer's philosophy to Baudelaire's poetics.[16] His most famous, and canon-defining, decadent work, *Against Nature* (*À rebours*, 1884), is written as an aesthetic exploration of various objects, grouped by types into chapters that move from one to another largely without any sense of plot or character development. For the 1903 reprint of his novel, Huysmans wrote a retrospective "Preface" in which he fit his infamous novel into a narrative of personal transformation from scandalous decadent aesthete to religious convert. There, he describes Schopenhauer as a primary influence on his early writing as well as a spiritual preparation for his eventual conversion:

> I never dreamt that from Schopenhauer (whom I admired more than was reasonable) to Ecclesiastes and the Book of Job was but a step. The hypotheses about pessimism are the same, only, when it is time to reach a conclusion, the philosopher makes himself scarce. I liked his ideas on the horror of existence, on the absurdity of the world, on the cruelty of destiny; I also like them in the Holy Scriptures; but Schopenhauer's remarks lead nowhere; he leaves you, so to speak, in the lurch; in a word, his aphorisms are nothing but a herbarium of barren plaints; the Church, on the other hand, elucidates origins and causes, points to conclusions, offers

> remedies; not satisfied with simply providing a spiritual consultation, she treats you and cures you, whereas the German quack, after having proved to you beyond any question that the condition afflicting you is incurable, turns his back on you with a sneer.[17]

Of course, Huysmans was writing retrospectively, after his conversion, and so from a perspective that wanted to chart a spiritual trajectory. He thus concludes his "Preface" by quoting from one of the early critical reviews of *Against Nature*, penned by Barbey d'Aurevilly for the *Constitutionnel* (28 July 1884): "After such a book, the only thing left for the author is to choose between the muzzle of a pistol and the foot of a cross."[18] Huysmans obviously opted for the latter, but the point that bears emphasizing is that in the decadent imagination Schopenhauer's philosophy occupied the same space as religion and that art pushed material life to its breaking point – carrying the destructive logic of modernity to its extreme. Indeed, where Joshua Dienstag has articulated pessimism as an acute awareness of decay that stops short of celebrating that loss, the decadent imaginary pushes pessimism to a next step and elevates it into an aesthetic principle, not simply celebrating decay but transfiguring it into something higher.[19]

It is for this reason that Schopenhauer's thought fits so well with Baudelaire's poetry of aesthetic attention that elevates even the mundane, the sordid, the ugly – a poetics that can delve with enrapt attention into the decomposition of a carcass as easily as it can represent the deadening power of capitalism's consumer materialism.[20] In Baudelaire's poetry, the decadent dandy looks out on the world as an object of aesthetic experience – a source not of pleasure, per se, but of fascination that elevates the mind from its own suffering and alleviates it of that enduring, terrible facet of modern life that serves as a subterranean springboard for such a wide array of decadent writers: *ennui*.[21] Thus, if, as Dienstag has argued, pessimistic philosophy opens an ontological gap between happiness and freedom, such that consciousness leads both to freedom and to unhappiness, decadentism can be seen as an attempt to use artistic practice to close that gap.[22] Decadent creators move toward a meta-level of artistic reflection focused on precisely those outcomes, producing a new dimension of freedom from boredom in the otherwise evacuated forms of artistic play.[23] The obsessive search for new objects of aesthetic experience is an objectification of that solution – the decadent seeks ever more sources of contemplation to maintain his ecstatic state of removal from the suffering of the world.[24]

Contrary to the implications of Huysmans's conversion narrative, then, decadent aestheticism actually offers a third choice to its believers, one besides death (suicide) and religious conversion. This alternative originates precisely in Schopenhauer's own response to the pessimistic world view of his metaphysics: ascetic renunciation coupled with aesthetic escape – what De Sanctis's dialogue ironically describes as Schopenhauer's notion of "dying without ceasing to live."[25] For the decadents, the deadness of modernity is transfigured into a special form of aesthetic rapture or ecstasy, so the renunciation or withdrawal associated with their pessimism is coupled with a turn toward aestheticism, thus complicating that pessimism. In this way, we should understand aestheticism as a necessarily hybrid position, a fusion of literature (or art) and philosophy that seeks to instantiate a metaphysical world view of artistic elevation that transfigures material vacuity. It is precisely this fusion that enables decadent aestheticism to offer more than just a nihilistic replication of modern crisis, developing an aesthetic response to modern rupture.

The Aesthetic Transformation of Modern Materialism: A Vexed Political Question

Coupling withdrawal into a world of art with aesthetic idealism has often been viewed sceptically as a dangerous replication and even elevation of crisis, both by thinkers in the modernist period like Norberto Bobbio and by contemporary theorists like Giorgio Agamben. Walter Benjamin likewise links it to the aestheticization of politics practised by fascism. But my contention here is that this fusion actually represents an effort to respond to the conditions of modern crisis – conditions that bely more than a simple (nihilistic) repetition of that crisis itself – and that the aesthetic transfiguration of modernity's decaying world is itself an effort to counterbalance the forces that give rise to modern deadness, from capitalist materialism to positivist materialism, from political crisis to existential crisis. And that effort is politically flexible: some figures align it to a politics of war and violence, as we will see in the case of D'Annunzio, while others like Svevo and Montale replicate key elements of that aesthetic paradigm with a wholly different political outlook.[26]

The early twentieth-century philosopher Norberto Bobbio saw the aesthetic self-absorption of *decadentismo* as the problematic endpoint of pessimistic, irrational philosophy – as a way of thinking that had drawn together existentialist philosophers with currents in artistic production represented by figures including (but not limited to) D'Annunzio and the Futurists. He coupled this outlook with the rejection of authority and a move toward anarchy in a political sense, viewing it as a form of self-abasement in an individual moral sense. Ultimately, he claimed, the literary-philosophical outlook of *decadentismo* had contaminated the human spirit by collapsing the world of the subject on itself, positing nothing higher than the individual consciousness and thus leaving the individual with an unbearable weight that eliminated the possibility of reaching beyond itself.[27] This trajectory had led, of course, to the constitution of the fascist state. At its extreme end, then, idealism had degenerated into a self-centred subjectivity that could not engage with the world rationally at all.

In this way, Bobbio was not far off from the way in which Gino Gori, an early twentieth-century literary critic, theorized the nature of art and aesthetic experience. Gori argued that the essential character of what art reveals is irrationality; for this reason, he recognized how Schopenhauer's aesthetics continued to resonate in modern art.[28] What Bobbio abhorred and Gori embraced, then, was a continuation of the debate we have already seen at work in De Sanctis's rejection of Schopenhauer: because Schopenhauer's idealism rejects a rational concept of the "idea" in favour of a blind notion of will, and in that way rejects Hegelian idealism to replace it with an irrational alternative, De Sanctis sees Schopenhauer's move as politically dangerous. Bobbio followed suit the better part of a century later, again condemning irrationalism as precisely a source of political resignation or, worse, anarchy. Of course, he did not simply attribute irrationalism to Schoenhauer; rather he saw a whole host of thinkers articulating that "nihilistic" view – including figures like Henri Bergson. This political withdrawal of the decadent aesthetic subject is precisely the key to Giorgio Agamben's critique of the trajectory of modern aesthetics and its culmination point in aestheticism's art-for-art's-sake, what he terms a "self-annihilating nothing" at its core that makes it politically dangerous.[29] Agamben's account of modern aesthetics is preoccupied with a metanarrative of decline to which he seeks to respond, like Leopardi (in De Sanctis's reading), through a return to classical praxis.[30]

But while a quasi-religious elevation of aesthetic experience to an ideal may strike critics as fostering an inward turn that results in merely aestheticizing the existential and political crises of modernity, in fact it is a more complex operation. This form of artistic consciousness, which renders life into art, is more than just an escape from consciousness's suffering; it is also a means of transfiguring experience from the form of its quotidian, instrumental (interested) state into an object of disinterested aesthetic contemplation.[31] To show how this is the case, and thus ultimately to offer a partial response to some of these critiques, it will be necessary to delve deeper into the complex, conflicting dynamics at work in decadent aestheticism and its response to modern loss.

A Sublime Death: Suicide and Decadent Aestheticism

The decadent paradigm has at its core an encounter with destructive forces. Post-conversion Huysmans figured that encounter as a world-annihilating pessimism that could lead only to suicide or the cross. De Sanctis contrasted the suicidal impulse in Schopenhauer with a more heroic outlook in Leopardi, one that hearkened back to the classical ideals of Stoicism and thus elevated important moral principles that could be used to combat modern, demystifying rationality.[32] Political critics posit a pessimism that leads to anarchy, political disengagement, or inward-facing withdrawal that forgoes ethical engagement with the outside world. Yet some of the most politically engaged writers of the modernist period, from D'Annunzio to the Futurists, are at the core of this decadent paradigm and its aftermath. Their politics, of course, align with a deeply disturbing vision of how the world should be remade, but their commitment to remaking it is hardly the resigned, disengaged stance that it has sometimes been made out to be. How can we make sense of this divergence?

My contention here is that we must delve into the way in which decadent aestheticism itself addresses modernity's death drive in order to come to an answer. What we find is an aestheticism that seeks not just to repeat or amplify that death drive but to substantially transfigure it through its own aesthetic self-awareness. Yet even while that decadence obsessively returns to the deathly quandary perceived to be at the core of modernity's "decline," it integrates an essential stance from Schopenhauer's outlook by pairing aesthetic elevation with ascetic renunciation. In so doing, decadence articulates a key pole in the ambivalent mixture of modernist idealism; but that pole is likewise related in complex ways to a Hegelian commitment to transforming the world. This conjunction begins to emerge when we consider the Italian reception of Schopenhauer as it was channelled through D'Annunzio's decadence and its debt to Wagner, on the one hand, and Nietzsche, on the other.[33] The conjunction of aesthetic ecstasy and a suicidal cult of death was at the centre of this decadent reception.

Sublime Death: Suicidal Modernity and Ascetic Aestheticism

The power of suicide to take on a heroic character is central in the decadent work of Gabriele d'Annunzio, but it is a heroism decidedly different from the one De Sanctis divines in Leopardi's writing on the topic. Murder and suicide recur frequently as tropes in D'Annunzio's corpus.[34] But they come to the fore especially in the third novel of his early trilogy, his "Romanzi della Rosa," the tellingly titled *Triumph of Death* (*Trionfo della morte*, 1894). The novel is explicitly written in reference to Wagner as a musical model of Schopenhauerian pessimism, and its decadent aestheticism expresses itself in an obsessive interest in and ultimate desire for death. The novel culminates with the male aesthete-protagonist, Giorgio Aurispa, pushing his beloved off a cliff and then throwing himself off alongside her in an effort to recraft their death as a romantic suicide, following the Wagnerian *Liebestod* motif. Desperate to control his beloved and to make himself the artist of their own romantic tragedy, Aurispa fuses murder and suicide in an effort to likewise fuse art and life. A far cry from Leopardi's stoic heroism, suicide here becomes a romantic act of artistic self-creation, an effort to elevate mundane life into the eternal form of art by giving it a tragic narrative trajectory complete with the grand romantic gestures associated with aesthetic elevation.

That impulse to elevate life by bringing it to its end is articulated explicitly by D'Annunzio in an article he wrote on contemporary politics and philosophy for *Il Mattino*, "The Elective Beast" ("La bestia elettiva," 25 September 1892). There, he describes Ludwig II of Bavaria, the famous patron of Wagner who funded the composer's vision for the Bayreuth Festival and who is perhaps even better known today for his construction of the romantic fairy tale castle, Neuschwanstein:

> After communicating for many years with the luminous heroes that Richard Wagner provided as companions in supernatural realms, Louis II [Ludwig II of Bavaria], the virgin king, immune from every feminine poison, hostile to all intruders, and sensing that the intensity of his joys was beginning to exceed the resistance of his organs, decided to transform himself into a higher being through death. So he descended to the bottom of his lake in search of the supreme vision.[35]

Ludwig did, indeed, manage to capture the imagination of a whole generation across Europe, with the French Symbolist Paul Verlaine going so far as to assert, in a sonnet dedicated to his memory at the news of his mysterious death ("A Louis II de Bavière"), that he was "the only king of this century."[36] D'Annunzio's point echoes Verlaine, highlighting how the king's dramatic suicide in 1886 is integral to his "eternal" fame. According to this outlook, his suicide was an act of self-elevation, allowing him to became something higher and achieve "the supreme vision." The language here speaks of transcendence, but the implication is that the transcendence is at once spiritual – a culmination within Ludwig himself, who has committed himself to an act of seemingly unimaginable proportions – and aesthetic – his elevation into a symbol for an audience, for us, into an object of beauty or, more accurately, the sublime.

This sublime beauty of self-destruction resonates in a complex way with Schopenhauer's combination of ascetic renunciation and aesthetic elevation. Schopenhauer's somewhat shocking praise of suicide was a topic of discussion in the nineteenth century much as it is today, with a contemporary philosopher like Dale Jacquette contending that Schopenhauer's view posits death as the purpose and fulfilment of life such that his rejection of suicide seems philosophically inconsistent.[37] Indeed, in both his collection of essays, *Parerga and Paralipomena*, and his major book, *The World as Will and Representation*, Schopenhauer concludes that life is not worth living and that suicide would seem a rational response to that fact; however, what complicates this rational response, according to Schopenhauer, is that at a metaphysical level suicide does not succeed in its goal. This is because the justification for it presupposes that life is not worth living because it is constituted by individual suffering, and thus that if an individual brings her life to an end, that suffering will likewise end. But according to Schopenhauer's outlook, this is a mistake in two senses: first, suffering is not, in fact, the experience of a single individual but is rather constitutive of metaphysical reality as such – *all* existence is suffering. Second, ending the existence of a single individual abates suffering neither for the individual nor for the whole – it is insignificant to the whole system, but following his metaphysical view of rebirth, it also is only an illusory resolution for the individuated subject. Thus at its core, suicide fails to bring an end to the chain of desires that brings with it perpetual suffering:

> Conversely, whoever is oppressed by the burdens of life, whoever loves life and affirms it, but abhors its torments, and in particular can no longer endure the hard lot that has fallen to just him, cannot hope for deliverance from death, and cannot save himself through suicide. Only by a false illusion does the cool shade of Orcus allure him as a haven of rest. The earth rolls on from day into night; the individual dies; but the sun itself burns without intermission, an eternal noon. Life is certain to the will-to-live; the form of life is the endless present; it matters not how individuals, the phenomena of the Idea, arise and pass away in time, like fleeting dreams.[38]

The result is that suicide actually undermines its own intended effect: instead of quieting will, it is just one more instance of will's manifestation, another unsatisfied desire in the endless chain, which exists not just for individuals but for all of the universe (will in each of its objectifications). Schopenhauer concludes that suicide is only apparently reasonable but is in actuality metaphysically untenable. Schopenhauer's outlook is thus pessimistic to the point that it appears pessimistic even about suicide – not even suicide succeeds. The only real solution to life's suffering is to use will against itself, to commit oneself to ascetic renunciation and so bring the cycle of desire to an end. The key, he concludes, is not ending life but ending life's desire.

That commitment to renunciation is finally a kind of ascetic heroism in Schopenhauer's thought. He depicts the image of various holy men, the saints who serve as models for the difficult (but not impossible) ideal of directing will toward its own extinction. As Schopenhauer argues, such models are essential, for

> my description, given above, of the denial of the will-to-live, or of the conduct of a beautiful soul, of a resigned and voluntarily expiating saint, is only abstract and general, and therefore cold. As the knowledge from which results the denial of the will is intuitive and not abstract, it finds its complete expression not in abstract concepts, but only in the deed and in conduct. Therefore, in order to understand more fully what we express philosophically as denial of the will-to-live, we have to learn to know examples from experience and reality.[39]

The saints understood, intuitively, that the will to live is the source of suffering and that only by turning that will against itself is it possible to be free of that burden. Schopenhauer's philosophy aims to lay bare the nature of the world and thus to use knowledge to motivate turning the will to live against itself, but the concrete example of saints is needed to help actualize that motivation – concrete examples that come not just from daily life but also from Schopenhauer's (aesthetic) representation of the will to live's self-extinguishing potential. His explanation of why this needs to be the case furnishes another key point in his outlook: quoting Spinoza, he states that "all that is excellent and eminent is as difficult as it is rare".[40] Indeed, the difficulty of attaining the level of self-mastery necessary to engage in true renunciation means that it is not feasible for the vast majority of people; it is so difficult that we cannot be expected to have encountered examples of it in our own actual lives, so we need representations of such action to furnish models.

Schopenhauer's philosophy thus points to a largely unattainable goal in its *ascetic* ideal. At the same time, however, it offers a form of consolation in a special kind of *aesthetic* withdrawal. For in aesthetic experience, Schopenhauer holds, the subject is removed from the world and thus removed from suffering:

> When, however, an external cause or inward disposition suddenly raises us out of the endless stream of willing, and snatches knowledge from the thraldom of the will, the attention is now no longer directed to the motives of willing, but comprehends things free from their relation to the will. Thus it considers things without interest, without subjectivity, purely objectively; it is entirely given up to them in so far as they are merely representations, and not motives. Then all at once the peace, always sought but always escaping us on that first path of willing, comes to us of its own accord, and all is well with us. It is the painless state, prized by Epicurus as the highest good and as the state of the gods; for that moment we are delivered from the miserable pressure of the will. We celebrate the Sabbath of the penal servitude of willing; the wheel of Ixion stands still.[41]

This aesthetic escape from suffering is necessarily fleeting, as the subject cannot long maintain its distance from the concrete reality of its individuated, embodied self. But in that moment of escape, the "subject of pure knowing" also has access to something else, a glimpse of the true forms of the world's becoming, what Schopenhauer understands as the "different grades of the will's objectification, expressed in innumerable individuals," which also "exist as the unattained patterns of these, or as the eternal forms of things."[42] Art's content objectifies some aspect of will's becoming into its visible/sensible form (as a representation for the subject); thus, aesthetic experience is both a withdrawal of the subject from suffering and simultaneously a glimpse of the true nature of the world in some limited aspect of its unfathomable reality – the unattained patterns that individuated existence only ever reflects in a partial way.

My contention is that decadent aestheticism combines these elements of Schopenhauer's outlook in its aesthetic self-reflection on death and loss. In so doing, it *realizes* two key ideas that we have seen were central to Schopenhauer's philosophy: his understanding that concrete models are needed to provide an intuitive grasp on the truth of his world view, which implies the need for artistic representation of that world view; and his ascetic push to quiet the will. This is what I refer to as *ascetic aestheticism*, and it is at the core of Schopenhauer's decadent legacy in modernist idealism.[43]

It is thus that D'Annunzio's (Wagnerian) cult of death seeks to elevate suicide itself to the heights of an aesthetic rapture, turning it from a dangerous lived experience into a safely distanced object of aesthetic contemplation and simultaneously idealizing the renunciation of life that it represents. Something similar might be said of Huysmans's aestheticization of decay in *Against Nature* or Wilde's aestheticization of murder-suicide in *The Picture of Dorian Gray*, or indeed of Baudelaire's earlier poem "A Carcass." What these examples finally reveal is an essential insight into the nature of decadent aestheticism and its mode of responding to modern loss by transfiguring it – the combination of ascetic and aesthetic impulses from Schopenhauer's idealism unfolds in a sublime transfiguration of modernity's death drive.

For Schopenhauer, the sublime entails contemplating an unfathomable or dangerous force at a distance, such that while it threatens the will it is nevertheless seen in a state detached from will's individuated interests. Describing how the subject of aesthetic contemplation encounters those hostile elements, he writes:

> The beholder may not direct his attention to this relation to his will which is so pressing and hostile, but, although he perceives and acknowledges it, he may consciously turn away from it, forcibly tear himself from his will and its relations, and, giving himself up entirely to knowledge, may quietly contemplate, as pure, will-less subject of knowing, those very objects so terrible to the will. He may comprehend only their Idea that is foreign to all relation, gladly linger over its contemplation, and consequently be elevated precisely in this way above himself, his person, his willing, and all willing. In that case, he is then filled with the feeling of the *sublime;* he is in the state of exaltation, and therefore the object that causes such a state is called *sublime.*[44]

Decadent aestheticism likewise involves transforming that which ought to frighten us, death and decay (which threaten us as embodied human subjects caught in the cycle of becoming and loss), into an object of aesthetic reflection. In this contemplation of loss there is a higher level of awareness, not only the experience of losing oneself in the object but also the awareness of one's own liberated subjectivity. The experience of aesthetic contemplation is also an experience of having detached oneself from the world of will. As such, the decadent sublime can function as an experience of self-overcoming integrated into aesthetic contemplation; it is thus the aesthetic realization of the moral heroism Schopenhauer portrays in his treatment of the ascetic saint.

Schopenhauer portrays this heroism but cannot fully represent it. It is in this sense that decadent aestheticism *realizes* Schopenhauer's philosophy, taking a next step and bringing it to fruition. Insofar as modernity itself is characterized by a threatening experience of loss and modern self-consciousness entails a historically self-aware understanding of one's self and society as constituted by that loss, the aesthetic rewriting of decay is actually a way of turning the terrifying into the sublime, allowing for a form of fleeting aesthetic pleasure. This transfiguration of modern death into sublime pleasure constitutes the (perverse) heroism of the decadent ideal, an ideal that is thus fundamentally *idealist,* following Schopenhauer's model, and likewise modernist, as a response to the temporal situation of modernity's perpetual coming into being (and thus loss).

Modernity as an Aesthetic Problem: D'Annunzio, Wagner, and Nietzsche

In light of this ascetic–aesthetic ideal, it should be no surprise that D'Annunzio identifies Wagner as the essential figure of modernity. In fact, he does so in a complicated way, at once lamenting the political and moral decadence of modernity and aligning himself with a revitalizing alternative, that suggested in Friedrich Nietzsche's new philosophy, but simultaneously returning to Wagner and aligning himself with this paradigmatic artist of modern decadence. It will be worthwhile to briefly examine this conflicted relationship in order to underscore the key point that D'Annunzio's decadence, and Italian *decadentismo,* is at once an affirmation and a rejection. In this way, it reiterates the dynamics at the core of Schopenhauer's philosophy in an ascetic aestheticism that sees itself as a deliberate transfiguration of modern deadness into a form of aesthetic pleasure rooted in the pain of loss itself.

In an essay he wrote for the newspaper *La Tribuna,* "The Wagner Case" ("Il caso Wagner," published in three instalments, 23 July, 3 August, and 9 August 1893), D'Annunzio stages a confrontation between Wagner and Nietzsche, borrowing from Nietzsche's own essay on Wagner, "Der Fall Wagner" ("The Wagner Case"; published in 1888). D'Annunzio's essay introduces Nietzsche's political thought to Italian readers. His aim is to bolster arguments that he had made a few months before in "La bestia elettiva," in which his description of King Ludwig II's suicide was part of a broader argument against what D'Annunzio characterized as the weakness and failures of Italy's liberal democracy. At the end of that earlier essay, D'Annunzio argues that the decline of the aristocracy has made it necessary to invent a new form of nobility, that of the "superuomo" (his word for Nietzsche's *Übermensch*). This new nobility will be rooted in inner freedom: "The essence of the 'nobleman' is his inner sovereignty. He is the free man, stronger than the things around him."[45] Nietzsche's "aristocratic" philosophy thus made for a natural ally, and so in "Il caso Wagner" D'Annunzio presents that philosophy as a response against the decadence of modern culture. Whereas in "La bestia elettiva" he had articulated decadence in political terms as the decline of nobility and concomitant rise of the demos, here he focuses on cultural decadence and a political-philosophical response. Thus in the first part of the essay he responds to what he characterizes as a modern cult of Wagnerism, which he says Nietzsche despises because of its link to the weaknesses of modern democracy.[46] In the subsequent parts of the essay, D'Annunzio traces out Nietzsche's argument. Wagner began as a revolutionary who fought to affirm life, but he was swayed by his encounter with Schopenhauer and became Schopenhauerian through and through, renouncing life and embracing death.[47] Nietzsche's response against Wagner is thus a rejection of that pessimism and its politics of supposed (democratic) weakness.

All the same, and perhaps surprisingly, D'Annunzio ultimately does not side with Nietzsche. While Wagner represents modern decadence, D'Annunzio argues that Wagner at least has the essential merit of bringing his vision to concrete realization, something that Nietzsche's "philosophy of the future" is unable to do: "Thus the philosopher places himself outside his time, while the artificer comes back to his time. But the former, even while glorifying life, ranges through a purely speculative domain; in contrast the latter *realizes* his abstractions in the concrete form of the work of art."[48] D'Annunzio thus ends his essay by praising Wagner's modernity – not just in spite of but *because* of its decadence. The artist's purpose is to make the present visible to itself. As such, Wagner is a consummate success, revealing the suffering of a decadent present, making modernity self-aware. It is in this sense that D'Annunzio points us to Wagner's *Tristan und Isolde* as a hallmark of modernity:

> In his work, Richard Wagner not only gathered together all of the spirituality and ideality dispersed around him, but by interpreting our metaphysical need he revealed to us the most occult part of our inner life. Each of us, like Tristan who listens to the ancient melody that the shepherd intones, owes to the mysterious virtue of great music the direct revelation of an anguish in which he thought he would catch the true essence of his own soul and the terrible secret of Destiny.[49]

Wagner, in other words, embodies a moment in the history of the world, synthesizes its spirit, and gives it aesthetic form that makes it real and powerful in a way that Nietzsche's desire for a positive, active alternative cannot. He reveals us to ourselves in the form of music. Modernity is Wagnerian.[50]

It is telling that D'Annunzio's essays I have cited here, from 1892 and 1893, were written in the run-up to *Trionfo della morte*. That suicide-obsessed novel is a study in modern Wagnerism, permeated by the cult of death that D'Annunzio in his essays has located as the fundamental feature of his contemporary, decadent modernity. By crafting an entire novel that elaborates on this musical theme (the *Liebestod* from *Tristan und Isolde*) in the language of prose, D'Annunzio is declaring his own modernity and taking up the mantle of the artist who must reflect the present to itself, in all of its diseased suffering, its Schopenhauerian renunciation of life.[51] D'Annunzio's protagonist, like D'Annunzio himself in his essays on Nietzsche and Wagner, is figuring the decadent project for aestheticism: the transfiguration of a deadening world into an aesthetic experience that is simultaneously self-reflective and distancing, decaying and sublime.

Ambivalent Idealism: Ascetic Aestheticism and Modernist Renewal

Tellingly, Giorgio Aurispa's project in *Trionfo della morte* is not a success. His effort to craft a sublime death in his exaltation of murder-suicide is undercut by D'Annunzio's representation of the final scene, in which the beloved, Ippolita, frantically screams out "murderer" as she tumbles down the cliff to her demise, pulling Giorgio with her.[52] Hardly exalted, the scene renders its grand poetic gesture as more grotesque than sublime. This novel is the end of D'Annunzio's decadent trilogy, after which he moves increasingly toward representations of a Nietzschean "superuomo" in novels like *The Flame* (*Il fuoco*, 1900), replacing the decadent (effeminate) aesthetes of the earlier trilogy.[53] This shift, I posit, serves as an indication of how D'Annunzio envisioned himself as a bridge between the decadence of modernity that he affirmed in his assessment of Wagner and a new future, such as the one he claimed Nietzsche philosophized about without knowing how to bring into reality. Put differently, D'Annunzio envisioned himself as a bridge between decadence and modernism – not as distinct historical periods but rather as alternative stances on the same moment of modern crisis.[54]

That D'Annunzio can be seen as both decadent and modernist in this way is telling, for it reveals the importance of an aesthetic stance in a modernist approach to crisis times. In fact, in texts less evidently "decadent" we see the same key dynamic, a modernist rearticulation of Schopenhauer's ascetic aestheticism. I thus offer two sets of comparisons that demonstrate how pervasive this paradigm became as a part of the modernist response to crisis time. First, I consider D'Annunzio's late work, *Notturno* (1916), together with Italo Svevo's famous modernist novel, *Zeno's Conscience* (*La coscienza di Zeno*, 1923). Despite their sharp political differences, the two writers shared in a Schopenhauerian aesthetic transfiguration of suffering and death in the service of a modernist temporal outlook affirming renewal. Second, I turn to the transnational case of the key category of modernist epiphany, where Schopenhauerian *Erhebung* is at the heart of an ascetic aestheticism of modernist redemption.

Modernity's Cult of Death as Affirmation of Renewal: D'Annunzio and Svevo

D'Annunzio's late novel/prose-poem, *Notturno*, in which the impulse to glorify death is articulated as part of the aestheticizing of violence and war, may seem to fall into a very different category from Italo Svevo's most famous modernist novel, *Zeno's Conscience*, which ends, quite literally, with a world-annihilating explosion that sets the universe back in order. However, they actually revolve around a similar shared problem and similar shared responses: the deadening force of modern materialism requires, in their view, an aestheticizing transfiguration that provides the push toward (imagined) renewal. This similarity reveals how the overlap of decadence and modernism is rooted in a shared philosophical impulse that ultimately not only transfigures suffering but also points toward renewal.

D'Annunzio's *Notturno* is a genre-defying prose-poem composition first written line by line on scraps of paper while the author was convalescing after an air mission in the First World War left him temporarily blind. From 16 January to 13 September 1916, he was taken out of action and blindfolded by doctors; he thus could not see the pages as he wrote and so had to invent a method of writing on single strips of paper, one verse/line at a time, to keep his words in order. The composition recounts visions, memories, and experiences with a lyrical intensity, elevating his wartime exploits and the sacrifices of his comrades in highly aesthetic language that treats battle as a religious form of martyrdom. He uses saints and even Christ as models, blending them together with the Italian soldiers fighting for the Fatherland. After D'Annunzio had regained his sight and returned to service, he eventually compiled the fragments (his daughter, Renata, helped him put together a partial version during his convalescence). He then wrote a prose *Post Scriptum* that brought the "Offerings" (chapter divisions) of his text together into a conclusive final image, one that traces the events of the years after D'Annunzio healed, from September 1916 through 4 November 1921. D'Annunzio chose that latter date for his *Post Scriptum* to make his book's "completion" coincide with the third anniversary of the war's end and the ceremony of interment for the unknown soldier, thus contributing to a monumentalization of the struggle, one that aimed to redeem loss while constructing what Laura Wittman has characterized as a new understanding – and fascist politicization – of mourning that loss.[55] These final pages are a hallucinatory interplay of images that can be difficult to track: the vision of his mother lying in her casket is interspersed with images of glorified war heroes, all of whom are converted into holy saints and martyrs, leading up to the final image of the unknown soldier being laid to rest in the new monumental tomb, which is blended with a memory of D'Annunzio's from when he and his comrades found a heroic, unidentified soldier who died and whose body they burned: "the flame was beautiful, and the soldier in his divine poverty was beyond all beauty."[56]

The Schopenhauerian element of this hymn to death is clear. Indeed, describing the unknown soldier before his funeral, as the soldier casts a net while fishing in a river surrounded by the graves of D'Annunzio's compatriots, the poet-warrior writes: "death was singing, life was singing. *O mors, ero mors tua*."[57] The vital rhythm of music mixes death and life, and the Latin phrase (Oh death, I will be your death) – a play on Hosea 13:4, "Oh grave, I will be thy destruction" – suggests precisely the shift from finitude to the infinite, the overcoming of death itself in (Christian) rebirth. This is the model for the vitalist rebirth that D'Annunzio aims to usher forth in his Fatherland, and here we see how the Schopenhauerian aestheticism of D'Annunzio's death-obsessed text commingles with a different impulse, one that repurposes the sublime martyrdom of self-renunciation as a tool to rekindle the patriotic spirit. As D'Annunzio puts it a few pages earlier, describing his invasion and occupation of Fiume: "To prevent the city from being undone in the spiritual space in which I had raised its towers and beacons, fraternal blood had to spill. The inexpiable crime, the insuperable trench, had to cleave the new Italy from the old. We had to bear witness, with wounds and deaths and ruins, that the new Italy forever rejected all reconciliation, all contamination."[58]

The nationalist fervour of these lines speaks to the darkest aspects of D'Annunzio's Fiume "adventure" and its prefiguration of Mussolini's fascism – a language of purity rejecting the "contamination" of other races (the Croats who were formerly subjects of Austria-Hungary and would now become part of Yugoslavia).[59] It also speaks to the modernist project to cleave a new Italy from the old one, deploying the aesthetic elevation of heroic violence as a tool in that larger nation-building project, one that unfolds in actuality and bestows upon itself a world-historical mission. What is at work in D'Annunzio's *Notturno* is thus the combination of the aesthetic heroism and renunciation of Schopenhauer's idealism with a messianic rearticulation of the political-historical impulses that motivated the Italian Hegelians to reject Schopenhauer. While this does not mean that D'Annunzio is in some sense directly embracing Hegelian idealism, what is clear is that beyond the question of direct reception we can see, through the double lens of these lineages, how the ambivalent character of modernist idealism's two sides combine to form one self-conflicted project.

Svevo's novel is likewise situated at the threshold of decadence and modernist renewal.[60] The novel's protagonist/narrator, Zeno, is attempting to exorcise his "sickness" through psychoanalysis and by writing out his inner thoughts and experiences as a form of therapy – the text's explanation for its own origin, as well as for its stream-of-consciousness style and fragmented structure.[61] The novel ultimately offers an ironic commentary on Zeno's effort to heal himself, depicting it as futile, and finally zooms out to a cosmic level in a pessimistic vision that turns into an ambivalent embrace of renewal through destruction. Near the end of the novel the protagonist claims that he has cured himself by giving up introspection and returning to the world of business, where he is able to "warm" himself "with struggle and above all with victory," then writing: "It was business that healed me and I want Dr. S. to know it."[62] But seen from outside the narrator's (repeatedly self-deluding) perspective, this "cure" is itself a form of sickness, as Antonella Braida argues.[63] He desires to show off his "cure" to Dr S., the name of his psychoanalyst (and an allusion to both Sigmund Freud and Schopenhauer), but this is merely an attempt to respond to a sense of pessimistic hopelessness that ends up embracing precisely the modern conditions that have given rise to the crisis he experiences.

In fact, on the very last page of the novel, directly following his assertion that he has been healed by business, the narrator launches into a final examination of the modern world and the human condition that radically shifts the perspective. Several paragraphs reflect obsessively on the sickness of the modern world, offering a scathing critique of our society and replicating the language typical of the discourse on decadence, both in a broad metaphysical sense – "unlike other sicknesses, life is always fatal" – and in more specific critiques of modern life – "present-day life is polluted at the roots."[64] He concludes that human beings have short-circuited evolution and made themselves unable to adapt so that no return to health is possible for them, except for a final, apocalyptic rebalancing: "there will be an enormous explosion that no one will hear, and the earth, once again a nebula, will wander through the heavens, freed of parasites and sickness."[65] Svevo's final picture moves from decadence to renewal, like D'Annunzio's, but in a way that is markedly less triumphant. The irony of his depiction of a peaceful, oblivious world, freed of human consciousness and wandering the universe, makes clear that the glorification of war as renewal is itself an instance of the human sickness that Svevo's novel confronts.

What we see at work in both postwar novels is thus a mixture of the aesthetic impulse toward decadence and the impulse toward renewal that is typical of modernist confrontations with that decadence. The aesthetic impulse is visible in the way that an obsessive interest in suffering, decay, and death is transfigured through the artistic process of creation itself. In D'Annunzio this transfiguration aims at crafting a secular religion of self-sacrifice in war, a cult of the hero that will supposedly lead to the emergence of a new Italy. In Svevo, the transfiguration is inward and refers to the way in which the self-analysing subject recrafts his own understanding, freeing himself from his sickness not by curing it but by seeing it as beautiful: "Mine was genuine meditation, one of those rare instants that our miserly life bestows of true, great objectivity… . I could smile at my life and also at my sickness…. How much more beautiful my life had been than that of the so-called healthy."[66] Yet at the same time, Svevo has chosen to set his novel in the moments at the beginning of the First World War, and instead of seeing the war as hopeful renewal his ironic prose likewise reduces it to a moment of boredom and finally to a thought experiment that reveals the inhumanity of the impulse toward renewal. This difference might actually, paradoxically, mark Svevo as more of a pessimistic decadent than D'Annunzio himself.

In either case, however, what is inescapable is the centrality of the outlook of philosophical idealism for the decadent aesthetic transfiguration of suffering, sickness, and death. Svevo figures this as the power of imagination to recreate history and the self or, in a moment in which he refers directly to Schopenhauer (and Goethe, in relation to their physiological theories of colour), the ability of the observing subject to literally recolour the world.[67] The obsessive interest in death and the deadening experience of modernity is thus not just a repetition of that decay but a strategy for converting it into something other, an effort to transform the world precisely through the power of the subject *qua* observer – and thus an implicit or explicit recognition of the precedence of the idea (and the observer's subjective stance) over material reality itself.

Idealist Erhebung *and Modernist Epiphany: A Transnational Paradigm*

This decadent legacy of Schopenhauer's thought extends beyond authors who were directly influenced by the philosopher, like D'Annunzio and Svevo, throughout a broader modernist context that receives and operates in terms related to his world view. In this sense, Schopenhauer offers not just a historical lineage but more importantly a conceptual lens for understanding the impulses at work in modernist production. To clarify what I mean, it will be useful to turn now to a constellation of writers from across Europe and the world who shared in the ascetic aestheticism of Schopenhauer's outlook and in the modernist impulse to transfigure modernity in aesthetic form. These writers engaged the idea of aesthetic *Erhebung* in the form of modernist epiphany – one of the most well-studied tropes of modernist creation, particularly in the context of James Joyce (1882–1941), from whose work the term comes, and British modernists like Virginia Woolf (1882–1941) and T.S. Eliot (1888–1965).

Post-Kantian German philosophy made significant use of the notion of *Erhebung*. In his *Logic*, Hegel deploys the term to describe the way in which the subject ("Ich") is elevated to the "standpoint of pure knowing where the distinction of subject and object has vanished."[68] This elevation takes the self beyond itself, from the finite to the infinite, the realm of God. Hegel's religious notion of *Erhebung* is shifted toward an aesthetic alternative in Schopenhauer's idealism. In *The World as Will and Representation*, he uses the term in his discussion of the sublime to refer to the way in which the sublime differs from the beautiful. As we have seen, when a knowing subject deliberately contemplates a threatening object as an aesthetic object, the result is not just beauty but the sublime. Here the notion of *Erhebung* becomes the way of pointing to that difference: "With the sublime, that state of pure knowing is obtained first of all by a conscious and violent tearing away from the relations of the same object to the will which are recognized as unfavourable, by a free exaltation, accompanied by consciousness, beyond the will and the knowledge related to it."[69] The free exaltation or elevation (*Erhebung*) described here is a heroic achievement, for the subject engaged in aesthetic contemplation has overcome the pressing actual relations of the object to the body (which is the individual's connection to the world of will) and sees it in the distanced form of unattached observation while simultaneously maintaining conscious awareness of this stance itself.

What makes Schopenhauer's version of *Erhebung* particularly powerful as a model for decadent aestheticism and, eventually, modernist epiphany is the way in which it is built out of the everyday, material world in its normal relations to us as embodied creatures with physical needs and wants. In transforming everyday experience into aesthetic rapture, aestheticism is not escaping modern life's material conditions but rather transfiguring them while remaining concretely aware of them, a process that is evident in the rapturous attention to *things* in a work like Huysmans's *Against Nature* or D'Annunzio's *Pleasure* (*Il piacere*, 1889). In a later modernist context, this same impulse emerges in the poetics of the epiphany, which Joyce described as a temporally isolated moment in which some essential truth is made manifest in aesthetically apprehensible form, akin to religious revelation.[70] It is thus fitting that Joyce chose the religious term, epiphany, which in Greek signifies the revelation of a deity and in the Catholic tradition is a feast day (6 January) commemorating the revelation of Jesus's divinity to the Magi.[71] But in modernist fashion, this religious revelation is channelled into aesthetic experience and linked to the disclosure of inner subjectivity or the sudden comprehension of an external set of relations that cohere into a deeper meaning for the observing subject. Thus, in *Stephen Hero* (~1903–5), as the aesthete-protagonist is walking down the street he overhears a "triviality" in the form of some snippets of conversation in which a Young Lady and a Young Gentleman flirt on the steps of a brown brick house.[72] The experience is banal, but it makes a deep impression on Stephen's "sensitiveness," leading him to determine that he will start his own collection of epiphanies, which he defines as "sudden spiritual manifestation[s]" and "the most delicate and evanescent of moments."[73]

These delicate, evanescent moments of sudden aesthetic revelation can be found in a host of writers, from Woolf's "moments of being" to Eliot's poetics of epiphanic revelation in his late work, *Four Quartets* (1943). Woolf describes such moments, which are at the heart of her poetics, in a journal entry from 4 January 1929:

> Now is life very solid or very shifting? I am haunted by the two contradictions. This has gone on for ever; will last for ever; goes down to the bottom of the world – this moment I stand on. Also it is transitory, flying, diaphanous. I shall pass like a cloud on the waves. Perhaps it may be that though we change, one flying after another, so quick, so quick, yet we are somehow successive and continuous we human beings, and show the light through. But what is the light?[74]

In a similar vein, Eliot's poem "Burnt Norton" (1936) from *Four Quartets* explicitly posits a kind of spiritual revelation as a core element of its epiphanic poetics, directly relating it to post-Kantian *Erhebung*. The word "Erhebung" appears explicitly in "Burnt Norton" II, where Eliot describes a mystical dance spinning "[a]t the still point of the turning world" (v. 62).[75] Being present in this dance means existing in a place and time that are removed from actuality, both moving and still, both spatially and temporally located while also outside of space and time (vv. 68–9). What occurs in this suspended moment is an epiphany in which the subject is freed from the shackles of desire that constitute what Schopenhauer terms individuated life (vv. 70–2), but something remains, as the poetic speaker is surrounded

> By a grace of sense, a white light still and moving,
> *Erhebung* without motion, concentration
> Without elimination, both a new world
> And the old made explicit, understood
> In the completion of its partial ecstasy,
> The resolution of its partial horror. (vv. 73–8)

Eliot is operating in terms of Schopenhauer's discussion of the sublime, as evidenced by his reference to these experiences of "partial ecstasy" and "partial horror" paired with the use of *Erhebung* left as an abstruse German term (in typically Eliottian fashion).[76] The dance is thus an aesthetic experience that pulls the subject out of itself, out of space-time, and out of the usual relations of causality and desire; the dance replaces these with a form of consciousness that ultimately is the meeting point of the present with history and with the future reminiscent of Woolf's "moments of being" and Joyce's epiphanies. The moment, as a "moment," is experienced as separate from normal time and space; however, the poem brings these moments back into relation with lived time, and the result is that the moment becomes a means of drawing together immanent reality with something transcendent. It pulls us up from the material realm, not destroying materiality but connecting it to something beyond itself, "concentrating" without "eliminating." Schopenhauerian *Erhebung* thus serves as a key term for understanding Eliot's exploration of time and quest to redeem modernity – and the modernist poetics of epiphany itself.

While the discourse on epiphany could be traced at much greater length, here I want to suggest only the way in which it exhibits a Schopenhauerian conjunction of heightened aesthetic experience and ascetic renunciation.[77] For Eliot the spiritual truth of *Four Quartets* is repeatedly articulated in terms of renunciation, drawing on the *Bhagavad-Gita* as well as Saint John of the Cross's *Dark Night of the Soul* (and other Christian mystical texts, such as *The Cloud of Unknowing* and Julian of Norwich's *Revelations of Divine Love*) in a negative theology of self-abnegation. But the ascetic element of epiphanic *Erhebung* does not require explicit theological intertexts to function, something that becomes clear in Eugenio Montale's modernist poetics of the secular miracle, as well as in two related cases: the Iranian modernist Sadegh Hedayat's (1903–1951) epiphanies of self-annihilation in his famous novel, *The Blind Owl* (*Buf-e Kur*, 1936), and Luigi Pirandello's (1867–1936) epiphanies of self-dissolution in his final novel, *One, No One, and One Hundred Thousand* (*Uno, nessuno e centomila*, 1926).

For Montale, epiphanic *Erhebung* appears as a secular miracle, absent in actuality but summoned for the reader through an aesthetic form that acts out its content. The clearest instance is his untitled poem "Maybe one morning …" ("Forse un mattino…") from his first collection, *Cuttlefish Bones* (*Ossi di sepia*, 1925):

> Maybe one morning, walking in dry, glassy air,
> I'll turn, and see the miracle occur:
> nothing at my back, the void
> behind me, with a drunkard's terror.
>
> Then, as if on a screen, trees houses hills
> will suddenly collect for the usual illusion.
> But it will be too late: and I'll walk on silent
> among the men who don't look back, with my secret.[78]

What this poem imagines is a possible but unrealized moment in which the speaker suddenly sees through everyday reality, "the usual illusion" that populates our sense experience with mundane objects of perception, what Schopenhauer would term the illusory world of representation. But while the opening word, "maybe," suspends the content of this vision in brackets – distancing what we might call its potential truth-claim in what Rebecca West has analysed as Montale's recurring insistence on uncertainty in a liminal poetics that situates itself as perpetually on the threshold – the poem nonetheless enacts its hypothetical vision lyrically, thus realizing it in the form of poetry if not in actual life outside of aesthetic experience.[79] The dry, glassy air already summons a tactile experience that is nevertheless distancing, reminiscent of the atmospheres depicted by a "metaphysical" painter like Giorgio De Chirico (1888–1978), whose works often express or imply an ideal or invisible level of reality beyond what is visible to us on the surface of things. The action of looking behind, introduced in the second verse and reiterated in the final one, shifts the field of vision and provides the opening for a fissure in the order of representation; it also implies a distinction, for the poetic speaker will, perhaps, hold this vision as a personal secret, separating him from those who don't look back. The secret is an emptiness ("il nulla" and "il vuoto," nothingness and emptiness) that strikes like a drunken terror, upending spatial perception and penetrating behind what Schopenhauer terms "the veil of Maya." But it also uproots the subject in some important way, emphasized by the enjambment separating the first-person object pronoun from those things behind the speaker, things which are themselves negations of things.

The self-annihilating aspect of this epiphanic vision is taken further when it becomes the obsessive theme of aesthetic reflection, as in the case of Hedayat's *The Blind Owl*. Here, the suicidal decadence running through Wagner and D'Annunzio becomes the hallucinatory framework holding together a set of confusingly intertwined narratives related more through the repetition of key words, images, and themes than by any clear linear plot. While this is not the place for a deep analysis of the novel's complexities, it is worth noting that it is structured in five sections that represent three apparently distinct fictional spaces (overlapping fictional worlds) and modes of discourse – and for this reason, Michael Beard claims that the novel should be considered "a series of love stories," which are in turn linked by metafictional spaces.[80] At the core of these love stories we find, in each instance, death: the death of the beloved, accidental or the product of homicide, but also the death of the aesthetic subject, who dissolves in an opium-dream of madness that breaks down the barriers normally separating self and world.[81]

Unlike in the moments of epiphanic revelation in Eliot and Montale, for Hedayat's protagonist the decentring effect of his fleeting contact with the transcendent destabilizes the self permanently. The ending of the epiphanic moment thus does not correspond to a return to "reality" – reality itself has been transformed and unsettled. Indeed, as if the ideal were an intoxicating substance to which one is addicted, the narrator-protagonist seeks out the terrible delight of making contact with it, and with the self-destruction and self-expansion that contact entails. Speaking near the end of the second narrative segment of the story (the fourth section of the novel), the narrator describes a scene in which his wife comes to his room to check on him in his decaying state of health. He berates her, and she leaves. This occasions an epiphanic moment described as madness in which deindividuation mixes with a delusion of grandeur:

> Several times I thought of getting up and going to her to fall at her feet, weeping and asking her to forgive me. Yes, weeping; for I thought that if only I could weep I should find relief. Some time passed; whether it was to be measured in minutes, hours or centuries I do not know. I had become like a madman and I derived an exquisite pleasure from the pain I felt. It was a pleasure which transcended human experience, a pleasure which only I was capable of feeling and which the gods themselves, if they existed, could not have experienced to such a degree. At that moment I was conscious of my superiority. I felt my superiority to the men of the rabble, to nature and to the gods – the gods, that product of human lusts. I had become a god. I was greater than God, and I felt within me the eternal, infinite flux… .
>
> How much time passed I do not know. When I came to myself she had gone. It may be that the space of time in which I had experienced all the pleasures, the caresses and the pain of which the nature of man is susceptible had not lasted more than a moment.[82]

The narrator's sense of superiority situates him above not only the common "rabble" but also nature and even the gods, whom he identifies as a projection of human desire in a psychoanalytically informed move echoing Freud's stance on religion.[83] At the same time, this delusion of grandeur is informed by and tied integrally to the aesthetic stance of *Erhebung* that sets apart a fleeting moment suspended in-and-out of time, demarcating a sublime combination of pain and joy, self-dissolving terror and self-expanding greatness. The elevation of the subject as a special site of refined reflection – the elevation extolled by aestheticism throughout the nineteenth century – is coupled with the self-erasure of modernist decentring. Put differently, the privileged situation of the pure subject of (aesthetic) knowing in Schopenhauer's aesthetics is combined with the ascetic impulse of his ethics of self-renunciation. The conclusion of that fusion of aesthetic and ascetic impulses is ultimately a (homicidal) immersion in death itself. The modernist epiphany becomes, in its limit case, an epiphany of death:

> Throughout our life death is beckoning to us. Has it not happened to everyone suddenly, without reason, to be plunged into thought and to remain immersed so deeply in it as to lose consciousness of time and place and the working of his own mind? At such times one has to make an effort in order to perceive and recognise again the phenomenal world in which men live. One has been listening to the voice of death.[84]

Hedayat's move to erase the illusions of the phenomenal world, and the very notion of an individuated self, is echoed in Pirandello's last novel, but there with a humorous twist of self-distancing that adds a final element to my comparison here. Pirandello's novel is recounted by a narrator-protagonist named Vitangelo Moscarda, who repeatedly describes his story as an account of his own madness, much as does Hedayat's unnamed narrator. This madness results from an irrational ideal shattering the sense of what constitutes "reality"; experienced aesthetically in an epiphanic moment, that shattering is a source of fear and simultaneously distances Moscarda from other, normal people – the people who, as Montale put it in his poem, fail to turn around and look at the world for what it truly is, or who Hedayat's narrator-protagonist would call "the rabble." In book II of Pirandello's novel, Moscarda has a vision of his dead father and imagines a conversation with him that ends with an epiphanic revelation of the irrational force that shapes the world, analogous to Schopenhauer's metaphysical vision of will:

> In the emptiness, now, a terrified silence, heavy with all the senseless and shapeless things that lie inert, dumb, impenetrable for the spirit.
>
> It was an instant, but it was an eternity. I felt inside all the horror of blind necessities, of things that cannot be changed: the prison of time; being born now, not before and not after; the name and the body that are given us; the chain of causes; the seed sown by that man, my father, without willing it; my coming into the world, from that seed; involuntary fruit of that man; bound to that branch, expressed from those roots.[85]

The usual features of the suspended moment of *Erhebung* are present – a temporal condensation that is also experienced as an expansion, tied to a sudden vision *through* things that reveals much more than what is present in the phenomenal world of material objects. But the horror thus revealed is a system of inevitable cause and effect characterized precisely as blind necessity, a surge of life giving rise to life accidentally, without purpose or rational structure – a Schopenhauerian vision of life as the irrational suffering of will.

At its limit, Moscarda's epiphanic vision expands to embrace the total dissolution of the individual as such, corresponding to an immersive transformation of the individual into the whole. The most extreme case comes at the end of the novel, where the protagonist has left the city and is living in a countryside poor home that has been established with his own money. It is from there that the narrator-protagonist writes his concluding lines, which insist that there can be no conclusion:

> I am alive and I do not conclude. Life does not conclude. And life knows nothing of names. This tree, tremulous pulse of new leaves. I am this tree. Tree, cloud; tomorrow book or wind: the book I read, the wind I drink. All outside, wandering… .
>
> The home stands in the country, in a lovely spot. I go out every morning, at dawn, because now I want to keep my spirit like this, fresh with dawn, with all things as they are first discovered, that still smack of the raw night, before sun dries their moist respiration and dazzles them… . And the air is new. And everything, instant by instant, is as it is, preparing to appear. I turn my eyes away at once so as to see nothing further arrest its appearance and die. This is the only way I can live now. To be reborn moment by moment. To prevent thought from working again inside me, causing inside a reappearance of the void with its futile constructions.[86]

The narrator's final state is set in opposition to that of his earlier epiphanies, which were rooted in thought – epiphanies about the nature of the world, the falsity of the fixed self, the "name" that is attached to things to assert an unchanging essence or self when in fact the self is mutable and transitory. Instead, he inhabits now what we might term a state of perpetual epiphany, where the boundaries of the self have been discarded so that the individual is deindividuated in perpetuity. Thus he identifies himself with the tree, the cloud, the book; and thus he asserts that he is always new, always coming into being in every instant and refusing to identify with anything fixed, which kills off the becoming of life. What has been achieved, in other words, through the aesthetic insight of *Erhebung*, is a dissolution of self – again, a modernist artistic articulation of the same conjunction of aestheticism and ascetic renunciation that is at the core of Schopenhauer's world view.

This examination of the modernist epiphany thus allows us to conclude with an insight into the way in which modernism can be read as the artistic fruition of a specific form of philosophical thought. Schopenhauer's metaphysical outlook is not only a bulwark in the romantic-modern theorization of the sublime but also an impulse that requires aesthetic form to be fully realized. His philosophy, as many critics and proponents have noted, operates not through argument but through a kind of world-creation: it evokes a reality and, in making it plausible and allowing it to map onto his reader's experience, persuades through showing rather than saying.[87] Yet Schopenhauer's aesthetically pleasing writing and world-creating approach to philosophy nevertheless confront the necessary limits of philosophical discourse, which can only show so much without a radical shift in form. In this sense, Nietzsche's writing surpassed that of his educator by moving toward a more literary union of philosophical thought and artistic form, and in this way he likewise set a pattern for the artistic production that would rearticulate Schopenhauer's view in literary and artistic form in the modernist moment.[88] In the modernist epiphany, the conjunction of a suspended temporal moment and the simultaneous psychological-metaphysical penetration it reveals offers one realization of that Schopenhauerian impulse and its sublime aesthetic experience. Terrifying, self-annihilating, and redemptive, the modernist epiphany's sublime form realizes what Schopenhauer's philosophy could only theorize. Ascetic aestheticism emerged as a key component of modernist idealism not only in the decadent reception of Schopenhauer's thought but also in the global rearticulations of it *qua* paradigm of modernist idealism.

Chapter Four

Avant-Garde Idealism: The Ambivalence of Futurist Vitalism

In the short piece of Futurist synthetic theatre "Before the Infinite" ("Davanti all'infinito"), written by Bruno Corra (1892–1976) and Emilio Settimelli (1891–1954), the Wild Philosopher ("Filosofo selvaggio"), a German-looking young man, paces the stage as he contemplates a stark choice: to sit down and read his daily newspaper (the *Berliner Tageblatt*), or to shoot himself dead with a revolver. After a moment of bored indecision, he opts for the revolver.[1] Scene.

The extreme brevity and lack of usual dramatic structure in this *sintesi* (synthesis) is typical of the genre, as is the violent action at its core.[2] There are only a few pieces of information to process, but each is multilayered and the effect is complex. The Wild Philosopher's everyday existence is represented by the *Berliner Tageblatt*, which was a wide-circulation liberal newspaper and thus stands in for the Futurists' favourite objects of derision: the stability and repetition sought by bourgeois materialism, liberal democracy, and the continued acceptance of German cultural supremacy.[3] The Wild Philosopher's decision to reject this and instead shoot himself with the revolver can thus be read in at least two, conflicting ways: on the one hand, read in the context of the recurring motif of suicide and modernity's death drive that I have examined in chapter 3, it would seem to be an embrace of the suicidal trajectory of modern crisis leading toward self-annihilation, here projected in heroic terms as a choice to take action against the backdrop of existential emptiness.[4] Indeed, the nonchalance of this self-destructive decision might seem to epitomize the almost nihilistic acceptance of modernity's trajectory toward catastrophe in the moment of the Great War.[5] On the other hand, the scene can be read in relation to the historical backdrop of Italian nationalism building toward an eventual push for war against Austria-Hungary and, as a consequence, Germany; in this reading, the "Wild Philosopher" might be more like a "Philosopher in the Wild," untamed but not for that reason a positive or heroic model. Instead, this philosopher epitomizes the emptiness of the dead world of idealist philosophy, the German school of Schopenhauerian pessimism that the Futurists rejected forcefully in other writings. Indeed, in his manifesto "Multiplied Man and the Reign of the Machine" ("L'uomo moltiplicato e il regno della machina," first published in *Le futurisme*, 1911), Marinetti directly describes Schopenhauer as the philosopher of the pessimistic revolver: "Thus our frank misogynist optimism is sharply opposed to the pessimism of Schopenhauer, that bitter philosopher who so often offers us the seductive revolver of philosophy in order to destroy in us our profound nausea for woman and love."[6]

The ambivalence we see in this short *sintesi* is also typical of the form: by condensing an entire play into a single synthetic moment, Futurist theatre aims not only to combine multiple, contradictory affective experiences but also to confuse or disrupt the traditional dominance of plot with its insistence on the logical progression of events that can be read and interpreted. The result of this formal strategy is necessarily an overdetermined representation of action that has the immediate force of irrationality and the affective power of the contradictory emotions and energies that the Futurists believed to be not only inherent to human existence but indeed its greatest strength. In this light, we can return to the ambivalent status of the Wild Philosopher and his suicidal act: it is both a heroic triumph and a pessimistic sign of decadence and the absence of meaning; it is, in other words, the ambivalent problem of modernity itself.

This ambivalence, I argue, allows us to rethink a core critical concept that has shaped understandings of Futurism. Scholars have tended to think of Futurism as developing from a first moment, in which it was defined by its anarchic rejection of the past and its (potentially utopian) vision for an alternative future, to a second moment, in which its violent and destructive impulses aligned it first with war and then with fascism. One of the most powerfully articulated versions of this narrative is found in Marjorie Perloff's foundational study, *The Futurist Moment*.[7] For Perloff, "The 'Futurist Moment' was the brief utopian phase of early Modernism when artists felt themselves to be on the verge of a new age that would be more exciting, more promising, more inspiring than any preceding one."[8] In this reading, the First World War marked a turn, a transformation in the movement, which would eventually lose this sense of revolutionary liberation and pivot toward a fascist alternative. The idea of the Futurist moment thus speaks to a utopian possibility that would be in some sense betrayed by the historical development of the Futurist movement. At the heart of the Futurist moment was a need to reimagine the world and its future, to find a new direction for progress in the face of the crisis wrought by modernity. Futurism engaged this need to restore meaning, direction, or purpose to the world by seeking ways to render the world spiritually vital.

Perloff's argument was fundamentally important in offering a different narrative of modernism, one that shifted away from those that focused on the artistic trajectory leading toward the pure, self-enclosed work of art.[9] However, my contention here is that if we examine the vitalist discourse of Futurism more carefully, taking into account the conflicting views of multiple Futurist authors, what we find is a vision of futurity in which the utopian possibility of the ideal was always already intermixed with the pessimistic irrationality it ostensibly opposed. As Christine Poggi has put it, Futurism embraced a cult of knowingly "artificial optimism."[10] That artificiality, I contend, was rooted in the fact that Futurism's ideal was always inherently ambivalent. I thus suggest that instead of embracing a narrative of temporal succession (a first Futurist moment of utopian anarchy followed by war, followed by fascist classicism and the "return to order"), we think in more phenomenological terms (or perhaps Futurist terms, if we have in mind the structure of the *sintesi*) and consider these "moments" as conceptually different and conflicting, but simultaneous and interpenetrating all the same.

The ambivalence that constitutes this simultaneous opposition within Futurism's own world view is rooted in what I have been arguing is the ambivalent character of modernist idealism: on the one hand, the material world and materialism are in need of a spiritual rejuvenation – matter needs to be brought in line with an ideal (more as an animating force than an organizing principle). On the other, however, this ideal remains deeply enmeshed in material reality itself. Theirs, in other words, is an idealism rooted in the long tradition of vitalist thought that understands the material world as animate, living, vibrating and pulsating to a rhythm of life that is simultaneously material and spiritual, actual and ideal.

This ambivalent fusion of spirit and matter emerges clearly in Marinetti's programmatic "Technical Manifesto of Futurist Literature" ("Manifesto tecnico della letteratura futurista," 1912). There he frames the Futurist project as a return to materiality: "Capture the breath, the sensibility, and the instincts of metals, stones, woods, and so on, through the medium of free objects and capricious motors. Substitute, for human psychology now exhausted, **the lyrical obsession with matter.**"[11] Yet this materiality is one that is fundamentally transformed through the Futurist artistic lens, as the rejection of traditional grammar, syntax, and form unearths something hidden within: "Profound intuitions of life linked together one by one, word by word, according to their illogical surge – these will give us the general outlines for an **intuitive psychology of matter**."[12] If standard grammar replicates a deadening logic that fixes meaning in a way that constrains it, the Futurist "words in freedom" ("parole in libertà") – the telling phrase they adopted to characterize their new mode of poetry – aim not just to break down the walls of logical grammar but also to thus liberate a vital impulse that has been trapped within those walls.

What emerges from this ambivalent fusion is thus a more complicated view of the Futurist project, one that helps me articulate the centrality of modernist idealism for a wide array of movements and figures with conflicting stances. The Futurists positioned themselves as fervent anti-traditionalists,[13] yet their smashing of libraries and rejection of stolid old philosophy masked a subterranean continuity with a complex of nineteenth-century idealist thought. To unearth that continuity, we must disentangle the drives underlying the Futurist engagement with vitalism in general and the philosophy of vitalism, *Lebensphilosophie,* in particular.[14] It is precisely their engagement with vitalist philosophy that helps us make sense of the conflicted stance we see in works like "Davanti all'infinito." Caught between an embrace of chaos and death (futurist anarchism and irrationalism) and a simultaneous rejection of the pessimistic death drive of cultural extinction, the Futurist project was situated at the threshold of two idealist world views, embracing both and rejecting both at the same time. On the one hand we find an optimistic idealism committed to realizing a teleological project unfolding immanently in world history – not necessarily derived from Hegel, but certainly sharing key traits with the idealist paradigm that he typifies. But at the same time, this teleological picture develops through a series of intertexts, including Bergson and Nietzsche, that complicate that paradigm, blending it with elements of the other strand I have identified in the Schopenhauerian pessimism of irrational idealism. These overlapping paradigms meet in the Futurist notion of a material reality suffused in vital energies. Ultimately, what this means is that the Futurists, for all their differences from modernist writers like Pirandello or Svevo, are nonetheless caught up in the same ambivalent struggle: the struggle of modernist idealism.

The remainder of this chapter will examine the ambivalent dynamics of modernist idealism in Italian Futurism by turning first to its "official" articulation by Marinetti, who directly engaged the legacy of nineteenth-century *Lebensphilosophie* but distorted that vitalist discourse by idolizing the machine in mystical terms. While this placed Futurism firmly in the discursive space of a broader modernist mysticism, it also emphasized not just the materiality of that mysticism but its inorganic mechanization. This version of vitalist mysticism thus contrasts with that of one of Marinetti's collaborators, the much less studied writer Bruno Corra, who participated in Florentine Futurism in the years around the First World War. Indeed, even in Walter L. Adamson's argument for situating Florence at the heart of Italy's avant-garde modernism, Corra is barely mentioned – a symptom of the broader critical tendency to overlook his significance.[15] Unearthing Corra's work here will provide a curious and important case of modernist ambivalence, offering insight into how Futurist vitalism engaged an anti-tradition of spiritual occultism that positioned it as a precursor to Grosz's "*new* new materialism" and thus revealed that materialism's continuity with idealist discourses.[16] Indeed, what held these seemingly divergent aspects of the Futurist movement together was precisely the underlying dynamic of modernist idealism, the effort to change materialism from a deadening force to the source of new, unforeseen, and irrational impulses of life that could be used to open up new possibilities for Italy's future.

Futurist *Lebensphilosophie*: Practical and Mystical Revitalization

Though Futurist thinkers and artists, particularly Marinetti, had a conflicted relationship with traditions and forebearers, it is possible to situate the vitalism animating the Futurist project firmly at the juncture of the two strands of idealist thought that have been at the core of this book's analysis. Their push to make artistic vitality into a vehicle to revitalize the political world through culture was linked to the immanent idealism that I have argued is typified by Hegel, for whom the historical becoming of actual reality was the immanent realization of the rational ideal. At the same time, however, the Futurists engaged a discourse of vitalism that had emerged out of the irrationalist move in nineteenth-century thought, thus engaging in the strand of idealism I have traced to Schopenhauer. The Futurists' language of vital becoming joined together these two conflicting idealist impulses: their notion of vital becoming offered a mystical, irrational, inhuman world view while simultaneously aiming toward political and cultural praxis, with the goal of actively guiding the development of the Italian nation and people as a historical realization of their ideals.

To understand this dual stance, we will need to consider how the Futurists are related to the legacy of a particular philosophy of life in its becoming. *Lebensphilosophie* was less a school of philosophical thought than a term used to signal the overlapping ideas of a group of philosophical thinkers, especially from the 1800s and the early 1900s in Germany and France. The figures most commonly associated with *Lebensphilosophie* are Henri Bergson (1859–1941) and Wilhelm Dilthey (1833–1911).[17] In some respects, Arthur Schopenhauer (1788–1860) can be considered the founding figure of this movement.[18] Likewise, one of Schopenhauer's most important "students," Friedrich Nietzsche (1844–1900), engaged with key aspects of this vitalist stance.[19] A unifying feature of these thinkers was their dedication to discovering the meaning of life by forgoing theoretical/intellectual knowledge in favour of a direct experience of the vital kernel of life – the unmediated flow of becoming underlying the actual world in which we think (intellectually, theoretically) and act.[20] According to the outlooks that overlap under the rubric of *Lebensphilosophie,* the significance of life is not conceptually explicated so much as vitally engaged.

Futurist production replicated this stance: life must be engaged rather than conceived intellectually. The irrationalism implied in this outlook (a feature present in *Lebensphilosophie* from Schopenhauer onward) informed their project from the start, though as the historical circumstances changed it took on new political dimensions. Marinetti's book, *Futurism and Fascism* (*Futurismo e fascismo,* 1924), opens with this telling epigraph: "I futuristi sono i mistici dell'azione" – "The futurists are the mystics of action" – a statement the author attributes to "the Theosophists."[21] This epigraph captures an ethos of vitalist dynamism, one that Marinetti wanted to project as the spiritual core of his artistic movement and its pursuit of practical, political action.

In this section, I examine two key elements of that dynamism as instances of the vitalist discourse of *Lebensphilosophie* that dialogued directly with Nietzsche and Bergson, even while the Futurists warped or distorted key aspects of their views. First, the Futurists' emphasis on creative-artistic action constituted what I term their form of *historical dynamism;* this element of their world view was tightly tied to Bergson's notion of creative evolution and also resonated with key elements of Nietzsche's philosophy of history. Second, their emphasis on action was also directly figured in cult terms as mysticism, and in this regard their vitalist dynamism was also characterized by a strain of *mystical optimism*. This mystical optimism, too, echoed key elements of the vitalist discourse deployed by Nietzsche and Bergson, albeit refigured in a reductively mechanical vision of human redemption through union with the machine. Seeing these two aspects in Marinetti's articulation of Futurism highlights how deeply the language and thought of nineteenth-century *Lebensphilosophie* penetrated the Futurist project and its combination of material and ideal reality. This in turn gives us reason to qualify scholarship that too readily accepts the Futurists' self-definition as anti-traditional, instead situating Futurism in a long modernist alternative tradition.

Revitalizing the World through Action: Futurist Spectacle as Historical Dynamism

What I am describing as historical dynamism is the particular approach Marinetti articulated in his quest to revitalize the dead world through artistic action. Futurism asserted that it could use "matter" (things existing in the actual, material world – artistic production and political action) to transform and spiritualize the material world. Futurists viewed matter and spirit as interpenetrating; thus, their art could unlock the spiritual potential within matter. Futurist art and action set out to bring the material world back to life by unlocking its buried energy through artistic and cultural action and using that unleashed vitality to rearrange the social and political world.

The Futurists thus called for the destruction of the barrier between art and life, an operation that would unfold in three steps. First, they would revitalize art itself through a revolution in artistic form, convinced that art could connect with the deep kernel of vital energy at the core of life. Second, they would use this revitalized art to vivify their audiences, drawing them into the spectacle and making them part of its vitality. Third, they would connect their art back to the realm of actual, lived life (beyond the aesthetic sphere) where practical politics occurs. A revolution in artistic form would thus become political and social revolution.

The unique form of performance art the Futurists invented, the *serata futurista* (Futurist soirée), served as a model for this three-step process and its connection to a broader notion of historical dynamism that had emerged in the Futurist ideal of actively shaping the world. The *serata* was a multimedia event bringing together Futurist artists to promulgate their movement in its early years, starting with the first *serata* in Trieste (12 January 1910).[22] These events were designed to foster audience participation as part of an overall program to revitalize Italian culture and Italian politics by pushing "passive" Italians toward a more violent, bellicose stance against Austria-Hungary, among other aims. As Marinetti describes in "Futurism's First Battles" ("Prime battaglie futuriste"), part of his 1915 publication, *War, Sole Cleanser of the World* (*Guerra sola igiene del mondo*), "it was precisely with fists and heavy punches that we fought in the theaters of the great Italian cities"; the

Futurist *serate* were battles "against the old, degenerate Italy that was rotten and corrupt."[23]

This statement was a metaphor for artistic revitalization as well as a literal affirmation, for a programmatic element of the *serate* was that they should cause violence to erupt to ensure that the audience participated actively in the vital energies of Futurist art. Street riots, police interventions, and brawls really did accompany these early manifestations of Futurist theatre.[24] Though the *serate* were designed to be unique events, certain traits of the typical *serata* highlight how the audience was pulled into the violent artistic spectacle. The *serate* were multimedia artistic performances held in large venues. They involved multiple Futurist artists who combined their efforts by, among other things, declaiming poems and manifestos (Marinetti generally taking the lead in this respect), exhibiting visual work (such as paintings by Boccioni and Carrà), agitating the crowd with loud sounds and music (Russolo's invention of ear-splitting noise machines, the "intonarumori," is an excellent example here), and directly interfacing with the crowd by hollering insults and provocative statements. The Futurists assumed that by inciting the crowds to participate in these events, they were enacting a new technique for liberating and revitalizing art.[25]

The Futurists hoped that the violent energy created at these event spaces would then spill out into the *piazze* or *osterie* of the targeted city.[26] The audience, having been revitalized within the frame of the aesthetic event, would then transform the social or political world beyond that frame.[27] This in turn was meant to snowball into a full political movement thanks to the way in which Marinetti crafted a public narrative that tied together the *serate* and other Futurist productions, not only through manifestos but also by authoring his own publicity narrative about these events. Earlier on he had pioneered this approach, which was rooted in crafting a public controversy into which he could then intervene: a disruption of the staging of his play *La donna è mobile* became the source of a controversy, and he used the media attention focused on it to draw notoriety to the subsequent publication of his first Futurist manifesto in *Le Figaro* in 1909. This strategy allowed him to depict Futurist artists as warriors in an ongoing, heated struggle against passé social and artistic norms.[28] In the same way, Marinetti followed up on his *serate* by writing his own reviews of the events, reviews intended to position Futurism similarly; in some cases he even bribed journal editors to use his exact words.[29] He thus constructed both the myth of his movement and the political and cultural capital that enabled it to have practical effects in the actual world.

As time marched on and the movement grew, the political aims of this practical revitalization were eventually linked explicitly to fascism. Marinetti went so far as to claim to be a founding father of the movement: "Fascism, born of interventionism and Futurism, fed on Futurist principles."[30] Anarchic irrationalism was thus channelled into a cultural project of nation-building that might seem radically opposed to such anarchism on the face. But what underpinned that transition was a basic commitment to the ideal of revitalizing the actual world of material life from within, using aesthetic practice to draw out its energy and then using that energy to transform social and political reality. Art became a conduit of vitality, reanimating our encounter with modernity as a response to the crisis of meaning inflicted by positivist, democratic, liberal-capitalist materialism.

This model of artistic revivification thus fit with a broader picture of historical becoming that was itself linked to vitalist narratives of progress and self-creation. This historical dynamism was in close dialogue with the language of *Lebensphilosophie*. The rejection of the past was a key characteristic of the movement. Marinetti's retrospective redescription of his initial "Manifesto of Futurism" from 1909 captured this clearly: "It [the manifesto] was the burning fuse of our great rebellion against the cult of the past."[31] In the founding manifesto itself, Marinetti had characterized the institution of museums in similar terms: "Museums, graveyards! ... They're the same thing, really, because of their grim profusion of corpses that no one remembers."[32] Against the culture of dead history and dead art, Marinetti set out an alternative ideal, one of violence as creation: "Admiring an old painting is just like pouring our purest feelings into a funerary urn, instead of projecting them far and wide, in violent outbursts of creation and action."[33]

This part of the Futurist attack on the past resonates significantly with one of Nietzsche's earliest works, his "untimely" essay "On the Uses and Disadvantages of History for Life" ("Vom Nutzen und Nachteil der Historie für das Leben," 1874).[34] There, Nietzsche develops a critique of sickly antiquarianism, which he contrasts to a healthier form of antiquarian relation to the past, a nuance lost in the Futurist version of the concept. Nietzsche's criticism of sickly antiquarianism makes use of the same language later found in Marinetti's manifesto to describe an obsession with the past that mummifies the present: "When the senses of a people harden in this fashion, when the study of history serves the life of the past in such a way that it undermines continuing and especially higher life, when the historical sense no longer conserves life but mummifies it, then the tree gradually dies unnaturally from the top downwards to the roots."[35] For Nietzsche, the past must serve the purposes of present life's striving and thriving; thus, while a strong historical consciousness can be useful, the weak or sickly man who misuses history will become mired in the details of the past for their own sake (much as Marinetti had characterized the admirer of an old painting as "pouring" his "purest feelings" into the dead past). Nietzsche then adds: "Man is encased in the stench of must and mould; through the antiquarian approach he succeeds in reducing even a more creative disposition, a nobler desire, to an insatiable thirst for novelty, or rather for antiquity and for all and everything."[36]

Of course, Marinetti's position was more extreme than Nietzsche's, for while Marinetti seemed to borrow language and ideas from his philosophical predecessor, he also insisted on a *total* rejection of the past. This why he refused to be considered a follower of Nietzsche, writing in an early manifesto, "Against Academic Teachers" ("Contro i professori") of May 1910, "I have no choice but to show how utterly mistaken the critics are in labeling us Neo-Nietzscheans."[37] He believed that Nietzsche's philosophy was too rooted in Greek antiquity for Futurist spontaneity and Italian genius.[38] As such, he took Futurism to be more legitimately future-oriented than even Nietzsche's "prelude to a philosophy for the future."[39]

In later works, Marinetti would describe the historical dynamism of Futurist art in terms that linked it not with Nietzsche but rather with Bergson's philosophy and his notion of "creative evolution." Marinetti underscored this claim of affiliation in a statement that he would repeat word for word, with one notable change, in two separate places, first in a manifesto and then in an interview the following year. Both in a manifesto from November 1914, "In This Futurist Year" ("In quest'anno futurista"), published the subsequent year in *War, Sole Cleanser of the World,* and in his January 1915 interview with *La Diana,* we read: "We, like Bergson, believe that 'la vie déborde l'intelligence,' which is to say that it overflows, swamps and suffocates the infinitesimally small faculty of intelligence."[40]

Bergson's theory, as he expounds it in his first major work, *Creative Evolution* (*L'Évolution créatrice,* 1907), is that evolution occurs as a result of the *élan vital,* or vital impetus, which animates the world by acting "on inert matter."[41] This impulse of life creates change not only in individuals but also in groups / species;[42] it realizes itself as an ordering force in two different directions: as instinct and as intelligence.[43] Humans rely on intelligence as a practical faculty for analysing, quantifying, and operating on the world.[44] But intelligence can only do this by displacing instinct – by focusing not on the movement of life but rather on its fixed instances, thus rendering intellect incapable of understanding life as movement.[45] Marinetti's quote, then, emphasizes the dual fact that, for Bergson, intelligence itself is only one form of the vital impulse's development and that intelligence enables human survival only by cutting us off from our instinctual connection to the vital impulse itself. If viewed intuitively (i.e., not through the lens of practical intelligence), however, life turns out to be much more than what we normally understand; hence Marinetti claims that life in this deeper form "swamps and suffocates the infinitesimally small faculty of intelligence."

Marinetti's claim directly replicates the conceptual vocabulary of Bergson's famous philosophical notion in both the manifesto and the interview. But at the end of this statement, the two different versions take different directions. In *La Diana*, Marinetti goes on to assert that "our intense focusing on the present is preparing the way for a Tomorrow which will emanate directly from us."[46] In contrast, in his earlier manifesto, he had claimed: "Our practical, effective Futurism is preparing the way for a Tomorrow *dominated* by us."[47] Where the manifesto uses the language of domination in a way that is perhaps reminiscent of Nietzsche's theorization of the will to power,[48] in the interview he instead draws on a spiritual language of light or energy that emanates. This latter formulation is closer to Bergson's notion of creative evolution, which is itself a response to and reconfiguration of a centuries-old discourse of light metaphysics.

As Bergson writes in an article from later in his career, "the continuous creation of unforeseeable novelty" is at the core of his philosophy of life.[49] That process of ongoing creation is in turn described in terms that draw on imagery related to the movement of light and energy. In his important early essay, "Introduction to Metaphysics" ("Introduction à la Métaphysique," 1903), one key passage describes the intuition of duration, his notion of lived time, as an instance of self-transcendence: "It [the duration of eternity] would be a living and consequently still moving eternity where our own duration would find itself like the vibrations in light, and which would be the concentration of all duration as materiality is its dispersion. Between these two extreme limits [pure material repetition and the duration of eternity] moves intuition, and this movement is metaphysics itself."[50] What Bergson is articulating is thus a reconfiguration of the traditional vitalist discourse of the world as a living energetic force. As Bergson puts it in his essay on "The Possible and the Real," which he composed by way of apology for not attending the 1928 Nobel Prize ceremony in Stockholm, the material world system can be understood in relation to the Neoplatonic notion of the World Soul (*anima mundi*).[51] This concept, drawn from Plato's *Timaeus* (30c), was repeated and developed by a series of Neoplatonic thinkers including Plotinus and Marsilio Ficino. At the same time, Bergson's notion of an emanating light force is also connected to another Neoplatonic tradition, this one following from Plato's analogy of metaphysical forms in terms of sunlight and vision (*Republic* VII).[52]

What these resonances show is that the Futurists' discourse of energy, light, and spiritual movement was entering into a rich, century-spanning tradition that had recently returned to a kind of popular philosophical vogue when Marinetti was writing. At the same time, Marinetti syncretically combined Bergsonian and Nietzschean thought.[53] The result was an immanent idealism whereby the Futurists' creative vitality reanimated artistic production, and that artistic production in turn called forth a new reality – the Futurists claimed that by operating in and through matter, they were connecting with the vital energy that allowed matter to take on new form and meaning. This was a much more ambitious project than readings that focus on Futurist politics tend to suggest: the Futurists were seeking to establish themselves as the self-conscious mechanism ushering ideal spirit into actuality – the apex of what progressive idealism from Hegel to Bergson envisioned as the telos of world-historical becoming.

Mystical Optimism: Vitalism and the Cult of the Machine

This idealist-inspired vision of a fusion between energy and matter that revitalizes the world leads not only to a dynamic picture of world-becoming but also to a messianic, mystical optimism. Marinetti's narrative rewrites destruction, death, and suffering in a positive light; to quote what is probably the most famous phrase to emerge from the movement, war becomes the "sole cleanser of the world." That is, death and destruction are the privileged site of healthy renewal; war's cleansing, a purification of life, is valued as the good or as an end in itself.[54] In this way, Marinetti's philosophical outlook again approaches that of Nietzsche: for both, the praise of violent, deindividuating action is optimistic and ultimately – to borrow from Habermas's analysis of Nietzsche – "messianic."[55] Nietzsche's concept of the Dionysian, developed in *The Birth of Tragedy* (written in 1870–71), already suggests something like an aesthetic messianism of the destructive impulses. In later works like *Thus Spoke Zarathustra* (1883–91) this messianism expands into a narrative of human progress from the ape through a transitional phase of humanity to the famous *Übermensch*, the higher race of man for whom Zarathustra is a prophet. The *Übermensch* is thus located rhetorically in a space between Christ and Dionysus: both the god in arrival and the salvation of humanity in the form of something higher –

a salvation not from beyond human life but emerging from within the struggle of life itself.[56] Insofar as the Futurists positioned themselves as the realization of the messianic impulse of human progress, they were participating in a similarly optimistic discourse of vitalism.

Likewise, Marinetti's outlook shares an element of fundamental optimism with Bergson's vitalist philosophical system, but here that optimism is less messianic and more mystical. Bergson's notion of creative evolution envisions a Darwinian struggle of life as a movement of creative energy, the *élan vital*, and pictures our ability to connect to that movement in a way that finally takes on mystical characteristics. While in *Creative Evolution* (1907) and earlier works, Bergson does not explicitly refer to mysticism, his descriptions of philosophical intuition nonetheless resonate with it, especially insofar as philosophical intuition is described in Schopenhauerian terms as being "at one with nature" and immersed in the "becoming which is the life of things," below the individuated sphere of scientific knowledge.[57] By the time of his last major work, *The Two Sources of Morality and Religion* (*Les deux sources de la morale et de la religion*, 1932), Bergson describes our intuitive connection to the creative movement of life directly as a "mystic intuition" ("une intuition mystique").[58] The mystical valence of the intuitive connection by which humans reactivate the fringe of instinct surrounding our intelligence bespeaks a fundamental optimism at work in Bergson's philosophy: life, which is really the movement of the *élan vital*, is endlessly creative, and we can participate in that creativity.

Futurism's messianic and optimistic vitalism thus borrows from aspects of both Nietzsche and Bergson; but it also distorts both by creating a new object of messianic hope – the machine. From the founding manifesto, which features a long description of an exhilarating car-ride and crash, Marinetti's writings idolize the mechanical world for its vitality. The energy that was originally associated with organic life has been transferred to the inorganic force of the machine. The machine is fast and powerful; it vibrates continually; it is strong. In "Multiplied Man and the Reign of the Machine" ("L'uomo moltiplicato e il regno della macchina," published in *War…*, 1915), Marinetti describes the machine as a love object to replace women and simultaneously envisions a version of Lamarckian evolution that will lead to the glorious self-realization of man (only man) as himself becoming a machine – a description that echoes the plot of his infamous novel *Mafarka the Futurist* (first published in French as *Mafarka le futuriste: roman africain*, 1909), in which the protagonist seeks to create a mechanized son who will be born without a mother and will herald the violent future of the machine.[59] In "Multiplied Man," the aim of this love of the machine is to capture the strength of vital energy, here figured as mechanical electricity, without the weaknesses that traditional eroticism supposedly introduces to man's libidinous vitality.[60] As such, the language of spiritual vitalism is channelled from the natural and human to a different object entirely, apparently in order to purify life of the weaknesses of sentimentalism.[61] Yet the language of vitalism is evoked in even its most spiritual senses – indeed, Marinetti goes so far as to invoke spiritualist séances ("sedute spiritiche") as an analogous instance of the way in which human will is to be externalized into the machine.[62]

While this vision is often written in terms that emphasize a masculine virility, it is telling that even Futurist women writers who feminized such images retained the vitalist fusion of human and mechanical energy. For example, in "The Creative Anxiety of the Hydroelectric Plant Nera Velino" ("L'ansia creatrice della idroelettrica Nera Velino," published in *L'Aeropoema futurista di Umbria*, 1943), Franca Maria Corneli wrote: "Is it your turbines or my arteries that in amassing calories and crushing avalanches of molecules tempt search out the bottom of the earth where no doubt your secret heart beats or mine filled with the divine and the satanic fighting?"[63] Here we see an interesting rearticulation of the motif – pulsing energy figured as matter, in molecules, but also drawing together not only organic and inorganic energy but also transcendent energies of violence that participate in a spiritual plane of reality.[64] What Marinetti saw in terms of spiritualist séances is now a demonic and heavenly force – a connection to an immaterial ideal. It is perhaps in this sense that Marinetti could have the "Theosophists" supposedly say that the Futurists were the *mystics of action*. Such was the cult of the future at the heart of their optimistic historical dynamism – rooted in nineteenth-century philosophical vitalism, engaged with the aspirations of idealism, but distorted into a bizarre worship of something altogether different.

Modernist Mysticism: A Dangerous Ideal(ism)

The mystical dimension of this historical dynamism and its mechanized messianism positioned Futurism in a continuity between two poles: decadent aestheticism and fascist ideology. Both poles were, notably, animated by idealist commitments to counteract the perceived deadening of modernity wrought by unrestrained materialism, positivist models of social and political function (which reduced human agency and thus rendered the future an automated outcome rather than a human creation), and the democratic-capitalist institutions that realized these impulses.[65] Both poles were also situated in a tense conflict with what was likely the most prominent institutional force charged with guarding a traditional vision of idealist thought, not only in Italy but across Europe: namely, the Catholic Church. In fact, the mysticism of Futurist vitalism was actually a subset of a larger trend in the period, one identified by the Church and targeted for censorship and contestation – modernist mysticism.[66]

An excellent historical account of how the Church identified this threat and attempted to counteract it has recently been charted by Matteo Brera. What emerges from his argument is an image of the difficulties the Church authorities faced as they sought to exert moral control over a changed society with the limited tools at their disposal. Their ability to operate was constrained by the expansion of state power after the Risorgimento and the simultaneous transformation of the public sphere in the Enlightenment and post-Enlightenment world, which resulted in a new, more liberal circulation of ideas and texts outside of Church control.[67] The Church in the early twentieth century identified two concurrent threats to orthodox understandings of the ideal. First, these threats emanated from cultural figures associated with the literary and artistic movements of *decadentismo* and modernism, including Antonio Fogazzaro (1842–1911) and Guido da Verona (1881–1939) as well as, most prominently, Gabriele d'Annunzio (1863–1938). Second, the rise of fascism in the 1920s posed an increasingly difficult challenge to Church authority and power over the moral life of the nation, as the fascist regime increasingly sought the means to shape society around its own system of values, conceived of in terms of an idealist philosophy that mystified the state.[68]

Both of these threats can be seen as aspects of modernism, which in the Catholic tradition has taken on a meaning rooted in an encyclical issued by Pope Pius X, *Pascendi dominici gregis* (8 September 1907). In it, the Pope condemned modernism as the synthesis of all heresies in the faith. Catholic modernism thus referred to a movement within the body of the Church to transform doctrinal approaches to modernity, effectively "updating" church teachings to account for the new knowledge and ideas that had taken hold in modern society in the wake of the Scientific Revolution, the Enlightenment, and now the age of positivism.[69] These heterodox views sought to align the revealed truth of the biblical ideal with a material empiricism that could seem categorically opposed to it. This tension had been vigorously fought across centuries of Church history: it was not just scientists like Copernicus and Galileo who had come up against Church censorship; so too did those philosophers who sought to mix the ideal and the real. This was the case for Tommaso Campanella (1568–1639), for example, whose empirical idealism proclaimed a fundamental union of material reality and divine will, and who argued that the world is the book of God in which divine truth is written for us to see.[70] For ideas like this, which led him to the practice of natural magic, the Calabrese thinker spent most of his life imprisoned by the Inquisition. A similar fate, or worse, awaited many others who dared theorize their own ways to bridge the transcendent and the actual.

Modernist mysticism, which combined spiritual mysticism with sensual experience in the decadent-aesthetic pattern, followed this model and was thus situated dangerously at the cusp of Church doctrine and a heretical immersion in the senses. As Laura Wittman has shown, mysticism not only is "at the heart of the modernist crisis" but also represents a way in which literary modernism overlaps with and informs religious modernism, contributing the idea that the formal dimension of an epiphany might itself be the mystical experience of the divine.[71] Bridging the ideal and the real, this mysticism feeds off the forbidden allure of a heretical reconfiguration of Church mystery.[72] In this sense, I argue, the Futurists, those self-proclaimed "mystics of action," occupied a space slightly different from but foundationally similar to D'Annunzio's modernist mysticism – one that complicates Mimmo Cangiano's argument that Catholic modernism represented the effort to establish a new form or centre for regrounding modernity in the wake of relativist thought.[73] Indeed, Marinetti too ran into censorship trouble for his scandalous novel *Mafarka il futurista*: in 1910, its Italian translation was put on trial in Milan for "oltraggio al pudore," an offence against moral decency. It is interesting that in this case the litigant was the state, not the Church; all the same, the trial ended in increased publicity for Marinetti and his book – an outcome that matches what the Church censorship of D'Annunzio "accomplished," as well as the outcome of some earlier proceedings against other works of literature, such as Umberto Notari's *Quelle signore* (1906).[74] The Futurist push to transform politics through art by revitalizing the material world coincided with the same fusion of matter and spirit, actual and ideal, that made D'Annunzio's modernist mysticism so dangerous in the Church's eyes.

The redirection of idealism away from a divine ideal toward a secularized, materialized ideal happened not only in artistic practice but also in political ideology and action. The limit case of this action and its mystical development was the cult of the leader and the auratic apparatus accompanying Italian Fascism as a political religion.[75] Indeed, fascist philosophers like Giovanni Gentile and Sergio Panunzio theorized the totalized state precisely in religious terms, and contemporary historians like Emilio Gentile have developed that connection into an analysis of Fascism as a civil religion.[76] Thus it was not only the artists of modernist mysticism but also the Fascist state itself that posed a threat to the Church's moral and spiritual authority, and the Church spent years attempting to strike a balance that would maintain as much of its autonomy and influence as possible. The Concordat of 11 February 1929 (the *Patti Lateranensi*), in which the Vatican and Mussolini's regime achieved a peace treaty in that struggle, represented the Church's best effort to preserve its influence over the direction of public morality and belief.[77]

The Church, the Futurists, D'Annunzio, and the Fascist state itself were thus locked in a battle over how to respond to the threat of modern materialism. Each held a different conception of how to understand a revitalized reality in connection with the ideal. Their different approaches to conceiving how to activate the ideal in actual, political reality created a conflict in which they sought to establish their primacy; and this primacy took the form not only of institutional power but also of influence over the social imaginary that would guide institutions and their practical reshaping of the world. The stakes of modernist mysticism, in other words, were both ideal and simultaneously very real.

Futurist Ambivalence and Modernist Idealism: The Case of Bruno Corra

Futurist mysticism bridged the political spirit of fascist actual idealism and the vitalist notion of a creative evolution redirected toward Marinetti's mechanical messianism, which sought to revitalize material reality. However, this mechanized fantasy of "official" Futurism came into a conflicted relationship with some of the ways in which other Futurist figures developed the spiritual ideal at the movement's core. For that reason, I turn now to a figure who has often been marginalized in histories of Futurist production, Bruno Corra. Corra's ambivalent spirituality and its connection to a metaphysical idealism without an emphasis on the machine offers further insight into the degree to which Futurist ideology was rooted in an ambivalent modernist idealism.

Corra (the pen name of Bruno Ginanni Corradini), was born into an aristocratic family together with his older brother Ginna (Arnaldo Ginanni Corradini, 1890–1982). Both participated in the avant-garde moment of the early 1900s and were active in shaping the Florentine circle of Futurists, who sometimes found themselves in opposition to the Milanese group. Corra founded two literary journals in the period of the "first" Futurism, *Il Centauro* in 1912 (with Mario Carli and Emilio

Settimelli) and then *L'Italia futurista* in 1916 (with Settimelli as co-director).[78] Again alongside Settimelli, he was especially active in Futurist theatre – including the short *sintesi* "Davanti all'infinito," which I considered in the opening pages of this chapter.

While not at the centre of Marinetti's group and not well-known today, Corra played an important role in the development of Futurism, allowing it to stretch in directions that highlight the conceptual tensions at Futurism's core.[79] He is best remembered for his "synthetic novel" ("romanzo sintetico") *Sam Dunn Is Dead* (*Sam Dunn è morto*, first published in 1914 by Marinetti's Edizioni di Poesia and then serialized in Corra's *L'Italia futurista* in 1916). This work has received some critical attention, particularly since it was republished in 1970 by Einaudi thanks to the collaborative effort of Corra's brother and a leading scholar of Futurism, Mario Verdone.[80] Corra, like many Futurists, both belonged to and exceeded the movement: his circle of collaborators in *L'Italia futurista* often debated against and openly disagreed with Marinetti, and after the First World War he shifted away from the movement and toward his own style – one defined by a blend of the grotesque, the paranormal, and a decidedly black humour, on the one hand, and engaged in an Orientalist exoticism with explicitly racist elements that can be seen as coinciding with fascist imperial politics and their representation, on the other.[81] Examining the case of Corra more carefully reveals not only a tension within Futurism but also an aesthetic sensibility rooted in precisely the dynamics of modernist idealism I have been outlining in this book. Corra, like those who adopted a more Schopenhauerian approach to counteract the deadening impact of modernity, turned toward spiritual revitalization not just through the material activity of Futurist interventions into political culture but also through a different sort of ideal, one at once more metaphysical and more magical.[82]

In their "Manifesto of Futurist Science" ("La scienza futurista," 1916; republished in 1920 in Corra's *Battaglie*, which I cite and translate here), Corra and a group of like-minded collaborators (his brother, Ginna, along with Settimelli, Remo Chiti, Mario Carli, Oscar Mara, and Vieri Nannetti) direct us toward one of the logical end points of the irrationalist approach the Futurists take to revitalizing the world: their "science" aims not to clarify and elucidate but rather to impress upon us the weight of the unknown, underscoring the pervasive force of irrational mystery.[83] They thus call on scientists to abandon the usual subjects of their research in favour of exploring and unleashing new vital forces:

> We call on the audacious to turn their attention toward that least fathomed part of our reality, comprising phenomena related to mediums, psychics, rhabdomancy, divination, telepathy… . Without doubt it is in this realm that we are about to grasp a certain something that will enrich our life with the unexpected. The energies acting in this field are certainly endowed with a higher level of intelligence than any others: this is made clear by the complicated way in which they act. While we can always predict, for example, the way in which a force like gravity will behave (it does nothing but infinitely repeat the same logic), we are not always able to guess how these more complex energies will act, as they know how to advance from the simplistic logic of a fluid motor (Tromelin, Fayol) to the intricate cerebrations of a medium cabinet.[84]

The vitality of the material world is understood here in terms that resonate with the nineteenth- and twentieth-century discourse on the spirituality of the material world, the discourse of vitalist spiritualism. They seek to abolish one scientific tradition and to replace it with another, an anti-tradition that is nonetheless a form of continuity with the past.[85] Their manifesto thus highlights the fact that Futurism does not simply reject tradition but also engages a tradition of its own, one that is focused on positing an alternative to the mainstream understanding of the phenomenal world.[86] This was true for Marinetti, who made copious recourse to the language of vitalism and understood the practical aims of his movement in terms that related to both a Hegelian and a Schopenhauerian paradigm of idealism. This was likewise true for the Florentine Futurists like Corra, who saw the spiritual as an anti-tradition opposed to modern materialism.

But Corra's stance is not identical to Marinetti's. If both can be said to operate on the same metaphysical spectrum, Marinetti envisions a Futurist practice in which matter is spiritualized through material artistic action: the spiritual is thus immanent to the material, and Futurist art liberates it. In contrast, Corra gravitates toward a spiritual view that is more abstractly metaphysical or intangible, where occult energies operate a spiritual transformation of material reality (more from the top down, we might say). This view is at the centre of Corra's *Sam Dunn Is Dead*, which recounts a bizarre occult "episode" where Sam Dunn, a man who apparently *does* nothing in the visible, material world (he hardly even moves), channels mysterious energies to create a burst of madness in Paris with the potential to transform the whole world. In one description, Corra writes that "the unleashing of occult energies generated by Sam Dunn" appeared to set in motion a tremendous revolution such that:

> The old, material appearances were falling away. In the world of men, craters of unpredictability were opening up, forests of strangeness were emerging and torrents of new laws and new forms of logic burst forth. The worn-out immobility of matter was on the point of being replaced by a brilliant multiform capacity for the new, gushing with phenomena that were elegantly transitory… . Twelve more hours of this feverishness would have been sufficient to bring to maturity the rebirth of life and of the world itself.[87]

Here, in contrast to the more concrete notion of artistic renewal of the material-actual world that Marinetti's *serate* pursue, Corra is envisioning a transformation in which occult energies gather, invisible and intangible, and not as the result of any form of material artistic action but rather through Sam Dunn's mere concentration of thought, though Dunn is in no way special other than in his mysterious ability to channel these energies. But those energies have the power to unleash the Futurist ideal – dynamic, explosive, multiform, transitory. The rebirth of life into a new spiritual dimension operates through the artist as medium (i.e., someone who communicates with spirits, or perhaps simply the spirit); in this way, a more abstract emphasis is placed on the notion of artistic action, which for Marinetti was much more directly physical and pragmatic.

Corra's irrationalist occultism resonates with a tendency within Futurism toward the esoteric where the action-based vitalism of the cultural politics sought by Marinetti and others comes into conflict with an alternative that emerges from the same set of principles. When Marinetti declares the Futurists to be the "mystics of action" and then attributes this phrase to "the Theosophists," he is recognizing this tendency and, implicitly, its continuity with forms of nineteenth-century spiritualism and magic. Corra points us toward the way in which the tension within Futurism is indicative of a broader move in modernist culture as it seeks to reanimate the dead world. In this sense, it is telling that when Corra collected and republished *Sam Dunn* a few years later, he grouped it with a set of strange short pieces, many of them prose-poems, under the not terribly Futurist title *Madrigals and Grotesques* (*Madrigali e grotteschi*, 1919).[88] Here, *Sam Dunn* (which he dates as being published in 1915) occupies some seventy pages (117 to 188) in between the longer section *With Glass Hands* (*Con mani di vetro*, dated 1910–14 and running from pages 7 to 113) and two subsequent writings, *Zig-Zags of Reality* (*I zig-zag della realtà*, 1916, 189 to 206) and *Words Written on Pages Soaked in Oregano: A Symphonic Poem of Sensations* (*Parole scritte su fogli inzuppati di Origan: Poema sinfonico di sensazioni*, 1916, 207 to

217). Rosa Rosà's (1884–1978) bizarre and magical illustrations of *Sam Dunn* are reproduced here, as are additional illustrations to accompany *Con mani di vetro*, these attributed to both Rosà and Corra's brother, Ginna (Arnaldo). While elements of this collection certainly resonate with the Futurist aesthetic of the period, in the end it juxtaposes statements seemingly straight from the founding manifesto with others that evoke a more tenuous sense of the mysterious unknown closer to the aesthetic styles of decadentism, along with the static nostalgia of *crepuscolarismo*. In this respect, Corra resembles aspects of Aldo Palazzeschi (1885–1974), whose Futurist works were resonant with symbolism and *crepuscolarismo* yet were accepted by Marinetti – in part at least because of Palazzeschi's formal innovations.[89] Official Futurism thus showed a degree of flexibility to embrace various forms of "anti-traditional" writing even when they might embody a temporality (past-facing rather than future-oriented) opposed to Marinetti's articulation of the movement.[90]

An instance of a relatively straightforward, "Futurist"-sounding phrase can be found in the short prose-poem from *Con mani di vetro*, "Plains" ("Pianure"), which reads, in its entirety: "Atoms of shivers erupting from the grass amass in vibrating hills that wound the sky with their acute peaks frozen with lucid trills: skylarks" ("Gli atomi di brividi erompenti dalle erbe si ammassano in colli vibranti che feriscono il cielo coi loro vertici acuti ghiaccianti di lucidi trilli: le allodole").[91] A simple landscape has been rewritten in a pulsating language of violent scientific and natural imagery. A few pages later Corra includes a poem (in verse) titled "Old People" ("I vecchi," 1910) that berates the elderly and enjoins them, ultimately, to just hurry up and die: "we pray: old people, finish it, old people, DIE!" ("noi preghiamo; vecchi, finite, vecchi, MORITE!"), clearly echoing the typical Futurist anti-passéist stance.[92] Corra would tackle the same theme in a theatrical *sintesi* written with Settimelli, "Passéism" ("Passatismo"), in which old people watch multiple centuries of world-historical events pass them by and then suddenly drop dead, having accomplished nothing.[93]

Yet despite these clear Futurist themes, Corra's collection begins with a "Diabolic Madrigal" ("Madrigale diabolico," dated 25 November 1911, Bologna), a short page-and-a-half prose-poem in which an abstract poetic speaker addresses his unnamed beloved, about whom we learn nothing of concrete detail other than that she has sworn to love the speaker forever. This piece is interesting not for its Futurist characteristics but rather for its reference to typical motifs of romantic love with an ironic distance that subverts them. The opening sentences place us firmly in the realm of romantic-decadent love: "'*Yours eternally.*' You promised that to me a thousand times, and I too swear, my lady, that not even Death will be able to separate me from you" ("<<*Vostra per l'eternità*>>. Mille volte me l'avete promesso, ed anch'io vi giuro, o signora, che neppure la Morte potrà separarmi da Voi").[94] Yet by the end of the "madrigal," this poetic image has been transformed from a testament of the power of love into a testament of the power of death. After describing how he will have two graves dug so that he can be buried next to an open hole, the speaker's insistent voice details how his beloved will inevitably choose to give up her life to be with him, drawn by the power of that open grave:

> In the tomb where I will be enclosed there will be a kind of emptiness, *the emptiness of you, your non-presence.* And that emptiness will attract you, inexorably. And you will have to give in. Perhaps it will be on a springtime night when life on earth is most intense. A wave of scents will pull you down into the cemetery, livid and trembling. And you will uncover the tomb and the coffin: and there you will stretch out, within, within, at my side.
>
> Never will a living man have had a more pallid and quivering lover in his arms.
>
> And you will still be mine, *eternally.*

> In quella tomba in cui io sarò rinchiuso ci sarà come un vuoto, *il vuoto di Voi, la vostra non-presenza.* E quel vuoto vi attirerà inesorabilmente. E voi dovrete cedere. Sarà forse in una notte di primavera quando la vita sulla terra è più intensa. Un'ondata di profumi vi abbatterà livida e tremante nel cimitero. E voi scoperchierete la tomba e la bara: e vi ci distenderete, dentro, dentro, al mio fianco.
>
> Mai uomo vivente avrà avuto fra le sue braccia un'amante più pallida e più palpitante.
>
> E sarete mia ancora, *per l'eternità.*[95]

It is not the power of love (a word that never actually appears in this poem about eternal "love") but rather the power of Death that summons the beloved and brings the two into eternal union. The beloved is not an agent of action but the receiver, and not of love but rather of some mysterious power associated with Death itself. It is in this sense, perhaps, that the piece can be termed a "madrigal" – as with an early-modern madrigal, a single line ("Vostra per l'eternità," the opening italicized phrase repeated at the end) is expanded to articulate its emotional content – although in this case, there is only a single, otherworldly voice. What we see here is a mix of misogynistic fantasy and the decadent cult of *Liebestod* written in a self-avowedly "diabolic" mode. What results is something I have elsewhere termed "vampire aesthetics," a form of decadent aesthetic fantasy in which the male lover empties out his beloved, consuming her (or him) as an aesthetic experience that helps constitute the life or subjectivity of the male aesthete. In this case, that vampiric relationship follows the pattern of *Liebestod,* where the irrepressible draw of their eternal love pulls the "beloved" woman to her death, drawing with her the scents and vibrations of life. It is thus no accident, I would argue, that the poetic voice here is eerily reminiscent of the poetic speaker, "A," in Kierkegaard's *Either/Or,* the founding figure of this vampire aestheticism.[96]

Kierkegaard's A articulates an aestheticism in which the subject of aesthetic reflection constitutes himself through an interaction with the (usually) female other, who is an object feeding into the construction of his aesthetic subjectivity. This vampirism, in which the aesthete literally feeds off the vitality of the other, aestheticizes misogyny. The gender dynamics in Corra's poem reveal a similar aesthetic misogyny that denies a voice or subjectivity to the female, who is only an object in the dynamics of romantic love. In this respect, it mirrors not just Marinetti's declared anti-feminism but, more fundamentally, the long trajectory of romantic-decadent love imagery that develops the male subject of reflection in part out of its relation to a female other who is, ultimately, a projection or construction of the male subject's aesthetic reflection. This penchant is echoed in other pieces collected in *Madrigali e grotteschi,* such as "Happiness" ("Allegria," n.d.), which charts the poetic speaker's fascination with a mysterious femme fatale who is drawn to his poetic greatness only to die suddenly of an aneurism.[97] The bathos of this reversal makes the mysterious woman into an object, just part of the speaker's poetic collection of sense experiences – replicating the typical image of the decadent dandy as an aesthetic collector. Indeed, as John Walker has noted in his introduction to the English translation of *Sam Dunn,* even Corra's explicitly "Futurist" novel is deeply tied to the nineteenth-century ideal of the dandy-aesthete, a refined connoisseur whose time is spent in leisure if not tedium.[98] For Corra, then, the decadent notion that modern deadness calls for aesthetic revivification remains a central component of his poetics even in the midst of works that attempt to establish themselves as Futurist.

The "Madrigale diabolico" opens Corra's collection by highlighting three key elements that are developed throughout the remaining pieces: first, it figures death or a realm beyond life as the locus of true power or meaning, thus evoking a sense of the ideal over and against the real (a separate ideal that can reach down, or up, into the actual world); second, it insists on the magical, fatal way in which the ideal beyond operates on the realm of the living, thus positing an alternative to the mechanics of positivist materialism; and third, in its sense of mysterious fatality it resonates with a pessimistic irrationality that undermines the ideal as a positive content while nevertheless operating in terms of an idealist logic. In other words, it opens the collection in the key of an ambivalent modernist idealism where the need to revitalize a dying world is pressing and the means to accomplish that task are aesthetic, vitalist, and occult.

The remainder of *Con mani di vetro* follows through on this opening, making the impulse even more explicit as it evokes magical alternative worlds, overlapping timelines, and grotesque distortions of reality. What *Madrigali e grotteschi* reveals is thus a complicated picture. On the one hand, we see here an ambivalence within Futurism itself. While Marinetti's work ultimately embraces a mechanized vitality, Corra's writings shift toward a more organic spiritual investigation, turning Futurism inward, we might say. This dovetails with his own evolving relationship to Futurist forms and ideals, an evolution he charts in works like *Battles* (*Battaglie*), his 1920 book that gathers together his theoretical writings and manifestos from 1911 through 1918. There, in the preface, he asserts his dissatisfaction with both the content and the form of some of these earlier works while nevertheless insisting on the importance of his collaboration with Marinetti and Settimelli in the renovation of Italian theatre through Futurist aesthetics.[99]

Corra's departure from the mechanized vitality of Marinetti's Futurism is thus less a full rejection than a way of pointing to a tension within the core ideology of the Futurist project itself. By pairing vitalist irrationalism with a more practical idealism, the Futurists' notion of the progressive ideal always already opened into the realm of mysterious spiritual forces blending the diabolic and the scientific. On the other hand, though, Corra also opened a window onto the ways in which Futurism was really just one inflection of a broader cultural moment, one in which the "Futurist Moment" was only a single side. While Marinetti's insistence on political praxis might set him apart from many of the other movements that constituted this broader, modernist moment, Futurism was driven by the same core desire, the need to respond against a deadened world reduced to material(ist) component parts. The spiritualism of Corra's "grotesque" collection signals one of the primary directions in which that desire pulled writers, thinkers, and artists from seemingly divergent sides of the modernist moment. Seeking a truer connection to life's vitality, it was an idealist beat that pulsed through modernism's veins.

Chapter Five

Occult Spiritualism and Modernist Idealism: Reanimating the Dead World

As the ambivalent idealism orienting Futurist vitalism suggests, the modernist engagement with the vital kernel of life was situated along a complex spectrum running from positivist materialism to occult spiritualism; clearly, then, these avant-garde projects had already destabilized any supposed bifurcation between matter and life. My focus now will be on how these two sometimes conflicting and sometimes overlapping outlooks constituted the frame within which modernist creators approached the task of reanimating the modern world. Modernism placed material and spiritual beliefs in the service of an ambitious aesthetic project to channel the ideal into and through the actual, aiming to restore meaning or fullness in the process. Part of what gave these responses to modernity cultural purchase was rooted in the broader discourse on spiritualism, which took on new prominence in the nineteenth century and the beginning of the twentieth. In fact, the aesthetic impulse to transform the material world worked in tandem with, and sometimes in tension with, the (re-)emergence of various systems of occult spiritualism.

The growth and spread of spiritualist beliefs and practices throughout the second half of the nineteenth century is a well-established facet of the period's intellectual and cultural history.[1] Occult and magical beliefs were pervasive; and as a special issue on "Decadence, Magic(k), and the Occult" in the new journal *Volupté* has recently argued, the artists and thinkers of decadence were fascinated not only with Church mysticism but equally with the mystery of occult practices and beliefs as part of their search for ever-new ways of stimulating unusual aesthetic experiences.[2] The same influence of "occulture" (the complex of beliefs, practices, and discourses attached to occult or esoteric traditions) can be seen in the formation of modernist poetics. As Leigh Wilson argues, examinations of how these belief systems functioned in relation to modernist experimentation have traditionally emphasized three motivations: a loss of faith in representation that dovetailed with the occult emphasis on the invisible, a shift toward science as the dominant model for modern thought, and the resituation of modernity in terms of an occult history of ideas.[3] For Wilson, however, these explanations fall short, and in fact the "non-mimetic" aspects of modernist production aligned with spiritualism precisely because, far from losing faith in representation, both emphasized the power of a "second" form of mimesis, one focused on the invisible (spiritual) realm.[4] Wilson's argument suggests an image of modernism steeped in magic as a form of experimentation: far from being an embarrassing blip of "regressive" thought, modernist magic was a way of opening modernity to new understandings of a higher reality and reconfiguring mimetic representation accordingly.

The characterization of magical thought as "regressive" is rooted in an enduring myth supplied by Enlightenment rationalism according to which the progress of reason entailed the teleologically oriented unmasking of mythological (or magical) thought. Yet as Jason Josephson-Storm has powerfully argued, this notion of progressive disenchantment was itself a myth and not a reflection of empirical fact. The nineteenth and early twentieth centuries were in fact suffused in cultures of magical thought and practice. This magical thought was not a regression; rather, it was a form of continuity with something that had never actually been "overcome" by the powerful rays of Enlightenment reason. Indeed, even the theorists who helped craft and disseminate this myth often operated in spiritual terms. For example, Hegel played an important role in the formation of the progressive narrative, writing decades before Nietzsche about the death of God and defining modern religious sentiment around this feeling of an absent divinity at its core.[5] At the same time, Hegel's notion of *Geist* – spirit or mind, but also ghost – drew on a language of spiritual entities in a rationalized form; thus, Josephson-Storm ultimately characterizes his philosophical project as a "disenchanted mysticism."[6] Drawing on this analysis, I suggest that we should see the myth of modern disenchantment operating in conjunction with the Hegelian picture of world history as consciousness's progressive coming into self-awareness – a connection that clarifies the sense in which Bergsonian vitalism (with its emphasis on an even mystical intuition) can resonate with such a seemingly different, rationalist predecessor.

Josephson-Storm and Wilson both help us see why we cannot understand the history of modernist production without accounting for the deep influence of magic on how it conceived art. However, as Thomas

Steinfield has argued, Wilson's study raises unanswered questions about *why* the occult is so important as a component of modernity and modernization: "one must go further to discover why modernity creates its own kind of spiritual fundamentalism and what this spiritual fundamentalism has to say about modernity itself."[7] My argument in this chapter aims to take this next step, showing how the turn toward spiritualism can be understood as part of the operation of modernist idealism. Just as decadent artists used the excess of materialism as a subject for aesthetic self-reflection that pushed material reality toward a connection with the absent ideal it eclipsed, so too did modernist production use occult belief to reanimate modernity. Underlying the penchant for magic was a sophisticated recognition that what modernity needed but struggled to furnish itself with was a connection to spiritual vitality that would ground it in a purposeful relation to some form of ideal.

The spiritual beliefs that modernist idealism activated unfolded along a spectrum, moving between positivist science and occultist irrationalism; and the two poles of this spectrum were not always as separate as one might expect. I thus want to examine three key Italian writers of the long modernist period – including some whose work might not traditionally be thought of as formally modernist – to show how they are situated along that spectrum: Grazia Deledda's anthropological study of magic treats it as a primitive remnant in popular Sardinian folk culture, but with the aim of preserving magic's vital force in the face of modern loss; Luigi Capuana's positivist-spiritualist blend seeks to expand the realm of the empirical by integrating spiritual phenomena into our conception of the real, in this way conversing interestingly with Schopenhauer's contention that scientific studies of magic demonstrate the reality of his metaphysical principle of will; and Luigi Pirandello's ambivalent spiritualism blends something like distanced scepticism with the kind of direct epistemological engagement championed by Capuana. Despite these differences, all three ultimately align in a shared project to rehabilitate nineteenth-century genres (fantasy, the gothic, vampire stories) and thereby rearticulate the dimensions of spiritual reality through literary imagination. I thus argue that despite differences in style, they can all be seen as having participated in a modernist reconfiguration of genre, on the one hand, and the broader stance of modernist idealism, on the other.

The occult spiritualism of these literary forms fits into a broader trajectory in modernist thought where the repurposing of apparently "surpassed" traditions both highlights and complicates the temporal self-awareness of modernity's self-reflection.[8] This spiritualism likewise enters into an ambivalent discourse where occult magic moves between religion and politics in the fascist reshaping of modernity. What holds these complex trajectories together is the enduring legacy of modernist idealism: both political praxis and the aesthetic transformation of life aim to channel the ideal into the real and thereby reanimate modern existence.

Occult Irrationality and Material Positivism: Spirits at the Juncture in Deledda, Capuana, and Pirandello

As was the case elsewhere in Europe, in Italy the fascination with spiritualism was situated between competing scientific and metaphysical drives. This complexity emerges clearly in *Psychology and "Spiritism"* (*Psicologia e "spiritismo,"* 1908), in which the Italian psychiatrist and anthropologist Enrico Morselli (1852–1929) offers a long list of contemporary notables who attested to first-hand encounters with the spirit world: not only political leaders, princes, the wealthy, and various cultural elites but also a range of scientists, mathematicians, and philosophers.[9] Their engagement with spiritualism ranged from a positivist-scientific interest in spirits to a more generally metaphysical one. That range reflects Morselli's argument from an earlier book, *Animal Magnetism* (*Il magnetismo animale,* 1886). There, he delineated three historical phases in the understanding of spiritual phenomena such as animal magnetism: a mystical/occult phase in antiquity; an empirical scientific approach in the mid-nineteenth century; and then the re-emergence of the mystical impulse in the metaphysical spiritualism of his contemporaries.[10] This narrative is clearly subject to the limitations that Josephson-Storm has articulated in reference to post-Enlightenment accounts of supposed cultural disenchantment; all the same, it highlights an important fact that will be my point of departure here. While on the one hand spiritualism can be seen as a rejection of the growing materialism and positivism of European culture in the wake of the Industrial Revolution, on the other it actually feeds on and becomes part of the discourse of positivist research in the late nineteenth century.[11]

This conjunction began even before the Fox sisters launched the nineteenth-century craze for mediums from their house in upstate New York, where they claimed to hear spirits "rapping" and thus to be able to channel messages from a metaphysical beyond. Their claims set off a craze that quickly spread across the ocean, speaking to the ripeness of this historical moment for what presented itself as the empirical demonstration that it is possible to overcome death itself. In a matter of decades, famous mediums like the Neapolitan Eusapia Palladino (1854–1918) were garnering the attention not only of Italy's literary and cultural elite but also of French scientists like Marie Curie and her husband, Pierre.[12] From mediums interacting with the spiritual dimension to experiments designed to measure and understand the hidden laws of magnetic forces, spiritualism attracted both popular and scientific interest. So, the position advocated by Bruno Corra and his co-authors of the "Manifesto of Futurist Science" ("La scienza futurista," 1916) was less extraordinary than it might at first seem: the idea of broadening the field of empirical research to encompass phenomena attributed to forces like spiritual energy and animal magnetism already had a storied nineteenth-century history.[13]

In this complex overlap, there was a bifurcation between two tendencies in spiritualism: what in English would be denoted as the spiritualist and parapsychological understandings of "spiritual phenomena" – though interestingly, in Italian the same word is used for both, "metapsichica" (which is generally translated in English as "parapsychology").[14] The spiritual side of this bifurcation referred to those ideas that required affirmative belief in a metaphysical spiritual realm, something necessarily beyond the scope of material science, while the parapsychological side saw spiritual phenomena as unexplained but not unexplainable and in this way maintained a firm grounding in materialist realism while nonetheless remaining open to stretching the bounds of that materiality. There was thus a tension within spiritualism, a tug-of-war between occult beliefs and practices whose re-emergence would seem to attest to an impulse toward modern "re-enchantment,"[15] and empirical or positivist beliefs and methods that helped establish spiritualism's cultural legitimacy and also pushed it in the direction of science.[16] However, whether the energies in question belonged to a spirit world beyond our actual, material existence or whether they were thought of as heretofore unexplained natural phenomena, the mania for studying these mysterious forces highlighted the effort to overcome a simplistic materialism that was perceived as having limited the horizons of modernity's epistemology while hollowing out its spiritual and moral core, rendering life an inauthentic external shell rather than a true, inner unfolding.

The modernist engagement with this complicated interface between positivist science (material realism) and occult or magical beliefs (spiritual idealism) can be seen in the complex relations among several overlapping but distinct stances on how to engage those beliefs. In her writings, Grazia Deledda responds to the positivist outlook with an ethnographic account of folk beliefs as local and "primitive." Capuana's examinations of the new vitalist/spiritualist science show the limitations of positivist epistemology and seek to correct them by integrating the unexplained phenomena that traditional science leaves out. And in a related but distinct move, Pirandello applies epistemological scepticism to both scientific positivism and spiritual beliefs while nonetheless ultimately affirming something like a spiritual notion of the ideal as it manifests itself in the creative imagination. All three stances fall along the spectrum of modernist idealism's ambivalent approach to the problem of modernity, hovering in the same spiritual space at the heart of Eusapia Palladino's mediumship – the juncture of the dead and the living.

Deledda's Anthropological Approach to Magical Culture

Grazia Deledda (1871–1936) is best-known as the recipient of the 1926 Nobel Prize in Literature.[17] Her prize citation highlights her "idealistically inspired writings which with plastic clarity picture the life on her native island and with depth and sympathy deal with human problems in general."[18] That citation recognizes a union of realism and idealism, although perhaps not in the full sense I will be describing here. To better understand that conjunction we should examine the ambivalent spiritualism of one of her earliest works, a collection of anthropological observations on the city of Nuoro, her hometown in Sardinia.[19]

After being published serially in the anthropological journal edited by Angelo De Gubernatis, the *Rivista delle tradizioni poplari italiane,* between 1894 and 1895, Deledda's study of folk practices, traditions, and beliefs was collected into a volume titled *Popular Traditions of Nuoro* (*Tradizioni popolari di Nuoro,* originally 1894). In that work, she undertakes what Peter J. Fuller has characterized as a "personal campaign or mission to combat what [she] regard[s] as the misunderstanding and misrepresentation in Italian national culture of [her] island's traditional values."[20] As Margherita Heyer-Caput has shown, this fits into the broader trajectory in Deledda's writing that aims at "liberating Sardinia from stereotypes derived from positivistic culture in unified Italy."[21] Yet this should not be read as Deledda attempting to naturalize Sardinian folk beliefs simply to explain them away, so to speak. The impulse is rather to enumerate local traditions and beliefs in order to demonstrate what Deledda sees as the atavistic folk wisdom of a "primitive" people who are separated from the processes of industrial modernization transforming the mainland. Amidst the people of Nuoro, "civilization" may be overshadowed by "barbarism," yet civilized culture (modernity) is erasing the customs of the people.[22] This, she claims, is a loss not only for the people of Nuoro but for the general repository of human experience:

> I do not intend to weave a panegyric of them here; rather let me say that the people of Nuoro are no more wild than any other group of people who are forgotten and abandoned on their own. They have the defects and virtues and passions of primitive man as well as the superstitions, which are likewise the general patrimony of all peoples and were not held in disdain even by great spirits, beginning with Luther and running all the way to many great men who are still living.[23]

Deledda's early ethnographic study of her native city thus reproduces common positivist notions of human progress and the unilinear unfolding of civilization. These notions, it bears emphasizing, not only reflect an Enlightenment belief in unilinear progress but also overlap with the discourses of colonial rule that seek to define colonized people as "primitive" others who require the intervention of a more advanced "civilization." While this discourse is most pronounced and systematically developed in the contexts of European colonialism abroad, as Franco Cassano has argued there is an intra-Italian equivalent that emerges in the difference between the industrialized, modern north and the traditional, agrarian south.[24] For Cassano, the different way of thinking built into traditional life offers an opportunity to resist the monolithic logic of industrialized modernity; likewise, Deledda recognizes the repository of traditional folklore not as an obstacle to progress but rather as an alternative to the secular logic of modernity.

In this way, Deledda's approach resembles but also finds itself in opposition to that of Ernesto De Martino (1908–1965), the Italian anthropologist whose studies of magical folk culture in the south of Italy have recently re-emerged in contemporary academic discourse.[25] De Martino was a student of Croce, and thus it is little surprise that he adopted a Hegelian logic of historical progress similar to the one underlying Max Weber's idea that modernity is defined by rationalization, intellectualization, and the "disenchantment of the world."[26] According to Weber, modern progress has resulted in sublime values retreating from public life and being relegated to "the abstract realm of mystical life or into the fraternal feelings of personal relations between individuals."[27] For De Martino, the primary question is how "primitive" forms of natural magic have managed to survive in modernity, and his ethnographic approach examines those beliefs and practices while also situating them in relation to historical developments in Catholicism, Enlightenment culture, and in particular the unique situation of southern Italy and Naples in this trajectory.[28] De Martino develops a psychological account of the function of these supposedly "surpassed" beliefs to help explain their unexpected longevity in modernity, contending that they offer individuals a means of combating the dangers of a hostile world not through reason and self-control but through reliance on superstition and ritual. He thus reinscribes a metanarrative of progressive historical development while simultaneously offering an account of the Italian south as outside modernity's rationalization and therefore unable to enter into its logic of productive self-reliance rooted in empirical science.[29]

Deledda's approach might seem to mirror aspects of De Martino's, but ultimately she arrives at a contrasting vision of what the south's (or the island's) difference means. Her recuperation of local belief in *Tradizioni popolari* spans a wide range of customs and practices, from traditional prayers and local idiomatic expressions to translations of poems, songs, and riddles, and also to a two-part section on "Popular Superstitions, Beliefs, and Medicines" ("Superstizioni, credenze e medicine popolari").[30] This long section takes up a significant portion of the book and includes a subsection specifically on "Magic and Spells" ("Magie e incantesimi").[31] In this scope and in her ethnographic approach, Deledda seems to mirror (or rather prefigure) De Martino's analysis. What is fundamentally different, however, is her insistence on the value of magical beliefs – they are not mere relics of a pre-modern world but rather sources of the fullness or value that modernity threatens. In this way, Deledda is actually closer to Weber's characterization than to De Martino's: for Weber, the rationalization of modernity, and thus its supposed disenchantment, poses a problem in that it relegates what he thinks are sublime values to the sphere of mystical belief. Likewise, for Deledda, modernity threatens not just culture but also a wisdom buried within that culture, forms of knowledge that express values that are at risk of loss.

Deledda's section begins by highlighting how magic or spells are blamed for mysterious illnesses or misfortune. This provides a transition between the previous subsection, on folk medicines, and the new one on magic. It also underscores a positivist narrative implicit in her anthropological approach: the enchanted world is seen as a primitive way of explaining that which science has not yet been able to explain. This narrative about the epistemological value of magical or superstitious beliefs as proto-explanations in the absence of scientific knowledge has a long history – one that continues to this day.[32] Deledda's examples seem to fit nicely with such a narrative, suggesting ways in which magic stands in for ignorance: from describing how priests use the power of sacred books to make spirits enter the body to accounts of love potions, magic emerges as a practice designed to enable the user to gain a kind of power over the material world that is otherwise unavailable.[33] The spiritual, in this view, serves as a resource to enable material changes. What Deledda is cataloguing are thus practices that can be understood functionally.

At the same time, however, her broader aims in cataloguing these examples run counter to the logic of positivist approaches that want to reduce the meaning of magical practices to mere phenomena of underdevelopment or delayed development: she sees the legacy of magic not as an embarrassment or a problem to be overcome, but rather as a source of value and a legacy to be preserved. While the work published in a journal like De Martino's *Rivista* naturally tends toward this perspective and could be seen as part of a "scientific" drive toward anthropological cataloguing or classifying that necessarily seeks to "preserve" its objects of study (as if they were items in an imaginary museum of historical practices), it is clear from Deledda's broader corpus that she is personally invested in these traditions not just as objects to examine but as lived realities, components of how a society makes meaning. Her view thus prefigures the approach argued for perhaps most forcefully by Hans Blumenberg in his monumental *Work on Myth* (*Arbeit am Mythos*, originally published in 1979). Blumenberg holds that enlightenment and myth are not antithetical but rather are mutually necessary in the larger project of cultivating meaningful human life – both are functional components of responding to the threat of the external world, not just by mastering it technologically (scientifically) but also by comprehending it through symbolic means. The mythological function of symbolic comprehension is not static but develops over time in our "work on" myth, its continuous re-elaboration in each contemporary moment of historical change. In the same way, Deledda's view recognizes the functions of "primitive" magical culture not only in how magic is used by people (as means to achieve ends that are otherwise unavailable) but also as part of a larger form of life that needs to be preserved against the monolithic impositions of a rationalizing modernity.

Indeed, the metaphor borrowed from Blumenberg helps us think about the role of magic in Deledda's fiction. Her literary works make recourse to and repurpose familiar generic tropes from nineteenth-century fantasy. While she sometimes wrote directly about magic and the occult, as in her short story "The Sorcerer" ("Il mago," published in *Racconti sardi* in 1894), her works often resonate with the magical traditions that she describes in her anthropological study more generally.[34] Thus in a novel like *Ashes* (*Cenere*, 1904), the island seems to be almost haunted; she presents an animated world in which an invisible, fatal power operates in the background, drawing the protagonist into an ill-fated attempt to track down his lost mother at all costs. A story like this resonates with Théophile Gautier's earlier definition of fantasy from his interpretation of Hoffmann's "contes fantastiques." Highlighting the overlap of the real and the imaginary in fantasy, he links the genre to "occult sympathies and antipathies; singular forms of madness, visions, magnetism; and the mysterious and malevolent influences of an evil principle only vaguely evoked."[35] If Deledda's writing often generates a Freudian feeling of the uncanny, I would contend that it is precisely because of its resonance with this fantastic tradition, which it draws on but also repurposes in the face of modern scepticism. The fantastic occult becomes a generic means of accomplishing something parallel to what I have described in my analysis of Deledda's anthropological study: in the face of modernization and rationalization, Deledda asserts the enduring fascination and thus imaginary power of an irrational alternative steeped in spiritual belief.

Spiritualism, Positivism, and the Question of True Knowledge: Capuana and Pirandello

Deledda's anthropological approach to magical culture is thus in close conversation with positivism, embracing positivist narratives of the primitive versus the modern while simultaneously resisting the totalizing impulse of modernity's logic. She carves out a space for the value of traditional cultural practices without, however, suggesting that these should change our model of positive science. This, I contend, places her at one end of a spectrum connecting materialist logic and spiritualist belief.

By turning now to examine the relation between Luigi Capuana (1839–1915) and Luigi Pirandello (1867–1936), I propose to illustrate other points on this spectrum. Capuana, who was older than Pirandello by several decades, engaged in an open discussion with his younger Sicilian compatriot about the reality and importance of spiritual phenomena. Both partook in séances in Rome and were fascinated, perhaps even haunted, by the claims of mediums and others affiliated with the various schools of spiritualist and occult beliefs. Yet Capuana's stance, perhaps reflecting the logic of his own literary realism, ends up closer to that of Deledda's anthropology, and he attempts to use unexplained spiritual phenomena as a mode of scepticism designed to extend the realm of positive scientific knowledge. Pirandello, by contrast, whose view of those phenomena seems much more ambiguous, ultimately presses further toward a metaphysical idealism that ends in a mediumistic theory of artistic creation itself.

Capuana wrote a series of prominent essays on the subject of occultism, spiritualism, and modern scientific belief, most notably his *Spiritism?* (*Spiritismo?*, 1884) and *The Occult World* (*Mondo occulto*, 1896). In these works, he recounts personal experiences, describes cases of spiritual phenomena, and dialogues with contemporary positivists such as the famous criminologist/anthropologist Cesare Lombroso (1835–1909). But his engagement with spiritualism was more far-reaching: he also wrote numerous short stories rooted in paranormal or spiritual events, which have today been collected in Capuana's *Stories of the Occult World* (*Novelle del mondo occulto*, 2007). My aim here is not exhaustive; rather, I seek to reconstruct the main ideas from this decades-long engagement with the occult and spiritualism, highlighting how he fuses a personal belief in spiritual phenomena with his positivist outlook.

In *Spiritismo?*, Capuana takes rhetorical distance from the beliefs he discusses, as indicated by the title's interrogative status – a last-minute addition made in cooperation with the publisher; all the same, the piece had a rocky reception, igniting significant interest from spiritualist circles but doubt and criticism from more sceptical readers,[36] including a figure as prominent as the famed poet Giosuè Carducci.[37] In his later essay, *Mondo occulto*, Capuana casts off that rhetorical hesitation, embracing a less "objective" tone and referring directly to the recent, highly publicized case of the Neapolitan medium, Eusapia Palladino, who had managed to convince numerous prominent figures such as Cesare Lombroso of the seriousness of the psychic phenomena that motivate spiritualist beliefs. In both works, however, Capuana justifies his interest in terms of the scientific grounding for studying these spiritual phenomena. For example, in the preface to *Mondo occulto* he writes:

> The question mark of *Spiritism?* signaled my prudent reservations at the time. However, thanks to the unprejudiced wisdom of many scientists, since that time so-called spiritual facts have taken on a sufficiently scientific value that I can leave aside those reservations that seemed necessary when I took on this thorny topic and was perhaps the first in Italy to do so – the first, that is to say, among those who were not apostles or unreasonable opponents.[38]

Capuana thus articulates a positivist approach to spiritualism that aligns with parapsychology in its effort to ground strange psychological phenomena in empirical explanations.

Interestingly, he chose to develop this view not only in his critical essays but also by authoring a short story, "A Vampire" ("Un vampiro," 1904), that acts out the debate between a sceptical scientist and a "poetic" figure who experiences these paranormal phenomena in his own life. The story's plot is relatively straightforward: it opens *in medias res* during a tense exchange between two friends, a failed poet, Lelio Giorgi, and the scientist Mongeri. Through their exchange we learn that Giorgi and his wife, Luisa, are terrified by a parapsychological phenomenon, and he wants Mongeri's help to solve the mystery. For some time now, the family has been haunted by the spirit of Luisa's first husband, who appears to be lashing out from beyond the grave to exact revenge on Giorgi for replacing him and on Luisa for having had a child with Giorgi. The case is laid out in detail, citing various events in an escalating series that culminates in the spirit attacking their newborn child in his crib and speaking to and through Luisa while her terrified husband watches – seeing nothing but Luisa's interactions and the physical evidence of the crib moving and the child apparently being suffocated or sucked dry of his life force. Mongeri's response to this account is sceptical, but that scepticism is put to the test when Giorgi convinces him to come to their house for the night and see for himself. Mongeri then witnesses all this and more, coming away convinced that the phenomena are real but not accepting a metaphysical/spiritual interpretation of their origin. He thus advises that they disinter the dead husband's body and cremate it so that the lingering energy associated with his not-yet-decayed corpse will be dispersed and the phenomena will stop. They do just that, and the phenomena do in fact disappear along with his remains.

The story thus enacts a debate over the nature of spiritual or parapsychological phenomena, and the primary outcome is that the scientist, Mongeri, ultimately has to shift his view (something he was at first loathe to do). His initial working theory held that these spiritual phenomena were merely psychological suggestions arising from Giorgi's hysterical wife and influencing him to experience hallucinations in sympathy with her own. When the scientist is finally confronted with direct evidence to the contrary, he alters his theory somewhat, but he retains his commitment to reducing these spiritual phenomena to a material/energetic explanation:

> "I ought to add that though science has been shy about taking up phenomena of this nature, for some time now it hasn't been treating them in the same dismissive way as before: science is now trying to bring them

> into the ambit of natural phenomena. For science nothing exists beyond this material world. Spirit ... science leaves spirit to the believers, mystics, and eccentrics who are now called spiritists ... For science nothing is real but the organism, that assemblage of meat and bones that constitutes the individual and breaks up when he dies, reverting to the chemical elements that allowed it to live and think. Once these have broken up ... But then according to some the question becomes precisely this: does this putrefaction, the breaking up of atoms, or better of their organic function, end instantaneously with death, thus annulling all individuality, or does it persist, depending on the case and circumstances, for some time after death? One is beginning to suspect that this could be the case."[39]

The positivist outlook of the character dovetails not only with Capuana's critical writings on spiritualism but also with the intellectual trajectory of one of the most prominent figures on Italy's positivist intellectual scene, Cesare Lombroso. Lombroso was famous at the time as a psychologist, anthropologist, and founder of a positivist approach to criminology. Capuana's story was initially published on 1 July 1904 in *La lettura;* in 1907 it was reprinted as part of a two-story collection with the title *Un vampiro* (Rome: Voghera) together with the story "Fatal Influence" ("Fatale influsso"). This collection was prefaced with a dedicatory letter to Lombroso, emphasizing the development of Lombroso's views regarding spiritual phenomena: the stories, Capuana claims, "relate to your most recent and utterly dispassionate studies into psychic phenomena, which we have discussed in Rome every time that I have had the pleasure of seeing you again."[40] The choice to dedicate the story to him thus subtly refers to how Lombroso has come closer to Capuana's own ideas while also acting as an authorizing gesture, in that he is naming a prominent scientist whose views on and apparent long-standing interest in the topic give greater substance to the ideas articulated by the fictional scientist in his narrative.

The view proposed in this story, however, is not fundamentally different from the one Capuana had already advocated as early as his 1884 essay, *Spiritismo?* There, he had argued that parapsychological facts exceed the bounds of our knowledge of nature and require us to revise our scientific views. He also contended, however, that scientists are in a poor position to make these revisions because they have inherited a legacy of theoretical commitments that they are unwilling to alter. It is thus the job of imaginative poets to reconceive the world so that science can follow suit:

> It is undeniable: certain facts seem to go well beyond the limits of human nature. They allow the most vivacious imaginations to see the infinite spaces of the marvelous unfold before them, where they lose themselves and enjoy losing themselves. Cold, observing minds, particularly those free from preconceptions, investigate, study, and attempt to give a reasonable explanation.
>
> In this case, the non-scientists have an advantage: they are not dominated by the need to defend at all costs the theories in vogue, and they aren't defeated by the fear of watching as the scientific edifices they have so laboriously constructed crumble before their eyes. It is well known that the prejudices of scientists have always been more tenacious and more dangerous than popular prejudices.[41]

Capuana places artistic creation at the head of social progress, suggesting that artistic imagination is necessary to push scientific and other advances forward. In this respect, he is rearticulating a romantic idea advocated already by Henri de Saint-Simon (1760–1825), whose late work placed the artist's imagination at the forefront of scientific, technological, and thus social change.[42] That view, in turn, was integral to developing notions of how avant-garde art could lead cultural revolution, dovetailing with the Hegelian impulse toward realizing the ideal in world-historical transformation.[43] Indeed, Capuana's embrace of the poet's imaginative leadership might seem similar to the view articulated by Bruno Corra and his co-signatories of the "Manifesto of Futurist Science," where a call to abandon old scientific prejudices coincides with a battle cry to open the empirical to the realm of spiritual phenomena.[44] The difference, however, is that for the Futurists the goal was mystification, a shattering of the positivist-rational ideal, whereas Capuana is hoping to save that ideal by finding a new way of clarifying and enlarging our understanding of the material world.

That fundamental goal helps explain why Capuana felt that taking spiritual phenomena seriously was of the utmost importance; it is thus not surprising that he felt compelled to enter into an open polemic against his literary friend, Luigi Pirandello. Pirandello had published an article in Turin's *Gazzetta del Popolo*, "Extravagant News: A Ghost" ("Cronache stravaganti. Un fantasma," 24 December 1905), in which he described the current fad for mediums and belief in ghosts with a humorous eye, poking fun at the seeming irrelevance of the ways these spirits apparently spent their time, playing little tricks on the living and sending messages to them. A few days later (the piece is signed 29

December 1905, Catania), Capuana sent a rejoinder, also in the *Gazzetta del Popolo*, "Open Letter to Luigi Pirandello: Regarding a Ghost" ("Lettera aperta a Luigi Pirandello: A proposito di un fantasma," 2 January 1906). Capuana's letter is interesting for several reasons. First, he reaffirms the same positivist stance we have seen elsewhere, but here going even further and asserting that humans are evolving to communicate with spirits from the beyond: "I am convinced that one day or another, within a few or many centuries – time makes no difference as nature is very slow to evolve – the mediumistic faculties that are now the privilege of just a few will become common by way of heredity through organic development."[45] Capuana's stance resonates unexpectedly with the Futurists' (later) assertion that human beings would one day evolve into cyborgs through a process of Lamarckian evolution in which we would grow metal wings.[46] Both evolutionary metaphors were deployed to highlight a progressive view of humanity reaching toward a higher future, one in which we would connect directly with the ideal in and through transformations in our actual material reality.

Beyond this resonance, however, Capuana's view is also significant in that it envisions a future in which human society is changed by new scientific knowledge of spiritual life, including what he terms the reality of reincarnation. After repeatedly making recourse to scientific authorities (not only Lombroso, but also Wallace, Crookes, and Richet) to ground his claim that positive science has begun to expand its horizons, he insists that scientific knowledge will one day achieve absolute certainty about the nature of spiritual reality, reiterating claims we have seen from earlier works but also adding the idea that when we use the words "matter" and "spirit" we are referring with imprecision to something we do not yet understand. When our vision of matter and spirit changes in light of a better, clarified understanding, the result will be "a social transformation such that it is impossible to form an even approximate idea of it in advance."[47] Capuana's vision again resonates broadly with the ideals of the Futurists, who believed firmly that unlocking the interpenetration of spirit and matter would usher in a revolution of the unforeseeable in Italian society and politics (and not just art).

Finally, Capuana's letter is important as a source of insight into the practical engagement that not only he but also Pirandello shared in these paranormal investigations. Capuana refers in a pair of paragraphs to how Pirandello had accompanied him to a séance (held in the house of a "Roman prince," according to Capuana's description) during which a prominent medium, Augusto Politi, channelled spirits with visible effects that both of them experienced empirically.[48] He thus questions why Pirandello has become so sceptical when he has seen the proof in person.[49] He hypothesizes that perhaps Pirandello's article shouldn't be taken seriously, that it is something of a joke; but he reaffirms that the issue is a serious one with potentially important consequences for the future of human society. In this way, Capuana's stance, bringing spiritual phenomena under the umbrella of positivist materialism, ultimately dovetails with the positivist (and avant-garde) quest to use reason (and art) to restructure society.

As we might imagine from this exchange, Pirandello's outlook is more complicated. The ironic tone he took in his article is hardly a lone instance in Pirandello's work. In fact, in his major novel of two years earlier, *The Late Mattia Pascal* (*Il fu Mattia Pascal*, 1904), and in a short story published a few months after this exchange with Capuana, "Characters" ("Personaggi," published in *Il Ventesimo* on 10 June 1906), Pirandello's humoristic eye falls on a pair of Theosophist characters, neither of whom is taken entirely seriously by the respective narrator-protagonists. In *Il fu Mattia Pascal*, the narrator-protagonist (Mattia Pascal) takes on a new identity after a dead body is mistakenly identified (by his wife) as being his own; freed from the constraints of his life, he leaves and eventually seeks lodging in Rome, where he rents a room from Anselmo Paleari. Paleari is an avowed Theosophist, but the narrator (Mattia Pascal himself, looking back in retrospect) paints him in comic brushstrokes as a kind of addle-brained idealist floating in the clouds and unaware of what is going on right around him, in the material world. Similarly, the prominent character in the story "Characters" is a certain Leandro Scoto, who comes to the narrator-protagonist (Pirandello) for an "audience" in which he begs the writer to use him as a character in a story and thus to make him real and grant him eternal life through artistic form. Scoto wants to be a doctor, but he comes armed with only a book by the prominent British Anglican-priest-turned-Theosophist, Charles Leadbeater (1854–1934). He draws on the conceptual vocabulary of this book to argue for a spiritual theory of artistic creation that mirrors what Leadbeater actually wrote in one of his best-known works, written with Annie Besant (1847–1933), *Thought-Forms*.[50] Despite this resonance with Theosophical ideas that Pirandello clearly had read and knew, the narrator in "Characters" dismisses Scoto with an ironic joke, deflating his pretensions and seemingly his Theosophical beliefs along with them.

On the one hand, then, it seems that Pirandello was indeed sceptical of spiritualism, as Capuana had suggested; this emerges particularly in reference to his apparent suspicion of the growing prominence of Theosophy in the early twentieth century. Theosophy is perhaps best defined by its most important proponent and modern founding figure,

Helena Petrovna Blavatsky (1831–1891), descendant of an aristocratic Russian-German family, who eventually moved to New York, where she founded the Theosophical Society based on principles she claimed to have learned in world travels that had brought her into contact with esoteric gurus, the "Masters of the Ancient Wisdom" or "Mahatmas," who occupy a revered place in Theosophical writings and histories.[51] Blavatsky was one of the most famous mediums of the period. She was also a prolific author, who mixed her own spiritualist practices with ancient and modern traditions to chart a unique view of world history that she claimed unveiled the perennial truth constituting the "Divine Wisdom" of Theosophy's name. And she wrote fantasy works as well.[52] In 1889 she published one of her last books, *The Key to Theosophy*, which is structured as a dialogue between a sceptical "Enquirer" and a "Theosophist" and outlines the main ideas of her movement. There, she describes Theosophy as a wisdom religion that aims "to reconcile all religions, sects and nations under a common system of ethics, based on eternal verities."[53] She traces this syncretic impulse from ancient esoteric thought (such as Hermes Trismegistus) through Western and non-Western variants, including Neoplatonism and Buddhism, but distinguishes the modern Theosophical Society from all of these, describing Theosophy as a system in which "we cull the good we find in each [religion and philosophy]."[54] The syncretic doctrine that results is a version of esoteric occultism tied to the metaphysical theories of various philosophical and theological traditions. The book includes some forty-six pages of glossary definitions to help the neophyte understand its secret teachings. The fact that nearly 20 per cent of this guide to Theosophy is occupied by a glossary speaks to how abstruse the Theosophical doctrine might seem to outsiders. It is no great surprise that a sceptic like Pirandello would see this as overwrought theorizing, as building artificial systems to assure us of that which we cannot really know or understand.

But if Theosophy and its ilk are treated sceptically, this hardly amounts to a privileging of positive science or "hard evidence." Pirandello's scepticism is critical of these impulses as well.[55] That scepticism is central to *Il fu Mattia Pascal*, where the idea that we are able to clearly define even something as personal as our own identity is dismissed with the same sceptical humour that relativizes the claims of the Theosophist character, Paleari.[56] Mattia Pascal loses his identity, adopts a new one, loses that identity, too, and ultimately attempts to return home to his first, "true" identity, only to discover that is impossible. He ends up as just the *late* Mattia Pascal, somewhere hovering between death and life – and in this way acting out the ambivalent juncture of material and spiritual reality that Paleari's Theosophical theories attempt to describe. In other words, looking at the trajectory of the novel as a whole, it is impossible to claim that it affirms any certain knowledge – the scepticism that Capuana identifies in Pirandello's stance on ghosts is actually just a subset of a larger scepticism about both the possibility of certainty and the way in which we place ourselves at the centre of the universe as the measure of meaning.

It is thus reductive to see Pirandello as affirming either scientific knowledge or Theosophical/spiritual knowledge in any strong sense. I contend, rather, that both positivist and spiritualist knowledge fall into the same broader category for Pirandello's thought: they are examples of what he considers necessary illusions that support our ability to continue living meaningfully in an absurd world bereft of inherent meaning. Pirandello developed this stance in a 1921 article (published in *L'Idea nazionale* on 22 June), which he then converted into the postscript of *Il fu Mattia Pascal*, "A Warning on the Scruples of the Imagination" ("Avvertenza sugli scrupoli della fantasia"), which accompanied the reprint of that novel by Bemporad in Florence (also in 1921). In this text, Pirandello engages with the philosopher Adriano Tilgher (1887–1941), who had become one of his most ardent supporters. Pirandello both accepts and responds to Tilgher's interpretation of his world view, according to which our experience is shaped by a dialectical relation between two forces: Life, which is the perpetual flux of becoming, and Form, which is the fixity of static identities (of people, things, institutions, etc.). Pirandello's point in this "Avvertenza" is that we humans adopt the forms of fixed identity not accidentally but knowingly, donning the masks that are available to us in order to make ourselves intelligible to the outside world. A closer investigation – the kind of investigation that Pirandello undertakes in his own work, relentlessly and repeatedly – reveals that the masks are just that; but the unmasking that his humour performs does not result in the disclosure of some hidden authentic subject "underneath." Rather, what is revealed is just the naked mask, for without the exterior form that we assume, there is no intelligible substance underneath.

This argument would seem to suggest a deep and abiding scepticism of all forms, all knowledge of fixed (identifiable) things.[57] But it is actually more complicated than that. In fact, while these forms are always false, conventional, exterior masks, they are also necessary in order for us to live with and act with one another. Life's primal surge generates forms, and even if each of these is insufficient to express the inner content of the life that gives rise to it, such forms are also necessary in order for us to have any intelligible access to that content. This is the fundamentally Schopenhauerian aspect of Pirandello's outlook, one that resonates deeply with Tilgher's Schopenhauerian vision of the dialectic between Life and Form and perhaps makes sense of why Tilgher finds Pirandello so compelling.[58] Life itself, like Schopenhauer's will (and like Kant's thing in itself) is unintelligible. It might be the true or authentic core of our being, but we cannot make sense of it or understand it in the conceptual categories available to the forms of human reason (space, time, causation). All we can experience and make sense of is what is available in forms, as representation (in the phenomenal world). The mask may be false, but it is also necessary. Illusion itself is a necessary condition of our ability to live in and know the world.[59]

For scholars like Mary Ann Frese Witt and Martin Puchner, Pirandello's stance on the necessity of form is the definitive characteristic of his thought. Witt contends that because Pirandello sees form as the way in which the chaos of life can take on shape and substance, his outlook is aligned with fascism in what she characterizes as its aspect of "aesthetic fascism."[60] She reads a series of his plays to argue that Pirandello turns to tragedy and myth in an effort to create illusions in a way that mirrors the fascist sacralization of political myth through the figure of the dictator.[61] Puchner connects this notion of aesthetic fascism to what he contends is the larger, core dynamic underlying all of Pirandello's dramatic production, which he terms "aesthetic Platonism."[62] For both, the point is that Pirandello, far from being a radical sceptic – as so many have assumed – is in fact deeply aligned with a project of finding some way to make sense of an otherwise unintelligible reality. Responding to the problem of relativism as a modern epistemological condition, Pirandello is engaged in an effort to restore the possibility of meaning. These readings have the merit of overcoming the superficial character that too often goes along with assertions of Pirandello's "relativism."[63] More in line with a Nietzschean perspectivism, Pirandello acknowledges the uncertainty of claims to knowledge even while affirming the need for such claims, the need to choose and live an illusion *while knowing it is illusory*.[64]

This is the situation of the famous protagonist of his play *Henry IV* (*Enrico IV*, 1922) – a character who very knowingly embraces the falsity of his own fixed mask, performing both the role of a historical character as well as, ultimately, the role of his own self (performing that historical character).[65] In a very different sense, it is also the situation of Pirandello's female protagonists written for Marta Abba, such as Elma in *As You Desire Me* (*Come tu mi vuoi*, 1930): Elma recognizes the falsity of her identity yet adopts her own "self" as a character, knowing all along that there is nothing to make it essentially true and in this way embracing the flexibility of changing her character as needed. As Daniela Bini has pointed out, this explains how Elma, like Pirandello's female protagonists in general, represents a more fluid, malleable sense of identity and truth; by contrast, his monolithic male characters like *Enrico IV's* unnamed "king" are rigid and ultimately brittle. Bini also contends that this flexible sensibility aligns with artistic creation in Pirandello's outlook.[66] Yet in both the male and female cases the end point is epistemologically similar: despite the absence of fixed truth, certainty, or authentic form, the human condition is such that one must find a way to inhabit the masks of those false forms that are available to us. The only other option is madness – an alternative pushed toward its limit case in Pirandello's final novel, *One, No One, and One Hundred Thousand* (*Uno, nessuno e centomila*, 1926) – leading to an epiphany of self-dissolution that, as I argued in chapter 3, ultimately corresponds to Schopenhauer's ascetic aestheticism.[67]

Pirandello's position is thus much more complicated than words like "relativism" or "scepticism" would seem to allow. At its core is an ambivalence that negotiates the fraught connection of a strong epistemological scepticism with an existential affirmation of the very truths that scepticism questions.[68] The result is the seeming paradox of a non-affirmative affirmation: at the end of his story, Mattia Pascal stands outside his own life, recognizing his identity as an illusion yet inhabiting it all the same.[69] He is a contradiction in terms. And in the final scene he stands over his own grave, speaking to a child who asks him who he is, coaxing him to pronounce the title line, affirming not that he is Mattia Pascal but rather that he is the *late* Mattia Pascal – a line uttered, however, with a laugh.

This non-affirmative affirmation gives us insight into the nature of Pirandello's spiritualism and helps us resolve the quandary posed by Capuana's open letter. Pirandello has seen the "evidence" of spiritual reality in his encounters with mediums and his attendance at séances, yet he will not affirm that reality any more than he will affirm any other. Every truth is subject to the ambivalence of his humour. All the same, that notion of spiritual reality plays an increasingly central role in how Pirandello articulates his own poetics as well as in the content that his writing and theatre seek to portray. Beyond the Theosophical theory of Leandro Scoto's understanding of artistic creation, Pirandello adopts a corpus-spanning metaphor in which artistic creation is a spiritual process. Pre-existing characters come to the author, demanding that they be ushered into actual reality. They exist in some realm separate from the author's actual reality, yet they are *not* the products of his imagination – they present themselves first, and only then does imagination begin to operate on them, making them into the fixed forms of a literary or dramatic representation. The character's reality is thus *ideal*, emerging from the realm of life that precedes fixed forms, and artistic creation becomes a process of ushering the ideal into actuality, using imagination as a mediating force.[70]

Pirandello not only theorizes this understanding of imagination in works like *On Humor* (*L'umorismo*, 1908) but also, obsessively, plays it out in his meta-literary production.[71] *Six Characters in Search of an Author* (*Sei personaggi in cerca d'autore*, 1921/1925) is the most famous example, and an apt one since it begins with a "Preface," which Pirandello added to the later version of the play. In that preface he explicitly theorizes this notion of fantasy as a medium – a spiritual intermediary between the characters' ideal reality and the author's actual reality.[72] But the metaphor is pervasive, and it takes on an even more explicitly magical instantiation in his final, unfinished play, *The Mountain Giants* (*I giganti della montagna*, 1937). There, artistic creation is the topic of the play's content, and one of the main characters is a hybrid between a theatre director and a mage, ushering the world of art into being through magical powers that act out the mediating force of the spiritual imagination and its creative means of connecting the actual to the ideal.[73]

Pirandello's spiritual aesthetics thus go much further than Capuana's positivist parapsychological version of spiritualism. In fact, Pirandello relocates "truth" to an ideal, immaterial realm and then posits artistic creation as a process through which that ideal truth attempts to emerge into actual reality. Tellingly, that ideal is never fully realized in the actual world. The paradigm case, *Six Characters*, is notably a "play in the making" or a failed play, and the Characters, insofar as they manage to act out their inner story or drama, do so by shattering the fictional frame of the work so that for a brief moment the ideal and the real are intermingled. But this can only be for a brief moment, and it will always be incomplete. In this respect, Pirandello's stance echoes another key element of Schopenhauer's aesthetics, in which aesthetic subjectivity gives us fleeting access to the ideal (which Schopenhauer links to Plato's Forms).[74]

Even if the fixity of form can only capture the fluid becoming of life in a single, insufficient aspect, Pirandello's view nevertheless goes much further than Capuana's in affirming the reality of the spiritual. For Capuana, spiritual phenomena are used to expand our scientific models. For Pirandello, the spiritual points us toward an ideal realm, one that emerges into material actuality only through the work of artistic creation, in a way that might expand the material realm but only by transforming it.

This same relationship can likewise be traced in the way that both authors reuse and repurpose nineteenth-century fantasy genres in their encounter with modernity. Capuana, a key figure in Italian *verismo* (the Italian version of Naturalism), was also the author of a large number of fantasy stories.[75] These span from typical ghost stories to strange accounts of magical musical performances and uncanny doublings. As we saw in his rewriting of the vampire story genre, Capuana uses these genres to address the epistemological limits of positivist science, not for the purpose of rejecting science but as a move to expand its scope. Likewise, he draws on fantasy genres in order to expand the scope of realism, integrating strange phenomena and seemingly magical elements to push realism's sense of the everyday in new directions. In contrast, Pirandello's engagement with these genres is tied to a push toward formal experimentation. His revenant story, *The Late Mattia Pascal*, integrates the doubling and displacement of its content into its formal devices, as well, with a dizzying plot where structures double and loop back on one another.[76] Likewise, his projected rewriting of *Six Characters* for its (unrealized) film adaptation drew on Gothic and fantasy elements to refocus the story on the act of artistic creation as a spiritual process of imagination that would become the meta-fictional focus of the film itself.[77] In this regard, what Capuana and Pirandello share is an impulse to draw on fantasy-genre tropes and forms in order to accomplish a self-aware intervention into modern realism. This shared interest in repurposing fantasy stories as one way of intervening into and reconfiguring positivist materialism speaks to how such different formal styles can both be thought of as specifically modernist.

Spiritual Creation and Modernist Idealism

What I have traced here then are three views that span the spectrum of ways in which positivist scientific culture and spiritualism intersect. In Deledda's account of Sardinian magical beliefs, a positivist framework positions those beliefs as part of a "primitive" or "pre-modern" society that needs to be preserved in the face of modernization. In Capuana's, spiritualism points to unexplained but not inexplicable phenomena that, properly understood, will expand our notion of reality. In Pirandello's, spiritual phenomena and material phenomena are both subject to scepticism and are both likewise affirmed as necessary illusions that constitute our reality. While the first two thus value literary and scientific realism, Pirandello's engagement with spiritualism goes further in its move to unground reality. All three authors are part of the long modernist period, reworking nineteenth-century fantasy genres and responding to the problems of modernization. However, it is Pirandello who takes modernist idealism furthest – he not only expands realism but develops a spiritual-ideal alternative that operates through the metafictional dimensions of what is typically seen as modernist form.

It will thus prove valuable to zoom in on how Pirandello's notion of artistic creation dovetails not only with Schopenhauer's broad metaphysics but also with the German philosopher's specific interest in magic as a manifestation of that metaphysics. What ultimately emerges is a deep connection that positions Pirandello's idealist notion of artistic creation in transnational dialogue with other modernist and avant-garde perspectives. As we have seen, Pirandello's theory of artistic creation and his understanding of life and form map onto a Schopenhauerian theory of will and representation – a connection emphasized in Tilgher's formulation. Pirandello had read Schopenhauer, but the debt here is as much indirect as it is direct.[78] Pirandello's view also echoes another facet of Schopenhauer's idealism – its interest in magic. In *On the Will in Nature* (*Über den Willen in der Natur*, 1836), Schopenhauer argues that empirical science and the natural world it studies confirm the doctrines of his idealist speculation, and he goes through copious examples that he believes correspond to how he has described will. In the volume of fifty essays that he added as a supplement to *The World as Will and Representation* in its second edition (1844), he states that his short study *On the Will in Nature* is essential to understanding his metaphysics, as it accounts for "the transition from the phenomenon to the thing-in-itself."[79] In this way, as he describes it in the Preface added to *On the Will in Nature* for its second edition in 1854, Schopenhauer contrasts his use of empirical science with mainstream natural science's "crass and stupid materialism," in which "even vital force is denied, and organic nature is degraded to a chance play of chemical forces."[80]

Schopenhauer thus seeks to examine how the natural world manifests aspects of will's core "character," insofar as such an examination is possible within the knowable limitations of the world as representation.[81] His short book includes examples ranging from anatomy and physical astronomy to the study of linguistics, but what is of particular interest for us here is his section on "Animal Magnetism and Magic," where his account of spiritual phenomena and their manifestation of the metaphysics of will can be linked to the developing discourse on parapsychology.[82] The chapter opens with a disquisition on how the study of animal magnetism has entered into scientific knowledge, contending that empirical evidence shows that magnetic suggestion is effective not because of some material cause–effect relation (as Mesmer had hypothesized) but rather solely through the operation of a "magnetizer's" will.[83] Thus, he concludes "we see the will, which I have stated to be the thing-in-itself, that which alone is real in all existence, the kernel of nature, achieve through the human individual, in animal magnetism and beyond it, things that cannot be explained according to the causal connection, viz., in accordance with the law of the course of nature."[84]

Working from this premise, Schopenhauer then examines magical beliefs and practices of various sorts, drawing parallels to the prototypical case of animal magnetism and contending that magic is indeed possible and real. So if all societies and ages have believed in the reality of magic, this is not a sign of primitive thought but rather a reflection of how our material reality is actually just a sensible manifestation (the representation) of something else, something immaterial, unavailable to the senses but nevertheless having agency and efficacy.[85] Perhaps one of Schopenhauer's most striking contentions here is that nineteenth-century society is prepared to recognize the possibility of magic in a way that Enlightenment society was not precisely because of the legacy of Kantian philosophy: thanks to Kant, we know that we only understand the world as an appearance to our subjective faculties and not as it truly *is* independently of such subjective perception, as a thing in itself. The result is that we cannot confidently reject the possibility of occult correspondences and relations among things, such as the "appearances of absent, dying, or even dead persons, and all magical influence."[86] And indeed, the idea of magic is so widespread, Schopenhauer continues, that it reveals to us how at some deep level people of all places and times have felt an intuitive connection to the omnipotence of will as a metaphysical principle. This feeling explains the pervasive belief in magic, which challenges the reductive materialism that does not make room for occult (invisible, undetectable) connections that go beyond material causes and effects.[87]

Schopenhauer's argument for a philosophically metaphysical understanding of magical belief gives us added insight into the importance of spiritualism and magic for the authors I have examined here. Like Deledda, Schopenhauer is interested in the pervasive character of superstitious beliefs and insists on looking at them not simply as failures of empirical knowledge but as revealing some different source of wisdom and value. Capuana's interest in somnambulism, clairvoyance, and mediums and the genres associated with them resonates with this idealist conviction that our sense of reality is limited and needs to be expanded – although for Capuana that expansion doesn't rely on a metaphysical philosophy. Thus he shies away from the idealism that Schopenhauer maintains is the source of the nineteenth-century resurgence of magical belief.

But the link is clearest and most significant in the case of Pirandello, where we can see the deep confluence of modernism and idealism: for Pirandello, like Schopenhauer, spiritual phenomena reveal the workings of a higher reality or a reality "beyond" our experience of the world, and in so doing they implicitly reiterate the limitations of our own material existence. The great Neo-Idealist of Pirandello's age, Benedetto Croce, fought against an association between idealism and spiritualism in a more rationalist, Hegelian vein, declaring that what was needed was not just idealism but also naturalism and thus scepticism of spiritualist claims: "Idealism, yes, but also a bit of naturalism is called for."[88] But Schopenhauer's irrational vision of the ideal permeated the modernist imagination, and Pirandello's openness to spiritualism as a way of understanding the link between real and ideal is thus a subset of that larger, irrationalist idealism.[89] It is enough to think of the ending of his famous *Six Characters*, where the multiple layers of fictional reality that have been developing across the whole performance suddenly interpenetrate in a chaotic moment (the gunshot) that leaves the Characters, actors, and audience simultaneously confused as to the status of their (respective?) realities. Here modernist form – meta-literature's self-reflexive aesthetic awareness – coincides with a spiritual model of artistic idealism, with the fact that the Characters pre-exist, come into reality, and seek to rearrange or influence it through an imaginary/spiritual intervention into the real. In his revisions to this ending, Pirandello added stage directions specifying that after that chaotic scene the Characters should reappear as shadowy silhouettes in a strange green light as the Stepdaughter's laugh echoes through the theatre.[90] This suggests that something pre-exists and likewise continues beyond the duration of the performance: the ideal reality of the Characters, who enter into our own world as shadows, intermediary spirit forms that can only strike us as uncanny.

Of course, such a view is hardly limited to Pirandello, and here we see another way in which modernist idealism exceeds national boundaries. The idea that the artist functions as a medium channelling a spiritual reality from beyond was important for a multitude of figures and movements in modernism, and we can compare Pirandello's spiritualist conception of the artistic project to that of T.S. Eliot, whose famous essay "Tradition and the Individual Talent" (1919) develops a similar metaphor of artistic creation as a mediumistic procedure, where the individual artist channels the artistic tradition (and thus the dead) to reconfigure that tradition through his or her own creation.[91]

As Stan Smith has argued, this notion is further developed through Eliot's poetry, with his late poem "Little Gidding" (1942, collected in *Four Quartets* in 1943) realizing it in the image of "the communication / of the dead" (vv. 51–52) as a form of historical knowledge transmitted through the privileged consciousness of poetic experience.[92] Likewise, the Surrealists explicitly envisioned their artistic practice as a magical communication with the dead. As Breton wrote in the first "Manifesto of Surrealism" ("Manifeste du surréalisme," 1924), in a section on the "Secrets of the Magical Surrealist Art": "Surrealism will usher you into death, which is a secret society."[93] The unconscious dream-creation to which Surrealism aspired was not simply outside of consciousness – thus corresponding roughly to the position of the unintelligible thing in itself that Schopenhauer's will redeveloped from Kant's transcendental idealism; more than that, this other reality that Surrealism attempted to connect to our conscious life was situated precisely outside of life itself. As Breton wrote in the concluding lines of the manifesto: "It is living and ceasing to live that are imaginary solutions. Existence is elsewhere."[94]

This, I argue, points us toward a fundamental metaphor for the spiritual creation of Surrealist art, situated between unconscious and conscious creation and seeking to channel the inaccessible, irrational surge of unconscious life into visible form in a way that mirrors both Pirandello's notion of the artistic process and Schopenhauer's account of magic as a manifestation of will. For Pirandello, as for Breton and the Surrealists, and for Eliot, what this spiritual process of artistic creation ultimately points to is an idealist conclusion: existence is *elsewhere* – not in a definite (or definable) other location, but in a beyond that is only intelligible in fleeting glances of intuition. Artistic creation is a privileged site of that fleeting glance, hidden and magical.

Modernist Idealism as Outsider Theory? Remembering What We Choose to Forget

The case studies I have considered here showcase the complex ways in which modernist occultism implies a revision of both positivist materialism and literary realism through recourse to nineteenth-century alternative models of spirit and their fantastic genres. More than that, however, they point to two key facets of how we can understand Italian, and European, modernism in a more expansive mode. First, focusing less on specific stylistic or formal similarities and more on the shared conceptual landscape and aims of these authors allows us to expand our notion of modernist production. Thus it was not just Pirandello's meta-literary formal innovation that was modernist in this sense; so too was the more traditional nineteenth-century style of Capuana's vampire story; and so too was Deledda's fatalist folk-culture realism. Second, these examples highlight how a complex effort to respond against the crises of modernity entailed a variety of possible positions, all of which, however, related to the broader confrontation with idealism that was so definitive in this moment of attempted renewal. Modernism, in other words, unfolded along a continuity with idealism, and literary engagements with spiritualism played an important role in positioning modernist writers within that continuity.

Of course, there was another side to modernist idealism that I have been tracing throughout this book that likewise drew on the discourses of nineteenth-century occult spiritualism. I am referring to the practical, political reception of idealist thought that we saw animating efforts to reconstitute and reanimate the Italian body politic. While I have thus far placed primary emphasis on the Hegelian aspect of that reception and those efforts, in the context of modernist occultism a disturbing complication emerges: there was a school of political thinkers and actors whose thought seems to have emerged from an intermixing of the practical aims characterizing the Hegelian approach to idealism and the irrationalist pessimism of Schopenhauer's metaphysical alternative. This confluence emerged precisely in the space where modernist political thinkers engaged with esotericism and occultism. There has long been a general association between magical and esoteric beliefs and political fascism, not only in Italy but also in Germany and beyond. In the Italian case, the connections were many and complex, speaking less to a direct line of influence and more to an overlap of shared outlooks, which I contend were rooted in the idealist commitments of both the nationalizing push of Italian fascism and the metaphysical outlooks of various esoteric or occultist traditions.[95]

A case in point is a problematic fascist theorist who has until very recently remained largely in the shadows: Julius Evola (1898–1974, Baron Giulio Cesare Andrea Evola). Evola sought to redevelop the notion of absolute idealism by focusing on the individual subject in a turn toward what he termed "magical idealism" ("idealismo magico").[96] He contended that the individual both is and creates the world as the only existing absolute – a version of something like Fichte's absolute idealism – and that magic is thus entirely real (a position resonating with the argument Schopenhauer makes in *On the Will in Nature*).[97] Evola's magical beliefs were tied to his efforts to influence the evolution of Mussolini's fascism, including through the foundation of the esoteric-occultist Gruppo di Ur (1927) and two short-lived journals, *Ur* and *Krur* (1927–29).[98] The new man needed to reshape the world was thus a kind of mage, one who recognized in his own total independence the power to bend the world to his will.[99] The resonances with the fascist cult of the dictator are evident enough – though it would be a simplification to simply link Evola to Mussolini and Gentile as straightforwardly espousing the same idealist outlook.[100] Rather, what we see in this instance is another case of the family resemblances that make Hegel and Schopenhauer into productive lenses for refracting the overdetermined conceptual content linking diverse thinkers together.

It is of little importance to dig deeper into Evola's theories here. What bears mentioning is just how they fit into a broader articulation of the history of problematic "outsider theories" that have circulated on the fringes of mainstream culture but nonetheless exerted important influence.[101] My point is to illustrate another sense in which idealism was implicated in the redevelopment of occult-spiritual beliefs – beliefs that were never really "surpassed" by modernity in the first place. Modernist idealism must be understood as more than the "official" or respectable philosophical positions that often take centre stage in intellectual histories of the period. The search for an alternative to modern crisis brought magical, occult, esoteric, and spiritualist beliefs (back) to the surface in ways that took on both aesthetic and political poignancy.[102] The occult return to the perennial tradition preceded and prefigured but also was not limited to the so-called "return to order" of postwar modernism; it was this element that for Surette constituted modernism as a kind of atemporal transcending of history, both tradition and innovation.[103] And the Fascist movement itself was even more temporally complicated, as Mussolini's revolutionary program for modernization and modernism became entangled with the resurgence of an Imperial Roman imaginary.[104]

In both cases, I would suggest, what we see is a dynamic similar to the one that haunted the uncanny expressions of Deledda and the broader modern(ist) interest in ruins: modernity situated itself as having surpassed, perhaps by force, a primitive other. But that "primitive" other abides, resurges, and colours the imaginary of modernity and its temporal self-constitution.[105] From the ruins of Walter Benjamin's *Arcades Project* to official efforts to deal with the "Southern Question" in post-Unification Italy, modernity had to forge a constant newness that was nevertheless obsessively haunted by the spectre of its own repressed history. In a figure like Evola, that historical ghost re-emerged with frightening consequences. But that re-emergence was not limited to what strikes us today as the unhinged speculation of an extreme fascist idealism: indeed, in Deledda's obsessive fatalism the logic of the island as "primitive" other likewise haunts and challenges the progressive logic of modernization, just as in Capuana's encounter with positivism age-old superstitions take on an "updated" scientific light in order to subvert the totalizing claims of modern materialist thought.

What these disparate instances all shared, then, was a profound need to respond to the perception of a crisis in knowledge, in social order, in religion, in institutions, and in the transformed conditions of individual life. The response they forged drew its power directly from what was meant to be forgotten. As T.S. Eliot put it in "The Dry Salvages," reflecting on precisely this ethos of modern progress as it confronts the brown god of an ancient river (whose power is to rage in the form of uncontrollable floods):

> The problem once solved, the brown god is almost forgotten
> By the dwellers in cities—ever, however, implacable.
> Keeping his seasons and rages, destroyer, reminder
> Of what men choose to forget. ("The Dry Salvages" I, vv. 6–9)

The dead world resurges to exert itself against this modern forgetting. The task that modernist idealism's self-awareness set for itself was to channel that resurgence into actuality through aesthetic form, thus harnessing its power to challenge our reality in a way that aimed to reanimate rather than destroy.

Chapter Six

Cinematic Idealism: Modernist Visions of Spiritual Vitality Mediated by the Machine

In the moment of *fin-de-siècle* spiritualism and parapsychology, technological advances were harnessed with an aim of expanding our conception – and perception – of material reality by developing new notions of the invisible forces shaping our world. It is no surprise, then, that the invention of a new medium of aesthetic representation, a new means of recording and viewing the world, should dovetail with that spiritualizing impulse.[1] The cinema offered previously unimaginable possibilities not only for capturing reality but also for altering how it was displayed – slowing it down, speeding it up, zooming in and out, and juxtaposing through montage, just to name a few of the early techniques that radically transformed our ability to envision the world.[2] Together with this new technology came a burst of intellectual activity theorizing cinema and reconsidering the "system of the arts." In the context of this theorization, the technological impulse of modernization and the anxiety of dehumanization it crystallized both became key elements of modernism's idealist project. The camera lens wields the power of the machine to reduce human agency; yet drawing on an idealist outlook, modernists reappropriated that mechanical lens as a part of their shift toward meta-representation, and in this way they responded to dehumanization by turning the reductive materiality of the machine into a tool for revealing a reanimated and revitalized world of human engagement.

The early years of film, the 1900s to 1920s especially, were in many ways focused on a heated debate about the status of the moving picture and its place in the system of arts.[3] Cineastes across Europe were engaged in this contentious effort to understand film, which emerged first as a fairground attraction and only gradually developed into a respected form of art.[4] All the way through the 1920s and 1930s film theorists found it necessary to defend cinema as an art form, contending with attacks from those who saw it as a copy or imitation and thus as lesser, particularly in comparison to theatrical performance and/or the written, literary text. This anxiety about cinema's disruption of the arts was paired with a broader fear of modernization's disruption of social life and order. As industrialization resulted in an accelerating alienation of human life from its social activities and mechanized labour reduced agency in ways that threatened to transform humans into mere machines, the spectre of an art form constituted by that same process of mechanical reduction was for many a danger to be fought.[5] This fear is perhaps best encapsulated by the metaphor repeated throughout Luigi Pirandello's film novel, *Shoot!* (*Si gira…*, 1916): the camera is a mechanical black spider devouring the lives of the actors who perform before it, reducing them to mere images on cellophane.[6]

Yet Pirandello's negative portrayal in *Si gira…* was hardly a total rejection of cinema; like many modernist intellectuals, Pirandello sought to reconfigure cinema and its technology so that instead of reducing human life to bare materiality, it would be harnessed to restore or expand the possibilities of human experience.[7] In this sense, Pirandello's turn toward an experimental art cinema mirrored that of ideologically divergent groups of modernists such as the Futurists. Their notion of *cinepittura* sought to use mechanization to revitalize the world by freeing objects from their mundane function in anthropocentric art and developing a new, object-based aesthetic of rhythmic motion. My project here is to read these divergent forays into experimental film in light of early theories that offered an idealist lens for understanding cinema's meaning, as well as its potential for (existential) renewal.

In fact, already in "The Philosophy of Cinematograph" ("Filosofia del cinematografo"), a newspaper article published in Turin's *La stampa* on 18 May 1907, the Italian philosopher Giovanni Papini had declared that despite the common perception, cinema was actually well-suited to philosophical reflection and metaphysical consideration. I will later examine Papini's argument to show how it provides a different way of understanding these early debates about film's artistic status. Cinema's transformation of the aesthetic rethinks the place of human existence. Papini opens a new discursive space, prefiguring later (and more famous) critical interventions by theorists such as Walter Benjamin while also serving as a conceptual grounding for us to consider subsequent experimentations. The most interesting intertext here, I contend, is not Benjamin but rather the early avant-garde film theory of the French Impressionist filmmaker Jean Epstein, whose notion of *photogénie* offers another articulation of the idealist approach to using the mechanical lens to reveal what is otherwise hidden within the world of human life. This notion of cinematic unveiling operates in conjunction with a broad modernist discourse on intermediality that positions film together with music and the visual arts in an effort to capture the vital rhythm of modern experience, a project theorized in film by Epstein's Italian contemporary, Sebastiano Arturo Luciani.

These theoretical interventions work hand in hand with experimental cinema and its literary image, both of which operate in terms of an idealist framework. Pirandello's own turn toward cinema and his interactions with film adaptations of his work, especially his novel *The Late Mattia Pascal* (*Il fu Mattia Pascal*, 1904) and his famous play *Six Characters in Search of an Author* (*Sei personaggi in cerca d'autore*, 1921 / 1925), are directly engaged with the theory and practice of French Impressionist cinema. At the same time, like the Futurists, Pirandello theorized "pure" cinema as an intermedial visualization of music. Reading these experimental views of cinema in relation to Papini's philosophical analysis enables two primary insights: first, these views of cinema work together with modernist renewals of occult-spiritualist discourses to posit a way in which modern art can attempt to bridge the ideal and the actual. Second, this effort at uniting seemingly disparate realities clarifies the modernist obsession with meta-representation, an obsession that is also at the core of experimental views of cinema. If film offers a new means to reflect on the process of artistic creation itself, then it also allows for the materiality of artistic production to become a revitalized subject of aesthetic self-reflection. The discourses of vitalism and spiritualism that we have seen as key subsets of modernist idealism thus come together in projects to reimagine the technical possibilities of the new medium of film. To speak in terms borrowed from Caroline Levine, the medium of film affords new ways of connecting the response to a perceived modern crisis to the project of experimental formal innovation developing across the modernist arts.[8] In contrast to narratives of modernism's turn toward "pure art" – art focused on its own materiality as such – I thus propose that cinematic self-reflection offers a case study for how modernism's engagement with idealism pushed it toward harnessing materiality for the purposes of transfiguring our perception of reality – a continuation and transformation of the decadent aesthetic impulse I examined in chapter 3.

In a moment when technology developed alongside a belief in paranormal phenomena that aimed to stretch the bounds of science and materialism, experimental cinema became the perfect fusion of both. From Papini's theorization of cinematic idealism to Luciani's theories of film and Epstein's notion of cinema's *photogénie*, and from Futurist cinema to Pirandello's engagement with the medium, I contend that the transnational reception of spiritualist thought reinforced the fundamentally transnational character of modernist idealism. Vitalism's spiritualization and the reception of magical thought dovetailed in a cinema whose material dimensions intersected with spirit, seeking to reanimate modernity and restore a sense of self-conscious meaning to existence.

Cinematic Idealism: Existential Thought Experiments and the Vision of *Photogénie*

Recent scholarship has finally turned more attention to early film theory, yet there has still been startlingly little discussion about what these theories can tell us regarding the development of modernism more generally. While Laura Marcus has done key work initiating a discussion about the relationship between early film culture and modernist literature, her study focuses exclusively on an archive of British texts and film institutions (especially the London Film Society and the magazine *Close Up*).[9] The burgeoning discourse, led by John Welle and others, on how early cinema and other art forms overlapped in the birth of modern celebrity culture marks another fruitful direction in this discussion, but one that is still developing.[10] These rich treatments focus on the links between film production, film criticism, modernist literature, and cultural transformations. A more direct link to a new philosophy of the image that was emerging in the late nineteenth and early twentieth centuries has been established in Mitchell's seminal work describing what he terms the "pictorial turn."[11] What has not yet been accounted for is the way in which the philosophical world view of early film theory provides not only a window into a transforming discourse of the image but also a new lens for understanding what was a broader philosophical tendency in modernism's idealist project and self-conception. That lens is provided by what I am referring to here as cinematic idealism.

I will now examine three under-studied theorists of early cinema who were ostensibly quite different, came from different backgrounds and contributed to different "phases" of the silent film era – if I may call them that, recognizing that narratives of discontinuity in the period are often overstated.[12] The characters at the centre of my analysis are the philosopher Giovanni Papini, who wrote the earliest contribution to Italian film theory; Sebastiano Arturo Luciani, a musicologist who was a forerunner in Italian film criticism and participated in film production; and Jean Epstein, a French filmmaker and theorist at the heart of the early narrative avant-garde movement in French film, known as French Impressionist cinema. Despite their differences, what holds these theorists together is a shared notion that the technological apparatus of film can be used not to dehumanize the world but rather to reanimate our perception of it. In this regard, all three participated in the unfolding logic of modernist idealism, seeking the means to revitalize modernity through a new art that would provide previously unavailable experiences of vision as well as new possibilities for developing a visual language of movement and rhythm that could offer what these thinkers envisioned as truer, more authentic insights into or intuitions about human life and the animate as well as inanimate world.

Papini's Theorization: Schopenhauerian Cinema and the Existential Crisis of Modernity

Giovanni Papini (1881–1956) was one of Italy's most widely known figures in the early twentieth century.[13] A philosopher, poet, and prolific essayist, over a period of decades he collaborated with numerous Italian intellectuals to establish journals of culture and criticism, including *Leonardo*, founded in 1903 with Giuseppe Prezzolini with the aim of combating the climate of philosophical and scientific positivism, and *La Voce*, founded in 1908, which was one of the most important periodicals circulating in the pre-war context. While *La Voce*'s tenor changed through its various phases of direction between 1908 and 1916, it was consistently opposed to the prevailing bourgeois culture of the liberal democratic era. In 1913, Papini collaborated with Ardegno Soffici to found another new journal, *Lacerba*, a Florentine publication that aligned itself with Futurism and made Papini a prominent voice in favour of war, a position he would later recant.[14] As is evident even from this brief overview, Papini was a very well-connected figure, polemical and eager to push for the renovation of Italian culture, not only in the arts but in politics as well.[15] He was also at the beating heart of not only Florentine but also Italian modernism, a central proponent of what Cangiano has identified as the avant-garde conviction that cultural action could reshape consciousness and thus history.[16]

Papini's stance was also tied to a broader polemic against academic philosophy more generally. In addition to his work with various journals, Papini wrote numerous philosophical or anti-philosophical works, such as *The Twilight of the Philosophers* (*Il crepuscolo dei filosofi*, 1906), which I discussed in chapter 2; these publications came to serve as major avenues for the dissemination of foreign philosophers' ideas that had not been integrated into the mainstream of academic philosophy – indeed, one of Papini's perpetual nemeses in the philosophical world was that giant of institutional philosophy, Benedetto Croce, who at first saw Papini as an ally in a shared idealist struggle, having identified Papini's position with Bergsonian idealism.[17] Papini's general outlook was in fact in many ways aligned with the vitalist and spiritualist dimensions of Italian modernist culture that I delineated in chapters 4 and 5: engaging with Bergson's thought on the one hand and the irrationalist tradition coming from Schopenhauer more broadly, Papini also played a role in Theosophical circles, attending meetings of the Theosophical Society led by Giovanni Amendola, with whom he co-founded *L'Anima* (published only once, in 1911), a blisteringly ephemeral journal that engaged spiritualist questions.[18] Having started out as an anti-ecclesiastical atheist, a vitalist, and a spiritualist, Papini would evolve in the subsequent decades into a converted Catholic and a fascist. These duelling trajectories may seem conflicted and strange, but they actually fit squarely into the pattern of modernist idealism that I have been tracing throughout this book: while Papini's notion of how to combat positivist materialism, academic institutionalism, bourgeois liberal democracy, and the other "deadening" forces of modernity may have changed over time, the fundamental impulse to recuperate a lost ideal and thereby revitalize modern culture and society was typical of the authors and thinkers who participated in this intellectual constellation.

Papini, then, was a thinker of modernist idealism. It is thus all the more interesting that he was also the first to theorize cinema through a philosophical lens. Indeed, Papini's essay "The Philosophy of Cinematograph" is notable for how early it came in the articulation of the new medium, long before the works that today are often considered touchstones of early cinema theory (itself a somewhat overlooked subset of film theory).[19] That essay was, as John Welle has noted, one of the most prominent early instances of Italian "cinema literature" and integral to fostering public reflection on the new technological form and its reception in popular, mass society.[20] Yet despite its early entrance on the scene, it sidestepped many of the preoccupations regarding cinema's relations to the other arts that often dominated the early discourse.[21] Though he does begin in that essay by comparing the cinema to other established art forms of mass modernity – the theatre, the newspaper, the illustrated magazine – Papini's focus is not on this comparison but rather on the specific kind of vision produced by the cinema and the specific philosophical and existential questions it poses for the philosopher of modern life.

The piece occupies two pages in the Turin daily, and it addresses itself to an imaginary reader who thinks of himself (the piece is typical of the period in its male focus) as a wise man or philosopher. After noting the sudden success of the cinema and the way that its popular character has led thinkers to discount it as an art form, Papini poses a question that motivates the rest of his argument: if cinema has suddenly become so popular, what does that tell us about it and about ourselves? The first answer he offers considers the question sociologically while taking a swipe at both the cinema and modern life: films take less time, effort, and money for their audience, so they both reflect and appeal to modernity's economizing tendency ("tendenza all'economia").[22] The moviegoing audience is in turn described in disparaging terms as "boys, women, and common men" ("dei ragazzi, delle signore e degli uomini comuni") – the modern urban masses, in other words, who are all defined by some element of cultural lack (immaturity, gendered assumptions about inadequacy, or class-based assumptions about inadequacy for philosophical refinement).[23]

However, this sociological answer doesn't satisfactorily resolve the question, so Papini proceeds to a second way of considering it, focusing on the technology of the cinema and its new aesthetic capacities. The cinema, he notes, offers advantages over other art forms like theatre: it can condense large-scale action (in time and space) so that it is available to us in a brief time and a single spot; and it can capture reality, giving us access to actual knowledge in a way that bridges a newspaper's reporting and an illustrated magazine's visualization, exceeding both by displaying how things unfold in "scenes of transformation" ("le scene di trasformazioni"). Both of these features focus on the cinema as a superior form of realistic mimesis: it is a new technology that allows us to see reality better in terms of scope, actuality, and the reproduction of life's vitality – in motion rather than in static images or snippets.

While these first points suggest an approach focused on cinematic realism, Papini goes on to complicate matters by examining how the technology of cinema enables a type of vision akin to the marvellous. He devotes more space to discussing these features, in language that seems to point toward a greater rhetorical emphasis on their significance. Cinema, he argues, can make use of technical "secrets" and "tricks," like those used in the "fake spirit photographs" ("le false fotografie spiritiche") of previous decades; these bestow imagined reality upon the most fabulous sorts of illusions. In this way, the cinema is able to contribute to the "development of the imagination" ("sviluppo della immaginazione"), like a "kind of opium without the negative consequences" ("una specie di oppio senza cattive consequenze"). The cinema thus enriches our world, not only giving us new access to our actual reality but also giving us the chance to envision a more marvellous one. Here Papini's argument dovetails with the modernist interest in "spirit" as a means of revitalizing or reanimating the modern world. His notion of cinema thus goes beyond the documentary impulse of early film, which often offered exciting new "views" of the actual world and thus drew in crowds attracted to the exotic or large-scale images they could not otherwise see.[24] As an opium for the imagination, the cinema enters into the vaunted space of decadent-romantic poetic creation, the sphere of aesthetic creation that cultivates the marvellous in and through the material reality of modern society.

This description of cinematic imagination draws on an idealist framework and is clearly situated in the same decadent lineage that I traced in chapter 3. There is a long romantic-decadent tradition of recourse to intoxication in general and opium in particular as models for a new creative subjectivity that blurs the distinction between imaginary and actual life, hovering at the border of the ideal and the real. Baudelaire is, as ever, a key node in the development of this discourse, with two of his most important contributions being the article "On Wine and Hashish" ("Du Vin et du haschisch," in *Le Messager del'Assemblé*, 1851) and the subsequent book *Artificial Paradises* (*Les paradis artificiels, Opium et Haschisch*, 1860), although the theme frequently recurs in his poetry and prose-poems. Baudelaire is not the originator of this discourse, however, which had already made Thomas De Quincey famous for his *Confessions of an English Opium-Eater* (1821). As Vincent Sherry notes, this discourse is tied to decadent modernism's encounter with a kind of spotted time: "Opium is indeed the medicinal for the sickness of time. The drug is a substitute for the otherwise unaccomplished possibilities, the aims unmet by the redemptive temporalities of the spot-of-time consciousness."[25] The artificial heaven of the opium dream allows access to invisible or impossible realms in the imagination; it likewise can be used to restructure the actual world by redirecting or redeveloping aesthetic attention. Papini thus theorizes cinema as a way of reanimating the modern world by connecting it to spiritual vitality via the imagination.

As I will argue later, this vision of cinema as an opium dream fostering the imagination connects directly to how Pirandello and the Surrealists would conceive of film in their engagement with the medium. Here, though, I turn to the final point that Papini makes in his article. He now insists that to understand the philosophical importance of the cinema it is necessary to think about how it transforms life into nothing but images constituted of light and then allows us to view life in/as those images. This third argument moves toward an existentialist perspective on the meaning of modern life, which is ultimately grounded in a metaphysical thought-experiment that he contends the cinema naturally produces. The existential aspect of the cinema comes from how it reduces living reality to *"little images of light"* (*"piccole immagini di luce,"* emphasized by Papini). In this way, the world is "spiritualized," which is to say "reduced to its most basic, made out of the most ethereal and angelic matter, without depth, without solidity, like a dream, quick, fantastic, unreal" ("spiritualizzato – ridotto al minimo, fatto colla materiale più eterea ed angelica, senza profondità, senza solidità, simile al sogno, rapido, fantastico, irreale"). All the same, we look at this reduced image and see life. Reflecting on this illusion and its impact on our senses gives us reason to question how solid and real we think life actually is. Human life is no more real or solid than this illusion of light and air. Following a post-Kantian idealist vein, the insight here is that cinema confirms to us that what we take to be reality is merely an effect, processed through the subjective faculties of our mind.

The final step of this third argument now moves into an expanded account of its existential and metaphysical significance. As we watch images of human life on screen, Papini says, we are in the position of a god watching its creation unfold before it. Understanding that metaphor as we watch, however, also entails relativizing our own existence, projecting ourselves as a dance of light and shadow being performed for *someone else*.[26] The universe itself may just be a grandiose cinematic spectacle for some unknown viewer(s), revealing the inane reality of our existence by making it visible in the way that cinema makes visible unexpected features of human life for our own consideration – "the imperfection of certain movements, the ridiculousness of certain mechanical gestures, the grotesque vanity of human distortions" ("l'imperfezione di certi movimenti, il ridicolo di certi gesti meccanici, la grottesca vanità delle smorfie umane"). Papini here reconfigures the familiar metaphor of life as a stage upon which human beings are merely actors, that famous Shakespearean motif that is just one familiar instance of the larger early-modern concept of the *theatrum mundi*.[27] The interesting part of how Papini reconfigures that familiar metaphor here is that he joins it with the technological focus of his investigation and its philosophical significance: the flickering light creates a seemingly living image, and our perceptions of life likewise flicker through our consciousness in a way that composes the semblance of a coherent whole. Cinema's tangible production of representation allows for a microcosm/macrocosm experience that is not explained or argued but rather made present as a perceptual fact.[28]

What this outline of Papini's argument should make clear is how he combines a starkly existential outlook on human life with the idea that aesthetic representation not only explicates the content of such an outlook (thematically, in words or images) but also *shows* that outlook.[29] What I mean is that cinema as a technology enacts a process of reducing life to a play of light and shadow, and that is itself a glimpse of the ephemeral illusion of existence. Thus for Papini, cinema is the technological conduit of an unintelligible truth, a revelation of the world as it is (as a process of becoming or series of relations, thus its "form" in the Platonic sense). As such, I would contend that Papini is reading cinema in a way that directly echoes Arthur Schopenhauer's notion of how aesthetic experience gives us fleeting insight into the underlying nature of the world, piercing the veil of Maya and revealing will in its forms.[30] If cinema can be read as an idealist medium, then, it is not the optimistic sort of idealism that we see in the Hegelian dialectic, where the development of/toward reason unfolds progressively through world history. Rather, it is the pessimistic, irrationalist alternative articulated by Schopenhauer, where art gives us a fleeting glimpse of the brutal reality that constitutes life beneath the sensible world.[31]

Ultimately, then, Papini's argument reveals both a sense of film's technical and spiritual possibilities and a frighteningly modern vision of the familiar notion that life is a mere performance, all the world a stage, and what we take to be deeply serious and important facts or events may be nothing more than the flicker of light against a black backdrop. In this way his exploration of the new medium speaks to two sides of an idealist discourse on the material progress of film as technology: on the one hand, he fits film into a larger view of human life that relativizes and thus decentres it, echoing the idealist traditions that contrast a fleeting material existence to some truer ideal form; on the other, though, he projects the possibility that film can mediate our connection to that ideal through its spiritual dimensions, forging a connection that transcends the limits of materialism. Film is both symptomatic of modernity's ailments and a glimmering, flickering image of something more.

Luciani's Cinematic Idealism: Visual Music and Rhythm Revitalizing Modernity

Papini's vision of cinema's possibilities was an early version of a discourse that would develop and become more complicated over subsequent decades, gradually building a notion of experimental, avant-garde, or art cinema that aimed to forge a new path for the medium – a path that, importantly for my considerations here, was seen as connecting the material apparatus of film production with a spiritualized or transcendent ideal that would give it deeper meaning.

In the development of that discourse, a key interlocutor was the early film theorist Sebastiano Arturo Luciani.

Luciani (1884–1950) was a musicologist whose work focused especially on the rehabilitation of Enlightenment-era musical figures and traditions. He moved to Rome to complete his musical training, and there in the 1910s and 1920s he became friends with a number of leading figures in the Italian avant-garde, from D'Annunzio to various Futurists. In 1924 he, Anton Giulio Bragaglia, and Franco Casavola co-signed the Futurist manifesto "The Visual Syntheses of Music" ("Le sintesi visive della musica").[32] His musical research was closely identified with an avant-garde intermedial sensibility, and he was interested in finding ways for music to connect to and manifest itself within the other arts. It is thus no surprise that as one of the leading Italian theorists of cinema in the early silent period, Luciani authored a number of texts that dovetailed with avant-garde articulations of the medium and its possibilities, conceiving it especially in terms of its resonance with music and grounding it in the principle of rhythm.

Luciani's film theory offers two important points of both conjunction and re-elaboration of the idealist stance that Papini's early article articulated. First, he insists on thinking of cinema as a medium that can be conceived in idealist terms that push it beyond the more limited commercial/popular vision of cinematic entertainment, although his notion of what that idealist cinema entails is strikingly different from Papini's. Where Papini saw the cinema as an idealist thought experiment on modern human life, Luciani opts for a more circumscribed aesthetic interpretation of its "ideality" as the possibility of achieving the purest and most transcendent form to which modernist art can aspire. Second, Luciani develops a narrative of how cinema will achieve that pure form, rethinking the relations among authors, directors, and actors with the aim of converting film into a rhythmic visualization of musical motion and thus unlocking the inner movement and vitality of material life. Thus he, like Papini, focuses on how cinematic vision suggests the marvellous and operates through visual imagination; however, where Papini's interest is in how this vision affects the audience, producing a heightened development of human faculties of imagination, Luciani focuses instead on the medium and its practitioners. Despite these differences, what emerges from a comparison of their early theories is the centrality of idealist paradigms for understanding the possibilities of film as a medium.

In January 1919, Luciani published a short article in the cinema journal *In penombra* titled "The Ideality of the Cinematograph" ("L'idealità del cinematografo").[33] This article summarized and redeveloped arguments he had previously made in a number of other pieces, especially in two articles published in consecutive issues of the journal *Apollon* in April and May 1916 ("Scenic Impressionism" and "The Poetics of Cinema," respectively).[34] In the first of those earlier pieces, Luciani begins by arguing that silent film functions like ancient pantomime and that both forms represent "decadent" stages in artistic development. However, he contends, cinema can renovate itself and become the only true form of modern art by forgoing theatrical narrative and relying instead on music as the dominant element, with cinematic choreography, gesture, and scenic elements (including light and colour) following and manifesting the music rather than vice versa. This is what he terms "scenic impressionism," which he situates as a cinematic refinement of the effect Wagner was attempting to achieve in the static form of theatre. In the second article, published the following month, Luciani revisits his argument and elaborates on its key implications with the goal of spelling out the compositional paradigm that can guide cinema to achieve the status of a true art form. He argues that cinema is essentially the visual unfolding of images through time and that it should thus be governed by compositional laws of rhythm and proportion that result in verisimilitude.[35]

Both these arguments inform his article on "The Ideality of the Cinematograph." Here, the notion of the "ideal" in question is explicitly framed in terms of idealist philosophy and aesthetics, with Luciani referring to the ideal as Platonic and then reworking and expanding on his previous articles to argue that cinema can become ideal only by redirecting itself away from the model of theatre and embracing the specificity of its medium.[36] This entails eliminating the hybrid nature of theatrical representation, where the actor serves as an intermediary between the poet's vision for the artwork and what is realized on stage; for Luciani, the cinema offers the potential to erase the individuality of the actor, making her instead what he terms – drawing on the language of Edward Gordon Craig's earlier article on theatre actors as "über-marionettes" – a "super-marionette."[37] The marionette actor is fully controlled by the director's vision, enabling a less individuated or personal form of representation. Likewise, Luciani argues that the author and director must be merged into a single figure, who will control all aspects of the production, including the actors' every gesture. In this way, it will be possible to control the rhythm of the vision unfolding on screen, offering a kind of melody in the form of human gesture that makes film into a spatial analogue of musical movement through time.[38] This outcome is explicitly labelled "transcendent," in that it brings the work of art into contact with a higher or truer rhythm of life than the particularities of individual actors or of narrative action would allow.[39]

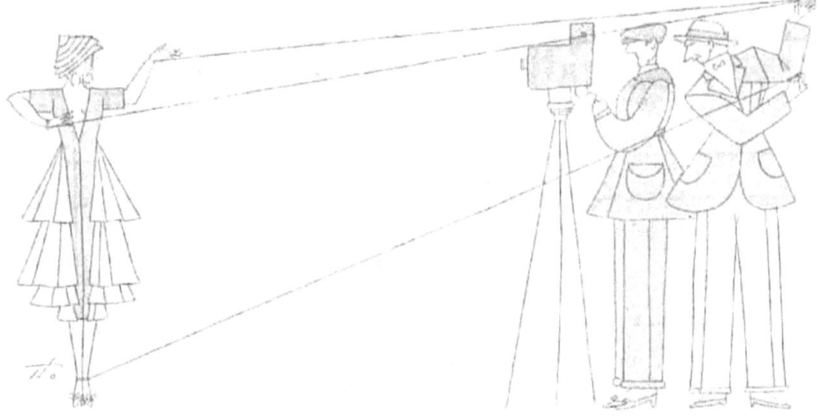

Figure 2. Illustration from "La idealità del cinematografo," *In penombra* (January 1919), 3.

For Luciani, in other words, the cinema is *ideal* precisely insofar as it becomes a pure musical expression in visual terms – it encompasses the movement of life, and in this sense it is "verisimilar" despite forgoing narrative structure and the reliance on language that he sees as more properly the domain of poetry. It is evident here how the discourse of modernist vitalism is operative in Luciani's ideal: the absence of the actor's voice in silent film makes the entire focus fall on "the visual and especially rhythmic elements of life. And life, in its most fundamental expression, is movement."[40] This emphasis on vital movement accessed through film's visual rhythm coincides in turn with the discourse of modernist spiritualism. Luciani writes that where "photography generally brings to light nothing more than the animality contained in the person represented, the cinematograph is able to bring to light its spirituality instead."[41] The technological apparatus becomes a material bridge to the ideal beyond, ironically not thanks to the living vitality of the actor but rather because of her marionette-like gestures, which are mechanically orchestrated to produce a vital rhythm that is itself the "spirituality" of the person. In this way, if film unlocks vital or spiritual truth usually hidden in a static view of reality, then the director is its god-figure – both the designer and the conductor of this orchestra of vital vibration.

This notion is brilliantly captured by one of the five illustrations accompanying the article (though others touch on the same theme) (see figure 2). Placed above the title at the beginning of the piece is a hand-drawn cartoon in which an actress stands before a camera mounted on a tripod. A man stands at the camera, operating its crank, and another man stands behind him. We can tell this second man is the director, for he is holding three strings that extend to the actress' arms and her feet, which are bound together so that she is effectively held in place. This is Luciani's ideal director, the man behind the camera, literally pulling the strings so that his "super-marionette" will perform precisely the gestures needed in order for his film to unfold a sequence of images orchestrated to the ideal music of his cinematic vision.

Though Luciani begins his article on cinematic idealism by referencing the Platonic ideal, it is clear enough that his interpretation is coloured by the post-Kantian vision of that ideal as it was articulated by Schopenhauer. Music, the purest form of expression and ineffable in its essence, is the privileged form of vital expression, and cinema's goal is to convert that ineffable movement into visual form through rhythm.[42] The particularities of the actor are to be erased in a universal gesture that speaks to an ideal form rather than an individual accident. The mechanical apparatus is to become a conduit to something higher by transfiguring actual reality into a form that lays bare its inner rhythm, the vital kernel of becoming underneath mere external form. In this respect, Luciani's notion of an ideal cinema is not as far removed from Papini's as it might at first appear. Likewise, it is in clear dialogue with experiments in Futurist cinema and the theories later developed by Pirandello. What holds all of these variations on the theme together is an abiding idealist commitment tied to the modernist desire to reanimate modernity.

Photogénie as an Idealist Realism: Epstein and French Impressionist Cinema

Luciani and Papini both focused on the spiritual element of cinema, its ability to speak to the imagination and render visible things that are actually impossible or at least invisible. This is one respect in which their approach bridged the realism of cinema's photographic-documentary capacities with a spiritualized notion of imagination and fantasy. Both authors, in other words, participated in the modernist-spiritualist endeavour to expand our perception of reality and the scope of realism – an impulse I have traced in the literary contributions of figures as seemingly diverse as Deledda, Capuana, and Pirandello in chapter 5. In this regard, I contend that we can see both as precursors to the subsequent discourse on *photogénie* that would develop in the context of French Impressionist cinema, the first wave of avant-garde French silent film that has perhaps too often been eclipsed in considerations of both film theory and film practice.[43] For Jean Epstein (1897–1953), the filmmaker and theorist most closely associated with the concept of *photogénie,* this special vision rendered possible by the camera was situated at the juncture of realism and idealism. *Photogénie* emerged as a key category for understanding the potential of cinema in a phenomenological mode, revealing a new spiritual, even mystical, kind of seeing that the camera lens and work of montage brought within reach.

The precise contours and periodization of French Impressionist cinema, also sometimes called the "first avant-garde," have been a matter of some historical contention: Bordwell dates the movement to 1918–28, while Abel argues that it should be subsumed into the larger category of the "narrative avant-garde," which he dates around the decade 1919–29.[44] In either case, its primary practitioners included Louis Delluc (1890–1924), Germaine Dulac (1882–1942), Epstein, Abel Gance (1889–1981), and Marcel L'Herbier (1888–1979).[45] These filmmakers took part in an avant-garde effort to establish an anti-tradition in film with its own networks of distribution and reception, including cine-clubs and journals / magazines that opened up discursive space for their interventions. In typical avant-garde fashion, they sought to renovate the cinema by changing its aesthetic task; but at the same time, they perceived this transformation as a way of elevating it into a pure art form.[46]

It is in this context that the notion of *photogénie* emerged and took on significance. First described by Louis Delluc in his book *Photogénie* (Paris: M. de Brunoff, 1920), this special form of cinematic vision was supposed to capture more than what was visible to the limited faculties of human perception. This was possible thanks to cinema's ability to manipulate or operate differently with space, time, and causation.[47] While Delluc may have invented the notion,[48] it was Jean Epstein who became its most significant proponent.[49] Most of our contemporary discussion of the concept focuses on Epstein's elaborations, particularly in two essays: "On Certain Characteristics of Photogénie," published as part of his 1926 book *Le cinématographe vu de l'Etna,* and "Photogénie and the Imponderable" ("Photogénie de l'impondérable," 1935).[50] In the former, *photogénie* is conceived as the essential principle of cinema as an art form, akin to the abstract principle of colour in painting.[51] As such, *photogénie* demarcates the specificity of cinema as a medium. At the same time, however, it is mysterious, undefinable, ineffable.[52] That characterization endures into his later writing, such as *Le cinéma du diable* (1947), in which he asserts that "the 'filmmakers' quest collided with the first of those great mysteries of the cinematograph: *photogénie.*"[53] While Epstein's insistence on the mysterious and ineffable qualities of cinema's special vision likely explains why subsequent theory has tended to ignore or downplay his concept (seeing it as mystifying and thus unhelpful or even suspect), this association reveals a key aspect of Epstein's modernism as well as his connection to idealist thought.

There is, in fact, an important connection between *photogénie* and idealist philosophy. Epstein repeatedly describes the concept not only as a kind of mystery but also as a kind of special insight into something that is absent from the reductive logic of verbal arguments that attempt to use words precisely so as to denote conceptual meanings. *Photogénie* uses the visual language of cinema to create an intuitive understanding that reaches beyond, or beneath, what mere constructions of words would be able to convey:

> Unattended, without words, an air of conviction alights from the screen on eighteen hundred pairs of eyes. Words slither like wet cakes of soap around what we try to say. This evening a friend, trying to put everything too precisely into words, suddenly shrugged twice and said no more. I believed him, as others might have been persuaded verbally, on the strength of this wearied silence. And when a scientist takes pains to use words with precision, I no longer believe.[54]

On the one hand, this stance clearly resonates with the tradition of *Sprachkritik* prominent in early twentieth-century thought: language fails to adequately signify what it attempts to convey, the true inner life or experience it cannot capture.[55] At the same time, it resonates with *Lebensphilosophie*: a purely mechanical, material, rational understanding of reality and our perception of it fails to account for the "vital kernel" that animates, structures, or gives meaning to that reality.[56] *Photogénie* intervenes by attempting to restore an experience of what has been lost in the era of materialist mechanization and positivist precision – "All details that are expressed without recourse to words simultaneously trigger the words that lie at their roots as well as the feelings that precede them."[57] In this way, cinema's special vision follows in the footsteps of the various spiritualist technologies that aimed to utilize mechanical and technological advances to help expand or transform our understanding of material reality itself. Beyond things, we see and experience an affective dimension of reality that exceeds the limits of logic; indeed, as Malcom Turvey has convincingly argued, Epstein's picture of cinematic vision dovetails with Bergson's vitalist philosophy of movement, in which the world is understood as a vibrating energy that exceeds the limitations of our material perceptions of it.[58] Epstein, too, turns to rhythm and movement as the core components of cinematic "language," replacing the false fixity or precision of verbal constructions with a fluid becoming of images operating at a strange juncture of space and time.[59]

In Epstein's articulation of cinematic language, the unique role of movement is a window on how cinema deconstructs a type of (positivist, materialist) logic. In "The Logic of Images," from *Esprit de cinema* (1955), Epstein contends that "in movement, which is the essence of cinematographic representation, fundamental principles of formal logic are mobilized, relaxed, wrecked, reduced to a very relative validity."[60] These principles include the notion of logical identity as well as concepts of "non-ubiquity and simultaneity," all of which are eroded by the new and previously impossible relations of space and time in cinematic language.[61] What is more, our notions of causation are likewise upended, a result of film's technical tricks such as reversing the direction of a sequence or otherwise manipulating the relations among images.[62] Epstein is directly utilizing the terms of Kantian and post-Kantian idealism both to think about how humans normally process and understand sensible reality and to express the way in which cinema's mysterious vision penetrates beyond those limits: the fundamental categories of space, time, and causation become not the delimiting border of human knowledge but rather a kind of illusion or barrier. In a move reminiscent of Papini's assertion that the way we view images in the cinema makes us wonder about how we ourselves are viewed (by God?), Epstein suggests that cinematic special effects impact not only our immediate perception of causation but also the very category itself: "However, a doubt can linger in our mind: is normal causality (which constitutes one of the items – not least among them – of our daily, logical act of faith, and that physicists already repudiate to replace it with statistical laws) another *trompe l'oeil* just like the absurd causality of the film recorded in reverse?"[63] While the human mind may, by necessity, process things in terms of a limited understanding of space, time, and causality, cinema gives us an intuitive experience, materially present, of how the world might consist of different relations that exceed those limits. This is the vitalist, idealist alternative pursued by both Schopenhauer and Bergson. Epstein's notion of *photogénie* develops into a concept of cinema as an idealist shock to the materialist system of logic, performed through the medium of film.

This cinematic idealism is also in an important sense aligned with the discourse on magic that I examined in the previous chapter. This is not only because Epstein associates *photogénie* with a mysterious and ineffable quality of film but also because the idealist shock to materialist logic entails a transformed relationship of idea and matter, one that is, indeed, magical. This emerges clearly in Epstein's description of *photogénie* in opposition to verbal language:

> The film shows a man who betrays; nevertheless there is no man and no betrayer. But the ghost of something creates an emotion which nevertheless cannot come to life unless the thing be for which it was created. So an emotion-thing is born. You believe in more than a betrayer, you believe in a betrayal. Now you need this betrayal; because you feel it, and feel it so precisely that no other betrayal but this imaginary one will satisfy you.[64]

The idea that the false reality imagined by the cinema gives rise to a real reality is striking. There is no man, just an image of one. Yet this image functions as a "ghost," one that gives rise to an actual emotion in the viewer. Epstein here insists that the cinema gives rise to an intermediate realm of things, "emotion-things." Rather than a bizarre particularity of his *photogénie,* we can see this as a component of the larger modernist discourse on occult/spiritual aesthetics. It functions here in the same way Pirandello uses Theosophical notions of "thought-forms" to explain how his characters exist *before* they come to the author and demand to be represented artistically (see the discussion in chapter 5). *Photogénie* thus describes a process of imaginary creation in which a reality that does not exist in the actual world nevertheless reaches into and modifies the actual world of material things.

Epstein's theory of cinema as art thus places the technological mechanisms of the lens firmly at the intersection of idealist philosophy and modernist reactivations of vitalist and spiritualist discourses. On the one hand, his focus on cinema as movement and rhythm pushes the medium toward a form of "pure" cinema linked to music,[65] echoing the trajectory of Luciani's idea of cinema as art. Indeed, the broader French Impressionist cinema was conceived in terms not necessarily of pictorial Impressionism but rather in relation to musical Impressionism – so much so that Epstein's like-minded contemporary, Marcel L'Herbier, defined cinematic Impressionism as an instance of its musical precursors, focusing on how the image produces a rhythmic experience that is in essence musical.[66] So one tendency in this outlook on modernist cinema is to articulate a vision of cinema as a pure art, theorizing art as an autonomous sphere and abstracting from the project of realist representation.[67]

On the other hand, though, Epstein's *photogénie* also traces a different modernist trajectory, one that seeks not to abstract from representation as such but rather to cultivate an intuitive experience that expands the capacities not just of representation but of our ability to perceive the world as it truly is. Epstein's rejection of logic, conceptual identity, and both verbal and intellectual understanding puts him squarely in the midst of the modernist engagement with both vitalism and *Sprachkritik,* replicating a preoccupation central to writers as diverse as Pirandello and the Surrealists, Woolf and the Futurists, Eliot and Svevo. If there is a true reality we can intuitively experience that nevertheless remains ineffable, then the aim of not only modernist literature but also modernist film (according to this idealist stance) is to unlock a means of encountering that experience and reproducing or communicating it beyond the bounds of everyday logic.

This connection to the legacy of idealism allows me to make one final distinction here: neither documentary nor anti-realist in a straightforward sense, modernist cinematic idealism is better understood as an attempt to use the ideal to intervene in reality. Ian Aitken offers a similar account: for him, in contrast to the usual divisions between realism and Impressionist or modernist cinema, early cinematic "intuitionism" can be seen as part of a realist-impressionist continuum defined by outlooks derived from German idealism and a modern concern with representing and countering instrumental rationality and its disenchanting effect on modern life.[68] Despite differences in ideology and approach, avant-garde filmmakers from movements like Surrealism are thus in a kind of philosophical continuity with the first-wave Impressionist filmmakers (whom the Surrealists themselves often mocked, a point of divergence emphasized in accounts by other critics, like Dudley Andrew).[69] In Aitken's reading, then, *photogénie* functions as an auratic means of not just reproducing reality but producing an experience of perception that expands our insight into reality. My contention is that this is not specific to French Impressionist cinema but rather is a symptom of the degree to which Epstein and his colleagues are enmeshed in the conceptual outlook of modernist idealism more generally. Like Papini and Luciani, Epstein articulates a vision where cinematic technology, the mechanized reproduction of reality, becomes a means of seeing not just more but more truly *into* the vital rhythm and illusory solidity of human existence.

Seeing Vital Rhythm: An Irrational Ideal in the Cinema of Futurism and Pirandello

Cinematic idealism has multiple iterations that thus share certain traits, especially the understanding that cinema is a special form of vision that unlocks a vital undercurrent of experience, which the cinematic idealists claim is unavailable within the traditional limits of (material) human sight. The flickering light of the film projector uses the movement of energy to create and reshape our vision of the world and our relation to it. For those like Luciani and Epstein, this notion of cinema led to new speculations about how the medium could be developed into its pure artistic form, joining with music as a rhythmic expression of some vital truth constituting a Schopenhauerian irrational ideal.

With this vision of the cinema in mind, I turn now to two case studies in the Italian context of experimental modernist approaches to film that show how the legacy of this cinematic idealism unfolded both in theory and in practice: the early Futurist notion of an experimental cinema of vital rhythm (*cinepittura*), and Pirandello's notion of cinema as musical rhythm visualized (*cinemelografia*). I do not intend to imply a relationship of historical cause and effect – although there is no doubt that both the Futurists and Pirandello were well acquainted with Papini's work and that Luciani and Epstein both garnered significant attention in the period and were likely known to the modernist artists in question.[70] Such historical reception aside, my interest here is in how these theorists' insights into cinematic idealism help us identify a key trend in early film experimentation and in modernists' engagement with the medium: the cinema is thought of, in Schopenhauerian terms, as a special form of representation that reveals an inner core of life, its vital underbelly, in a fleeting moment of truth by penetrating beyond the limits of human reason. Cinematic representation thus gives us access to an irrational ideal that is conjured into presence, musically or rhythmically, rather than explicated or described. In this way, cinema performs a technological transformation of the nineteenth-century discourse on vitalist spiritualism that can be thought of as *realizing* the aesthetic impulse in Schopenhauerian idealism through artistic creation.

Futurist Film and Cinepittura: *Vital Rhythm, Violent Modernity*

The Futurists' experiments with cinema and writings about cinema have both seen significant scholarly attention in the last several decades.[71] As early as 1911 the Florentine Futurist brothers, Ginna (Arnaldo Ginanni Corradini, 1890–1982) and Corra (Bruno Ginanni Corradini, 1892–1976), were engaged in practical experiments, shaping a *cinepittura* that sought to animate coloured images with rhythmic movement in a kind of chromatic music.[72] Futurist film was thus conceived as an intermedial experiment from the start, drawing the pure movement of musical experience into the visual realm – a conjunction that clearly prefigured Luciani's later articulation of film as visual music rooted in rhythm. As Mario Verdone has argued, the Futurists' films were in fact based not in principles of visual representation but rather in the idea of rhythm itself.[73] The Futurists articulated this musical / rhythmic drive in their manifesto on "The Futurist Cinema" ("Il cinema futurista," 11 September 1916, signed by Marinetti, Corra, Settimelli, Ginna, Balla, and Chiti). There, they proclaimed the need to "**liberate film as an expressive medium** in order to make it the ideal instrument *of a new art*" that would create a "**polyexpressive symphony**."[74] This musical metaphor was followed by a list of new expressive elements to be exploited in film, ranging from images recorded from actual life to streaks of colour or poetic words, and "from chromatic and plastic music to the music of objects."[75] As they went on to list the features that would distinguish Futurist cinema, their fourth point was that "**cinematic musical researches** (dissonances, harmonies, symphonies of gestures, events, colors, etc.)" would contribute to freeing the medium from the dominance of prose theatre models that had stultified it.[76] Both in its earliest experimental forms and in its subsequent theorization, Futurist cinema would seek to free the visual language of the new medium from the logic of plot, enabling new kinds of associations and new access to "the inner and outer rhythm" of the life represented by cinema.[77]

In this respect, the Futurists' innovations clearly dovetailed with the larger discourse on musical rhythm that I have been tracing as an element of these modernist approaches to an intermedial cinema. While the Futurists' experiments prefigured the later theorizations of cinema by Luciani and Epstein, they coincided more or less exactly with a key articulation of this musical intermediality by the prominent artist-theorist who reshaped modernist visual art, Wassily Kandinsky (1866–1944).[78] Kandinsky's famous essay *On the Spiritual in Art* (*Über das Geistige in der Kunst,* 1911), which Thomas Harrison has aptly termed the "most philosophical manifesto for abstract art," argues against positivist materialism and enjoins artists to lead human spirituality toward the highest levels of advancement (he envisions a pyramid rooted in base materiality and developing upward toward spiritual expression).[79] In that essay, Kandinsky asserts that musicians, whose art is necessarily non-representative and immaterial, have typically been at the forefront of pushing the spirit toward this advancement against the forces of materiality.[80] Indeed, he contends that visual artists will naturally attempt to emulate music in this regard, replicating it in their own medium: "From this derives some of the modern search in painting for rhythm, mathematical abstract construction, colour repetition, and manner of setting colour into motion."[81] In precisely the same year, Luigi Russolo (1885–1947) was completing his painting *Musica* (1911) (figure 3), in which musical rhythm takes on visual form in static

Figure 3. Luigi Russolo, *Music*, 1911.

paint. Kandinsky's essay became a major theoretical statement and thus inspired a host of other modernist artists of various movements, spanning all the way to Georgia O'Keeffe (1887–1986) in the United States, whose *Blue and Green Music* (1921) took on the same challenge a decade later with an even higher degree of formal abstraction. These artists were attempting to merge painting with musical rhythm in order to express an inner spirituality rather than a material exteriority. That quest dovetailed with the experimentations of Ginna and Corra, who went the next step and sought a moving depiction of musical rhythm in colour and shape through their *cinepittura*.

But the musical rhythm of an experimental cinema is more than just a repetition of this broader discourse on the spiritual potential of music and its intermedial possibilities; it also fits into a broader pattern that encompasses not only the vitalism motivating Futurist art and thought from the very start of the movement but also a broader philosophy linking that vitality to the principle of rhythm. That philosophy would be articulated more fully a few years later by Gino Gori (1876–1952), whose *Aesthetic Studies of the Irrational* (*Studi di estetica dell'irrazionale*, 1921) was published by Bragaglia's press. In that work, Gori argues for a historical account in which irrationality has emerged as the primary principle of modern thought, tracing its development from Kant through Hegel and Schopenhauer, whose philosophy resonates throughout modern art, and finally arriving at Nietzsche, whom he figures as the beating heart of this modern outlook.[82] Gori then examines how art embodies this irrational principle, focusing on the way in which vital rhythm has become the essence of aesthetic structure and expression. The rhythmic vibration of a work of art is what allows it to reveal something true,[83] and in this way the work of art reverberates (physiologically) with the principle of harmonic rhythm that structures the universe down to its atomic particles.[84] Against a materialist picture of reality he thus posits what he takes to be a scientific understanding of the spiritual-energetic forces that shape our world;[85] it is these forces that Gori sees as the true vital core of artistic expression, its rhythmic vitality allowing art to connect man with the whole.[86]

What Gori articulates as an aesthetic trajectory leading toward irrationality and its vital rhythm is thus a broad-strokes, idealist articulation of the same guiding principles that the Futurists placed at the heart of their own experiments with cinema. Their vitalism was likewise rooted in an irrational ideal, and it likewise entailed spiritualizing matter, or rather unleashing the spirit within the material world that had been constrained there, as I argued in chapter 4 of this book. And while Gori's work was written in the wake of the Futurist intervention, a similar world view preceded it in Papini's early theorization of cinema, which operated in terms of the same irrationalist aesthetic outlook. But where this irrationalism could seem to entail a pessimistic view of humanity's place in the world – one like the existential stance in Papini's zoomed-out thought experiment where human life is but a flickering illusion against the black backdrop of the cosmos, entertainment for a god viewing from beyond – these thinkers likewise moved against the ascetic conclusions that occupied Schopenhauer in his metaphysics and ethics. Instead, the Futurists embarked on a project of what Christine Poggi has aptly termed "artificial optimism."[87] While they may not have made recourse, like Gori, to a language of unity in which rhythm connects man to the whole, in the end their efforts revolved around a similar axis: modernity has furnished us, through processes of biological and cultural evolution, a new, mechanized reality. Futurism employed a frenetic language of mechanical energy to connect the beating pulse of the human body to the steel rhythm of the new era. Cinema, the first moving art entirely mediated by a mechanical lens, was a natural point of juncture, ready to capture and create that rhythm in order to reshape human sensation and sensibility.

Pirandello's Cinemelografia: *Music Visualized*

Film was a much more vexed question for Pirandello than it was for the Futurists. He was a vociferous critic of cinema in many respects, a defender of the terrain of theatre in the face-off between the two sister arts, proclaiming that "both classical theater and the music hall can rest easy in the certainty that they will not be abolished for one simple reason. Theater is not trying to become cinema; cinema is trying to become theater."[88] The Futurists, in contrast, wanted theatre to evolve into cinema, to cast off the limitations of its prose tradition.[89] In this regard, Pirandello's stance might seem more traditional and anti-modern (passéist, as the Futurists would call it), with the perspective in his essays aligning with the way his film novel, *Shoot!*, took a critical stance on the life-sucking "black spider" that devoured actors and turned them into mere images on celluloid. Yet Pirandello was deeply engaged with the cinema: he eagerly allowed his works to be adapted, including by the French Impressionist filmmaker Marcel L'Herbier, who created a fascinating film version of the novel *Il fu Mattia Pascal* (1904) titled *Feu Mathias Pascal* (1925);[90] Pirandello also wrote his own screenplays and scenarios for possible films; and he had an almost obsessive interest in adapting his most famous play, *Six Characters in Search of an Author*, into a film – he wrote three separate treatments or scenarios for the adaptation from the mid-1920s until his death in 1936, at which point he had arranged but not yet signed a contract with MGM. While that adaptation was never realized, it is a testament to the importance Pirandello placed on being part of the new industry.[91] His criticism of film is thus complicated by his simultaneous engagement with it.[92]

In fact, Pirandello aligned in many ways with the avant-garde filmmakers and theorists of the first decades of cinema's growth and transformation. Like the French Impressionists or Luciani, Pirandello wanted to see cinema move away from the narrative arts (literature and theatre) and develop into its own, pure form. The epitome of this, he argued, would be a cinema of sound, what he termed *cinemelografia* – not a score to a narrative representation, but a film in which the music *is* the content represented in colour, shape, and visual form.

> Thus, pure music is pure vision: two paramount aesthetic senses of sight and hearing united in one sole pleasure. The eyes see, the ears hear, and the heart senses all the beauty and variety of feeling expressed by the sounds and represented in the images that such feelings arouse. They stir the subconscious with its inconceivable pictures, sometimes as terrible as those in nightmares, or as mysterious and changeable as those in dreams; images can come in vertiginous succession, or softly and restfully in time to the music. The name for this true revolution is Cinemelography – a visible language of all kinds of music.[93]

Pirandello's concept of a cinema that visualizes the movement of sound is profoundly intermedial and speaks to the important visuality of his outlook on art – his theory of humour ("umorismo") as well as his practical production.[94] In this regard, his stance seems to echo Luciani's quite closely: for both, the specificity of cinema is its ability to visualize pure movement, the capacity that was previously seen as unique to music in Schopenhauer's prominent assessment of the hierarchy of arts.[95]

For Schopenhauer, music is the highest form of art because it abstracts from the illusory side of our everyday life (the kinds of things represented by narrative plots and particular characters with verisimilar qualities): music moves in the way will does, manifesting its true nature without however giving it a concrete or fixed form.[96] It is the way music abstracts from concrete content that appealed to the Futurists and to Pirandello as well. This highlights what Papini's article had already underscored by pairing a focus on cinema's technologies of representation with the idealist stance that views reality as a surface illusion covering over a true, hidden, inner core of life. That core, irrational and unintelligible to the conceptual language of representation, is a vital movement or surge – what Schopenhauer called will, what the Futurists saw in terms of rhythm and movement (in parallel to thinkers like Gori), and what Pirandello understood as a form of spiritual life seeking form in representation.[97] The effort to push cinema toward a different, "pure" form of the medium thus coincided with the irrational idealist impulse to uncover the true essence of life that exceeds the bounds of rational comprehension and intellectual analysis.

That vitalist philosophical idealism aligned in turn with the ways in which these early theories of cinema made recourse to a language of spirit and spiritualism to articulate how the new technological medium could bridge the gap separating material from ideal reality. In Pirandello's treatments for a film adaptation of *Six Characters*, representing the creative process becomes central to the project. In his *Film-Novelle: Sechs Personen suchen einen Autor*, written with Adolf Lantz, Pirandello reimagines the story, not only changing the characters and plot but also changing the focus of the play's meta-representation. [98] Now, in scenes that draw from Gothic visual tropes, Pirandello seeks to make visible the ghostly process of artistic creation itself, the emergence of new realities from a realm of imagination that exists independently, it seems, beyond the confines of the artist's mind. As Thomas Harrison has argued, for Pirandello (and, I would say, for modernist idealism more generally), knowledge of life becomes a kind of trap, what his novel *The Late Mattia Pascal* figures in the metaphor of a puppet show acting out the tragedy *Orestes*; the only solution to this trap is to become self-reflectively aware of it, not thus taking control of the strings but rather understanding how the strings are pulled.[99] This impulse toward a meta-representational self-reflection is thought through in his earlier novel, and now it takes a next step into the visual realm via a filmic meditation on the process of artistic creation.

In the *Film-Novelle*, the emergence of the characters is meant to be achieved by combining the Gothic tropes of ghosts with new special effects that align with techniques emphasized by French Impressionist filmmakers to visualize spirits.[100] These techniques are a part of the legacy that Papini had already noted in cinema's debt to fake spirit photographs, and they serve as one small example of a much larger phenomenon. If cinema's *photogénie* allows it to look into the world differently, seeing what the eye cannot, then perhaps the same special vision functions in the place of Schopenhauer's intuition of will. The technical apparatus becomes the means to bridge two sides of reality, one accessible to our senses and rational faculties, the other escaping both.[101] At the same time, that reality is bridged in and through meta-representation: Pirandello's play about the failure to make a play has become a film that envisions both an author creating a story and the creative process of the artistic imagination itself.

What my reading ultimately suggests, then, is that Papini's view of cinematic idealism reveals a fundamental outlook shared by modernist experimenters who sought to harness the technological capacities of the new medium to enact or respond to a philosophical problem. That problem has both an existential and a metaphysical side, and while different theorists and practitioners may have emphasized those sides to differing degrees, there is a common core beneath them. Turning back to the ideas of pure cinema as a fusion of vision and music, then, we can redescribe that project in similarly "spiritual" terms: if music manifests the blind movement of life's hidden reality, then the visualization of music is something like an attempt to point representation's focus at the moment of transition between ineffable vitality (outside the realm of conceptual intelligibility) and concrete materiality in the actual world. This is why, in the end, Schopenhauer admits that he cannot provide a rational argument for his understanding of music's power:

> I recognize, however, that it is essentially impossible to demonstrate this explanation, for it assumes and establishes a relation of music as a representation to that which of its essence can never be representation, and claims to regard music as the copy of an original that can itself never be directly represented. Therefore, I can do no more than state here at the end of this third book, devoted mainly to a consideration of the arts, this explanation of the wonderful art of tones which is sufficient for me. I must leave the acceptance or denial of my view to the effect that both music and the whole thought communicated in this work have on each reader.[102]

It is likewise in this ineffable sense that the rhythmic music of an experimental cinema can serve as a bridge between the ideal and the real. Rather than *saying* something that exceeds the bounds of the sayable, it is left to modernist techniques of meta-representation to *show* that artistic truth, displaying a glimpse of the ineffable nature of imaginative creation itself.

Cinematic Idealism Repurposing Mechanization: A Surreal Coda

Modernist cinematic idealism conceived film as a means of capturing aspects of reality that exceed our normal perception of it, of representing beyond the usual limits of representation. This belief drove an avant-garde approach to the new medium both in its theorization and in its practical application, thus marking the confluence of at least three broad discourses that were all central to the constitution of modernism: idealist philosophy, vitalism, and spiritualism. Engaging a decadent elevation of aesthetic sensation – as an opium for the imagination – and Gothic fantasy, it also committed itself to reshaping modernity through cultural production. In the midst of this overdetermined confluence, the mechanical lens was transfigured from a reductively dehumanizing force into one that liberated our sensibilities, expanded our imagination, and (re)enchanted our world.

That modernist impulse to revitalize the world using precisely those tools that risked deadening it connected cineastes from across Europe and from varying, and often conflicting, aesthetic and ideological movements or frameworks. A telling instance of these nuanced connections was that of the Surrealist stance on cinema. This example thus serves as a fitting conclusion to my project here, for it highlights how even those artists who criticized the impulses of avant-garde art film toward a synesthetic fusion of pure music and vision nevertheless orbited the same ideal star and thus constellated a vitalist horizon of spiritual renewal for modern materiality.

The Surrealists were in many respects opposed to the French Impressionist approach to art cinema, seeing it as exceedingly interested in creating a "pure" cinema that abstracted in a problematic way.[103] For example, Salvador Dalí (1904–1989), responding to his disagreements with Luis Buñuel (1900–1983) over their collaboration on the film *L'Âge d'Or* (1930), decried the way in which avant-garde cinema "deliberately takes the absurd and stupid path of abstraction" that relies on "a cumbersome visual rhetoric of an almost exclusively musical nature culminating in the rhythmic utilization of close-ups" and other techniques.[104] Dalí's assessment resonates with the categories I have deployed here to understand avant-garde art film, but while he rejects that approach to the pure or ideal cinema he nonetheless emphasizes another aspect that aligns with an idealist outlook, the typical Surrealist drive to uncover the "real functioning of thought."[105] As André Breton (1896–1966) had written in the first "Manifesto of Surrealism" (*Manifeste du surréalisme*, 1924), Surrealist techniques like automatic writing aim to produce something as close as possible to "spoken thought," giving us access to "the true thought in search of itself" in place of the usual exterior logic of representation.[106] In his reflection on cinema, Dalí was asserting that avant-garde art film had become its own external language – not a true revelation of inner thought's workings but a codified visual language of signs that were thus in some important way inauthentic and merely exterior.

Yet despite this rejection of Impressionist cinema and its culture of avant-garde narrative film, the Surrealist stance on the medium resonates deeply with the core animating ideals of modernist cinematic idealism: precisely idealist philosophy, vitalism, and spiritualism. One need only look to the Surrealist impulse to "spiritualize" film as one of their "magical" techniques for representing an invisible/intangible/unrepresentable existence beneath or beyond our quotidian world.[107] The surreal is in principle unrepresentable or ineffable – something that is emphasized repeatedly throughout the manifestos and perhaps best captured by the impossible, ghostly image that haunted Breton, the "soluble fish" (which was the name of another manifesto/document published in 1924).[108] Surrealism *must* be magic precisely because it must conjure the presence of that which cannot be present for us – it must summon the soluble fish, using the imagination as an intermediary for channelling the impossible/invisible ideal into actual reality, where it takes on material form not in itself (there is no actual soluble fish, though imagination conjures one) but through its effects, which are operations of human consciousness. The idea here is strikingly parallel to Epstein's articulation of the operation of imagination through "emotion-things" in film, and to Pirandello's desire to represent the process of representation as a ghostly creation in his project for *Six Characters*. We respond to the imagined soluble fish, even though no such entity exists as a part of the actual, material world. The imagined entity exists not as a "state of affairs" but through the reality of its effects.

This helps us understand why so many of the Surrealist writings on cinema emphasize aspects of magic and impossibility – what Albert Valentin ("Introduction to Black-and-White Magic," 1927) refers to as "black-and-white magic" – describing what Benjamin would theorize as aura and comparing the cinema to a church, a space where an aesthetically mediated deception humbles us.[109] Antonin Artaud ("Sorcery and Cinema," ca 1928) goes further, not criticizing cinematic magic but rather envisioning cinema as the solution to the modern crisis of representation, where artistic forms have become spent and are in need of revival. His analysis is replete with the language of vitalism as well as spiritualist notions, which he marshals to argue that cinema restores life to objects through their movement, resulting in an intoxicating effect in the viewer's brain that is both physical and spiritual.[110] Cinema thus "reveals a whole occult life, one with which it puts us directly in contact" allowing "insensate substance" to acquire form, revealing the inner workings of consciousness and the dream.[111] Cinema unveils something, it reveals the vital kernel of life that surface appearances obscure – it gives us access to the occult through a spiritual process that operates via imagination and thus ushers the ideal into the real.

The Surrealist stance on cinema, in other words, replicated all the key facets of what we have seen in Pirandello and in the Futurists. In Surrealist films, we can see this in practice. At base, the illogic of something like Buñuel's *Un Chien andalou* (1929) represents the functioning of the unconscious mind – not its contents, but its movement, its rhythm, the way it makes itself known through interventions in the real world. We can thus say that it represents the process of representation in the idealist sense intended by Schopenhauer, for whom music was the highest art because through it we gain intuitive access to the surge of will, which is precisely the movement that results in what we perceive through representation as forms.

This continuity explains how despite apparent divergences and disagreements, the broader constellation of modernist approaches to the cinema bespoke a fundamentally shared world view – not at the level of ideological particularities (it is enough to think of the broad ideological divergence between Futurism's fascist-aligned politics of war and Dada or Surrealist rejections of both) but rather at the level of what we might term a shared philosophical project for modern representation.

Thinking of that continuity also helps us reassess the status of the technological apparatus of film. Where Pirandello's *Shoot!* seems to decry the mechanized death of humanity – modernity's all-consuming, dehumanizing impulse – what actually emerges from avant-garde theories of film and engagement with film is a way of reversing that dynamic. The inhuman element of the cinematic apparatus becomes an opportunity, a tool for revealing something that human faculties do not see. Surrealism's invisible ray, Epstein's *photogénie*, and Pirandello's transfiguring *cinemelografia* operate on the same wavelength, using the mechanical to revitalize and respiritualize the modern world.

The fleeting glance of the cinematic instant can provide a sudden revelation of the world as it really is – an existential metaphor for the relative lack of substance in human reality, to return to Papini's image, or a penetrating experience of an inner rhythm that goes beyond mere representation to reveal the vibrating vitality of life itself. In either case, it operates at an epiphanic threshold, as if by magic, connecting immanent materiality to something that transcends or exceeds it. Existence, cinematic idealism insists, is elsewhere.

Conclusion: Overdetermined Idealist Legacies

But do you not see that this is the greatest title of praise that you can give to our century: this unanimity of doctrine hidden under the bark of so many differences, professed by philosophers, represented in art, seeping into science, entering into history, attested by martyrdom, such that it has become in some sense the religion, faith, character, and one might even say the soul of our time?

– Francesco De Sanctis, "Schopenhauer and Leopardi: A Dialogue between A and D."[1]

The optimistic ideal of revolution animated not only nineteenth-century struggles to forge a new Italy but also a host of literary, artistic, and philosophical projects that took shape across the nineteenth and twentieth centuries – and not only in Italy. Such projects saw themselves as fundamentally opposed to a corrosive force that had weighed down the possibilities of modern progress, the power of materialism. Thus one of the hallmarks of not just modern thought but modern life – from capitalist materialism to scientific materialism – became an essential element spurring efforts to re-form modernity, to cast it in a different shape or make it from a different mould. What De Sanctis called the religion, faith, character, and soul of modernity, then, was a spiritual core that underlay seeming disparities as it sought renewal. It was the spirit of idealism.

This book has encompassed a relatively wide range of thinkers, writers, and artists from across more than a century and traversing national and linguistic borders, gathering them together under the common heading of modernist idealism despite what might appear to be significant differences in formal technique, political and ideological alignment, and even (at times) historical circumstances. Likewise, it has identified two major "types" (we might say characters, to draw on the language of both Schopenhauer and the *commedia dell'arte* tradition) within the constellation of modernist idealism: on the one hand, a rational, optimistic notion of the ideal unfolding into and through actual reality, structured as a progressive historical process; on the other, an irrational, pessimistic vision of an ideal beyond the material world that manifests itself into actuality, taking on forms that represent moments or glimpses of some surging process of endless becoming. To typify that first outlook I have used the figure of Hegel, and for the second, Schopenhauer – not because they are the only thinkers or even the "most important" ones (perhaps just a judgment of taste) to articulate those ideas, but rather because they crystallize major traits of the key outlooks, we might even say dispositions, of these battling, overlapping stances in modernist idealism. As should now be clear, while Hegel and Schopenhauer saw themselves in stark opposition, the legacies of their thought are inescapably intertwined. Modernist idealism is not a coherent philosophical argument but rather an ambivalent amalgamation – in this sense, not totally dissimilar to D'Annunzio's eclectic collection of art and objects decorating (perhaps constituting) the museum-mausoleum-theatre-house that he erected in honour of his own self-mythologization during the final years of his life, the Vittoriale degli Italiani on the shores of Lake Garda.[2] Somewhere between a bedroom shrine to St Francis and a recovered First World War fighting ship built into the hillside overlooking his gardens, modernism's multiple and conflicting ideals take shape.

While I have used two post-Kantian idealist philosophers to characterize the intellectual strands of modernist idealism, the instantiation of their outlooks in artistic production draws together a host of forces that are idealist in a much broader sense. Thus while chapters 1 and 2 of this book trace the reception of Hegel's and Schopenhauer's thought in modern Italy to situate the intellectual history of modernist idealism, the subsequent chapters complicate any effort at a neat delineation, perhaps against the will of their various philosophical interpreters, from De Sanctis to Croce and beyond. The complexity of this overdetermined idealism is evident in the decadent-romantic elevation of art and interest in epiphany as a form of aesthetic–religious–philosophical insight (chapter 3), which draws explicitly on Schopenhauer to transfigure modern life into an aesthetic spectacle that is thereby freed from the grinding logic of (capitalist) materialism. It likewise emerges in the multifaceted notions of vitalism that were developed and redeployed by avant-garde artists like the Futurists, whose political nationalism and activism coexisted with irrational aesthetic impulses that transformed everything from art to science (chapter 4). So too is it an idealist stance that animates the modernist fascination with spiritualism and magic, from occult and esoteric traditions to theories that view the creative act itself as a mediumistic channelling of something immaterial into the realm of actuality, informing modernist interest in repurposing genres and in meta-representation (chapter 5). And parts of each of these views took on a new, mechanized life in the era of the moving picture, when the cinema became both a figure representing and an experiment enacting idealist efforts to reshape modernity and recapture a lost sense of authentic fullness (chapter 6). While my engagement here has focused on the Italian reception of German thought, contextualizing it in terms of European discourses on key modernist concerns including decadence, avant-gardism, vitalism, spiritualism, and the cinema, what I ultimately propose is a case study for a concept that can bear fruit in our consideration of modernism around the globe.

Each stop in the itinerary of my case study has revealed a different sense in which modernism is shot through with idealist impulses, not as a single coherent philosophical outlook but rather in an ambivalent combination of views that highlight an irrepressible pressure to reshape the forms of modern life – by force, if necessary. The renovation of modernity coincides with a rejection of traditional forms of representation, of course; but more than that, and going beyond any stylistic elements of experimentalism, it entails a fundamental hybridity that brings together literature, the arts, and philosophy. In this respect, again, modernism follows the model of Schopenhauer's aesthetic thought, which presents its philosophical system not as a logical argument but rather as a descriptive depiction that either will or will not inspire its reader. When a writer like Pirandello conceives of imagination as an intermediary realm where "thought-forms" or "emotion-things" emerge into being, what he is recognizing is precisely the power of aesthetic form to usher the immaterial and incorporeal ideal into actuality. Like ghosts that do not exist as actual entities in the material world, ideas nevertheless manifest themselves and become real as a result of their impact on us. They shape and reshape human actors, and as such they inform historical change in society and the broader world. This is the meaning of the vitalist picture of an inner kernel of life that manifests itself in the forms of our everyday reality, and it colours the aspirations of a subset of artistic creators who seek not just to interrogate and critique modernity but to reshape or reanimate it through the power of their words, their images, and their ideas. Where a materialist approach to history would scoff at such ambitions, perhaps offering a political critique or perhaps simply dismissing the pretension out of hand, modernist idealism replies not with a propositional claim but with a demonstration.

No one, after all, has ever really proven the existence of the soul. And these writers, thinkers, artists, and political agitators – so often defined by their scepticism, their relativism, their atheism, their anarchism ... – are counterintuitively people of great faith.

What is left to us, then, is to assess what that faith has achieved; and the results are as ambivalent as their causes. Beautiful, powerful, moving, complex, compelling, disastrous. Just as the decadent artist might seek to transfigure the brute ugliness of modern life into a refined spectacle for the senses, so too might aesthetic beauty usher in its own terrors. Yet this coincidence of modernist idealism and modernist nationalism does not imply, I think, an irredeemable pairing of aestheticization and fascist totalitarianism. It rather speaks to the confluence of forces that was always underneath that overdetermined impulse toward aesthetic action in the first place. It is this, then, that constitutes the double sense in which the legacies of modernist idealism are fundamentally ambivalent.

Appendix. Schopenhauer and Leopardi: A Dialogue between A and D

FRANCESCO DE SANCTIS
TRANSLATED BY MICHAEL J. SUBIALKA

Translator's Note

De Sanctis' dialogue, "Schopenhauer e Leopardi. Dialogo tra A e D," is the first work in Italian to offer any significant engagement with Schopenhauer's thought; in fact, published in the pages of the Turin-based review of philosophy, literature, science, and the arts, the *Rivista contemporanea* (vol. 15, no. 61, December 1858: 369–408), De Sanctis's long essay is among the earliest significant treatments of Schopenhauer outside of Germany.[1] Like many of Schopenhauer's earliest critics, De Sanctis is nervous especially about the political conservatism of Schopenhauer's outlook and the apparently disengaged affect that seems to result from his philosophical pessimism. This criticism is heightened by De Sanctis's involvement in the revolutionary politics of Italian liberalism, which had experienced a recent defeat after the revolts of 1848, which led to De Sanctis's exile in Switzerland during the time he wrote this dialogue. All the same, he gives a thorough and largely accurate reconstruction of Schopenhauer's thought. I offer a close analysis of the dialogue and its use of Leopardi to critique Schopenhauer in chapter 2 of this book. Here, I want to note only a few important points about its formal qualities and the special challenges that they have posed for translation.

The dialogue is written in a loosely colloquial, literary form, with a strong sense of tongue-in-cheek irony throughout. Lines are full of pithy jokes, jabs, and occasional plays on words, all of which can of course be difficult to render in translation. I have opted to maintain the tone where possible, which has sometimes required straying from literal meaning; I have, however, been careful to balance that effort to maintain the tone with attention to the specificities of De Sanctis's language and use of terms, which is not casual but rather engages directly with the language and ideas from Schopenhauer's works. Playing with words like "idea," "will" (and its variations – "desire," "want," and so on, many of which can be rendered in Italian with the same verb, "volere," or its nominal or adjectival forms), De Sanctis achieves some of his comic effect simply by redeploying Schopenhauer's philosophical language in a way that is consistent with Schopenhauer's overall world view while also making light of it. Some of these games cannot be captured in English, and a choice has had to be made between rendering the conceptual meaning and rendering its ironic wordplay. I have added notes in a few places to signal such moments where a choice has been inevitable.

One final note on the notes: De Sanctis sprinkled his dialogue with brief parenthetical references to show where in Schopenhauer's corpus he was finding specific ideas and, in some cases, the sources for his quotations or paraphrases. He also added a few short footnotes of his own. I have preserved all of De Sanctis's notes and citations – all of which, however, appear in endnotes here. To distinguish these from the translator's notes that I have added, all of my own interventions in the endnotes are contained in square brackets. I have left citations as De Sanctis wrote them, pointing to the editions he used to compose his study; the exception comes in those citations that are of Leopardi's works, where De Sanctis has not indicated the edition to which he is referring. I have thus added updated bibliographical references to his citations from Leopardi. In some places, and without any seeming consistency, De Sanctis renders parts of a title into Italian to make them accessible for his audience, while leaving the rest in German. In those instances I have translated any segments that he himself translated, rendering his Italian versions of German titles in English. The full bibliographic information is then noted in brackets.

An ironic, jocular, multilingual text "translating" and domesticating Schopenhauer's foreign philosophy for his Italian audience, "Schopenhauer and Leopardi" is a unique testament to the ways in which philosophy and literature coincide in the moment of Schopenhauer's rising international fame. Of course, De Sanctis was not only a literary critic but also a wide-ranging "man of letters" whose life and work spanned literary, philosophical, and political concerns; it is thus little surprise that his dialogue would move so adeptly among all three. The success of that pairing can perhaps also be gauged by the response of one philosopher in particular: Schopenhauer was excited to read De Sanctis's essay and see himself compared to the great Italian poet, whom he thought of as sharing a kind of spiritual brotherhood.[2] That De Sanctis's dialogue has maintained its notoriety for more than a century and a half is further testament to the resonance of these combinations today. It is time that this essay, which has been reprinted for decades and decades in Italy, was published for an English-reading audience, as well.

Schopenhauer and Leopardi: A Dialogue between A and D[3]

D. All the way to Zurich?

A. Why not? One travels to gather ideas.

D. Well then at this point you must have enough of them to fill your pockets.

A. You mean my notebooks. Here's one that's still entirely blank. You can help me fill it up. What are these books?

D. Arthur Schopenhauer.

A. Who is that?

D. The philosopher of the future. In Germany there are great men of the present and great men of the future, the misunderstood. Schopenhauer is one of the latter.

A. I've never heard his name.

D. Your grandchildren will have. Truth walks with a limp, but in the end it gets there.

A. And you're studying all this stuff?

D. I have been for three months, my friend. I promised an article to the *Rivista Contemporanea*.

A. You'd study three months for an article? You are too simple. The more you study an author the more you find yourself in the dark. As if it were something solid … A philosophical treatise?

D. Do you scorn philosophy?

A. I too once felt that itch. I studied philosophy, poetry, history. I thought that to be Plato all you had to do was learn him by heart. I wrote hymns, short stories, dissertations. Many times, I applauded myself. I thought that I would become a Cantù or at least a Prati.[4] But one fine day when I was huffing and puffing to demonstrate the Idea, that ugly mug Campagna, who no one here has heard of, gave me a counter-demonstration.[5] And when I saw – what a miserable sight! – the beard that I had cultivated with such care lying on the ground, it seemed that together with my hairs all of my ideas had been dispersed, one by one. What miraculous scissors were those that converted me. I had been a boy; I became a man. I no longer believe in philosophy, and I have become an astronomer. De Gasparis got it right: a gentleman, professor, and plenty of money, too.[6] Let's talk about the stars and leave the earth be. Philosophy leads a gentleman straight to the noose.

D. That's why children believe in philosophy.

A. Children and madmen. The way that today we laugh at the puerile explanations ancient philosophers gave of the world, those who come after us will laugh at all the ruckus that is made about the Idea. Theology and philosophy are destined to disappear in the face of the progress of the natural sciences, just as astrology, natural magic, etc., all disappeared. The more that observation advances, the more the circle of speculation constricts. Many things used to belong to the sphere of theology and philosophy that now belong to physics, chemistry, astronomy, and mathematics. Once the sun was Apollo and was part of mythology; then with Pythagoras it entered into the realm of philosophy and became a musician and dancer. A good telescope put an end to all that idiocy. When I don't know something, rather than daydreaming and racking my brain, instead of explaining a mystery with other mysteries that are even more obscure, whether they be theological or philosophical, I simply say: "I don't know." If all the time that had been wasted imagining these things had instead been used to cultivate the natural sciences, we would be further ahead. But you've become pensive.

D. While this century began with so much faith, so much fervour, we've only traversed the half of it and yet most people now think the way you do.

A. A sign that we're making sense. I can't help but laugh when I think about all those great professors with their systems of thought. Two good cannon shots were enough to make their ideas flee. Who do you expect to believe in them anymore? As for myself, when I mention the Idea, I seem to see Campagna with his scissors. It was a revolution of professors and scholars. Who do you expect to believe in professors anymore? And consider this: the ideas abandoned us and put themselves in the service of the victors, who make this one or that one pop back out, as it suits them. War is waged against Russia (1853–56), and out pops "civilization." There is a coup d'état (1851), and "progress" covers the coup up with its shadow. Emigrants are hunted down, and here comes "order" to say hello. We are puppets made to dance to another's tune and – just look at the irony! – in the name of the ideas that we ourselves proposed and defended. What value can these ideas have anymore, when once they were so beautiful and now they have turned into old procuresses?

D. Arthur Schopenhauer is just your sort of thing.

A. Still with this Arthur Schopenhauer! I already told you in what account I hold philosophers and philosophies. The Idea no longer does it for me.

D. But Schopenhauer is the enemy of the Idea.

A. A philosophy without the Idea? That sounds impossible to me. I'm beginning to appreciate Schopenhauer.

D. There's more: he's in agreement with you on many things. According to him, philosophy should not concern itself with that which is beyond experience, like what the world is, where it comes from, where it's heading, etc. His subject isn't the *what*, but the *how*: only that is knowable and observable.

A. Well done, Saint Thomas. To see and touch. We're already fully in the realm of natural history. But God? With which telescope will he observe God?

D. God goes the way of all things that are beyond experience. Schopenhauer says: "Let's discuss the things of which we can have experience and leave the rest in peace, since it's a waste of time." Proudhon is of the same mind.

A. Wonderful. That way we can be at peace with the priests. After a great deal of boasting, philosophy beats its retreat. What the world is, where it comes from, where it's heading – the priests will tell us all that. The day that the philosophers sign their names to this act of abdication would give cause for much celebration in Rome. Well enough. Let's leave father Curci to explain the Catechism to us, and we can busy ourselves with physics, chemistry, and astronomy, which are less risky.[7] I'm starting to like Schopenhauer.

D. Since I have to write this article, and we have to chat about something, I want to explain Schopenhauer's system to you.

A. My friend, you are tempting me. In the end it is still a philosophy. And I want to suggest an observation to you. All of these modern philosophers quarrel, they make a show of arms, but in substance they agree about certain maxims that stink of the gallows. Robespierre, or whoever else, discovered the secret with his goddess Reason. They made reason into a sort of governor: reason governs the world. This is the bad seed from which sprout the theory of progress, the divinized world, the triumph of the Idea, Doctor Pangloss's everything is the best,[8] the inviolability and dignity of humanity, freedom, and similar such frights. And to think that I believed in all this, and I was practically about to risk my hide. I forgot the theory of sacrifice and how the individual must precisely let himself be killed for the greater glory and prosperity of the species. Squeeze and squeeze and then tell me that this isn't the juice of all modern philosophies. There are those who say it cheekily, those who advance various temperaments, those who come out with the possible being; those with the creator being, those with the logical being, those with intuition, those with demonstration, those with the dialectic; one is an ontologist, the other a psychologist; some are realists, some are idealists ... my dear philosophers, you can go so far as to glare at each other menacingly, but you won't fool me: you're all of the same ilk.

D. But do you not see that this is the greatest title of praise that you can give to our century: this unanimity of doctrine hidden under the bark of so many differences, professed by philosophers, represented in art, seeping into science, entering into history, attested by martyrdom, such that it has become in some sense the religion, faith, character, and one might even say the soul of our time? Those who come after us will not be able to deny their admiration to a century that professed such a noble philosophy, vivifying it with faith and sealing it with blood. It is difficult to find two generations of men so heroic, industrious, and faithful as the generations of '89 and '30.

A. I see that the rivers of '48 have not been drained from your head. You must have been in need of a pair of scissors.

D. On the contrary, I owe this service to the Lieutenant Duke of San Vito, one of the most well-educated and courteous lieutenants and dukes in the kingdom.[9]

A. I don't believe that lieutenants and dukes are required to be courteous and well-educated. I see that you have no hope of recovery. And of course you ought to have understood from your own example that what governs the world isn't reason but rather the Duke of San Vito. Reason, or the idea, as she's called, is a wonderful governess.[10] She appears like a comet, and at the first sign of a beating, she beats it, leaving her loyal subjects in a tough spot. They say that these beatings are "accidents;" whatever they don't know how to explain by means of the Idea they call an accident, and the accident has no reason to exist, it's like it never happened. Let's take consolation, then: the hangings, the imprisonments, the blows, and the haircuts didn't exist, or to put it better, they did exist, but they didn't have to exist. Damn these philosophers![11] Our descendants, since you're talking to me about descendants, will have to heave a great laugh when they think that for the better part of a century people believed in the identity of thought and being, which gave rise to all of these lovely doctrines. As if all the rubbish in my head must exist because I think it, and as if all the things that happen won't exist if I don't think them, won't have the right to exist, and are accidents. But when has such an absurdity ever before been uttered? You can make ideas jump around like bullets here and there as you wish, because they don't have cannons and cannot defend themselves and they contain one another such that it's enough to take out one of them and all the others will follow as in a procession. Philosophical systems seem to be like castles made of pebbles that children build, take apart, and rebuild in a thousand different ways. And up to this point there's nothing wrong because, given that we've got a brain and there's no way of getting rid of it, it's a good thing for it to take up this pastime. But the joke becomes serious when one conflates ideas with things and places his hands on those things in the hopes of repeating that game. Because things do have cannons, and they don't just allow themselves to be built or made. If you persist in this regard, you'll leave with a split head. So long as you're just putting things on paper, it's doable, given that each thing presents itself to you in various aspects, and you can pull it to the right or the left and place it under whichever idea you like. For this reason facts are like the poor boys who ended up on Procuste's bed, mangled and twisted: read the philosophers and you'll find the same fact under the most disparate ideas, according to the requirements of each system. And wherever it doesn't fit in, it's an accident. It's wonderful to write all that, but when you want to come to the facts.... It is so clear, and I can't understand why no man of resolution and good sense has ever said so. This has been an age of illusion, or rather of general imbecility.

D. But there has been such a man of resolution and good judgment, and he's Arthur Schopenhauer. You seem surprised? Do you think Arthur was just born yesterday? Arthur was born in 1788, and he published his principal work – these two volumes here – in 1819 in Leipzig.[12] And this work was like Cassandra's prophecy. At that time Fichte, Schelling, and Hegel ruled the scene; the world was practically hypnotized; no one paid him any attention at all. Arthur, heavy with indignation, squared his shoulders, and with a sardonic laugh he put on the airs of a merchant and banker and said: "Just wait and you'll see."

A. And we've seen some good ones. If I had had his judgment, by now I too would have a full purse. How much time I wasted on Schelling and Hegel, on Gioberti and Rosmini, on Leroux, Lamennais, and Cousin! And how I went on imagining things! How simple it seemed to me to flip the world on its head using the idea as a stick! I wish I were twenty years younger with the judgment I have today. If only the young could see the future!

D. But Arthur, who was still young, saw it very clearly and, scorning his contemporaries' scorn, he made his appeal to the future. And this future, after so many disillusionments, seems finally to have arrived, if I can judge based on you and many others who think the same way.

A. It is the singular destiny of man not to understand the truth until it is too late.

... And when
You begin to repent
The shameful error, then you die.[13]

Metastasio has a golden pen, and his good sense is worth more than intuition and the dialectic. If only I had kept to my Metastasio, which a good old uncle of mine put in my hands! But you know what? The propagators of falsehoods are animated by what I would call an infernal genius, and they have an incredible grasp on the art of leading dupes along by the nose. And dupes are in the majority. So the friend of the truth is modest, simple, and unlucky.

D. That is precisely the case. Listen to how Schopenhauer himself explains the reason for which his contemporaries ignored him for so long. A great many histories of philosophy have been written, and in them you can find many extremely mediocre men mentioned without a word about Schopenhauer. You might even think they are afraid of him. And so you start to suspect that underneath it all is a conspiracy, a conspiracy so formidable that it can kill a man: the conspiracy of silence. On the other hand all of these histories make a great din about Fichte, Schelling, and Hegel, who are praised as the educators of the human race.

A. Or rather their executioners. After all, they are the first cause leading so many people to go off and get themselves killed. And as for me, while I was talking about the absolute, I lost my beard.

D. Charlatans and sophists, "rather than philosophers," Schopenhauer says.[14] "For they wanted to appear not to be," and they sought not the truth but Government employment and money from students and bookshops. They are truly excellent in the art of fleecing the public and making their wares valuable, which is doubtless of merit – just not a philosophical one. At one moment they put on airs of passion, at another airs of persuasion, at another severity. Obscure and bristling with formulas, they sold words that they baptized as thoughts. In vain do you search them for that calm, clear exposition that makes a philosopher beautiful. They look to the effect; they want to seduce, carry you away; they adopt the tone of an oracle to make themselves understood. Kant had demonstrated that the world is a phenomenon of the brain, but that underneath the phenomenon there is yet a thing in itself, beyond consciousness. Here was his mistake: if he had baptized that thing in itself, he would have laid the final stone in the temple of philosophy.

A. The devil with it! Is that all that's left, baptizing the thing in itself?

D. Of course, and Schopenhauer laid that final stone. But listen. Since Kant closed the door and had the imprudence to announce that behind it was the thing in itself, the transcendent, the unknowable, everyone gathered around that door desiring to taste the forbidden fruit. So there you have the charlatans. Fichte, not a disciple but a caricature of Kant, goes to the front and says: "Fools! Leave that door alone. Kant played a trick, and there's nothing inside. The thing in itself, true reality, does not exist. Everything is a product of the brain, of the I."[15] It was Fichte who introduced the formulas, the oracles, and all of the apparatus of charlatanry into philosophy, and it was Hegel who brought them to perfection. But the kernel was too big to swallow. And once again people came to knock on that door and say: "Give us the real." At that point Schelling, who was more crafty, said: "It's useless to come knocking. There is nothing inside there. The real exists, and there's no need to go in there to find it. The real is all around us, but you don't see it, like the man who has his hat in his hand but goes all about the house looking for it. That which you call the ideal is precisely what you are looking for, the real. Thought and being are the same thing."

A. Here we go again with the identity of thought and being, the evil plant. If it were at least something new! My teacher used to cite these words of Spinoza to me: "Substantia cogitans et substantia extensa una eademque est substantia."[16] "Mens et corpus una eademque est res."[17]

D. But look at the sly dog, says Schopenhauer. Kant places the phenomenon in opposition to the thing in itself, and to misdirect the public from the thing in itself bit by bit he substitutes thought for being, and so he switches the cards right in your hand. But people realized it and went off in search of the real in the ideal, only they couldn't find it. "I see it, I do," he said, "because I have a good telescope called the intellectual intuition. If you all don't see it, rub your eyes." Hegel took pity on those poor eyes and said: "Wait, I want to let you see it even with your eyes shut." And so he proposed the dialectical process, which is the same as saying he removed thought from the brain and made it a thing in itself, the absolute, the idea, which is endowed with an internal restlessness that allows it no repose. He made it a true, living being that walks on its own impulse and follows its own laws of evolution; it walks across the centuries. Thus Hegel's doctrine was substantiated, predicated with impudence, and believed in with nonsense. Hegel bestowed upon the world all of the qualities that we attribute to God, including omniscience; and confounding metaphysics with logic he made the universe into an animated logic.

A. Which the governments dispersed with blows from bombs, rifles, and scissors.

D. Fichte was a caricature of Kant. Hegel was the buffoon of Schelling, and he made him ridiculous with that idea that moves of its own accord, and with those concepts that become, those contradictions that generate. Do you want to make a young man into an imbecile, rendering him incapable of thought forevermore? Put one of Hegel's books in his hands. And when he reads that being is nothingness, the infinite is the finite, the general is the particular, and history is a syllogism, he'll end up heading to the madhouse....

A. Or to the Vicaria to make a syllogism with the thieves – where I myself nearly ended up.[18] Give it to 'em, give it to 'em, Schopenhauer!

D. Hegel is the greatest sinner, and Schopenhauer is upset with him most of all. Fichte's sin is being the peddling disciple of Kant,[19] and Arthur gets angry with a public that can never seem to mention Kant's name without lumping Fichte on his back – a public with Midas's ears, unworthy of Kant, unable to ever understand him, that places Fichte alongside him, rather on top of him, as the person who not only continued but carried to perfection that which Kant began. Thus it happened that today we say Kant and Fichte, but we ought to say Kant and Schopenhauer: the first great sin of the century. The second sin was committed by Schelling. Philosophy had found its foundations thanks to Locke and Kant, resting on the absolute difference between the real and the ideal. And here comes Schelling who does precisely the opposite, confusing black with white, and he tosses you the real and the ideal in the abyss of his absolute identity. Error after error comes from this: sowing the bad seed gives birth to the corruption and perversion of philosophy. Schelling's sin is a big one, but, as I told you, Hegel is the biggest sinner because intellectual intuition would have had a hard time making its way into the public mind, but Hegel with his dialectical process gave the appearance of harmony to this philosophical monster; he gave it order and was its architect; he made the sin durable. And Schopenhauer tans his hide: charlatan, insipid, stupid, nauseating, ignoramus,[20] whose impudence was hailed as wisdom by his coward followers, he is the true author of the century's intellectual corruption. And here Schopenhauer cannot contain his indignation: "Oh admirers of this philosophy ..." but how can I say it? I cannot translate for you the energetic epithet that Arthur assigns to this philosophy. The Italian language is chaste ...

A. Oh come on!

D. Since you are curious, recall the epithet that Dante gives to Thaïs's fingernails, and you'll have an equivalent. "Oh admirers," Schopenhauer shouts, "the scorn of your descendants awaits you, and already I hear the prelude! And you, public, for thirty years you have taken my works for nothing and for less than nothing, while you honoured and divinized a wicked philosophy that is absurd, stupid, and contemptable! The one is deserving of the other. Go to the imbeciles and get yourselves praised. Clever, bought idiots, ignorant charlatans without spirit and without merit, that's what it means to be German. Not men like me. This is the testimony that I leave you before my death. Wieland says that it is a disgrace to be born German;[21] Bürger, Mozart, Beethoven, and others would have said the same thing. And so do I: *Il n'y a que l'esprit, qui sente l'esprit.*"[22] All of which means: "You all are imbeciles, and you are unable to understand me, Arthur Schopenhauer."

A. For God's sake, I feel myself becoming smaller, I feel like I'm becoming an imbecile.

D. Now you understand why no one thought about him for the space of thirty years: his contemporaries were not *à sa hauteur*. They preferred the sophists and the charlatans. The new, more intelligent generation threw Hegel away like a rag and gathers around Arthur. If you go to Frankfurt, go into the big hotel and you'll see how many Austrian officials are there with their mouths ajar to listen: it's Arthur who's preaching.

A. Schopenhauer must have a big head. He understood an important truth: to propagate a doctrine above all it's necessary to render the sword philosophical. Muhammad's sabre made more conversions than our shouting in the square. A good smack with the broad side of a sword would make me shout out immediately: "Long live Schopenhauer!"

D. But Schopenhauer has other followers, too. First off all those men of the future, the malcontents, the misunderstood, the unsatisfied, who take themselves to be the great man's brothers and say: "Our time too will come."

A. Formidable followers, because being impatient with the silence that surrounds them, each of them speaks with the voice of a hundred.

D. Add in the women, especially after Arthur called them myopic overgrown girls bereft of memory or foresight, living only in the present, endowed with the intellect common to animals, with just barely a bit of reason, liars par excellence, and born to remain under perpetual tutelage.[23]

A. These are no sugar-coated pills.

D. But my dear friend, today women no longer wish to be treated to sugar-coated pills: gallantry has gone out of fashion. Women want to feel force, and the more you say and do so, the more she likes you. If you stand there before her, timid and respectful, in her heart she will immediately baptize you as an imbecile and begin to teach you a lesson. You must round your mouth, behave like an important man, animate your gestures and voice, and keep three or four paradoxes in reserve, as those are the best for tickling the attention, and spit them out at the right moment in quick and imperious ways. Plus, today women want to be held as people of spirit, rather of strong spirit, and so they'll act like an atheist just as once they acted devout. Women, too, want to be able to philosophize and theologize, and how is that done? Put Hegel and the other sophists in front of them, and wandering among those formulas and abstractions they'll see the ground missing from under their feet and be overcome by dizziness. They want science, but at a good price, losing as little of their own capital as they can.

A. And they're right. I believe it would be better that way for us men, too. Does it seem to you that a poor gentleman should sweat away half his life with these philosophers? And if there were at least some certainty of getting something out of it. You read one, and when you let out a great sigh and say "it's finished" you pick up another and find yourself back at the beginning: a new language, new formulas, a new method, new opinions – such that it seems like you're advancing, and really you're always in the same place. A philosophy ought to be such that even women would happily read it.

D. Which is the case with Schopenhauer. After taking frequent trips and keeping his distance from teaching, there's nothing professorial or scholastic about him. He writes well, banishing formulas and any kind of scientific apparatus, using current, popular language. As is the case with those who are a bit dense, he repeats the same thing to you until you're satisfied. After having philosophized a bit, so as not to tire you, he switches things up, as if he were telling you: "Let's go and get a tea." Then, in place of reasoning, he gives you a bit of conversation and pours out insults, invectives, comparisons, anecdotes, citations from Spanish, Greek, Latin, Italian, English, French, which are like the sauce of his science. As such, it is a pleasure to read, particularly for philosophical dilettantes, both male and female. He boasts of his clarity and originality, and if you don't notice it yourself he announces it to you with trumpets. He's not satisfied with being clear but wants to make sure you know it, and for that reason he has the coquetry of clarity, going over the same thing again and again in many ways. He says things that are often older than Adam, but he thinks them with his own head and says them in his own manner: the originality is in the way he dresses them up. Beneath the philosopher's overcoat the man is visible – full of bile, passionate, sure of himself, a provocateur, spiteful, such that you seem to see him with one hand busy throwing punches and the other preening and admiring himself. He stimulates you, amuses you, and warms you up. Just think, then, how many followers he must have, especially in Italy where this time they won't be able to repeat the usual line about Germanic fogs. This philosophy is a solid thing, all flesh and bones.

A. And what's more, an enemy of the idea. It would be a great benefit to translate it for us. But I'm curious to know how he was able to form the world without the idea, because the idea scares me and I'd really like to throw it out, but I don't know how.

D. Schopenhauer threw it out with a swipe of his pen, such a simple thing. Listen here. Kant had said that everything is ideal, a phenomenon of the brain. The world is my image: I don't know the sun, nor the earth, but only an eye that sees the sun, a hand that feels the earth; everything that I know, the whole world, is not in itself but for another; it is an object for the subject, the vision of he who sees, in a word, an image, a phenomenon. It is Heraclitus's becoming, Plato's shadows, Spinoza's accident, the Indians' deceptive veil of Maya, similar to a dream or to that sunlight on the beach that you confuse with water from far away. Take away the subject, he who sees, and the world would no longer exist.

A. In this way we are puppets, and the world is a comedy.

D. Of course, but behind the scenes is the true reality, the thing in itself, beyond our sight. Now given that men aren't satisfied with being called puppets, even those who really are, and they've been after science for many centuries, it was too cruel a thing to tell them that science is behind the scenes and you'll never see it, what you'll see is appearance. The three sophists, wanting to satisfy the human race, said: "Take consolation: appearance is the same as essence; there is nothing behind the scenes." And so they went on scribbling volumes when, after Kant, there was nothing left to do except the simplest thing in the world.

A. What?

D. Take a peek behind the scenes. And here is the glory of Schopenhauer. He opened the door and there he found reality, the thing in itself: the *Wille*.

A. What does *Wille* mean?

D. Will.

A. How hard it must have been to find that![24]

D. It's Columbus's egg. Now it seems easy, and everyone says: "I would have found it, too." Schopenhauer's discovery is even more important than the discovery of America, because, as its inventor says with justified pride, it is the truth of truths, the ultimate discovery, the only thing that was left to do in philosophy. And yet this truth had been glimpsed for a long time. The Chinese and the Indians had raised it up into a religious principle. Christianity was saying nothing else with its story of original sin. We find this truth in the mouths of the people at large, when they say that the sky doesn't *want* to rain, attributing will not only to men but to the universe of things in all languages, which is to say not as a poetic figure but as a confused feeling of the truth.[25] Even the Greek philosophers, who were closer to the ancient Brahmin and Buddhist wisdom, got close to it, such that what you have is really the *consensus gentium*. Among others, Empedocles can be properly called the precursor of Schopenhauer because the philosopher from Agrigento, whom Arthur calls *ein ganzer Mann*, a complete man, places at the head of the world not intellect but love and hate, which is the same as saying the *will*, attraction and repulsion, sympathy and antipathy.[26] And since many maintain that Empedocles is a Pythagorean, we ought to believe that he stole this truth from Pythagoras, and if Gioberti had known this, enamoured as he was with Pythagorean philosophy, he would have become the most fervent propagator of this doctrine which was born as philosophy in Italy, and he would have made our primacy grow with another ingredient.[27] But Gioberti didn't think of this, and all the glory remains Schopenhauer's, because the true inventor isn't he who finds a truth but he who fertilizes it, applies it, extracts its consequences, as is said by some Frenchman or other whom Schopenhauer cites in a moment where he feared that his patent of invention might be contested.

A. What amazes me is that Kant didn't see it despite being mere inches from the discovery.

D. My dear friend, once Kant fell into the phenomenon he was no longer able to get back out. What amazes me is rather that he didn't conclude by the rigour of logic that everything is phenomenon. After all if it is true that the phenomenon presupposes the "noumenon" or the thing in itself, it is also true that according to his system this necessity is wholly subjective, based on the law of causality, which is itself a form of the intellect. I believe that what he lacked was not logic but rather courage. Because, having begun to philosophize in order to ground science, and finding himself finally in the void, just as he grasped for the categorical imperative in morality, so too did he ascend to the thing in itself in metaphysics. But this inflicted men with the punishment of Tantalus, saying to them: "the thing in itself exists, but you'll never know it because it transcends experience." Now Schopenhauer performed a whopper of a miracle. He said to experience: "Give me the thing in itself," and experience gave it to him. Philosophers had worn down their brains so much over this affair, and there was nothing to it other than undertaking a little interrogation. What am I? I am a phenomenon, like everything else, because I look upon myself in space and time, which are necessary forms of my intellect. My body is an object among objects; its movements and actions are as inexplicable to me as the changes in every other object. Kant stopped himself here, but this road doesn't lead to Rome, by which I mean it doesn't lead to reality. He needed to replicate the question: "What am I?" Then he would have got the response: "I am *Wille*." I move, speak, and perform actions because I will it. Nor is there a cause and effect relation between my body and my will, because in that way we would fall into the law of causality. The act of will and the corresponding bodily movement are not two objectively different states but rather the same thing in two different modes, in one case as immediate and in the other as an image offered to the intellect. Thus the bodily movement is nothing other than the act of will objectified, made into an image, as Arthur says: will is *a priori* knowledge of the body, and the body is *a posteriori* knowledge of the will.[28]

A. Knowledge! Knowledge! And so even the will falls under knowledge, and yet we said that everything that is known is a phenomenon of the brain. I know in such a way because the brain is made in such a way.

D. But the will is an immediate knowledge that is indemonstrable, outside the forms of the intellect, not logical, not empirical, not metaphysical, and not metalogical, which are the four classes to which Schopenhauer reduces all truths. It is a knowledge of its own genre, and it could be called the *philosophical Truth* par excellence.

A. This seems like a subtlety to me. Immediate or mediated, it's knowledge all the same. And it seems to me that cursed brain is involved a bit even here.

D. It seems to me, and yet it doesn't seem to me! You are on the side of appearance, and here we're talking about a truth that even children see. Now what is true for your body is true of all others, such that the *Wille* is the reality of the universe or the thing in itself, and matter is the same *Wille* made visible.

A. I would imagine that once the phenomenon has been overcome and true reality has been grasped, Schopenhauer ought to navigate with full sails in the sea of being.

D. You're fooling yourself. Schopenhauer opens Kant's door just a bit and looks at the *Wille*. Kant had said: "Nothing is known." To this the three imposters responded: "Everything is known." Schopenhauer pitched his tent between that absolute ignorance and this absolute knowledge and concluded: "Only one thing is known and can be known: the *Wille*." But no sooner had he learned its venerated name than he hurried to close the door. What is the *Wille* in itself, outside of the world? What does it do? How does it get along? Is there another order of things different from our own? Other worlds? And this world, what is its origin? What is its destination? What is its reason, its why? Don't ask, my dear friend, for the door is closed. You mustn't confuse

Schopenhauer with those charlatans who seem to have a conversation every day with the good Lord from which they discover all the secrets. He gives you a philosophy that is modest and serious.

A. A philosophy that isn't a philosophy, since it leaves unanswered all the problems that constitute philosophy.

D It is already a great merit to have demonstrated the unresolvable nature of these problems, the impossibility of metaphysics. Up to this point it has been believed that we were given intellect to know, and when a gentleman philosopher admonishes you that nature is unknowable, we usually respond: "Then why do we have reason? What use is the intellect?" Its use is in eating and drinking, making money, life's practical uses, Schopenhauer responds. Nature gives to each being what it needs to live and nothing more. The intellect is able to grasp relations but not the substance of things.[29]

A. Well done! So we are not able to live without metaphysics? But metaphysics has always been the stomach's enemy, not to mention the accounts it makes us settle with Campagna, if you take it seriously.

D. The intellect can understand that which nature is, but not nature itself.

A. It seems to me that bit by bit you're forgetting the *Wille* and falling in love with nature.

D. It's true. That happens to Schopenhauer, as well. I meant to say that the intellect cannot know the *Wille*, the thing in itself, and much less that which is further above it …

A. Leave that stuff to the theologians. It's as if I were hearing a holy father preach on the insufficiency of reason, and hence the necessity of revelation. But I confess that the more you speak the less I understand. You say that we cannot know the *Wille*, but before you said Schopenhauer did know it, however without the intervention of the brain it seems.

D. This is all cleared up with a *distinguo*. There's *Wille* and then there's *Wille*. The absolute *Wille* is unknowable, because knowing the absolute is a contradiction in terms. Everything that is known, as something known, falls under the form of our intellect and thus is relative. The *Wille*, which is free, can be at rest and can take on any form that it likes beyond our own; up to this point we know that it exists, but we don't know what it is. The *Wille* that we know is the *Wille* inside us, a relative *Wille* subject to the forms of space and time and the laws of causality, and for that reason accessible to the intellect.[30]

A. Which is to say it's a phenomenon like all the others.

D. The first phenomenon, which can make sense of the others.

A. But then don't go on preaching about how Schopenhauer discovered the thing in itself! Some thing in itself this is, if it's relative! I detect a whiff of charlatanry.

D. Schopenhauer is no charlatan: he himself showed you the limits to our knowledge of the *Wille*.

A. But then this *Wille* may not be the first thing but itself a product of something else that we don't know about and that would be the true thing in itself.

D. It could be. But what does that matter to us? What matters to us is that the *Wille* is found beneath all phenomena and is the thing in itself *for us*: in that way we can make sense of the world.

A. But that doesn't work for me either. Isn't it strange to say that inside a rock is *Wille*? It would make more sense to me if the idea were in there, if it weren't for Campagna.

D. Perhaps it's that you're accustomed to seeing the *Wille* or will with a vulgar eye. Plebian philosophers don't know how to conceive will except as being in the service of intelligence. Now, making an effort of abstraction, you must descend from the intellect to the will. And what's left? A blind and unaware stimulus that strains to act. That's Schopenhauer's *Wille*.

A. The principle of everything is thus a blind, unintelligent stimulus? I don't like it.

D. Otherwise you're going to run into the idea, or else even Campagna.

A. Therefore ...

D. Therefore look around a bit, and tell me whether you don't see *Wille* everywhere. In a world where everything is a phenomenon, it is the *Wille* that is the true reality and gives all things the power to exist and act. Not only the involuntary acts of animals but the entire organism, its form and condition, the vegetation of plants, crystallization in the inorganic realm, and in other words every primitive force that manifests in chemical and physical phenomena, even gravity, considered in itself and outside of appearance, is identical with the will that we find in ourselves. It is true that will is set in motion by motives in animals, by stimuli in the organic life of animals or plants, by simple causes in the strict sense of the word in inorganic life. This difference, however, regards the phenomenon and leaves the *Wille* intact. Now open your ears, as the best part is coming. It is generally held that the intellect is the principle of life, the essence of things – you can see that we're nearing the idea. From this derive order and universal harmony, progress, freedom, and that certain divinization of the world. But since Schopenhauer took humble *Wille*, believed to be a simple function of the intellect, and raised it to the highest level, intellect became completely secondary, a phenomenon that accompanies the *Wille* but is inessential to it, sticking its head up only when the *Wille* appears in organic life, thus an organ of the *Wille*, a physical product, a non-metaphysical being. The intellect can disappear without the *Wille* going away: indeed, in vegetable and inorganic life there is no vestige of the intellect, and for that reason it is not will that is conditioned by knowledge, as everyone maintains, but rather knowledge is conditioned by will, as Schopenhauer maintains.[31]

A. I understand, I understand. Up to this point I confess I was laughing to myself about the *Wille*, saying: "In the end it's just a word, the baptismal name for the thing in itself that Schopenhauer added to Kant's doctrine." But our friend is subtle, and I see where he's heading. Let's celebrate the funeral of the idea.

D. In effect the *Wille*, operating blindly, is not bound by any necessity like the idea, or like Spinoza's substance. Absolutely free, it can stand there with its hands in its pockets, amidst the majesty of tranquility. When it feels an itch, it leaves its immobility and generates ideas.

A. Dammit, him too, with the idea.

D. Rest assured, it's not Hegel's idea but rather Plato's ideas, *species rerum*, types and genres, outside of space and time.

A. Concepts, then.

D. Slow down there. The scissors haven't yet managed to extract philosophy from your head. You need to know that for Schopenhauer concepts are simple abstractions extracted from the phenomenal world, like being, substance, cause, force, and so on. They have a logical value but not a metaphysical one. They are thought, not contemplated. Struggle and press all you like, concepts can give you nothing other than concepts. And it took the impudence of a Hegel to found philosophy on concepts. In contrast the ideas are the first product of the *Wille*; they don't generate but rather are generated, and they are, so to speak, the outline or model of the world, perfect for contemplation.[32] As such in this theory you find all of the greatest truths of philosophy gathered together: Kant's thing in itself, Plato's ideas, and the immanent unity or monism of Spinoza. The *Wille* is one, immanent in all things, indeed things are nothing other than *Wille* itself put into motion; light is the appearance of *Wille*.

A. So Schopenhauer is a pantheist.

D. What does that matter?

A. Trifles! You forgot, I have to go back to Italy. The idea can venture down there every once in a while, with certain precautions, since even Governments have their ideas, especially if you pronounce it in the plural, with each minister wanting to have a bunch of them for his use. But with pantheism there is no way out.

D. Console yourself, then. Schopenhauer is not a pantheist, because his world resembles less God than the devil. Arthur says that a pantheist is someone who divinizes the world, transforming the idea into a substance or an absolute and making reason its organ. Idea as substance operates fatally and reasonably …[33]

A. I thought that pantheism consisted in admitting a single, immanent substance regardless of it name – substance, idea, or *Wille*. But since Schopenhauer assures me of the contrary, then what should I call him?

D. Call him a monist,[34] and you'll be rid of the bother. The idea, then, as I was saying, operates fatally, because it operates reasonably, from whence comes optimism, that movement always from good to better following immutable laws, which is called progress. But if it really is so, Schopenhauer asks, then how do we explain evil and error?

A. You've placed your finger in the wound. A fine God this world of ours is, a mix of madness and silliness and trickery. When it conceived of the world, the idea must have been in the mental hospital.

D. For that reason Schopenhauer dismissed the idea and substituted *Wille*, blind and free, which does good and evil as chance dictates. If it would just remain calm, it would be a respectable *Wille*, but because of its whims it often has the fancy to leave its generality and individuate itself. This is its sin: from this arises evil. Evil is generated by the *Principium individuationis*, what the Catholics call matter or the flesh. It could say "I don't want to live," and it would be God. But when it gets it in its head to say "I want to live," it becomes Satan. Life is a demonic work.

A. I see that this *Wille* must be an ass, a buffoon, and a rascal: I really did know what I was talking about when I said that the true idea of the world, that which governs it, is Campagna: the closer we get to that type, the closer we get to the truth.

D. The *Wille* is essentially an ass up until it produces the brain.

A. And how does it become so learned all of a sudden? I mean, if it doesn't have knowledge, how can it produce knowledge?

D. Can't a learned son be born to an ass of a father?

A. Enough with that joke. Why?

D. Because it wills it.[35] The *Wille* can do anything, and when it wants to know, it makes a brain. Didn't I say that the *Wille* loves life? As long as it wants to live as a stone or a plant it doesn't get the idea of a brain, because it can do without one. But once the idea of animals occurs to it, and it says "I want to be an animal," it makes a brain, since intellect is necessary to animal life, as I told you before. And the *Wille* married to the intellect is what we commonly call the soul.

A. An intellect that is born from an unintelligent *Wille* is a greater miracle than the one performed by Saint Januarius.

D. No bigger than what you find in the most ordinary events. A stone that falls by virtue of the law of gravity is just as big a miracle as the man who thinks. The *Wille* does all these miracles because it wills them.

A. Which is to say that if the stone falls, it's the case that it wants to fall?

D. Certainly.

A. And if I were to throw you from the window, would you want to go down to split your skull?

D. I am a complex being. My body would want to, because it too is subject to the law of gravity.

A. Up until now I believed that in inorganic life movement came from without and that if, for example, a stone falls, the reason is that I push it …

D. Not only that, but because it is a stone and not a bird. It falls because its nature is such, and in this sense we say that it "wants" to fall.

A. Well then I don't understand this *Wille* anymore. If it follows certain laws of physical order, it could also follow them in the moral order. And if it acts in accordance with fixed laws, it is no longer *Wille* but idea, it's an intelligent *Wille*.

D. Think of Campagna.

A. He can't hear us here. I thought this *Wille* was an ass and a buffoon, but now you're talking about laws.

D. The *Wille* is free so long as it doesn't will anything, but once it wills something …

A. Let's just stop here. A *Wille* that doesn't will is a contradiction in terms, because the essence of *Wille* is willing.

D. But in its freedom it can also will not to will.

A. That's a subtlety. But let's leave that alone. What pushes it to will?

D. An inner fancy.

A. That's some kind of witty remark. Will is a desire that presupposes need; need presupposes lack; lack presupposes absence, a being with certain determinations and its own nature. The *Wille* thus cannot be a first principle because it presupposes being, and thus the idea.

D. Think of Campagna.

A. You just say that when you have nothing to say.

D. If you keep interrupting me, we'll never finish. I was saying that when the *Wille* wills something, it is no longer free as it must make use of all the means that lead to what it wants. At that point it is subject to laws, which thus regard the phenomenal *Wille* and not the *Wille* in itself.

A. But then when it wills something, the *Wille* proposes an end and applies the means to that end. Do you think you'll get me to believe that the *Wille* is an ass, that it doesn't work reasonably, that it isn't intelligent?

D. But it does all this without knowing what it does, the way a bird wanting to lay its eggs begins to gather bits of straw and constructs a nest. The bird doesn't even know what use the nest is destined for. It does all this not because it thinks about it, but because it wills it.

A. That's just a word game. It's lacking consciousness, not intelligence. It's not enough to will, it must know, whether consciously or not doesn't matter much. Your *Wille*, if it is blind, can will as much as it wants without being any good for anything, even forming stones. Every formation presupposes that the means fit with the end, and this is the work of intelligence. A blind *Wille* that forms the world! Will is not enough, my friend, you need knowledge. I want to go to Paris, but if I don't know the road that leads there, it will just be by chance; out of a hundred roads ninety-nine times it won't lead there.

D. But the *Wille* is blind not because it is truly an ass but because one can't say that it thinks and reflects. It operates without consciousness.

A. Who ever told you that the idea operates with consciousness and that it thinks and reflects? We know that Nature operates spontaneously and unaware; must we draw the conclusion that it operates without reason? And when Hegel sees the idea in stones, do you think that the idea reflects on it and thinks about it? If the *Wille* does what is required by its proposed aim, it is a reasonable being, it's the idea. Don't interrupt me. Here there's nothing to say except another: "Think of Campagna."

D. If you want to see what difference there is between the *Wille* and the idea, focus your mind on the consequences. The idea gives birth to an unreasonable and thus awful world.

A. Which does not prove that the *Wille* is not the idea! It just proves that it's a rascal. Someone who wants something bad and makes use of the means to get it is called wicked, but not irrational.

D. For the idea, life is precisely its own progressive unfolding following its constitutive laws. For the *Wille*, life is a sin: cursed be the moment that it says "I want to live!" Living it ceases to be free, it imprisons itself in space and time, it enters the chains of causes and effects, it becomes individual, it condemns itself to suffering and lack, descending with its own legs into this valley of tears, as Empedocles and the *Salve Regina* call the world.

A. And why all this now?

D. Because the infinite *Wille* cannot satisfy itself under this or that form, where it always finds limits. Therefore taking on a form is its unhappiness. Its sin, its misery comes from saying: "I want to live."

A. It would thus be better off saying: "I want to die."

D. Certainly. Death is the end of evil and suffering, it is the *Wille* returning to itself, eternally free and happy.[36] Living to suffer is the greatest of all asininities.

If life is misery
why do we bear it?[37]

Life is a phenomenon, an appearance, *Pulvis et umbra*, vanity of vanities, where there is no reality other than suffering, and if you take away the suffering what remains is boredom.

A. It seems like you got distracted and passed from Schopenhauer to Leopardi.

D. Leopardi and Schopenhauer are the same thing. At almost the same time the one created the metaphysics of suffering and the other the poetry of suffering. Leopardi saw the world in this way, he just didn't know why.

[…] All is mystery except our pain.[38]

Schopenhauer discovered the reason why with his discovery of the *Wille*.

A. Doesn't Leopardi after all speak of a "brute hidden power that rules to common harm," and immediately afterwards attack "the boundless vanity of all."[39] It seems to me that this is precisely the *Wille*, underlying that whole series of vain appearances that is called the world.

D. With this difference: for Leopardi, power is eternal matter endowed with one or more mysterious forces, whereas for Schopenhauer power is a single force, the *Wille*, and matter is one of its appearances, the veil of Maya. The one is materialist and the other spiritualist.

A. How then did they manage to arrive at the same consequences? One can imagine how a bad world is born from matter. Materialism is one of those words that makes me as afraid as pantheism. But spiritualism is a word that sounds so good to the ear, the holy ark of religion, the palladium of Catholic civilization, a type of passport that allows you to enter without suspicion in Naples and Turin, in Austria and France, and even in Saint Petersburg, the true *Verbum*, the word of words at which the holy faith and true freedom both clap their hands with equal pleasure, both the absolutists and the liberals …

D. The liberals in Naples …

A. The right-thinking, honest liberals of every country. "What are you?" "I'm a spiritualist." With this talisman honesty is written on your forehead and enables you to make good acquaintances in all of civilized Europe. I'm a spiritualist, and Ferdinand II will write me a letter of introduction to the Pope; Luis Napoleon will allow me to go about Paris unaccompanied; and Cavour will make me a knight of Saint Maurice. Don't laugh as I'm speaking from the heart.

D. You see then that I suggested a good philosophy for you, since Schopenhauer is a spiritualist.

A. But he agrees with Leopardi, who is a materialist! I no longer believed in philosophy, but I did still believe in logic. Now I no longer believe even in logic.

D. Under the name of a Greek philosopher, Leopardi says: "Matter is *ab eterno*,"[40] and he sees the irrational appetite germinate from matter's breast – and hence ignorance, error, the passions, and in a word evil. Schopenhauer said: "Matter does not exist; it is a concept, an abstraction. The only thing that exists is the appetite, the *Wille*." Both thus admit the same principle, but one grounds it in matter and the other makes matter into a simple veil. Schopenhauer's *Wille* is almost like the Christians' soul, which descends into the body like a prison where it is constrained to live together with that body, but it keeps itself distinct and distant for fear of contagion, and at the moment it departs, which is called death but is true life, the soul lets out a sigh. Except that in religious doctrine the soul is good, and evil is in the body, whereas for Schopenahuer evil is in the spirit, in *Wille*, and matter is the same *Wille* when it deigns to appear, its ghost. That's why Leopardi and Schopenhauer agree in their consequences, placing the same blind, malign power as the principle of the world. It makes little difference that in the one it's a material force and in the other a force that manifests itself under the aspect of matter. The same *ergo* follows.

A. I understand. I'm beginning to become suspicious of spiritualism, and Schopenhauer spoiled this beautiful word for me. This is the destiny of all the words that are beautiful and celebrated upon their initial entry into the world, and then you throw them around and I throw them around and they are wrecked, they get old, they grow ugly, they become frightening. I know many words that once many years ago would fill your pockets and now they only empty them. Spiritualism was one of the few words that had remained afloat amidst all these shipwrecks, and now here comes the person who will ruin it for us. Today it's not enough to say "I'm a liberal," but you have to explain if your liberty is the true or the false one, that of honest men or that of rascals; in the same way, there will now be a true and a false spiritualism. The true, honest spiritualism presupposes the opposition, the inveterate war, between the spirit and the body. In contrast, in the false spiritualism spirit and matter are fraternal cousins.

D. Brothers born of the same parents, more like; indeed, they are the same thing in two different aspects. Because, according to Schopenhauer, the opposition between matter and soul is an ancient philosophical prejudice, introduced by Descartes and affirmed by charlatans under their other names, nature and spirit. The only true distinction is that between phenomenon and noumenon, or the thing in itself. The *Wille* is the *Wille,* and the world is its phenomenon, its shadow, its eyes. Everything is vanity: only the *Wille,* the spirit, is.

A. An impiety put in Christian language. Because here spirit is not reason but blind appetite, the origin of sin: it is the spirit of evil.

D. Precisely. The *Wille* is not only a sinner but the only sinner. It is he who commits all of our sins.

A. And we are impeccable?

D. Impeccable.

A. I'm starting to like Schopenhauer again, despite his false spiritualism. I already feel a child's innocence running through my blood. If he ends up demonstrating that man does not sin, from now on we'll be able to do whatever we want.

D. As if up until now we had been doing what we didn't want.

A. I can certainly say that up until now I have done many things that I would not have wanted to do.

D. That's an illusion. You are a phenomenon of the *Wille,* and what you've done your *Wille* wanted to do.

A. I often felt the whim to scream in the square: "long live liberty!"

D. So why didn't you do it?

A. Out of fear of Campagna.

D. That's the same as saying that if you hadn't been afraid you would have done it. We all act according to our nature. When it takes the form of an individual, the *Wille* is no longer free; instead it is this or that, which is to say it is conditioned in this way or that way, with this or that character. And once it has a character it acts in keeping with it. Now acting in keeping with one's character is doing what one wants.

A. This is an abuse of language, because doing what you want is substantially just doing what you are able to do. But in certain cases I can do both of two things, and if I do one I know that I could have also done the other but didn't want to. I am thus perfectly free.

D. An abuse of language, an illusion of the brain. Why did you do this and not that?

A. For this or that reason.

D. And this reason induced you with the same fatal necessity that the law of gravity applies to a stone. In falling, the stone does not sin because it obeys its nature. The thief who robs does not sin because he obeys his character.

A. But the stone cannot do anything but fall, whereas the thief could not rob.

D. You still don't understand. Suppose that the thief hesitates before robbing, considers hell, God's commandments, dishonor, prison, and so on. What will he do? If not robbing is not a virtue but just a necessary effect of his character, that is because he has such a character that those images have an effect on him. And if he does rob, it is not a sin because given his character, he could no more prevent himself from committing the theft than the stone could prevent itself from falling. Free man is a *contradictio in adiecto* because man is a conditioned, determined being, in such a way that it is enough to know someone's character very well in order to guess what he will do. Do you understand now why man is impeccable?

A. And what of morality? Duty?

D. Duty, Schopenhauer says, is another abstraction. No one has the right to say "you must," and one of Kant's defects is having come up with his categorical imperative. Having to and not having to suppose a freedom of choice that contradicts the concept of man. Go ahead and tell me: "you must not kill." I'll kill, if my character takes me in that direction. And I won't sin.

A. And what if they hang you?

D. They will hang me justly.

A. What? I'm beginning to wonder whether your brain is out for a stroll. And why should they hang me? Where there's no fault, there's no penalty. What would I have to answer for?

D. Not for your action, but your character. Why are you made like this?

A. Oh nice! And what have I got to do with that? It's the *Wille*, that trickster of a *Wille* that made me like this.

D. And if they hang you, it isn't you who they hang but the *Wille*.

A. That too! But I'm the one who's going to feel the pain.

D. Which is the same as saying the *Wille* feels it, because what in you is the true reality is the *Wille*. All the rest is phenomenon.

A. But the *Wille* in me is the same as the *Wille* in whoever hangs me.

D. Exactly.

A. I'm beginning to get dizzy.

D. In fact this is the basis of morality. Once we're persuaded that in everyone there is only one and the same *Wille*, we will feel like brothers linked to one another by reciprocal sympathy. And since the same *Wille* is likewise in animals, indeed in the whole universe of things, a universal sympathy will light up in our hearts …[41]

A. Even for the ass …

D. The ass is our brother, just like the rest. This sympathy will become a deep compassion when we think that because of the *Wille* we are all unhappy, all condemned irremediably to suffer. And instead of making war against one another we will have pity for one another in turn and get angry with the impious Nature that made us like this.

A. Just like Leopardi says.[42]

D. A good observation. For Leopardi the ethical or moral principle is compassion …

A. Even for the rascals!

D. Exactly, even a bit more compassion still, since they are not at fault, but rather impious Nature. They cannot do otherwise than they do, and they are to be pitied like the sick and the insane. If men looked at one another in this way, there would no longer be envy, resentment, jealousy, ambition, or hate. The dictionary would be reduced to a single word: compassion.

A. I see a rich young man full of wits and knowledge, loved by women, honoured, celebrated, and I ought to say to him: "I have compassion for you!" He would challenge me to a duel, thinking that I was mocking him.

D. He would be an idiot. But if he had even a bit of brains he would have compassion for himself and you and everyone else. Pleasure is negative, incapable of satisfying the infinite *Wille*. Just wait and beneath the most desired pleasures you'll see boredom and suffering seep out. Pleasure is an ephemeral appearance, beneath which inexorably stands the one, true reality: suffering. Now tell me on your faith if wealth, beauty, intelligence, and glory are anything other than shadows and illusions.

A. You sound like a Saint Paul.

D. Often when you hear Leopardi and Schopenhauer speak it seems like you're listening to a holy father.

A. A holy father in a mask. Look him good in the face, and you'll see the devil's horns sprout out.

D. In the end I thought that you would like a philosophy that was the enemy of the idea, the enemy of freedom, and the enemy of progress.

A. Yessir. I'll go to Naples, take Campagna by the arm, and tell him: "I have compassion for you! You're so content: wretch, what are you enjoying? You're so self-confident: wretch, what are you so proud of? You and the least *lazzarone* of Naples are the same thing."[43] Campagna will stroke my beard, if he let's me keep it, and he'll make a certain face as if to say: "you'll end up yet on the gallows." And then I'll say: "My dear, what will you gain from that? Don't you know, my sweet Campagna, that according to the new philosophy by hanging me you hang yourself. And if you smack me, that smack comes back to your face; and if you beat me with a stick, I'll assume an air of compassion and say: poor Campagna, don't you know you are beating yourself!"[44]

D. This sounds like a caricature, but it's the truth.

A. The difficulty is being believed.

D. Citing one of the ancients, Schopenhauer says that truth is down in the well, and when it wants to stick its head out, it gets a smack across the knuckles. Yet it ends up fighting its way through. And look at this other advantage: with this philosophy not only the idea and freedom go away, but also the fatherland, nationality, humanity, the philosophy of history, and revolution.

A. You're tricky. When I'm about to give Schopenhauer a good kick, you find a way to ingratiate him to me again.

D. You'll end up saying: "Long live Schopenhauer!"

A. And yet Kant, his master, predicted revolution and speaks constantly of right, of fatherland, of freedom. His morality makes you pardon his metaphysics.

D. On the contrary, you contradictory man.

A. Why do you call me contradictory?

D. Because sometimes you speak according to your thoughts, and sometimes according to your fears.

A. You're right. Sometimes I forget about Campagna.

D. The opposite happens in Kant, as his witty disciple noted. For, so long as he was at work constructing his metaphysics, he was thinking with his brain; but once he saw the complete, beautiful building before him, he got scared and remembered Campagna, which is to say the Old and New Testament, and he started thinking with fear and prejudice. Thus since in the Commandments of God's law you find a litany of "thou shalts" and "thou shalt nots," he imagined an absolute and categorical duty, though he had previously considered the absolute to be something transcendent and hypothetical. And alongside this duty came the immortality of the soul, reward and punishment, the egoistic foundation of vulgar morality, freedom conjoined to the concept of God the creator, as if being created and being free were not a contradiction and putting out of mind the maxim that *operari seguitur esse*, which is to say that everyone does such-and-so because he is such-and-so. In this way Kant, believing he was philosophizing, did nothing other than theologize, and he thus lost all merit and credit when he crowned his work with a speculative theology.[45]

A. Fear is a great philosopher.

D. Schopenhauer cast off this philosophy of fear and, minding metaphysics and adding in the *Wille*, he created – as he boasts with good reason – the only philosophy that can give you a moral theory and a political theory. I must answer for my actions because it is I who do them; my fault is being myself and not you, and not whoever else.[46]

A. How am I guilty for having been born this way?

D. It is the *Wille*'s fault since, making a wicked man, it had a wicked caprice.

A. But I'm the one who has to pay the price? This reminds me of that schoolmaster who, wanting to chastise a young marquis but not daring to touch his magnanimous backside, lashed the boy's schoolmates instead.

D. That's a silly comparison. You forgot that everything is *Wille* and you yourself are *Wille*, for which reason the punishment is always borne by the *Wille*. Here we have an unshakable foundation for morality, one that neither Judaism nor Catholicism, nor pantheism nor materialism managed to find. The glory is all Schopenhauer's. And he, having provided for morality, also plans on giving you a recipe for politics. Pay attention.

A. I'm all ears. This is the crux of it. For me a philosophy is true or false, blessed or cursed, based on whether it draws me toward or away from Campagna.

D. Imagine that Campagna were listening to us, and see if he wouldn't be the first to clap his hands. First listen to what he has to say about the liberals of today. Schopenhauer notes that they call themselves optimists believing that the world contains its own purpose within itself and that we are sailing straight toward happiness.[47] But since they see the world afflicted by every sort of evil, they blame the Governments and preach that if we took those away we would have earthly paradise, we would achieve the purpose of the world. And translating that purpose of the world into proper language, it turns out to be nothing other than their own purpose, which is to eat and get drunk, grow and multiply without giving a damn about the world.

A. Campagna says that he has said so many times himself.

D. It sounds like they are talking about humanity and progress, but in substance they are thinking about their bellies. They imagine that the State has a mission, that it is the organ and instrument of progress, which in their language means it is the dispenser of jobs and money for them. But here is the truth. Men are by nature violent rogues, and the earth would be populated by murderers and thieves if the State weren't there to assure property and life. This is its mission, and when a Government protects you from thieves and killers, you're a rogue if you contest its authority and tell it: "Give part of your authority to me, too." And for that reason all of the present governments in Europe are excellent because they all provide for security, and we, I meant to say the demagogues, are the true disturbers of the public peace.

A. Schopenhauer deserves the cross of Saint Januarius, Campagna tells me.[48]

D. Now, since men are inclined toward evil and violence and their actions are controlled not by reason but by *Wille*, that is by instincts and passions, in order to rule them the State should not use persuasion but rather violence. Because as much as men are violent, so too are they cowards, and they obey nothing other than fear: make yourself feared, and you will be obeyed.

A. Campagna says that logic ought to be reduced to this single argument.

D. Power must be in the hands of only one man, because wherever power is divided among more people, force is scattered and less effective. On the other hand the monarchic State conforms better to the *Wille*. First of all there is only one *Wille*. Then, look around. You will see that when they go in procession bees, ants, elephants, wolves, and the other animals always have a single one of them in front, as king. An industrial organization, an army, or a steamship will have but one head. The animal organism is monarchic because only the brain is king. Even the planetary system is monarchic. The king is the incarnation of the people, and he is perfectly able to say: "I am the people."[49]

A. Campagna says that he ought to be made director of the fund that subsidizes journalists.

D. Don't interrupt me. A king, a head of State who maintains justice for all, is however a simple ideal, and the ideal is by nature ethereal and evaporates easily. For that reason, in order to give it a bit of consistency, as with certain chemical substances that are never pure and isolated but always mixed with other substances, it is necessary that other elements be introduced to the State, such as the nobility, the clergy, and privileges. All of this feels a bit arbitrary and violent, but it's better this way than in a State ruled by pure reason, because it means you don't break with the usual way and can ensure greater stability. In contrast look at the United States, where legal rights dominate – pure, abstract, and free of every arbitrary element. From whence you have the most abject materialism with its indivisible companion, ignorance; and from whence also stupid Anglican bigotry, a brutal roughness combined with the most ridiculous veneration of women.[50] Add in cruelty against blacks, frequent and unpunished homicides, and brutal duels; contempt for rights and the law, greed for your neighbour's lands, assassin-style raids and expeditions, corruption, and immorality. These are the fruits of a republic. The republic should thus be rejected particularly by men of genius, who are always overpowered by the ignorant many whereas they are favoured and celebrated by the monarch. Monarchy conforms to the *Wille*; the republic is an artificial construction, a fruit of reflection, a historical exception that is not only of little duration but contrary to civilization, seeing as how in all times and in all peoples the arts and sciences have flourished only in monarchies. Don't you think?

A. There is a battle within me between *Wille* and brain. The *Wille* wants to say yes, but my brain grimaces and whispers: "Greece, Rome, Italy."

D. Greece was an ephemeral apparition. Rome is all in the century of Augustus. And Italy was truly a long barbarism, as was the whole middle ages. Anyway, if you want your *Wille* to defeat it, all you need to do is study Schopenhauer.

A. That would be for the best. But don't you think that today monarchy is insufficient to guarantee your neck, since it has been infiltrated by the poison of the constitution? What kind of monarchy does Schopenhauer mean?

D. Take heart, for Arthur has also thought about your neck. A constitutional monarch, he says, is as ridiculous as Epicurus's Gods who are concerned with getting fat in heaven and don't pay any attention to things down here. Leave him to England, which holds him so dear, since he suits their nature. But when we try to put on an English dinner suit, we are truly buffoons.[51] One of the stupidest institutions is the jury, for nothing other than a *calculus probabilium* can find its way in the crude heads of the common people, and they don't know how to distinguish verisimilitude from certainty, always thinking of their shop and kids. Juries are praised for their impartiality: the impartial *malignum vulgus*![52] Freedom of the press can be thought of as a safety valve against revolutions, the true vent for bad humours; but on the other hand it's like the freedom to sell poison. This is because all of the blunders that get printed imprint themselves easily in simpletons' minds. And what isn't a fool capable of when he gets something fixed in his head?[53]

A. My dear juries, my dear freedom of the press, my dear constitution, I bid you adieu. The hairs on my chin feel calmer. But we're left with the fatherland, nationality, which is something worse. He hadn't thought about that.

D. But Schopenhauer did think about it. The *Wille* exists only in individuals: fatherland, people, humanity, and nationality are all abstractions, empty concepts. The modern Spinozists think otherwise, and particularly that head-corruptor, Hegel, whose mediocrity the Germans would have been able to read written on the vulgarity of his forehead if they had studied the science of physiognomy. Nature had written on his face: ordinary man.[54] Now he and the modern charlatans along with him maintain that the world is harmonically ordered following pre-established laws and that history is thus a science and the facts of peoples rather than individuals are of philosophical interest. If they had read Schopenhauer they would have seen that only the facts of the individual have unity, morality, meaning, and reality because the *Wille* alone is the thing in itself. Multiplicity is an appearance; peoples and their life are abstractions, just as the genus is an abstraction in nature. And since only the individual and not humanity has real unity, the history of humanity is a fiction. Historical facts are the long, confused dream of humanity, and wanting to explain those facts seriously makes you like he who sees groups of men or animals in the clouds.[55] History therefore is not a science but a jumble of arbitrary facts where there can be coordination but not subordination. Likewise a biography is of more interest than the whole history of humanity, for there you can find the eternal page of the *Wille*: egosim, hate, love, fear, courage, frivolty, stupidity, cunning, spirit, genius.[56] In contrast in history you find a supposed spirit of the world, a pure shadow, fleeting facts without meaning that often result from the most futile causes, like clouds stirred up by the winds. Fools and malcontents of today trust in tomorrow, not seeing that time is a phenomenon and that the future is similar to the past, that nothing new happens under the sun, that the superfice changes but the depths remain the same, and that the world resembles certain Italian comedies where you find that underneath various plots made of events, Pantalone is always Pantalone and Colombina is always Colombina.[57] Let's even suppose that there is intellectual progress; men still wouldn't be changed by that. Neither learning nor upbringing will work to make them less wicked and less unhappy: *moral* progress is a dream.

A. We should thus close the universities and schools and abolish all history.

D. I'm not saying that. History isn't totally useless, because a people that does not know its own history is like a man who has no memory of his past life, tied to the present like an animal.

A. But there is *Wille* in the individual. *Wille* gives you your character, and your character gives you necessity and the subordination of events. The people is a poetic fiction; it has no *Wille* and no character, and its history is a mass of clouds of different shapes, and I don't know what resolution can be extracted from it.

D. A little bit of experience can always be extracted. A simple woman who has tried a medicine in one case, if she remembers it, can use it again in a similar case.

A. Which means that history is an empirical medicine.

D. Do you believe that it's really a medicine to treat the many evils that afflict humanity? They are incurable evils, inherent to our nature.

A. What about the monarchy with its nobles, priests, and privileges?

D. That serves only to assure rights.

A. Does that seem like a small thing to you?

D. Well, since pleasure is negative and only suffering exists, rights don't have any affirmative aspect to them, affirmation is an injustice.[58]

A. How clever! No means yes, and yes means no. This invention deserves first prize, and second prize we can give to Hegel, who says that yes and no are the same thing.

D. If injustice didn't exist, rights wouldn't exist either. A right is a negation of a wrong. The State is the guardian of rights, because it defends me against whoever wants to do wrong to me. For this reason it is a police commissioner, not a doctor. It cannot heal us of our sicknesses, and it would not even be desirable for it to heal us.

A. This is a real discovery, since no one has ever said it. Up to this point I was saying to myself: "Leopardi also said that." Because Leopardi does not believe in progress; he laughs at the philosophy of history; and he considers our sicknesses to be irremediable. It's only that business about rights and injustice that you don't find in him, but I do remember it in father Bartoli.[59] But neither in Leopardi, nor in Bartoli, nor anyone else have I found that our recovery is undesirable.

D. This is because if you are cured of suffering, what remains is not pleasure, which is a negation, but an enemy who is even more bothersome: boredom. It is likewise because were we all happy the result would be an increase in the population the frightening consequences of which terrify every daring imagination.[60]

A. I'm sorry, Gioberti. We must bestow the prize on Schopenhauer. Your brain would not have known how to dream this up, though it has certainly dreamt up plenty. So what type of world is this, then? The fatherland is an abstraction; humanity is a fiction; history is a little game of clouds; the individual is condemned irredeemably to suffering and boredom. Then why do we live? We should kill ourselves. Beautiful, adorable, piteous death.

Shut these sad eyes now on the light
O queen of time.[61]

D. Leopardi was in too much of a hurry to extrapolate the consequences. Schopenhauer figured out how to extract paradise from this hell we call life, and here it really is the case that an eagle's flight takes wing.

A. I challenge Schopenhauer to extrapolate any consequence other than suicide.

D. He's up to it. Listen and learn. The Indians and the Christians discovered the true medicine. You must die, but without ceasing to live.

A. Which is the most convenient way to satisfy life and death.

D. The *Wille* desires to live; it always runs toward life; life is its eternal present. And living signifies giving oneself to the satisfaction of every desire and need. At first it operates as a blind stimulus, without awareness, and says: "I want to live." Then it gives itself a brain endowed with intellect, recognizes itself in the cosmic image, and says again: "I want to live." In man it gives itself not only an intellect, as in animals, but reason, and it still says: "I want to live." And as life, that is to say the satisfaction of needs and desires, it is more difficult in the form of man, it has constructed itself a more artificial brain, such that the intellect is more acute and quicker, and it has added in reason, the faculty of the absolute according to the three charlatans, which in substance was placed by the *Wille* in the intellect's service for its needs. This is because the intellect only takes care of the present, while reason – the faculty of concepts – abstracts, generalizes, coordinates, subordinates, ties the present to the past and predicts the future. Armed with these two very powerful weapons, the *Wille*, in the form of man, gives itself over to the pleasure of living, and this is the source of its unhappiness: for desire swarms with desire, and need generates need, but there is no way of fulfilling it and so it lives in a state of agitation.

A. We need to find it a tranquillizer.

D. Reason does give it a sedative. This is because, in a man of good judgment who has experienced the suffering of life, reason speaks thus: "Don't you realize that individuals are disappearing dreams, that everything passes, that pleasure is an appearance, that the desire to live, the love of life is the root of all your evils?" There's no way out from this except waging war against the *Wille*, that is to say desires and passions. This means considering all of the things that men cling to – pleasures, honours, riches – to be empty phantoms, killing off your will to live or to take pleasure. *Sustine et abstine*: follow this principle and you will recover a peaceful soul.

A. The peace of the grave.

D. Now you understand what it means to say "dying without ceasing to live." You live, but renouncing the pleasures of life as something vain; only men endowed with reason are able to do so. Animals and all things want to live; only you can place yourself above life. This is because, once you have experience of that type of reason which does not stop at the level of individuals but rather gives you universal knowledge as if in a mirror with its memory of the past and anticipation of the future, you can then pose the following question: "what good is life? What gain do you get from so much trouble, running to keep up? *Le jeu vaut-il bien la chandelle*?" And when you have persuaded yourself that life isn't worth the pain that a gentleman suffers for her sake …

A. What will I do then?

D. You will kill off the *Wille* that attracts you to life.

A. That is to say the *Wille* kills itself.

D. Of course. The *Wille* affirms itself and denies itself in its freedom and omnipotence. By means of reason it ends up with its own negation. And since the generative act is at the centre of the *Wille* when it wants to live, you must first of all abstain from carnal pleasures and then castigate the flesh with fasting, shirts of hair, and abstinence.

A. Like Saint Anthony in the desert.

D. The Brahmins and saints shall be your exemplars, and you can reduce the recipe to these three famous words: "Chastity, poverty, obedience." In this way living is dying without having to make recourse to suicide, which is the refuge of weak souls.

A. Meanwhile the others will enjoy themselves and make fun of me?

D. Rather you will make fun of them, because from your height and calm you will look upon them as one in a safe harbour looks at men caught in the storm. You will do as Schopenhauer, who in '48, while everyone ran about like madmen fighting against one another, sat back observing them all through a telescope, laughing under his moustache and saying: "You all can go get yourselves killed, but I'm here contemplating the *Wille*." In effect, if men were to allow themselves to be persuaded that freedom, humanity, nationality, the fatherland, and all the other things for which they feel passion are abstractions and appearances, each one would stay at home in peace and cling to the contemplative life in private and public alike. Then instead of running out into the squares and toiling and tormenting himself and others, he would stretch out on a sofa, smoking with gusto like a Turk, and watch as his individuality evaporated bit by bit among the circles of smoke, and he would feel himself to be pure *Wille*.

A. The sofa and the pipe is overdoing it, since whoever wants to die living ought to do without those, as well. I imagine poor Schopenhauer like a Trappist monk, a martyr of chastity, poverty, and obedience, sweet as a lamb, and his body full of wounds from his shirts of hair.

D. Schopenhauer eats divinely; he takes advantage of all the pleasures that are still possible for him; and he's always shouting and making a din, tyrannized by the *Wille.* If you mention Hegel to him he'll become a storm, and to calm him you must praise his clarity and originality.

A. So what use is philosophy, then?

D. Philosophy is theoretical knowledge, which has nothing to do with praxis. Reason is as ill-suited to making you virtuous as aesthetics are to making you an artist. Everyone acts according to his nature. You can't be a saint if you don't have the vocation for it, which is to say if the *Wille* didn't give you that character. Just as one is born a poet, so too is one born a saint: *Welle non discitur*. For this reason Schopenhauer gives no precepts. He doesn't say: "you must kill off the desire to live within yourself." No prohibitions, no categorical imperative. He describes the actions of men; he doesn't impose them. The knowledge of the world as a phenomenon works as a motive, and it ties you to life. The knowledge of the world as essence works as a sedative, and it detaches you from life. It isn't necessary that philosophy give you this knowledge; it would be enough for you to have it immediately. What is necessary is that you have the predisposition to holiness – grace.[62]

A. We started out with Kant and ended up with Saint Augustine. I believe that I myself am lacking grace, because that philosophy of chastity, poverty, and obedience doesn't do it for me. I want to live happily, and when it's time to die, we'll die. Or if I come up against some circumstance that makes life unbearable for me, I would rather return to the womb of *Wille* all at once than slowly draw closer to it with a long death under the name of life. I prefer Leopardi to Schopenhauer.

D. You're wrong. Leopardi aligns with Schopenhauer in the substantial points of his doctrine, but he is beneath him in many respects. First of all, Leopardi is a poet, and men don't commonly lend credence to a doctrine developed in verses, since poets have a liar's voice.

A. But Leopardi philosophized in prose, as well.

D. He didn't exactly philosophize, since philosophizing requires a method. And this method is one of Schopenhauer's glories. There have been so many controversies about analysis and synthesis, psychology and ontology. Schopenhauer hasn't been read, but his work would have been Brennus's sword in the balance. Analysis and synthesis, Arthur says, are incorrect terms, and we ought to rather say induction and deduction. Now philosophy's method is no different from that of all the empirical sciences, and it must be analytical, which is the same as saying inductive – taking experience as its foundation and extracting judgments from it. To do this requires an appropriate faculty, which he calls the faculty of judgment, placed midway between intellect and reason, the intellect that sees and the reason that forms concepts. The philosopher sees, not demonstrates. The very word evidence proves as much, as it is manifestly derived from the verb "to see." But because of an ancient prejudice it is accepted that philosophy must start with the general and descend to the particular, which we call deduction and is done by means of demonstration. From this came the opinion that without a demonstration there is no true truth. But demonstrating is the easiest of things, requiring no more than common sense, whereas in order to extract truth from objects we need that faculty of judgement which is permitted to only a very few. This is because in order to do this it is necessary to have a good understanding of the two procedures that Kant and Plato discuss, homogeneity and specification, which is to say gathering together what objects have in common and what they have of their own, coordinating and subordinating, not skipping any steps, not leaving any lacunas, respecting every difference and similarity. You can add that the demonstrative method is exceptionally boring because, since all of the particulars are contained within the general, you already know from the very first page what is going to come next, and it's like going out every day to walk around Saint Mark's Square.[63] In contrast in Schopenhauer's books you find an infinite variety that excites your curiosity and is more like travelling from one city to another. What is more, a philosophy founded on general concepts like the absolute substance, God, the infinite, the finite, absolute identity, being, or essence is basically living on air and can never seize reality. And here, his chest full of holy scorn, Arthur heaps flames upon Schelling, Hegel, and all the modern fabricators of concepts.[64] They give you a philosophy of words, whereas he gives you a philosophy of things. Because from his observatory he looks at objects very clearly, seeing what is similar and what is different, and with his most potent faculty of judgment he is able to pull out the newest truths from them, such that you will remain silent in wonder. And how he strives to thrust them into your head! How well he handles them such that each takes the form of a paradox and entices your attention! And if you fall asleep, it will be him who wakes you up and says: "Look what erudition! And look here at this paradox! Wait and you'll see how clearly I explain Kant to you! You must know that I don't read histories of philosophy but always the original works! And I assure you that I always think with my own head!"

A. Is that true, at least?

D. Let's leave the joking aside. It is true. Schopenhauer has an uncommon mind: lucid, quick, hot, and often acute. You can add to that an unordinary doctrine. And even if you don't agree with all of his judgments, you run into many rare things here and there, acquire all kinds of knowledge, and pass the time with great enjoyment, as he is most pleasing to read. Leopardi reasons with common sense, demonstrating just like that, as it comes to him. He doesn't think about making an effect; he's too modest, too sober. His gaunt prose reflects the squalour of life that he wants to represent like a mirror; his style is like his world, an unlovable desert where you search for a flower in vain. Schopenhauer, on the other hand, when you cut through his loquacity, can't contain himself: he is copious, florid, lively, happy. He enjoys pronouncing the most bitter truths to you, because beneath it all is the thought: "The discovery is mine." He distracts and is distracted, and when he reasons sometimes you feel like you're in a pleasant conversation where, in-between a cup of tea and a glass of champagne, he declaims on the vanity and poverty of life. As such you read Schopenhauer with pleasure, and you esteem Leopardi.

A. I understand. Leopardi died young, a martyr to his ideas. Schopenhauer still continues to die without ceasing to live.

D. You're like a child who has been trusted with too much confidence, for this is a lovely and good bit of insolence.

A. You want a monopoly on joking. Let Schopenhauer live many, many more years, and he will regale us with a new treatise on the *Wille*. Indeed, I promise you that I will set myself to studying for real, and I would like to translate his principle work and propagate it in the Kingdom of Naples. Because I think that it would please Campagna a great deal if his most faithful subjects dedicated themselves to the contemplative life, took vows of chastity, poverty, and obedience, and leaving him to be the victim of life, spent their time meditating on death.

D. But if you want your edition to bear fruit, you must first burn all the originals of Leopardi.

A. It seems to me that Schopenhauer inculcated the sickness of paradoxes in you. We said that they both think the same.

D. I say this because Leopardi produces the opposite effect from what he intends. He doesn't believe in progress, and he makes you desire it. He doesn't believe in freedom, and he makes you love it. He calls love, glory, and virtue illusions, and he lights up an inexhaustible desire for them in your chest. You cannot take your leave of him without feeling better, and you cannot approach him without first trying to compose yourself and purify yourself so that you don't have reason to blush in his presence. He is a sceptic, and he makes you a believer; and while he doesn't believe it is possible to have a less-sad future for our shared fatherland, he awakens a vital love for that fatherland in your breast and inflames you toward noble deeds. He has such a lowly notion of humanity, yet his high soul, gentle and pure, honours and ennobles it. And if destiny had prolonged his life up to '48, you feel that you would have found him beside you, giving comfort and fighting. A pessimist and anti-cosmic thinker, like Schopenhauer, he does not preach the absurd negation of the *Wille*, the unnatural abstention or mortification of the cenobite – that philosophy of idleness that would have reduced Europe to an emasculated Oriental immobility if the freedom and activity of thought had not defeated Dominican ferocity and Jesuit cunning. Leopardi is certainly opposed to the passions, but only the wicked ones; and while he calls all of life a shadow and error, without knowing how, you feel yourself holding tighter to everything in life that is noble and great. For Leopardi idleness is an abdication of human dignity, cowardice. Schopenhauer requires activity as a means of preserving good health. And if you'd like to measure the abyss that divides these two souls with a single example, reflect that for Schopenhauer the difference between the slave and the free man is more one in name than in fact, for if the free man is able to go from one place to another, the slave has the advantage of sleeping peacefully and living without thinking, having his master to provide for his needs.[65] Had Leopardi read that sentence, he would have blushed at being, as *Wille*, of the same nature as Schopenhauer.

A. Up till now we've been joking. Now you're pulling a tragic face.

D. You could add that the deep sadness with which Leopardi explains life does not lead you to accept it, and you want and strive for the comfort of another explanation. As such were chance, or fortune, or destiny to have it that Schopenhauer were to peek his head out in Italy, he would find Leopardi there, who would attach himself to his feet like a lead ball and impede him from going forward.

A. It's getting late, and Schopenhauer has given me a big appetite, and since I lack grace, I cannot conquer the *Wille*. Goodbye.

D. You're going to just leave me like that? This whole discussion will remain without a conclusion?

A. I'll be the one to draw the conclusion. If you read Leopardi, you'll have to go get yourself killed. If you read Schopenhauer, you'll have to become a monk. If you read the rest of the modern philosophers, you'll have to be hung for love of the idea.

D. I understand. A young lady once told Rousseau: "James, leave women and study 'mathematics.'"[66]

A. Which means that for me it's the opposite. I'm leaving mathematics and studying women. I want to go back to Naples, burn every book of philosophy, and become friends with Campagna. I'll invite him to lunch, and we can have a philosophical conversation about beautiful girls. Goodbye.

D. And I'll get to work writing that article for the *Rivista Contemporanea*.

Notes

Introduction

1 Quoted in Hofmann, *The Fascist Effect*, 19. There is some variety in the capitalization of D'Annunzio's name. I follow the convention of capitalizing the 'D' when it is the first letter of his name and leaving it in lowercase, as D'Annunzio himself preferred, when it is a part of his whole name (Gabriele d'Annunzio): see Gochin Raffaelli and Subialka, "Introduction." Throughout this book, translations from Italian are my own unless otherwise cited.

2 Amano argues that Japan and Italy share both the experience of marginal modernity and paradigms of literary renewal: Amano, *Decadent Literature*, 28–9.

3 Woodhouse, *Gabriele D'Annunzio*, 315. A spate of recent scholarship uses the Fiume episode to examine D'Annunzio's experiment in nation-building, which prefigures fascist nationalism in important regards. Knipp, *Die Kommune*. See also Mondini, *Fiume 1919*; Salierno, *Nino Daniele*; Vogel-Walter, *D'Annunzio*; and Gumbrecht, Kittler, and Siegert, *Der Dichter als Kommandant*. Cf. Carli, *Con D'Annunzio*.

4 Emilio Gentile's account of the origins of Italian fascism shows the importance of D'Annunzio's pairing of poetic leadership and avant-garde aesthetics: Gentile, *The Origins*, 142.

5 Amano, *Decadent Literature*, 61.

6 Mishima read Western literature voraciously, with some emphasis on D'Annunzio: Yourcenar, *Mishima*, 21.

7 "Fascism thus cannot be separated from modernism; modernism and fascism together formed a lingua franca spoken as fluently in Japan as in Europe. An exchange of ideas – both modernist and fascist – across the globe linked Japanese fascism with German, Italian, French, and other fascisms, each of which employed its own ideological mechanisms

and drew on shared but also native rhetorical styles and images. The culmination of a conservative revolutionary tradition, with roots in Nietzsche and Bergson and intellectual branches that reached across national boundaries, fascism encompassed not only state intellectuals but also modernist writers such as Ezra Pound and Wyndham Lewis in the United States and England, Gottfried Benn in Germany, F.T. Marinetti and D'Annunzio in Italy, Georges Sorel and Louis-Ferdinand Céline in France, and Giménez Caballero in Spain" (Tansman, *The Aesthetics*, 18). I argue that this connection comes into clearer focus when we consider the underlying idealist outlook animating both modernist artistic production and fascist political ideology.

8 D'Annunzio has frequently served as an instance of the troubling connection between decadent aesthetics and fascist nationalism. For example, Umberto Eco observed that D'Annunzio's dandy aestheticism marks a distinct fusion not seen elsewhere: "The national poet was D'Annunzio, a dandy who in Germany or in Russia would have been sent to the firing squad. He was appointed as the bard of the regime because of his nationalism and his cult of heroism – which were in fact abundantly mixed up with influences of French fin de siècle decadence" (Eco, "Ur-Fascism").

9 On education, philosophy, and the Westernization of Meiji Japan, see Collins, *The Sociology*, 369–78; and Lincicome, *Principle.* On the lasting legacy of German philosophy in Japanese modernization, and German idealism in particular, see Maraldo, "The Japanese Encounter"; Ryōsuke and Katsuya, "The Kyoto School"; Takashi, "How Western Philosophy Was Received"; and Barcénas, "Modern Japanese Aesthetics."

10 Japanese artists also exoticized the modern West, blending various Western locales in a homogenizing way. For example, Utagawa Yoshitora's *North America* (*Kita Amerika shō*, 1866) depicts a church in Kent, England; similarly, Utagawa Hiroshige II's *A Picture of Prosperity: America* (*Amerika shin no zu*, 1861) depicts a castle in Copenhagen.

11 Burnham, "Introduction," 13.

12 Irvine, *Japonisme*, 229.

13 The Impressionist reception of Japanese art from the 1870s on was inspired by the sense of its "immediacy and (by European standards) seeming informality" (House, "Impressionism and Japan," 105). On Van Gogh's deep and multilayered engagement with Japan, see *Van Gogh and Japan.*

14 Genova, *Writing Japonisme.*

15 D'Annunzio's dual-faceted engagement with Japanese modernity is examined by Turoff, "Il Giappone."

16 Reinvention of sexuality was a key component of self-invention according to Reed, *Bachelor Japanists*, 4; though Reed does not mention him, his

account sheds further light on the connection between D'Annunzio (the dandy-poet-warrior who was also a Hellenist and participated in queer decadence) and *Japonisme*.

17 Schiermeier, "Imitation or Innovation?," 164.

18 The connection between Japanese decadence and D'Annunzio is only one facet of a broader cultural exchange, which includes the Japanese reception of Futurism. Marinetti's famous manifesto circulated by March 1909, just a month after its publication in Paris, in *Subaru*, the same journal in which D'Annunzio's *Trionfo della morte* was translated. See Omuka, "Futurism in Japan"; and Wu, "Transcending the Boundaries," 353. Japanese modernism connects to multiple Western writers and movements – especially Surrealism, as emphasized by Bush, "Contexts for Modernism," 17–19.

19 As Pericles Lewis points out in his introduction of the term, at least since 1927 critics have identified modernism as a movement or grouping (Lewis, "Introduction," 1), starting with Laura Riding and Robert Graves's *Survey of Modernist Poetry*. Orr, "Modernism," offers an overview of the viability of periodizing approaches to modernism, arguing that despite criticism that model retains its institutional power. Potolsky, *The Decadent Republic*, offers a network-based understanding of the cosmopolitan nature of decadence, which I consider here as an aspect of modernism.

20 Peter Gay's popular account of modernism defines it as precisely "the lure of heresy" (Gay, *Modernism*). Diepeveen, *The Difficulties*, examines modernism as a shift toward difficulty as a means of rejecting traditional aesthetic forms. The view of modernism as a shift in aesthetic paradigms is ubiquitous; interestingly, though, two of the most powerful critical theorizations of this aesthetic shift present themselves as counter-histories: Rancière sees modernism as a subset of a new "aesthetic regime" in art: Ranciére, *Aisthesis*, 62; meanwhile, Agamben, *The Man without Content*, depicts the historical emergence of an autonomous aesthetic sphere as a long shift beginning in the Renaissance *Wunderkammer* and culminating in the self-annihilating aestheticism of decadent modernism. Both accounts follow the Marxian line running through Walter Benjamin as well as Horkheimer and Adorno's critical modernist self-understandings: Horkheimer and Adorno, *Dialectic of Enlightenment*.

21 Eisenstadt articulates the need for a paradigm shift toward theorizing multiple modernities, separating the concepts of "modernity" and "Westernization" (Eisenstadt, "Multiple Modernities," 2–3). Fourie, "A Future," shows how the discourse on this multiplicity flourished in the 2000s, though sometimes at the risk of defining "modernity" too broadly. The notion of multiple modernities is at the root of Charles Taylor's articulation of modern social imaginaries (plural): Taylor, *Modern Social Imaginaries*.

22 Wollaeger, "Introduction," 14.
23 Mao and Walkowitz, "The New Modernist Studies," are at the centre of this paradigm shift, showing how the new modernist studies expand temporally, geographically, and beyond the usual division of high and low art. As Susan Stanford Friedman playfully and convincingly shows, this expansion results in "an archive of modernisms that is staggering in its global and temporal reach" (Friedman, "Planetarity," 491); yet an expansion beyond comfortable limits is necessary (Friedman, *Planetary Modernisms*, 3). Even so, stubborn disciplinary realities remain. For example, the special issue of *Modernist Cultures* dedicated to "Global Modernism" frames its task in terms of the spatial expansion of modernist studies, focusing on exchange, reception, and circulation (Jaillant and Martin, "Introduction," 2). Tellingly, however, these exchanges all involve a relation with the anglophone world, maintaining the anglocentric tendency of the new modernist studies even while promoting its geographical enlargement. There is still need to decentre the anglophone component – without eliminating it – and my elaboration of modernist idealism aims at just such a project. See also (though the list is incomplete): Ross and Lindgren, *The Modernist World*; J. Berman, *Modernist Commitments*; GoGwilt, *The Passage*; Ramazani, *A Transnational Poetics;* Pollard, *New World Modernisms;* and Gikandi, *Writing in Limbo*. Related projects that do not rely on the key term modernism but operate in the same discursive space include Saler, *The Fin-De-Siecle World;* and Potolsky, *The Decadent Republic.*
24 Hayot and Walkowitz, *A New Vocabulary*, 8.
25 Hayot and Walkowitz, *A New Vocabulary*, 9.
26 Sherry, "Introduction," 20.
27 See Taylor, *Modern Social Imaginaries.*
28 Sherry, *Modernism*, 32–3.
29 Sherry articulates that broader sense of "modernism" as relating to its English-language definition, which he claims "operates as a denominator for a more chronic pattern of consciousness and a more diachronic experience of history" than the European notion of modernity, which is a response to the specific crisis time after the French Revolution (Sherry, "Introduction," 6). He sees the temporal dynamics of modernism as allowing for a critical shift away from exclusivity (a historically restrained notion of where modernity lies) toward a promisingly inclusive alternative (18–19). In principle his argument thus understands itself as participating in the impulse to expand the new modernist studies.
30 Mazzini's political idealism was no doubt connected to his education and interest in the work of the German post-Kantian thinkers and romanticism: "He became attracted to and familiar with romantic poetry and idealist

philosophy: he read and admired the works of Vico, Herder, Goethe, Fichte, the Schlegel brothers, and Schelling, and he wrote some innovative essays on the character of Italian literature from Dante Alighieri to Ugo Foscolo" (Recchia and Urbinati, "Introduction," 4).

31 Burnett, "Giuseppe Mazzini," 514.

32 "Mazzini was a visionary and undoubtedly an idealist, in the sense that he deeply believed in the power of ideas to effect lasting political change" (Recchia and Urbinati, "Introduction," 30).

33 The characterization of Mazzini as propagator of a religion of altruism is Burnett's: "Giuseppe Mazzini," 523.

34 Oriani describes materialism as a base animal form of living, which he connects to Darwinism and positivism as opposed to the high idealist thought of Hegel in philosophy and Christianity in religion: Oriani, *La rivolta ideale*, 59.

35 The problem of locating a precise definition of idealism is illustrated in Beiser, "Romanticism and Idealism."

36 My overview here draws on the following for a general concept of idealism: Dunham, Grant, and Watson, *Idealism*; Bubner, *The Innovations*; and Ameriks, *The Cambridge Companion*.

37 Dunham, Grant, and Watson, *Idealism*, 10.

38 See the *OED* entry on "idealism, n."

39 Hampton, for instance, makes realism into a subset of idealism, defining "realism" as a way of describing "objective idealism," or the notion that ideals exist independently of subjective thought and are thus "real and constitutive of reality" (Hampton, *Romanticism*, 21).

40 Borges, *Ficciones*.

41 Kant's transcendental idealism is articulated throughout *The Critique of Pure Reason*.

42 Kant, *Prolegomena*, 40.

43 This is not to imply that Kant is a "relativist." All the same, an important philosophical source for later notions of relativism comes from precisely this move in Kant's first *Critique*.

44 Bubner, *The Innovations*, is an excellent example of this tendency to think of German idealism as the essential instance of modern idealist thought.

45 Schopenhauer offers his own history of the various philosophical approaches to the question of idealism and the relation it posits between the ideal and the real, insisting that the post-Kantians listed here are merely "sham philosophers" and that their systems of idealism are not dedicated to the pursuit of truth: Schopenhauer, *Parerga and Paralipomena*, I, 21. De Sanctis picks up on this invective and replicates it in his imaginary dialogue on Schopenhauer, which is translated in the Appendix here.

46 On German idealism and the relations among the various schools or derivations following Kant's thought, see: Gabriel and Rasmussen, *German Idealism Today*; Beiser, *German Idealism*; Hammer, *German Idealism*; Pinkard, *German Philosophy*; and Beiser, *The Fate of Reason*.

47 On the connection between idealism and romanticism, see: Breazeale and Rockmore, *Fichte*; and Behler, *German Romantic Literary Theory*.

48 It would of course be possible to argue that German romanticism constitutes a part of the long modernist period, a response to the conditions of modernity that, like so many others, relies on elements of an idealist outlook to motivate a heightened claim for the power of art to reveal truths of the world that are obscured by the forms of modern thought and life. See Bowie, "German Idealism," 241.

49 Beiser suggests that according to the standard narrative, German idealism ends with Hegel; nevertheless, idealist philosophy continues after his death in the work of Trendelenburg, Lotze, and Hartmann, who sought to ground idealist conclusions in new methods from the empirical sciences (Beiser, *After Hegel*, 10). My examination of German idealism is informed by this view, which does not see Hegel as a historical endpoint.

50 The term "absolute idealism" (*absoluter Idealismus*) was first used not by Hegel but by Schelling in his 1797 work, *Ideas for a Philosophy of Nature* (50). Even if Hegel is often seen today as its primary proponent, the term is nevertheless associated with a whole host of "romantic"-era thinkers (Beiser, "The Enlightenment," 18). De Sanctis describes Hegel in similar terms; see "Schopenhauer and Leopardi" in the Appendix here.

51 Hegel, *Hegel's Aesthetics*, vol. 1, 90.

52 Hegel, *Lectures on the Philosophy of World History*, 128.

53 There are numerous interpretations of Hegel's philosophy of history and of his phenomenology. I examine some of the key positions in chapter 1.

54 My summary traces the basic structure of *The World as Will and Representation* and draws on notions from his other works. More thorough overviews of Schopenhauer's philosophy can be found in (among others): "Arthur Schopenhauer" (2019); Wellbery, "Schopenhauer"; and Janaway, "Introduction." Cartwright, *Historical Dictionary*, defines key notions and terms in Schopenhauer's thought.

55 Schopenhauer is the "philosopher of art with the largest influence on artists, on their understanding of themselves, and on their artistic production" (Hammermeister, *The German Aesthetic Tradition*, 111). Cf. Jacquette, *Schopenhauer, Philosophy*. On the fundamentally aesthetic stance of Schopenhauer's philosophy, see Vasalou, *Schopenhauer*.

56 Taylor, *A Secular Age*, 12–14.

57 Taylor may offer the most philosophically systematic articulation of this crisis of fullness and attendant nostalgia in relation to the transformed

horizons of faith in European modernity, but he is hardly alone. George Steiner, for instance, asserted that the modern crisis of faith gave rise to alternative "mythologies," including Freudian psychoanalysis, Marxian politics, and philosophical irrationalism (Steiner, *Nostalgia for the Absolute*). Cf. Burrow, *The Crisis of Reason*.

58 Here I draw on Sherry's articulation of the deeply intertwined relation of decadence and modernism as a response to crisis time in modernity (Sherry, *Modernism*, 34). This theorization speaks to what David Weir already articulated in his study of modernity's debt to decadence: Weir, *Decadence*.

59 This is the argument advanced by Mimmo Cangiano in *La nascita del modernismo italiano*, which I address at greater length below. While this extreme characterization may hold true for some modernist writers such as Aldo Palazzeschi, whom Cangiano describes as the most extreme proponent of the "phantasmagoric spectacle of contingency" (269), or for some modernist thinkers, such as Ernst Mach (18), I take issue with Cangiano's repeated assertion that this constitutes the "hegemonic" position in modernist discourse (29). As my readings of Pirandello will exemplify, it simply is not the case that modernist writers who take perspectivism seriously all totalize a nihilistic view of absence as the only truth. All the same, certainly one of the limit cases of the modernist engagement with new notions of relativity, contingency, and so on, is expressed in this vision that makes vital flux the new centre of its decentred world view.

60 Lear, *Radical Hope*, 80.

61 The interrelations of decadence, the avant-garde, and modernism are central both in the general theorization of the concepts (Calinescu, *Five Faces*) and in the specific history of Italian modernism (Somigli and Moroni, *Italian Modernism*).

62 Key recent studies of vitalism in relation to modernism include Mitchell, *Experimental Life*; Ardoin, Gontarski, and Mattison, *Understanding Bergson*; Packham, *Eighteenth-Century Vitalism*, 207–16; and Jones, *The Racial Discourses*.

63 See Moses, *Out of Character*, which focuses especially on the vitalist legacy of Henri Bergson, William James, and Friedrich Nietzsche.

64. Nineteenth-century magical and occult beliefs are not an exception but a continuation of a long legacy (Josephson-Storm, *The Myth of Disenchantment*); indeed, the history of magic is rich, complicated, and enduring (Copenhaver, *Magic in Western Culture*).

65 Franklin, *Spirit Matters*, 2.

66 Rabaté, *James Joyce*.

67 Coole and Frost, "Introducing the New Materialisms," 3.

68 Jonathan Basile goes so far as to dispute the claim to novelty in Bennett's book, and in the new materialist studies more generally (Basile, "Life/ Force"). It is worth pointing out, however, that the lack of radical newness in Bennett's theory is already highlighted by Bennett herself in an essay on historical vitalism and the new materialism (Bennett, "A Vitalist Stopover," 47).

69 The complexity of these debates is visible in efforts to craft a scientific-philosophical theory of evolutionary emergence that could replace the mystical aspects of vitalist dualism with a mechanistic account of life's (conscious) emergence without, however, engaging in a materialist reduction – an early-twentieth-century ambition for "a synthesis of antimaterialist and antidualist thought" (Garrett, "Vitalism," 152).

70 Grosz, *The Incorporeal*, 13.

71 Grosz, *The Incorporeal*, 14.

72 In this respect my argument aligns with Amanda Jo Goldstein's suggestion that the investigation of material reality is already expanded and transformed as early as romanticism by conceiving of poetic knowledge as a form of empirical inquiry: Goldstein, *Sweet Science*. However, where Goldstein unearths a romantic materialism rooted in Lucretius's non-dualist atomism, my argument shifts the lens to consider the role of idealist thought.

73 I thus agree with the critique of new materialist ethics posed by Paul Rekret, who argues that the attempt to assert a direct connection between ontology (the reinterpretation of matter) and ethics fails in part because it ignores essential questions about the origins of thought/consciousness: Rekret, "A Critique."

74 I have in mind here Hans Ulrich Gumbrecht's notion of artistic materiality: Gumbrecht, *Production of Presence*; likewise, I draw on the discourse about how literature gives shape to thought by engaging the emotions (Nussbaum, *Upheavals of Thought*) and how literature trains our cognitive faculties (Landy, *How to Do Things*). In my view, a philosophical world view or conceptual outlook becomes *real*, part of the actual world and human interactions, because it is given a material form that can motivate human action through intellectual-affective engagement.

75 Vasalou, *Schopenhauer.*

76 Wellbery, "Schopenhauer," 327.

77 The centrality of artistic practice to Schopenhauer's afterlife is thus not a problem, as some critics suggest – for example, arguing that Schopenhauer "only" lives on in art and not in an explicitly philosophical reception and thus his ideas "remained isolated in the history of ideas" (Hammermeister, *The German Aesthetic Tradition*, 111).

78 See Jodock, *Catholicism*. Wittman, "*Omnes velut aqua dilabimur*," argues for the importance of Catholic modernism to understandings of modernism more generally.

79 The most recent overview and discussion of these debates is offered by Cangiano, *La nascita*, 11–29. While the recent theorization of Italian modernism has mostly been contained in Italian-language publications, the globalization of modernist studies has also brought Italian sources into view; Ram, "Futurist Geographies," and Rainey, "F.T. Marinetti," show the global dimensions of Futurism, while Somigli, "Italy," offers an account of Italy's place in European modernism.

80 Somigli and Moroni, "Introduction," 25.

81 Some key instances of this Italian-language debate: Castellana, "Realismo modernista," contends that modernism encompasses a realist vein, examining the work of Pirandello together with that of Svevo and Federico Tozzi. Cf. Castellana, *Finzione e memoria*; and Castellana, *Parole, cose, persone*. Baldi, *Reale invisibile*, groups Pirandello and Gadda in a consideration of modernist interiority. Donnarumma, "Maschere della violenza," analyses modernism in relation to critical humour. Luperini investigates Pirandello, the intellectual history of the period, and *La Voce*: Luperini, *Pirandello*, and Luperini, *Gli esordi del Novecento*. Cf. Tortora, "Verifica dei Valori," and Gazzola, *Montale the Modernist*. Of course specific figures have also been important to English-language scholars, though not usually in an effort to argue for and establish a canon of Italian modernism in the same way. See, for instance, Minghelli, *In the Shadow*, which reads Svevo as a lynchpin who opened Italian literature to "modernist experimentation and contamination" (13).

82 Adamson, *Embattled Avant-Gardes*, 3, 344; Perloff, *The Futurist Moment*.

83 Laura Wittman had already articulated a key way in which Catholic modernism's mysticism is integral to Italian literary and artistic modernism more generally, though Cangiano does not engage her argument directly: Wittman, "*Omnes velut aqua dilabimur*," 131.

84 Adamson, *Embattled Avant-Gardes*, 18.

85 Cangiano characterizes modernism explicitly as an expression of crisis, "la crisi filosofica che il moderniso esprime" (*La nascita*, 21).

86 Harrison, "Overcoming Aestheticism," 183.

87 Modernism's elevation of the incomplete privileges the essay as a mode of experimenting, setting forth something without affirming it in absolute terms: Harrison, "Overcoming Aestheticism," 187. His analysis thus points back to his earlier analysis of figures like Pirandello and Musil in Harrison, *Essayism*.

88 See Baioni, "*La lotta politica*," 187.

89 As Nicholas Goodrick-Clarke puts it, "influences from Schopenhauer, Hegel, and Nietzsche combined in [Evola's] philosophical idealism to

assert the 'the ability to be unconditionally whatever one wants' and 'the world is my representation'" (Goodrick-Clarke, *Black Sun*, 313). Here, again, it is clear that the way in which post-Kantian thinkers like Hegel and Schopenhauer were received does not always align with the best possible interpretation of their thought. Yet these influences characterize the particular forms of idealist thought that operate in modernism.

90 For example, Richard Spencer, a prominent white nationalist figure in the Trump era, lauded Steve Bannon's reading of Evola as an indication of Bannon's potential to usher in radical change to American politics: Beiner, *Dangerous Minds*, 11–12. The paradoxical union of radical or revolutionary opposition to the liberal order and the supposed conservative traditionalism of these far-right thinkers is typical of historical fascism, as well.

91 Eburne, *Outsider Theory*.

92 See the volume edited and translated by Massimo Verdicchio, Croce, *A Croce Reader*. This adds to the vast compendium of modern Italian thought translated and introduced in the volume edited by Brian and Rebecca Copenhaver, *From Kant to Croce*.

93 See Cangiano, *The Wreckage of Philosophy*; and Cangiano, *La nascita*.

94 Cassano, *Il pensiero meridiano*, sees his theory as a response to the hypotheses of thinkers like Fukuyama, who took up Hegel's notion of the "end of history" and applied it to the post–Cold War American hegemony: Fukuyama, *The End of History*. In a later interview, Cassano contends that Fukuyama's hypothesis is fundamentally flawed precisely because it understands history from a limited, Northern European/Western perspective (Cassano and Fogu, "Il pensiero meridiano oggi," 1). The idea that Italy's "Southern Question" has created a division in the country that otherizes the south in an instance of intra-national Orientalism is taken up in Jane Schneider's volume, *Italy's Southern Question*. Interestingly, as Cangiano has shown, some modernist intellectuals such as Piero Jahier located this "other" to the industrializing Continent not in the south of Italy but in rural alpine communities in the north; this became a part of their push to re-establish a lost moral and epistemic horizon through recourse to "surpassed" forms of life (Cangiano, *La nascita*, 432, 436) while at the same time embracing a cosmopolitan position akin to that of Woodrow Wilson or Giuseppe Mazzini (433, 438).

95 It is interesting in this regard that Pericles Lewis's relatively recent compendium of studies on European modernism, which divides Europe into "core" and "peripheral" modernisms, places Italy in the core (in distinction to other southern nations such as Portugal, Spain, and Greece): Lewis, ed., *The Cambridge Companion*. That placement is a testament

to the growing scholarly discourse on Italian modernism that ties it transnationally to other European modernisms.

96 The formation of a specifically modernist nationalism is described by the historian Emilio Gentile: Gentile, *The Struggle for Modernity*; Gentile, "The Conquest of Modernity."

97 For Suzanne Stewart-Steinberg, Pinocchio represents not only the difficulty facing individual subjects in the new era but also and especially the tricky task facing elite reformers attempting to forge a national identity: Stewart-Steinberg, *The Pinocchio Effect*.

98 As a sometimes Futurist like Bruno Corra suggests, a new nation needs a new art to express its spirit: Corra, *Per l'arte nuova*.

99 See Ziolkowski, *Kafka's Italian Progeny*.

1. Italy at the Banquet of Nations: Hegel in Politics and Philosophy

1 Gramsci, *Prison Notebooks*, vol. 2, 232 (Notebook 4, §56).

2 Gramsci, vol. 2, 232 (Notebook 4, §56).

3 My interpretation of modernism as a philosophical problem and idealism's role in rewriting modern subjectivity draws especially on Pippin, *Idealism as Modernism*; and Taylor, *Sources of the Self*.

4 H. Marcuse, *Reason and Revolution*, 3.

5 This interpretation is rooted in an outlook like the historical materialism that Marx advocates in *Capital*. It likewise fits with the brief narrative of the progress from feudalism to modern capitalism popularized throughout nineteenth-century Europe via Marx and Engels's *The Communist Manifesto*: shifts in relations of production provide the conditions of possibility for shifts in social and political relations, and these in turn require shifts in the intellectual / philosophical discourse. But these ideological shifts can also be traced to the social fabric of the basic structure of what Habermas has analysed under the rubric of the public sphere: Habermas, *The Structural Transformation*.

6 Pinkard, *German Philosophy*, 21.

7 Rockmore, *Before and After Hegel*, offers a broader historical account of how Hegel's thought develops in the context of Kantian and post-Kantian questions, leading to various afterlives and responses, from the Young Hegelians to Kierkegaard's rejection of Hegelianism.

8 Honneth, "Atomism and Ethical Life," begins his reinterpretation of the relationship between Hegel and the Revolution with an overview of the varied and complicated critical debate on the topic.

9 Habermas, "Hegel's Critique," 121. In his lectures collected as *The Philosophical Discourse of Modernity*, Habermas traces this link in greater detail, emphasizing the biographical importance of revolutionary politics

to Hegel and his "young contemporaries in the Tübingen seminary," who were informed not only by debates about religious Enlightenment but also by Kantian philosophy and the political ideals of the French Revolution (24). "Thus," he goes on to argue, "[Hegel and Schelling] turned against both the party of the Enlightenment and that of Orthodoxy" (25).

10 Comay, *Mourning Sickness*.

11 The debate has been long and wide-ranging, and these are only a few of the positions taken in it. See also: Ritter, *Hegel*; Wildt, "Hegels Kritik"; Lukács, *The Young Hegel*; and Steven Smith, "Hegel and the French Revolution."

12 The literature on German idealism and German romanticism in this regard is large. Lougee identifies a traditional list of romantic thinkers, arguing that in multiple respects their philosophies enable a conservative response against modernity while nevertheless insisting that it would be too much to insist on a connection between German romanticism and the nationalism of the absolute state developed in Nazi fascism: Lougee, "German Romanticism," 644–5. German romantic thought's role in the development of (an eventually authoritarian) nationalism is argued for by Kohn, "Romanticism"; and Snyder, *Roots of German Nationalism*. Morrow, however, in "Romanticism and Political Thought," contends that the similarities between romantic rejections of radical politics and the conservative response to the French Revolution obscure an important difference in their approaches to nature and the function of government.

13 Habermas, *The Philosophical Discourse*, 23–44.

14 Pippin, *Idealism as Modernism*, 8. See also: Pippin, *Hegel's Practical Philosophy*.

15 Burrow, *The Crisis of Reason*.

16 My analysis thus adds a new dimension to previous work on the relationship between modernism and nationalism, for example, Pericles Lewis's argument that the modernist novel can be situated as a response to the crisis of liberal nationalism in the aftermath of the Great War: Lewis, *Modernism, Nationalism*, 6.

17 Croce, "An Unknown Page," 170. Marcuse terms Hegel the "so-called official philosopher of the Prussian state" (Marcuse, *Reason and Revolution* [*Reason and Revolution*], 169).

18 Croce, "An Unknown Page," 170–1.

19 Hegel famously saw Napoleon as a manifestation of the world spirit, riding on horseback to transform history and the world. Eric Michael Dale argues that readings of this element in Hegel's thought give rise to the "contemporary myth of the end of history," an interpretation that he traces to Kojève's reading of the role that Napoleon and the Napoleonic

Wars played in what was supposedly the overcoming of the master/slave dialectic (Dale, *Hegel…*, 97).

20 Croce, "An Unknown Page," 170. Croce does not indicate any source for this quotation, which seems to be an inexact paraphrase of a paragraph from an Inaugural Address in which Hegel declares that Germany is the only place in which philosophy can now take place, saying "we have been given *custody* of this *sacred light*" though not specifying that it is God doing the giving (Hegel, *Political Writings*, 183).

21 Croce, "An Unknown Page," 171.

22 Croce, "An Unknown Page," 186–7.

23 The discourse on cosmopolitanism has grown significantly in the last several decades, and as Bruce Robbins and Paulo Lemos Horta emphasize in the introduction to their recent volume on the topic, it is now difficult to think of a singular cosmopolitanism; rather, we must identify the concept as plural – not a commitment to a single vision of world citizenship but something varied both in terms of the degree of its globality and in terms of its origins and dynamics. This is what they term the recent "turn to a descriptive, empirical, plural understanding of cosmopolitanism," one that recognizes not only an elite liberal version of it but also a cosmopolitanism of the poor, the refugee, those whose association to a locality has been uprooted (Robbins and Horta, "Introduction," 8).

In my use here, "cosmopolitan" implies a commitment to a larger whole and a belongingness to that whole – perhaps even a vision that the local can be constituted as particular only as a part of that whole. There is, however, ample debate about to what extent these cosmopolitan commitments overshadow or preclude local or partial commitments. Kwame Anthony Appiah offers an articulation of cosmopolitanism that attempts to negotiate that separation with a focus on balancing both: Appiah, *Cosmopolitanism*; Appiah, *The Ethics of Identity*, 222–3. Likewise, Appiah argues that cosmopolitanism and patriotism are both sentiments rather than ideologies, hence they are not fully mutually exclusive: Appiah, "Cosmopolitan Patriots," 23. His theorization thus dovetails with what I will identify in this chapter with Bertrando Spaventa's Hegelianism and his insistence on thinking of patriotic nation-building in consonance with a cosmopolitan philosophical ideal – though for Appiah patriotism is of the state and not the nation (29).

While a cosmopolitan like Martha Nussbaum takes a relatively robust stance on the precedence of the cosmopolitan whole over the partial locality (Nussbaum, "Reply," 135–6), she also recognizes the limits of the cosmopolitan tradition in terms of its tendency to abstract rationality at the cost of a more human, material approach (Nussbaum, *The Cosmopolitan Tradition*). Toulmin, *Cosmopolis*, likewise argues that modernity's notion of the cosmopolitan rational order reveals a struggle against humanism; in this regard, the rational idealism of Hegel's philosophy of history and its push toward a notion of the rational state may sit in tension with the Italian rediscovery of the Renaissance and return to humanism, both of which constitute a major part of the political project of the new Italy (Rubini, *The Other Renaissance*). For this reason, my use of the term "cosmopolitan" should be taken as weak rather than strong, an indication of a transnational notion of building the community in consonance with the whole.

24 On Neapolitan Hegelianism and the construction of a new state, see *Oldrini, Gli hegeliani di Napoli.*

25 Palmieri was a man of many talents and fields, as recognized by the eulogistic encomium published in the *Atti del Reale Istituto d'Incoraggiamento di Napoli* (vol. 9, Naples: 1896), an institute in which Palmieri had served as president. While Palmieri's career at the University of Naples began when he assumed the chair in physics that had previously belonged to Pasquale Galluppi, a philosopher who responded to modern epistemology from Descartes to Kant and who wrote about transcendental idealism, Palmieri was always more of an experimental scientist: *Atti del Reale*, 13. As Rocco Rubini observes, Palmieri's tenure at the University of Naples was marked by controversy, particularly given his insistence on the need for a thorough nationalization of knowledge and his simultaneous rejection of Hegelian idealism in precisely the moment that Francesco De Sanctis, as Minister of Education, undertook an effort to oust his line of thought from the university: Rubini, *The Other Renaissance*, 68.

26 Tellingly, Gioberti's *Del primato morale* was reprinted by the Fascist government in 1938 as a part of a national edition of his texts (the *Edizione nazionale delle opere edite e inedite di Vincenzo Gioberti*, under the direction of Enrico Castelli). The political dimensions of philosophical projects to create an Italian lineage in thought were perceived as very real.

27 Rubini examines the debate between Giobertian thought and the more open and transnational approach of thinkers like Bertrando Spaventa: Rubini, *The Other Renaissance*, 47–61. While Rubini's focus is on the reassessment of Italian humanism and the cultural reappropriation of the Italian Renaissance, his intellectual history of this period is an essential source more generally. Cf. Copenhaver and Copenhaver, *From Kant to Croce*, 36–44.

28 This text is translated in Spaventa, "Italian Philosophy."

29 Already in 1848 Silvio Spaventa was combining political activism with an investigation of revolutionary movements and the idea of a new Italian identity. This is attested by his articles in *Il Nazionale*, a Neapolitan journal he founded and wrote for starting in March 1848, which addressed topics

such as "The Idea of the Italian Movement" ("L'idea del movimento italiano," 5 March 1848) and "Italianness" ("Italianità," 18 April 1848), later collected by Benedetto Croce in S. Spaventa, *Dal 1848 al 1861*, 14–36. That volume also includes letters between the two brothers attesting to the rich overlap of political activism and Hegelian idealist philosophy at work in their shared outlook (216–34). Cf. B. Spaventa, *Opere*, vol. 2.

30 B. Spaventa, "Italian Philosophy," 48.

31 This theory that philosophy circulates across borders and historical moments is repeated across B. Spaventa's philosophical writings. See L. Gentile, *Coscienza nazionale.*

32 B. Spaventa, "Italian Philosophy," 49–50.

33 Hegel viewed tribal and foreign civilizations like those of India as pre-historical in the sense that they existed (so he believed) prior to the moment of history's development toward self-conscious freedom: O'Brien, *Hegel on Reason.*

34 In his *Lectures on the Philosophy of World History*, Hegel states that "history is the process whereby the spirit discovers itself and its own concept" (62). This relates to the famous way in which Hegel elaborates the necessary conditions of self-consciousness through the master/slave dialectic in his earlier *Phenomenology of Spirit* (108–16). Spaventa's idea of the "banquet of nations" is already implied in the phenomenological concept of mutual self-recognition, though Hegel's lectures on history provide a clearer blueprint for Spaventa's narrative.

35 The legacy of Hegelian intersubjective self-constitution is wide-reaching. Habermas's notion of intersubjectivity in communicative action (social action) is one example of that discourse's development. See Habermas, *Theory of Communicative Action*, vol. 1, 11; and, in relation to a cosmopolitan political project for contemporary Europe more broadly, Habermas, *The Crisis of the European Union.*

36 This is what Alessandro de Arcangelis sees as the active, domesticating reception of Hegel in conjunction with Vico, which he sees culminating in the private school started by Francesco De Sanctis between 1839 and 1848: de Arcangelis, "Towards a New Philosophy," 237.

37 Piccone, "From Spaventa to Gramsci," 99.

38 Rubini, "(Re-)Experiencing," 11.

39 Hoffmeister, "Hegel and Hegelianism," 65. Oldrini argues that Vera typifies the conservative reading of Hegel central to the strand of "right" Hegelians (as opposed to left Hegelians), who are guilty of a "unilateral absolutization of idealism": Oldrini, *Gli Hegeliani*, 13. These are the thinkers who, in Oldrini's analysis, close down the open dialectical system by fetishizing the categories that Hegel develops in that system.

40 Oldrini characterizes the reception of Hegel as something of a cult animating a whole circle of thinkers and revolutionaries in Naples in the years leading up to the Risorgimento: Oldrini, *Il primo Hegelismo*, 323.
41 Gallo, "The Rise of the Ethical State," 260.
42 "Hegel's Italian legacy during the Risorgimento presents itself as a continuous attempt to elaborate the non-metaphysical and historicist reading of Hegel, highlighting the union between philosophy and history, and the synthesis of idea and fact": Gallo and Körner, "Challenging the Intellectual Hierarchies," 216.
43 Croce, "An Unknown Page," 191.
44 In 1941 Croce published his work *Il carattere della filosofia moderna* (Bari: Laterza), in which the first chapter focuses on "Il concetto della filosofia come storicismo assoluto." In the preface to his recent English translation of this essay, Massimo Verdicchio describes it as a logical endpoint to the way in which Croce's concept of history developed throughout his career: originally Croce conceived history as aligned with art, in the realm of concrete intuition of life, and gradually he shifted it so as to align it with and finally identify it with philosophy itself: Verdicchio, "Introduction," xxiv. "This is a reworking of Hegel's definition of philosophy as absolute Spirit or Idea, which for Croce is didactic and metaphysical, or allegorical. Once philosophy is reformulated in terms of the identity of philosophy and history, there cannot be any metaphysical misunderstanding or didacticism, or allegory; absolute idealism becomes absolute historicism" (Croce, *A Croce Reader*, 40).
45 That domesticating move was also sometimes a way of taking distance from Hegel. Ciracì emphasizes the often overlooked fact that while De Sanctis certainly was a Hegelian in key respects, he also found Hegel's philosophy limiting and began looking for alternatives, eventually turning toward realism by way of French naturalist literature. In a letter to Pasquale Villari of 3 October 1857, De Sanctis uses Vico as an alternative model of history, seeking to supplant Hegel's linear picture of historical stages (religion–art-philosophy) with a view in which all three express the same underlying content and thus the historical forms become recurrent in a Vichian sense: Ciracì, *La filosofia italiana*, 32–3.
46 I draw here on the broad notion of form delineated by Levine in *Forms;* she highlights how social forms afford new means of acting or interacting.
47 As Invernizzi has pointed out, Spaventa and De Sanctis both had a two-phase relationship with Naples: they were there in the period around the failed revolutions of 1848, then left only to return with the unification in 1860 or 1861: Invernizzi, "Schopenhauer," 68.
48 For a comprehensive biography, see Croce and Croce, *Francesco De Sanctis*.

49 Drake examines the formative relationship between Spaventa and Labriola in the context of Labriola's developing Marxist views: Drake, *Apostles and Agitators*, 56–7.
50 Labriola's "Una risposta alla Prolusione di Zeller" was finished in 1862 but not published until after his death, in a volume of his works edited by Benedetto Croce: Labriola, "Contro il 'ritorno a Kant.'"
51 In Drake, *Apostles and Agitators*, 58. However, Labriola likewise wrote against prominent Hegelians like Vera and thus had a complicated or uneasy relationship with Hegelianism. Influenced by Johann Friedrich Herbart, Labriola sought to connect the large-scale Hegelian history with a more empirical and psychological approach: Copenhaver and Copenhaver, *From Kant to Croce*, 77–8.
52 Drake, *Apostles and Agitators*, 59.
53 There has been a contentious debate about the historical roots of Marxist politics in the Italian context and the respective roles of Labriola, Filippo Turati, and Antonio Gramsci: Jacobitti, "Labriola," 297.
54 Copenhaver and Copenhaver, *From Kant to Croce*, 80.
55 Verdicchio, "Introduction," describes Croce's approach to Hegel as one that develops and shifts but is always fundamental to how he establishes his own critical perspective.
56 Croce's involvement in education reform likewise became conflicted and complicated with the rise of Fascism, though even under Mussolini's government Croce continued to support the education reform movement spearheaded by his friend, Gentile: Rizi, *Benedetto Croce*, 52–4.
57 The description of Gentile as the official philosopher of fascism is ubiquitous. See, for example: Faraone, *Giovanni Gentile*; Moss, *Mussolini's Fascist Philosopher*; and Gregor, *Giovanni Gentile*.
58 Another unexpected conjunction can be traced linking Hegel to the fascist thinker Julius Evola, who was inspired by hermetic philosophy and mysticism. Glenn Alexander Magee argues that Hegel himself was likewise influenced by hermetic traditions, Magee thus draws on Evola's studies of alchemy and other forms of esoteric thought to establish another unlikely connection: G. Magee, *Hegel*. I point out this conjunction not to take a stance on the question of Hegel's relation to hermeticism but rather to indicate the diverse and far-reaching paths of influence the Hegelian legacy traces into opposing faces of Italian modernity's political self-imagination – its position not just as hegemonic theory but also in relation to "outsider theory."
59 Copenhaver and Copenhaver, *From Kant to Croce*, 7.
60 The institutional history I have traced is of course partial, its aim being not a complete depiction of the institutional channels of Hegel's reception but rather to broadly illustrate the varied and wide-spanning impact of

his thought and its character. Further consideration of the left-Hegelian legacy, in particular, would offer a different political lens. I have placed less focus on that element of Hegel's legacy not to indicate some relative unimportance but rather because the goal of my study is to chart the context that gives rise to the modernist push for regeneration and to examine the ambivalent relation of politics to aesthetics within that push.

61 This makes it all the more interesting that Hegel's philosophy of history has not always been seen as a central component of his thought. Writing as recently as 2001, Joshua Dienstag could sum up the resurgence of interest in Hegel's thought by saying that "while Hegel's philosophy of history remains as dead as ever, his Phenomenology of Spirit and Logic and even his historicism are the subject of an increasing number of inquiries" (Dienstag, "What Is Living," 262–3).

62 Meir Michaelis summarizes this transition nicely, writing that "Alfredo Oriani, whom Mussolini regarded as the sole precursor of Fascism, translated Mazzini's concept of 'mission' into the language of imperialism" (Michaelis, Italy's Mediterranean Strategy," 41). Cf. Oriani, *Fino a Dogali*. On the earlier Risorgimento project for national emancipation and its link to cosmopolitan ideals, see Moggach, "Italian Receptions," 325.

63 Croce claims Oriani as an idealist, noting in an essay from 1909 that Oriani makes reference to Hegel in each of his works; at the same time, however, Croce sees Oriani as essentially speculative: Croce, "Alfredo Oriani," 6, 8. The Fascist reception of Oriani then becomes the defining moment of his afterlife: Massimo Baioni, "*La lotta politica*," 191.

64 Hegel, *Lectures*, 62.

65 Taylor, *Hegel.*

66 See Beiser, "Hegel's Historicism," 272–3.

67 Rubini, *The Other Renaissance*, 31.

68 Cuoco was the author of important works on both the reception of Plato and the legacy of political revolution: see, respectively, his *Platone in Italia* (1806) and *Saggio storico sulla rivoluzione di Napoli* (1801).

69 Spaventa was also the author of an important essay that played a role in the diffusion of Hegelian thought in revolutionary circles, his "Studii sulla filosofia di Hegel" (*Rivista italiano*, 1850), which is now to be found in G. Vacca's edited collection of Spaventa's works, *Unificazione nazionale ed egemonia culturale*, 16–25.

70 For an analysis of this inaugural address with attention to this specific phrase, see Donati, "L'insegnamento della filosofia."

71 Croce, "An Unknown Page," 175. Earlier on in the same dialogue, Sanseverino praises Hegel directly: "Now your philosophy, Professor, is quite different, tending not towards the natural and mathematical sciences

but towards poetry – of which it is the complement –, towards religion – in which it brings clarity – and towards history, where it discovers its concreteness and actuality" (172). Ignoring, for the moment, the possibly double sense of the honorific "Professor" here, given Croce's criticisms of professional philosophy, it is worth noting that Croce conceives of Hegel's move as a push toward unifying the absolute and universal with the concrete, not only through history but also through poetry and religion. As Croce puts it in a passage from his *Logic*: "From intuition, which is indiscriminate individualization, we move to the universal, which is discriminate individualization, and from art to philosophy, which is history" (Croce, *A Croce Reader*, 23).

72 Croce, *A Croce Reader*, 45–6. Here we might note a similarity between Croce's approach to history and key elements of Nietzsche's famous essay "On the Uses and Disadvantages of History for Life": in Nietzsche, *Untimely Meditations*. As Croce writes in his book *La storia come pensiero e come azione*, "But historical thought has played a joke on this respectable transcendental philosophy and on its sister, transcendental religion, of which it is the reasoned or theological counterpart. The joke is to historicize it by interpreting all its concepts and doctrines, arguments, and disheartened sceptical renunciations as historical facts and historical statements borne out of certain needs that are left partly satisfied and unsatisfied. In so doing, historical thought gave them their due, which they deserved because of their long domination (which was at the same time their service to human society), and wrote their honest obituary" (Croce, *A Croce Reader*, 52). The historicization of transcendental thought is ascribed a critical function that buries that thought. In other words, what Croce shows here is how historicization can play the role that Nietzsche's genealogy plays in the critical reinterpretation of historical facts so as to shift the direction of contemporary life.

73 Fogu, *The Historic Imaginary*, 13.

74 See Bellamy, "What Is Living"; and Bellamy, "Croce, Hegel, and Gentile." Their debate leads to two different readings of Hegel and, ultimately, two different stances on the proper realization of the rational ideal in and through the state.

75 Gramsci, *Prison Notebooks*, vol. 2, 232.

76 Hegel, *Political Writings*, 183.

77 Hegel, *Political Writings*, 183.

78 Lewis, *Modernism*, 70.

79 Montesquieu, *The Spirit of the Laws*, 231. For Montesquieu this notion of national character and how it is suited to the laws is more complex than this quote might suggest. At the end of the same section of his book, pt 3, he examines why it is necessary for the spirit of a nation to be prepared

for the laws in order for those laws to thrive, saying that "even liberty has appeared intolerable to peoples who were not accustomed to enjoying it. Thus is pure air sometimes harmful to those who have lived in swampy countries" (308–9). As such, we might say that Montesquieu's outlook is similar to Hegel's in that it recognizes the interplay of circumstantial forces as well as something like "character" in the constitution of a nationality's "spirit," although the notion of "spirit" varies significantly. See Mosher, "The Particulars."

80 Hom, "On the Origins."
81 Lewis, *Modernism*, 212.
82 E. Gentile, "The Conquest of Modernity."
83 Adamson, "Modernism and Fascism."
84 Sherry, *Modernism*, 32–3.
85 This dynamic played out in the cultural sphere in the Church's struggle to maintain control over public morals through censorship, which conflicted with the Fascist state's effort to reshape public morality in its image: Brera, *Novecento all'Indice.*

2. Italy's Modernist Idealism and the Artistic Reception of Schopenhauer

1 De Sanctis, "Schopenhauer e Leopardi," 269. All translations come from the Appendix here.
2 Goya, *Los Caprichos,* Plate 42, my translation.
3 See Amann, *Dandyism*, 148. Goya's tie to the revolution is well established, as evidenced for example by the exhibition in Hamburg: Hofmann, *Goya*. Helmut C. Jacobs has argued that this etching, no. 43 in the series of *Los caprichos* completed between 1797 and 1798, and published in 1799, can be read as a symbol of its age: Jacobs, *El sueño de la razón,* 11. At the same time, it can serve as a visual metaphor for the process of artistic creation itself (32). Elsewhere, Jacobs traces the literary afterlives of this seminal image on modernity's aesthetic self-conception – for instance, in the poetic imaginary of a figure like Baudelaire: Jacobs, *Die Rezeption,* 36–7. As Robert Havard contends, Goya's etching aims to refocus artistic creation from rational imitation toward the visible expression of fantasy's inner workings: Havard, *From Romanticism to Surrealism,* 11–12.
4 This ambivalence is the starting point for Peter Wagner's *Progress.*
5 The earliest English-language studies to focus on Schopenhauer framed him as an anti-Hegelian iconoclast, illustrating how not just Schopenhauer's philosophy but also his reception have been deeply marked by his polemics against his German contemporary: "Iconoclasm in German Philosophy" (1853). Schopenhauer's vitriolic critiques of Hegel

have been the subject of much commentary, both from biographers and in philosophical studies. Fritz Richard Stern goes so far as to suggest that Schopenhauer's criticisms of Hegel helped inaugurate a widespread period of anti-Hegelianism in the latter part of the nineteenth century, paving the way for a new German ideal of the state ultimately leading to National Socialism: Stern, *The Politics*, 281–2.

6 Lukács's argument in *The Destruction of Reason* maintains that post-Hegelian thought moves toward an irrationalism that paves the way for the rise of fascism. In his perspective, Schopenhauer plays a role in this move, though he places special weight on the existential and phenomenological philosophies of Nietzsche and Heidegger. His assessment of the dangerous shift from the philosophy of reason (Hegel) to irrationalism thus aligns with what Italian philosopher Norberto Bobbio, in *La filosofia del decadentismo*, articulates as a connection between existentialist philosophy and Italian decadentism, a connection that he saw at the root of Italian fascism.

7 Earlier examples of this line in Schopenhauer criticism can be found especially in Wellbery, *Schopenhauers Bedeutung*; Henry, *Schopenhauer*; and Jacquette, *Schopenhauer, Philosophy.*

8 Wellbery, "Schopenhauer," 327–8.

9 Vasalou, *Schopenhauer*, 5, 57.

10 Shapshay, "Poetic Intuition," 225. Numerous scholars conceive Schopenhauer's thought in terms of its aesthetic representation of insight. Bryan Magee contends that because we never truly know will but only intuit it, Schopenhauer's style of argumentation actually aligns with Buddhist insight: B. Magee, "Misunderstanding Schopenhauer." Likewise, Peter Abelsen argues that both Schopenhauer's philosophy and Buddhist insight operate by revealing a *Weltanschauung*, despite the fact that in Abelsen's view Schopenhauer is much less Buddhist than is often assumed, at least insofar as his philosophy expresses a disgust with life that is not consistent with the Buddhist notion of suffering, *duḥka*: Abelsen, "Schopenhauer and Buddhism," 255. Christopher Ryan shows how Schopenhauer recognizes a distinction between the "immediate illumination" of mystical Indian insight and the modern philosophical process of idealist philosophers such as Kant, in whose footsteps he sees himself following: Ryan, "Schopenhauer on Idealism," 18–19.

A version of this idea that we can understand Schopenhauer's works as an aesthetic form using intuition to make insight available for philosophical reason was proposed to Schopenhauer himself by his friend and follower, Adam Ludwig von Doss, in a letter of 28 March 1858. In the same letter he also compares Schopenhauer to Leopardi, focusing on their shared outlook on the aesthetic constitution of philosophical insight: Schopenhauer, *Schopenhauer-Briefe*, 307.

11 Harms, "Arthur Schopenhauer's Philosophy," 113.

12 Harms, "Arthur Schopenhauer's Philosophy," 114.

13 Papini, *Il crepuscolo*, 96.

14 Papini describes his book as an attack on philosophy that aims at a general rehabilitation of the human spirit so as to make it more active and meaningful – thus capable of conquest: Papini, *Il crepuscolo*, 8–9.

15 See Ciracì, "Mainländer all'Inferno," 43. Despite Papini's rejection of Schopenhauer as a satisfactory endpoint, he comes back to Schopenhauer and his followers throughout his career: Ciracì, "Mainländer all'Inferno," 46.

16 Schopenhauer's significance for popular philosophical discourse can be ascertained by the fact that Papini decided to focus a chapter on him in the first place. As Papini writes in his introduction, describing his method, he aimed to put modern philosophy on trial in order to wipe it out; however, he wanted to do this not by discussing philosophy in the abstract but rather by attacking it through its leading representatives: Papini, *Il crepuscolo*, 9.

17 Segala, "Sulle traduzioni italiane," 168–9.

18 Ciracì, *La filosofia italiana*, 22. If anything, Ciracì is understating the case for this "effetto in ampiezza" here in order to emphasize the philosophical reception he privileges in his study.

19 Papini, "Schopenhauer in Italia," 130.

20 "For this reason the doctrines that are truly the *maîtresses* of his philosophy remain those that first made his name: the metaphysical vision [veduta] of will as queen of the universe and the ethical vision [*veduta*] of evil as king of all human things" (Papini, *Il crepuscolo*, 97). Here the word *veduta* connotes not just a normal vision but a kind of panoramic, encompassing view – somewhere between a vision, a view, a landscape, and a standpoint.

21 As Ciracì points out, there were, in fact, at least three publications prior to De Sanctis's essay that mentioned Schopenhauer, though only very briefly: two are single citations found in teaching textbooks (*manuali*) for high schools – Tennemann (1832–1835) and Turri (1854) – and the other is a translation of and commentary on Aristotle's *Metaphysics* that includes a note to Schopenhauer by editor Ruggiero Bonghi (1854): Caracì, *La filosofia italiana*, 595–6.

22 Settembrini's complete translation of Lucian appeared in six volumes in 1862 (published as *Opere* in Florence by Felice Le Monnier). *I neoplatonici* [*The Neoplatonists*], his homosexual love story set in ancient Greece and written as if it were a "found" document, was written in the period from

1851 to 1859 but never published during his life – indeed, even after Benedetto Croce became aware of its existence he kept it a secret for fear of besmirching the reputation of one of the Risorgimento's key heroic martyr figures, and the book was released only in 1977, edited by Raffaele Cantarella (Milan: Rizzoli). De Sanctis never completed a full translation of the *Logic*, but large parts were finished and are to be found in his *Opere. La crisi del Romanticismo.*

23 Here I have in mind Itamar Even-Zohar's notion of how translated texts enter into the target system in a way that can be either innovative or conservative: Even-Zohar, "The Position of Translated Literature." While Schopenhauer's popular diffusion would appear to offer an innovative intervention into the Italian system, in De Sanctis's philosophical reception we see a conservative effort to domesticate the foreign such that its innovative force is tempered.

24 The *Rivista contemporanea* eventually incorporated an earlier Torinese journal called *Il cimento*, with which De Sanctis had already begun to collaborate in 1855, during his period in Turin (1853–56) while he was teaching in a private school for girls after being released from jail in Naples (1850–53). De Sanctis wrote several pieces published in the 1855 edition of *Il cimento*, the penultimate published; he then continued his collaboration with the *Rivista contemporanea*, which endured for years and led to the dialogue on Schopenhauer and Leopardi.

Il cimento was founded in 1852 as a journal of "science, letters, and the arts." It was published in Turin by the Tipografia Ferrero e Franco and featured the work of politically engaged thinkers who contributed to the intellectual climate of revolution and unification, such as Gustavo Benso di Cavour, the prominent marquis who became a major Risorgimento figure and was an avid reader of Kantian philosophy (the first issue of *Il cimento* opened with Cavour's essay, "Saggio sui principii della morale," 3–22, 129–52, and also featured two more of his contributions). The journal continued to publish with this title for three years and a total of six volumes, 1852–55.

The *Rivista contemporanea* was likewise a journal dedicated to "science, letters, the arts, and theatre." It began publishing in Turin in 1854 (by the Unione Tipografico-Editrice) and positioned itself as an attempt to revitalize a broken and divided Italy by establishing a common literature. In the "Introduction" to the first volume, the editors justify the need for their work as an intervention into the formation of a national literature that is suited to the needs of social progress ("Introduzione," 1). It is for this reason, they go on to say in the next section, that they have decided to publish the *Rivista contemporanea*, which is meant to draw together writers and thinkers of various outlooks without imposing an ideological direction and in the hope of elevating the Italian spirit: "Introduzione," 1–2.

25 My references throughout this chapter are to the 1921 edition of De Sanctis' *Saggi critici*, edited by Paolo Arcari (Milan: Fratelli Treves).

26 Croce, "De Sanctis e Schopenhauer," 3.

27 Croce, "De Sanctis e Schopenhauer," 3.

28 Croce, "An Unknown Page," 191.

29 The title here is indicative of the reception of the essay, which is always grouped among De Sanctis's writings on Leopardi, showing that its afterlife is indeed tied to the Italian poet. De Sanctis collected the dialogue in his own version of *Saggi critici*, published during his lifetime. There, he situated it together with several essays on Leopardi, starting with the "Epistolario di Giacomo Leopardi," then "Alla sua donna – Poesia di Giacomo Leopardi," and finally the dialogue "Schopenhauer e Leopardi: Dialogo tra A e D" immediately after these two. This grouping suggests that De Sanctis saw its treatment of Leopardi as the essay's central feature, at least insofar as it was related to the rest of his own writings. That perspective is further highlighted in "La prima canzone di Giacomo Leopardi," published not in *Saggi critici* but in the *Nuovi saggi critici* (105–26). There, De Sanctis comments on the fact that there is not yet a concentrated critical study of Leopardi, and refers to his own dialogue as a partial and insufficient treatment of the poet ("La prima canzone," 109). From De Sanctis's own perspective, the dialogue on Schopenhauer is a part of his humble contribution to the study of Leopardi's work.

30 Margherita Heyer-Caput is the only scholar to offer a sustained discussion of De Sanctis's essay in English, writing a few pages on the topic in the context of her larger consideration of Schopenhauer's importance in late-nineteenth- and early-twentieth-century Italy: Heyer-Caput, *Grazia Deledda's Dance*, 213–16. She previously discussed De Sanctis's work in her essay on "Leopardi tra Schopenhauer e Nietzsche." In her chapter on "The Way to Britain: French and German Receptions," Daniela Cerimonia briefly mentions De Sanctis's essay in her articulation of how Leopardi was received outside of Italy, stating that De Sanctis's essay was "critically acclaimed" and leaving it more or less at that: Cerimonia, *Leopardi and Shelley*, 52. This brief mention is typical of the other (few) sources in English that refer to De Sanctis's essay, though they often refer to it as "famous," evidently describing its Italian rather than anglophone legacy.

31 Ciracì, *La filosofia italiana*, 37–8.

32 There have been multiple, though not entirely aligning, assessments of the role irony plays in De Sanctis's essay. My own position falls closest to that of Fabio Ciracì, who argues that De Sanctis is using Schopenhauer to counter Hegel, despite the fact that he never embraced Schopenhauer's

metaphysical pessimism, concluding that "De Sanctis makes use of Schopenhauer's works as an anti-Hegelian medicine, an effective antidote to Hegel's pan-logoism" (Ciracì, *La filosofia italiana*, 34). As such, even if the dialogue is ironic, it nevertheless also points to the merits of Schopenhauer's philosophy (50). In contrast, Heyer-Caput's analysis of the dialogue sees its irony as more pervasive and thus totalizing: "'D' initially declares himself a staunch supporter of Schopenhauer, 'il filosofo dell'avvenire' … misunderstood by his contemporaries. In the course of the conversation, though, 'D' infuses his presentation of Schopenhauer's philosophy with a corrosive irony, which reverses his judgment" (Heyer-Caput, *Grazia Deledda's Dance*, 213–14). Her reading thus aligns more with Croce's, who likewise saw irony as central to the dialogue's reversal.

Schopenhauer himself had read De Sanctis's essay as well as many of Leopardi's writings, all of which were brought to his attention by his growing group of disciples in the later years of his career. This is the topic of Giuseppe De Lorenzo's study, *Leopardi e Schopenhauer*, which stitches together a large volume of letters (translated into Italian) written between Schopenhauer and various members of his circle on the topic of Leopardi. For De Lorenzo, Schopenhauer's keen interest in De Sanctis's (apparent) praise was heightened by the philosopher's long-standing fascination with Italy, where he travelled and about which he wrote numerous enthusiastic letters (see 14–18 especially).

33 A note De Sanctis added to the piece when he first collected it in his *Saggi critici* explicates these characters thus: "The dialogue was written in Zurich in 1858. *D.* is the author, and *A.* is an old student of his who comes from Naples" (De Sanctis, "Schopenhauer e Leopardi," 227).

34 Calling him by an Italianized version of his first name, "Arturo," De Sanctis domesticates with a strategy that diminishes the sense of grandeur or authority that might be attributed to a prominent philosopher.

35 De Sanctis, "Schopenhauer e Leopardi," 259.

36 See the exchange between A and D on page 246. D then goes on to describe the whole third book of *The World as Will and Representation* as an "exaggerated aesthetic theory" (De Sanctis, "Schopenhauer e Leopardi," 247).

37 The first English-language review, "Iconoclasm in German Philosophy" (1853), focuses on Schopenhauer's pessimism and ethics of renunciation, making scant mention of aesthetics except in its focus on Schopenhauer's style. A number of similar treatments occur in the English-language literature of the following two decades, often condemning Schopenhauer for his pessimism as well as his atheism (or perceived pantheism). An 1863 article in *The Saturday Review*, for instance, treats Schopenhauer's thought as a "moment of dark genius" ("Arthur Schopenhauer" 1863, 325).

In 1864, *The Christian Examiner* published its own, much longer study of Schopenhauer's philosophy, which likewise emphasized the role of pessimism and atheism while underscoring the significance of his thought for its independence and its stylistic clarity ("Arthur Schopenhauer" 1864). These assessments align notably with De Sanctis's, in that they condemn the content of Schopenhauer's thought for its negative consequences while simultaneously praising his independence, originality, and style.

Today many critics instead focus on the role of aesthetic liberation. Some particularly interesting interventions into various facets of that discussion can be found in Clifton, "Schopenhauer and Murdoch," Wellbery, "Emancipation from the Will"; Vandenabeele, "Schopenhauer on Sense Perception"; and Nussbaum, "The Transfigurations of Intoxication."

38 De Sanctis, "Schopenhauer e Leopardi," 251.

39 Dienstag, *Pessimism*, 37. The earliest studies of Schopenhauer more or less universally examine him in terms of this notion of pessimism, as noted above, with the 1911 article in *The Edinburgh Review*, "Degeneration and Pessimism," marking a kind of culmination of that discourse. English translations of Schopenhauer often used pessimism as a key term to interest readers, an example being *Studies in Pessimism* from 1891, which a review in *The Spectator* of that year saw as the cream of Schopenhauer's philosophy with its pessimistic theology ("Studies in Pessimism" 1891, 251).

Leopardi's pessimism has likewise been discussed to the point that it is now codified in Italian high school textbooks, which classify it into two overlapping forms: historical pessimism and cosmic pessimism. Cosmic pessimism is rooted in a general (metaphysical) view in which happiness has not been granted to human beings, whereas historical pessimism is the result of viewing cultural decline through history (this is the aspect that Dienstag focuses on in his analysis). The traditional view holds that historical pessimism, which is more limited in scope, develops into an increasingly total pessimism as an evolution in Leopardi's view. Yet new scholarship suggests that there is nevertheless a close conceptual tie between the two "types" of pessimism in Leopardi, who sees not only revolution but history itself as inherently traumatic and thus aligned with a cosmic pessimism: Rennie, *Speculating on the Moment*, 140. Marco Moneta suggests that this distinction and its ramifications can be traced back to the early 1900s, seeing in Bonaventura Zumbini's 1904 *Studi sul Leopardi* a point of origin: Moneta, *L'Officina delle aporie*, 151. Zumbini did, indeed, suggest that Leopardi is unique as a thinker and poet of pessimism precisely because for him it is both deeply personal/biographical and also universal or philosophical: Zumbini, *Studi sul Leopardi*, vol. 2, 339. It is interesting to note for my purposes here that Zumbini's treatment of

Leopardi sees him as the unique Italian manifestation of a pan-European turn toward pessimism in which philosophers of human suffering are paired with poets of suffering. Thus in Germany, this is visible in the line from Kant to Hegel, which he sees reflected in Goethe and Schiller (Zumbini, 333–34); in England, we encounter it in a conceptual link between David Hume's pessimistic outlook and the poetry of Shelley and Byron (334–5). In the Italian case, he believes, Leopardi encompasses both sides of the equation.

40 Dienstag, *Pessimism*, 82–3.

41 As D says: "Often when you hear Leopardi and Schopenhauer speak it seems like you're listening to a holy father" (De Sanctis, "Schopenhauer e Leopardi," 256).

42 De Sanctis, "Schopenhauer e Leopardi," 251.

43 De Sanctis, "Schopenhauer e Leopardi," 252.

44 De Sanctis, "Schopenhauer e Leopardi," 232.

45 "Iconoclasm in German Philosophy."

46 Lawrence Venuti argues that domestication and foreignization are strategies that translators use in determining the way in which a text is fit into a cultural and linguistic system or allowed to remain foreign to it (and thus disruptive to it). For Venuti, foreignization plays an important critical role that domestication would erase violently: "The ethnocentric violence of translation is inevitable: in the translation process, foreign languages, texts, and cultures always undergo some degree and form of exclusion, reduction, and inscription that reflect the cultural situation in the translating language. Yet the domesticating work on the foreign text can be a foreignizing intervention, pitched to question existing cultural hierarchies" (Venuti, *The Translator's Invisibility*, 267). My argument is that De Sanctis can be read as domesticating Schopenhauer explicitly in a way that reveals precisely what Venuti has in mind, as De Sanctis *intends* to use this domestication as a tool for blocking access to the foreign. In that respect, he has chosen to avoid the foreign so as to render it inaccessible, a purposeful inversion of the dynamic highlighted by Antoine Berman's argument that accentuating the strangeness of a foreign text is "the only way of giving us access to it" (Berman, "Translating and the Trials," 285).

47 De Sanctis, "Schopenhauer e Leopardi," 268.

48 Here De Sanctis's dialogue again aligns with the prevailing tendencies of Schopenhauer's reception, which consistently focused on the philosopher's pleasing, refined style. As the author of a negative review of Schopenhauer's recently translated essays wrote for the American journal *Self Culture*, "The socialism and discontent of the times has of late given Schopenhauer a vogue, and editions of his writings have been numerous

in the past few years, their sale being helped, presumably, by the author's fine literary faculty" ("The Essays of Schopenhauer," 1897–98, 335).

49 De Sanctis, "Schopenhauer e leopardi," 269.

50 De Sanctis, "Schopenhauer e Leopardi," 268–9.

51 De Sanctis's political interpretation of Leopardi is rooted in his earlier study of the poet's letters. In 1849, De Sanctis was forced out of Naples and fled to Calabria; there, he wrote the introduction to an edition of Leopardi's letters, which he then revised and published in *Saggi critici* as "Epistolario di Giacomo Leopardi." In it, De Sanctis describes Leopardi as a manifestation of virtues that Nietzsche might term untimely: suffering greatly, the great man lifts himself above misfortune with the special dignity of magnanimity (208). Leopardi can thus be seen as a point of transition between the self-obsessed subjectivity of Enlightenment individualism and the patriotic movements building toward the Risorgimento: "His concept of things is so elevated that it will not cause us to marvel if he seems like a most severe judge and if, more than praising that which we have, he shows us that which we are lacking" (209). This notion of Leopardi's elevating effect is clearly prescient of how De Sanctis will later contrast Schopenhauer and Leopardi.

52 Antonio Negri's study of Leopardi as a critical thinker is of particular importance here. Considering how Leopardi is situated in the historical trajectory of nineteenth-century responses against dialectical thought, Negri argues that rather than seeing Leopardi as aligned with Schopenhauer we should rather see him in relation to left-Hegelianism's ways of redirecting the dialectic. Where Schopenhauer replaces dialectical thought with a phenomenalism that Negri sees as reintroducing nothingness through "the paradoxical overthrow of the absoluteness of spirit," Leopardi instead "traverses the nothingness of being in order to regain, in light of it, the reason of critical antagonism" (Negri, *Flower of the Desert*, 238). In contrast, Leopardi's ties to the Hegelian left are visible in their shared demystification of the dialectic: "They have in common a violent critical impulse directly inherited from the revolutionary tradition of the Enlightenment" (238). Negri, in other words, inadvertently confirms De Sanctis's position while rejecting what he perceives to be De Sanctis's assimilation of Leopardi to Schopenhauer. Ultimately, however, Negri argues that Leopardi's anti-dialectical thought should be understood as its own model, one that spans from Schopenhauer and the left-Hegelians to a Kierkegaardian existentialism in that it "combines a metaphysical predisposition to a materialist ontology with irrationalism, the sense of demystification and the pleasure of singularity" (239).

This vision of a revolutionary philosophical lineage contrasts with what Frank Rosengarten has described as Leopardi's ambivalent position. As Rosengarten notes, reading the *Zibaldone*'s entries on the French Revolution in relation to Leopardi's later entries and epistolary exchanges, his initial enthusiasm for the Revolution is limited to the ways in which it may have helped restore our contact with nature, whereas "there is nothing in Leopardi's writings after the mid-1820s that would justify considering him a militant revolutionary" (Rosengarten, *Giacomo Leopardi's Search*, 217). Indeed, he rejected the July Revolution in 1830, asserting that it had ruined Europe and with it literature. Leopardi's own view of historical revolution is thus much less positive than Negri's interpretation.

53 De Sanctis, "Schopenhauer e Leopardi," 265.

3. Aesthetic Decadence and Modernist Idealism: Schopenhauer's Literary-Artistic Legacy

1 I discuss Sherry's position in more detail in the Introduction. See Sherry, "Introduction"; and Sherry, *Modernism*.

2 Cf. "Iconoclasm in German Philosophy" and "Degeneration and Pessimism."

3 Potolsky, *The Decadent Republic*, 11. Cf. Wellbery, *Schopenhauers Bedeutung*; Jacquette, *Schopenhauer, Philosophy*; and Henry, *Schopenhauer*. I will not attempt to trace out all of the directions these studies examine regarding his European and global artistic reception, but it is notable that many of the figures treated in these studies are associated with decadence and/or modernism.

4 I also take to heart the critique of computational models in literary studies offered by Nan Z. Da, who demonstrates through statistical evidence that these computational methods result in either robust but obvious insights or else non-obvious but non-robust insights; there is thus "a fundamental mismatch between the statistical tools that are used and the objects to which they are applied" (Da, "The Computational Case," 601).

5 This tendency is still visible today, with the most recent reprint of De Sanctis's essay coming in a volume titled precisely *Schopenhauer e Leopardi e altri saggi leopardiani*.

6 Ciracì describes Croce's dominant position in Italian thought and his moves to block Schopenhauer with considerable detail, accounting for Croce's negative reviews of works on Schopenhauer, his refusal to include translations of Schopenhauer in the series he edited for Laterza, and other strategies: Ciracì, *La filosofia italiana*, 457–69.

7 Segala, "Sulle traduzioni italiane", 172–3.

8 Spackman, *Decadent Genealogies*, viii.

9 See Bettini, *La critica e gli scapigliati*.

10 Arcangelo Leone De Castris, for example, groups D'Annunzio with Svevo and Pirandello as the triad representing Italian *decadentismo*: De Castris, *Il decadentismo italiano*. Carlo Salinari offers a grouping of D'Annunzio, Pascoli, Fogazzaro, and Pirandello: Salinari, *Miti e coscienza*. Roberto Tessari's volume focuses on Pascoli, D'Annunzio, and Fogazzaro: Tessari, *Pascoli, D'Annunzio*.

11 Weir, *Decadence*, 9.

12 Spackman, *Decadent Genealogies*, 33. On D'Annunzio's debt to Huysmans, see De Michelis, "D'Annunzio e Huysmans" and De Michelis, "D'Annunzio e i plagi."

13 Lucia Re sees *decadentismo* as a transition between *romanticismo* and *modernismo* in her excellent examination of the actor in the moment of decadent aestheticism: Re, "D'Annunzio, Duse, Wilde, Bernhardt," 117. Her analysis of the Italian case thus aligns with David Weir's broader picture of decadence as a transition constituted by both rupture and continuity: Weir, *Decadence*, 14. Peter Jeffreys's move to unearth a Victorian genealogy to Cavafy's poetics likewise signals the recurrence of notions of decadence beyond those historical confines: Jeffreys, *Reframing Decadence*.

I would thus argue that approaches to decadence have in some sense mirrored the polarity of approaches to the concept of the avant-garde, with Peter Bürger and Renato Poggioli similarly describing that concept in terms of a historical period of transition (for the former) or as a mobile aesthetic category that recurs across historical moments and geographies (for the latter): Bürger, *Theory of the Avant-Garde*; Poggioli, *The Theory of the Avant-Garde*.

14 It is surprising, for example, that in Jeffreys's thoroughly documented treatment, which makes heavy recourse to anglophone Victorian decadentism as a source for Cavafy's poetics, Schopenhauer's name never appears – despite Schopenhauer's importance for a British decadent like Wilde, for example. Even Sherry's articulation of the concept, focused on the poetics of loss and its pessimistic view of history, makes only one brief mention of Schopenhauer: Sherry, *Modernism*, 185.

15 Stephen Romer goes so far as to assert that "in this feckless retinue of disabused young men, seeking to lose themselves in art and novel experience, the influence of Schopenhauer is all-pervasive" (Romer, "Introduction," xiv).

16 Likewise, in his 1883 study of decadence, *Essais de psychologie contemporaine* (*Essays on Contemporary Psychology*), Paul Bourget connects the decadent aesthetic to the conjunction of Baudelaire's poetic obsession with death and Schopenhauer's pessimism (15). For Bourget this is symptomatic of an excess of individualism and detachment from life: Nalbantian, *Seeds of Decadence*, 11. This detachment from life was what Nietzsche, reading

Bourget's essay, responded against in Baudelaire and the aesthetic cult of the dandy, which is connected to his response to Wagner and thus to Schopenhauer: Downes, *Music and Decadence*, 71–2.

17 Huysmans, *Against Nature*, 187.

18 Huysmans, *Against Nature*, 197. This forms an interesting point of comparison to the way Schopenhauer's German disciple, Adam Ludwig von Doss, compared his teacher with Buddhist thought, seeing Schopenhauer and Leopardi in relation to a "Buddhist" pessimism: see De Lorenzo, *Leopardi e Schopenhauer*, 20–2. Ciracì documents the copious literature linking Schopenhauer's Italian reception to interest in Eastern thought and Buddhism in particular: Ciracì, *La filosofia italiana*, 213–64.

19 Dienstag, *Pessimism*, x.

20 His poem from *Flowers of Evil*, "A Carcass," turns the usual poetics of praise devoted to the beloved's beauty into a praise of decomposition, transforming European love poetry and the baroque tradition of the *memento mori*. In *Paris Spleen*, by contrast, he depicts the misery of modern capitalist culture and its unfeeling deadness in "The Eyes of the Poor" (52–3).

21 Boredom is a ubiquitous topic in the literature on Baudelaire and decadence, central to Baudelaire's own framing of his poetics as reflected by Théophile Gautier's 1868 preface to the "definitive" edition of Baudelaire's *Fleurs du mal*, where he describes the opening poem to the "hypocrite reader" as accusing the reader of nourishing the "great monster of modernity, Boredom" (Baudelaire, *Les fleurs du mal*, 30). Cf. Dienstag, *Pessimism*, 30; "Degeneration and Pessimism," 148.

22 Dienstag, *Pessimism*, 35.

23 This is the poetics of what Gautier compares to the twilight stage of poetry in his preface: Baudelaire, *Les fleurs du mal*, 16.

24 While the aesthetic stance implies a necessary distance from its object – the modern world and its inhabitants – Baudelaire's poetics nevertheless invests in an ambivalent sense that poetry can influence its readers through the correspondence between beauty and the good: see Simek, "Baudelaire."

25 De Sanctis, "Schopenhauer e Leopardi," 268.

26 In this respect I disagree with Mimmo Cangiano, *La nascita*, insofar as he insists that modernism is essentially nihilistic and necessarily politically suspect, following in the trajectory of the critical theorists cited here. My analysis of how even decadent aestheticism functions beyond the realm of merely reproducing crisis and totalizing it suggests why such readings may prove to be overly simplified.

27 Bobbio, *La filosofia del decadentismo*, 4 and 22.

28 Gori, *Studi di estetica dell'irrazionale*, 42. Irrationality is frequently associated with decadentism in the Italian critical literature, both during the early twentieth century and in subsequent scholarship. See Tessari, *Pascoli, D'Annunzio.*

29 Agamben, *The Man without Content*, 52.

30 Agamben follows this same logic, arguing that the trajectory of modern art (starting with the Renaissance *Wunderkammer* and the inception of the museum as an aesthetic space) is a long process of turning away from classical praxis. Here Agamben is likewise borrowing from the tradition of Walter Benjamin's criticism of modern aestheticism and its transformation of the political – the "aestheticizing of politics" (Benjamin, "The Work of Art," 122).

31 I abbreviate *The World as Will and Representation* as *WWR*, and quotes refer to the classic translation by Payne, although a new translation by Norman, Welchman, and Janaway has made some important improvements.

32 This view of suicide emerges in multiple sources, from Leopardi's poetry (collected as *Canti* in 1835) to his philosophical reflections in the *Zibaldone* (published posthumously in seven volumes, 1898–1900, and newly translated as *Zibaldone* by Michael Caesar, Franco D'Intino, and Kathleen Baldwin in 2013), to his collection of prose essays and dialogues, the *Operette morali* (published in its definitive edition in 1835, translated as *The Moral Essays* in 1983). But nowhere is it clearer than in his "Fragment on Suicide," written around 1820 and published posthumously in the *Scritti vari inediti*. There, Leopardi contrasts the happiness of a direct connection to life fostered by ancient forms of illusion and the bleak experience of modern rationality, which has dispelled illusion at the price of being unable to bear life, concluding that: "back then, even when dying one lived, whereas now one dies living. No other means besides the ancient ones will allow us to return to loving and feeling life" (389). The search for a lost connection to vitality, interrupted by modern reason, is a hallmark of the romantic poetics at work in Leopardi's pessimistic world view – and likewise another possible source of the affinity between Leopardi and Nietzsche that Negri identifies in his reading of *The Gay Science*: Negri, *Flower of the Desert*, 297.

33 The importance of Wagner as a source not only for decadence but also for modernist innovation more broadly is underscored in Juliet Koss's impressive study of his legacy and the role of the Wagnerian *Gesamtkunstwerk* in European modernity: Koss, *Modernism after Wagner*.

34 The second novel in his decadent series, *The Innocent* (*L'innocente*, 1892), focuses on the protagonist's murderous desires and ultimate decision to commit infanticide; and the motif recurs all the way to his last novel / prose poem, *Nocturne* (*Notturno*, 1916), which is obsessed with heroizing death

in battle. In between are countless plays, poems, and other novels where themes of death, murder, and suicide abound. On D'Annunzio's obsession with decadent death, see Härmänmaa, "The Seduction of Thanatos"; on the role of murder-suicide, sexuality, and politics in *Triumph of Death*, see Galbo, "A Decadence Baedeker"; and Wood, "The Art of Dying." Rabiner, "Dannunzian Aesthetics," argues that D'Annunzio's aestheticism, culminating in the novel *The Virgins of the Rocks* (*Le vergini delle rocce*, 1895), is defined by precisely a necrophilic sexuality of death. Cf. Syrimis, *The Great Black Spider*, 14.

There is likewise a significant rise in rates of suicide and cultural interest in it as a phenomenon in the period: Bernardini, "Introduction," for an overview of the trend; and Bernardini and Virga, *Voglio morire!*, for a series of in-depth studies.

35 D'Annunzio, *Il caso Wagner*, 82–3.
36 Verlaine, translated in Borchmeyer, *Drama and the World*, 261.
37 Jacquette, "Schopenhauer on the Ethics of Suicide."
38 Schopenhauer, *WWR* I, §54, 280–1.
39 Schopenhauer, *WWR* I, §68, 384.
40 Cited in Schopenhauer, *WWR* I, §68, 384. The citation is to Spinoza's *Ethics*, V, Prop. 42.
41 Schopenhauer, *WWR* I, §38, 196.
42 Schopenhauer, *WWR* I, §25, 129.
43 My reading of Schopenhauer's combination of the aesthetic and the ascetic is informed by Julian Young's treatment of the sublime in relation to death: see Young, "Schopenhauer, Nietzsche"; and Young, "Death and Transfiguration."
44 Schopenhauer, *WWR* I, §39, 201–2.
45 D'Annunzio, *Il caso Wagner*, 96–7.
46 D'Annunzio, *Il caso Wagner*, 54–5.
47 Here D'Annunzio echoes Nietzsche's characterization of Wagner, which is certainly on this count accurate. Wagner's feelings toward Schopenhauer are captured in a letter that Wagner wrote to his friend, the painter Franz von Lenbach (1836–1904), in 1868, where he comments on Lenbach's portrait of Schopenhauer that Wagner's second wife, Cosima, had given him and that remained on prominent display in his study. After describing how Lenbach has succeeded in rendering a bodily representation of Schopenhauer's clarity and depth of thought, Wagner goes on to say: "I have a hope for the culture of the German spirit, which is that the time will come when Schopenhauer becomes the law of our thought and our understanding" (Schopenhauer, *Schopenhauer-Briefe*, 510). Indeed, Wagner and his circle made a direct link between Schopenhauer's person(a) and the spirit of a new German age.

48 D'Annunzio, *Il caso Wagner*, 65–6.
49 D'Annunzio, *Il caso Wagner*, 76.
50 Nietzsche had acknowledged something similar in his preface to *The Case of Wagner*: "Through Wagner modernity speaks her most intimate language: it conceals neither its good nor its evil: it has thrown off all shame. … I can perfectly well understand a musician of to-day who says: 'I hate Wagner but I can endure no other music.' But I should also understand a philosopher who said, 'Wagner is modernity in concentrated form.' There is no help for it, we must first be Wagnerites" (Nietzsche, *The Birth of Tragedy and the Case of Wagner*).
51 Bryan Magee has offered an excellent reading of Wagner's Schopenhauerian art, and in it he places due emphasis on the way in which *Tristan und Isolde* is a musical manifestation of the impossibility of satisfaction and the will to self-extinction at the core of book IV of Schopenhauer's *WWR* (B. Magee, "Schopenhauer and Wagner: Part Two," 54).
52 D'Annunzio, *Trionfo dellla morte*, 382.
53 On the role of the "superuomo" see Piga, *Il mito del superuomo*; on the literary afterlife of the Dannunzian *superuomo*, see Barnaby, "*Superuomini e no*."
54 Andrea Mirabile characterizes D'Annunzio as situated precisely at the threshold of decadence and modernism: Mirabile, *Multimedia Archaeologies*.
55 Laura Wittman's study of Italy's tomb of the unknown soldier emphasizes D'Annunzio's central role in the creation of the new rituals commemorating national loss: Wittman, *The Tomb*.
56 D'Annunzio, *Notturno*, 305.
57 D'Annunzio, *Notturno*, 304.
58 D'Annunzio, *Notturno*, 297.
59 Woodhouse addresses the nascent fascism of D'Annunzio's Fiume episode: Woodhouse, *Gabriele D'Annunzio*, 324–5. He also argues that the "Carta del Carnaro," the new legal framework he crafted for Fiume, reveals a poetic and aesthetic impulse in his project that is more liberal than fascist (345). The complex issue of race and colonial aspirations in D'Annunzio's writing and the development of fascism is treated at length by Welch, who argues that "D'Annunzio tethers rhetorics of race and (re) productivity to a variety of other formulations about Italian modernity and preeminence. Race is inscribed within a poetic constellation that figures blood and territory as the rhetorical conditions for Italy's conquest of modernity" (Welch, *Vital Subjects*, 130). Cf. Re, "Italians and the Invention of Race."
60 Svevo's broader world view likewise poses a critique of modern decadence and responds with a shift toward a modernist alternative.

Across Svevo's corpus, two key notions recur – senility and ineptitude; these ways of framing his characters as outsiders or failures in modern culture offer not only a critique of modern decadence (Santi, "Ineptitude as Cultural Senility") but also a contrasting alternative insofar as ineptitude represents a kind of resistance to the reductive logic of bourgeois modernity and its practical aims, beliefs, and conventions (Di Nunzio, "La differenza"). That resistance, I argue, speaks to the power Svevo attributes to the creativity of the written word, which Terrile identifies as central to *Zeno's Conscience* in "La parola all'ombra." This creativity, I would add, functions precisely as an alternative frame for rewriting modernity – consonant with Caselli's notion of Svevo's development toward plurality: Caselli, "<<Bisogna isolare…>>" – and in this way it likewise functions in consonance with the aesthetic response to crisis that I have articulated throughout this chapter. The strategies of decadent aestheticism are thus mirrored in modernist deconstructions of fixed logic.

61 Contarini offers a classical Freudian interpretation of the novel's function in her "<<Vedere l'infanzia>>"; Annavini expands on this to suggest that psychoanalysis not only is in the content but also is an integral component of the hybridization of genre that is a hallmark of modernist production more generally, thus putting Svevo in contact with modernists across Europe: Annavini, "<<Un filo di fumo>>," 81.

62 Svevo, *Zeno's Conscience*, 434.

63 Braida, "Salute o malattia?" Godioli offers a recent approach to Svevo's irony that emphasizes how it is both corrosive and self-corroding, providing the space for laughter: Godioli, *Laughter.*

64 Svevo, *Zeno's Conscience*, 435, 436.

65 Svevo, *Zeno's Conscience*, 437.

66 Svevo, *Zeno's Conscience*, 419.

67 Svevo, *Zeno's Conscience*, 411.

68 Hegel, translated in Stephen Houlgate, *The Opening of Hegel's* Logic, 185.

69 Schopenhauer, *WWR* I, §39, 202.

70 While the term appears in his most prominent work, *Ulysses* (1922), he had been toying with the idea of epiphany some two decades earlier, while he was working on *Stephen Hero* (~1903–5, published posthumously in 1944), the partly lost autobiographical precursor to his *A Portrait of the Artist as a Young Man* (1916). Likewise, around the years 1904–6, Joyce was jotting down a series of *Epiphanies*, held in manuscript form by the University of Buffalo's Lockwood Memorial Library and published in 1956. The dates 1904–6 are offered by O.A. Silverman in his introduction to the *Epiphanies* (xv), which consists of twenty-two short notes of epiphanic moments that Joyce wrote out on separate sheets of paper and kept together.

71 See Hu's entry on 'Epiphany' in the *Routledge Encyclopedia of Modernism* for the etymology and development of this term.

72 Joyce, *Stephen Hero*, 210–11.

73 Joyce, *Stephen Hero*, 211. The centrality of epiphany as a concept in modernist studies is attested in a number of sources. See, for instance, Beja, *Epiphany*; and Gillespie, "Epiphany." Joyce is an originating figure at least of the critical term if not of the practice itself; see Aubert, *The Aesthetics of James Joyce*; Rabaté, *James Joyce*; and Delville, "Epiphanies and Prose Lyrics." That being said, the practice is much broader than Joyce's specific poetics and encompasses multiple dimensions, not only of suddenness and condensed temporality but also in relation to the spiritual and the psychological. On the temporal dimension of epiphany, see Morel, "The Modernists' Commitment." On the centrality of the amorphous category of the spiritual, see Kim, *Literary Epiphany*.

74 Woolf, *A Writer's Diary*, 138. See also the volume that uses this concept for its title, Woolf's *Moments of Being*.

75 Quotes from Eliot's *Four Quartets* are in *The Poems of T.S. Eliot*; throughout I cite by verse number.

76 Aakanksha Virkar-Yates has noted that the usual association of these verses with Hegel seems unconvincing when considered in light of the numerous ways in which Eliot is directly engaging Schopenhauer's theory of the sublime in particular and aesthetics more generally: Virkar-Yates, "*Erhebung*." That association to Hegel is so common as to be asserted without further discussion in the commentary in Christopher Ricks and Jim McCue's edition of Eliot's collected poems, Eliot, *The Poems*, "Commentary on 'Burnt Norton' II 28: 'Erhebung.'" As Virkar-Yates also shows, *Four Quartets* is likewise in close connection with the legacy of Wagner in its sense of musical asceticism: Virkar-Yates, "Absolute Music."

77 Though I am calling it a "Schopenhauerian" conjunction, this is not to imply that Schopenhauer is the only source of that aesthetic notion but rather that looking through the lens of his philosophy helps us recognize and unpack the family resemblance holding together various instances of modernist epiphany. For Montale, for example, Boutroux's reading of Bergsonian duration plays a fundamental role in establishing the secular miracle so central to his epiphanic mode. Cf. Rosada, "Il contingentismo di Montale."

78 Montale, translated by Jonathan Galassi in *Collected Poems*, 55. Eugenio Montale, *Ossi di seppia* © 2015 Mondadori Libri S.p.A., Milano. Published by arrangement with the Publisher and The Italian Literary Agency.

79 West likewise emphasizes the importance of the word *forse* in her readings of Montale's collected works: West, *Montale*, 62–4.

80 Beard, The Blind Owl *as a Western Novel*, 49.

81 Hedayat's novel is thus an intensification, in a more hallucinatory and complex style, of themes that are also pervasive in his short stories. See *Three Drops of Blood*.
82 Hedayat, *The Blind Owl*, 128–9.
83 In his late writings on religion, especially *The Future of an Illusion* (1927) and *Civilization and Its Discontents* (1930), Freud emphasizes that the notion of God / gods is a psychological projection that functions to shore up society and as a defence mechanism against the overwhelming superiority of powers that cannot be controlled. Freud, of course, is another channel through which Schopenhauer's outlook is transmitted into the imaginary of modernism. See Gupta, "Freud and Schopenhauer."
84 Hedayat, *The Blind Owl*, 117.
85 Pirandello, *One, No One, and One Hundred Thousand*, 83.
86 Pirandello, *One, No One, and One Hundred Thousand*, 217–18.
87 Shapshay argues that Nietzsche's analysis is only partly right and that Schopenhauer himself already combines aesthetic intuition and philosophical argumentation in a novel way: Shapshay, "Poetic Intuition."
88 Nietzsche, of course, operates with multiple formal models throughout his writing, with a work like *Thus Spoke Zarathustra* (1883–1885) approaching literary myth while many other texts adopt an aphoristic form. Certainly some are more discursively oriented than others, but in general they embrace a literary-philosophical hybridity that is broadly noted in the criticism.

4. Avant-Garde Idealism: The Ambivalence of Futurist Vitalism

1 "Davanti all'infinito" is collected in Marinetti, Settimelli, and Corra, *Il teatro futurista sintetico*, 42.
2 In the manifesto signed by Marinetti, Settimelli, and Corra on "The Futurist Synthetic Theater" (11 January 1915), they outline their idea for this new art form; see Marinetti, *Teoria e invenzione futurista*, 113–122, translated in Rainey, Poggi, and Wittman, *Futurism: An Anthology*, 204–9. This theatrical form builds on Marinetti's earlier praise of variety theatre as the only salvageable theatrical form in Italy since its speed and dynamic aspects make it anti-traditional and align it with the Futurist aim of inventing new modes of astonishment. See "The Variety Theater" (29 September 1913) in Marinetti, *Teoria e invenzione futurista*, 80–7, translated in Rainey, Poggi, and Wittman, *Futurism*, 159–64.
3 On the shift from German cultural identification to its bellicose rejection, see Subialka, "Modernism at War."
4 This reading coincides with the second conclusion drawn in "The Futurist Synthetic Theater" that their invention of this new form aims to "put onstage all the discoveries (no matter how unrealistic, strange,

or antitheatrical) that our talent is discovering in the subconsious, in ill-defined forces, in pure abstraction, in pure conceptualism, the purely fantastic, in record-setting, and body-madness" (Rainey, Poggi, and Wittman, *Futurism*, 208).

5 As Thomas Harrison notes, 1910 and the build-up to the First World War saw an increasing trend of suicide among young men in the Habsburg Empire: Harrison, *1910*, 91. Harrison links this to the proliferation of new theories on the death instinct (Freud, Jung, etc.) and hauntingly concludes: "Nineteen ten is the spiritual prefiguration of an unspeakably tragic fatality, heard in the tones of the audacious and the anguished, the deviant and the desperate, in the art of a youth grown precociously old, awaiting a war it had long suffered in spirit" (7).

6 Rainey, Poggi, and Wittman, *Futurism*, 92 (Marinetti, *Teoria e invenzione futurista*, 301).

7 Perloff's description of the Futurist Moment dovetails with Poggioli's theory of the Futurist phase of various avant-garde movements as a "prophetic and utopian phase, the arena of agitation and preparation for the announced revolution, if not the revolution itself" (Poggioli, *The Theory of the Avant-Garde*, 69).

8 Perloff, *The Futurist Moment*, 36.

9 On medium specificity, see Greenberg, "Towards a Newer Laocoön," 8. This concept allowed him to trace modernist art to a conceptual development in abstract expressionism, which showcases the self-critical logic of modernism: Greenberg, "After Abstract Expressionism," 30.

10 Poggi, *Inventing Futurism*.

11 Rainey, Poggi, and Wittman, *Futurism*, 122 (Marinetti, *Teoria e invenzione futurista*, 50). Bold type in original.

12 Rainey, Poggi, and Wittman, *Futurism*, 123 (Marinetti, *Teoria e invenzione futurista*, 52). Bold type in original.

13 I thus disagree with Frank Kermode's demarcation of modernist production as anti-traditionalist or traditionalist: Kermode, *The Sense of an Ending*, 103–4.

14 While Futurists would often attempt to downplay the influences of previous models on their poetics, they were clearly well aware of them: Gordon, "The Italian Futurist Theatre," 349.

15 Adamson mentions Corra briefly in two places in reference to one of the Futurist periodicals he ran, *L'Italia futurista*: Adamson, *Avant-Garde Florence*, 220, 223.

16 Grosz, *The Incorporeal*. My intervention here into the debate over the new materialisms is clarified in the Introduction.

17 See Dilthey on how the "enigma" of life's meaning leads humans to attempt to intuit a world view that offers them a cosmic sense of their

place and purpose: Dilthey, *Dilthey's Philosophy of Existence*, 48. Life as immediate experience furnishes the motivating question that makes it necessary for the subject to activate a "cosmic picture" that helps render the world meaningful.

18 The discourse on vitalism has its own long history, and Schopenhauer's notion of the world as will (the deep, vital core of the world), while unique, is in conversation with earlier forms of spiritual vitalism such as those developed by the ancient and Renaissance Neoplatonists (see, for example, Ficino's account of the unending system of love's desire in *El libro dell'amore*, VI.10). But insofar as *Lebensphilosophie* is seen as a particular approach to the experience of life, Schopenhauer is foundational for later thinkers like Dilthey and Bergson. In addition to his most famous work, his essay *On the Will in Nature* (*Über den Willen in der Natur*, 1836) also gained significant notoriety; I discuss that essay in more detail in chapter 5.

19 Nietzsche famously dubbed Schopenhauer his "educator" while simultaneously taking distance from him in "Schopenhauer as Educator," in Nietzsche, *Untimely Meditations*. He thus positioned himself as a response to and cure for Schopenhauerian pessimism, which represents something like the fundamental problem at the root of Nietzsche's turn toward the will to life and his famous thought experiment for affirmation, the eternal recurrence: see Conant, "Nietzsche's Perfectionism." Karl Albert places Nietzsche as an origin point for *Lebensphilosophie* alongside Bergson and Dilthey, all of whom are responding not only to Schopenhauer but also to Friedrich Schlegel and the far less-known French philosopher Jean-Marie Guyau (1854–1888): Albert, *Lebensphilosophie*.

20 See Gaiger for a definition of *Lebensphilosophie* as the opposition to conceptual intellect via intuition: "The central claim underlying its various manifestations is that life can only be understood from within" (Gaiger, "Lebensphilosophie," 487–8). Fellmann offers a more complicated picture of German *Lebensphilosophie*'s historical manifestations: Fellmann, *Geschichte der Philosophie*, 269–349.

21 Marinetti, *Teoria e invenzione futurista*, 11.

22 A good summary of the *serate* and their development is Berghaus's chapter, "The Beginnings of a Futurist Performance Art: The Early *serate*" in Berghaus, *Italian Futurist Theatre*. On the first "battles" in Trieste, see Berghaus, *Italian Futurist Theatre*, 86–91.

23 Marinetti, *Critical Writings*, 153.

24 Berghaus, *Italian Futurist Theatre*, 95.

25 Livio argues that far from being truly participatory and active, the audience is subjected to the political agitations of the Futurists in a way that limits the revolutionary form of the *serata* (Livio, *Il teatro in rivolta*, 39).

All the same, Marinetti himself theorized his *serate* as instances of public participation and interaction.

26 Berghaus, *Italian Futurist Theatre*, 90.

27 The schematic overview I have given here simplifies the changing contours of the Futurist *serate*. In fact, the first *serata*, held in Trieste on 12 January 1910, was quite different from later events. There were fewer committed Futurist artists available to take part in the *serata*, with only Marinetti, Palazzeschi, and Mazza declaiming that evening. The whole event involved *only* readings and speeches of various sorts. During later *serate*, the integration of visual and musical art would add further confusion and chaos, and the reactions of the audience-turned-crowd were sometimes much more hostile, violent, and active. See Berghaus, *Italian Futurist Theatre*, 85–145, esp. 86–91.

28 Antonucci, *Cronache*, 24; Livio, *Il teatro in rivolta*, 12–13.

29 Berghaus, *Italian Futurist Theatre*, 138.

30 Marinetti, *Futurismo e fascismo*, 18.

31 Marinetti, *Critical Writings*, 152.

32 Marinetti, *Critical Writings*, 14–15.

33 Marinetti, *Critical Writings*, 15.

34 This is the second essay (begun in 1873 and published in February 1874) collected together under the heading *Untimely Meditations* (*Unzeitgemässe Betrachtungen*). The notion of "untimeliness" is important to Nietzsche's philosophical project, which undertakes a diagnosis of the sickness plaguing modern culture. As such, it is essential for Nietzsche that the modern philosopher inhabit a multiplicity of perspectives, both belonging to and also seeing from outside of his contemporary social world. In his later, retrospective, philosophical self-description (*Ecce Homo*, written in 1888), Nietzsche writes: "To be able to look out from the optic of sickness towards healthier concepts and values, and again the other way around … If I became the master of anything, it was this. I have a hand for switching *perspectives*: the first reason why a 'revaluation of values' is even possible, perhaps for me alone" (in Nietzsche, *The Anti-Christ, Ecce Homo*, 76, emphasis Nietzsche's). This comment on his philosophical method in general is likewise relevant to his rereading of the historical sense in "On the Uses and Disadvantages of History for Life," with regard to which he declares, still in *Ecce Homo*: "In this essay, the 'historical sense' that this century is so proud of is recognized for the first time as a disease, as a typical sign of decay" (112).

35 Nietzsche, *Untimely Meditations*, 75.

36 Nietzsche, *Untimely Meditations*, 75.

37 Marinetti, *Critical Writings*, 81.

38 As Marinetti puts it in an interview with *La Diana*, "Germanism must be opposed in order to defend the imaginative spontaneity of Italian creative genius, which has everything to fear from libraries, museums, and professors" (Marinetti, *Critical Writings*, 144).
39 This phrase is the subtitle of his book from 1886, *Jenseits von Gut und Böse*: "Vorspiel einer Philosophie der Zukunft" (Nietzsche, *Beyond Good and Evil: Prelude to a Philosophy of the Future*).
40 Marinetti, *Critical Writings*, 233.
41 Bergson, *Creative Evolution*, 107.
42 Bergson, *Creative Evolution*, 95.
43 Bergson, *Creative Evolution*, 149.
44 Bergson, *Creative Evolution*, 169.
45 Bergson, *Creative Evolution*, 167.
46 Marinetti, *Critical Writings*, 146.
47 Marinetti, *Critical Writings*, 234 (emphasis mine).
48 This term appears in Nietzsche's later writings, but the notion of a "will to life" or of some kind of striving for higher life is central already in his first publications from the early 1870s. Thus, for example, in his first book, *The Birth of Tragedy out of the Spirit of Music*, the power of tragedy is precisely that it enables the Greeks to simultaneously experience the truth of the Dionysian (which pulls against individuated life and speaks through the wisdom of the satyr, Silenus, to decry human life) and nonetheless affirm life itself (Nietzsche, *The Birth of Tragedy and Other Writings*, §3, 22–5). In other words, already in Nietzsche's early work, affirming life is the characteristic activity of healthy culture. Likewise, in his essay "On the Uses and Disadvantages of History for Life," positive life is figured as a striving for greatness (Nietzsche, *Untimely Meditations*, 67), and this depiction resonates closely with the later picture of a noble will to power, as it is developed in his *On the Genealogy of Morality*, II, §12.
49 Bergson, *The Creative Mind*, 73.
50 Bergson, *An Introduction to Metaphysics*, 158.
51 Bergson, *The Creative Mind*, 74.
52 The rearticulations of this Platonic discourse on light as a metaphysical principle are many. See Moevs, *The Metaphysics of Dante's* Comedy, on Dante Alighieri's light metaphysics (esp. 19–21). See also Walker, *Spiritual and Demonic Magic* (chapter 2 especially) on Ficino's philosophy of spiritual and natural magic rooted in notions of splendour and emanation, which are visible in his *De amore* (Ficino, *El libro dell'amore*, V.4).
53 On the relation of Bergson's *élan vital* and Nietzsche's will to power, see François, "Life and Will," 107–8.
54 The rhetoric of sickness and rebirth in Futurism echoes the dynamics of convalescence that Barbara Spackman delineates in the rhetoric of

decadentism, not only in D'Annunzio but also in Baudelaire, Huysmans, and Nietzsche: Spackman, "The Scene of Convalescence," in *Decadent Genealogies*, 33–104.

55 See Habermas, *The Philosophical Discourse*, 83–105.

56 See Nietzsche's *Ecce Homo*, where he describes his philosophy as offering an alternative to the Christian God: "Have I been understood? – I have not said anything that I would not have said five years ago through the mouth of Zarathustra" (150); and then: "Have I been understood? – *Dionysus versus the crucified …*" (151).

57 Bergson, *The Creative Mind*, 104. These remarks come from his lecture on "Philosophical Intuition," given at the Philosophical Congress in Bologna in April 1911. Bergson is fundamentally working within the same metaphysical horizons as Schopenhauer, but with a different result. His account is close to Schopenhauer's idea that suffering is the individuated experience of will's movement. The difference is that for Bergson intuition enables a person to engage *sympathetically* with life as a whole, indivisible movement (though this sympathy is achieved only after intellect becomes disinterested – another borrowing from Schopenhauer's aesthetics (*The Creative Mind*, 194)). In Bergson's last book, *The Two Sources of Morality and Religion*, he characterizes the outcome of this sympathetic engagement as a state of spiritual joy (317). For Schopenhauer, even if aesthetic experience can allow a momentary, disinterested escape from will, that escape is never a positive state of joy but is at most the momentary absence of suffering (*WWR* I, §38, 197–8). Thus Bergson's philosophy of life operates with a metaphysical system similar to Schopenhauer's but has developed it toward an optimistic possibility of spiritual redemption that is absent in Schopenhauer's philosophy.

58 Bergson, *Les deux sources …*, 317.

59 On the homophobic elements of Marinetti's ideal, see Spackman, "Mafarka and Son." Rebecca West examines the gendered aspects of the modernist-era metaphor of artistic creation as a process of giving birth without biological limitations: West, "Diventare un aggettivo."

60 Marinetti, *Teoria e invenzione futurista*, 299.

61 Christine Poggi explores the tensions of this fantasy of mechanized love: Poggi, *Inventing Futurism*, 150–80.

62 Marinetti, *Teoria e invenzione futurista*, 300.

63 Rainey, Poggi, and Wittman, *Futurism*, 471.

64 On the gender dynamics of Futurism and the role of women writers in the development of its rhetoric of energy and power, see: Re, "Women, Sexuality, Politics," and Re, "Mater-Materia."

65 See chapter 3 and chapter 1 on how decadent aestheticism emerges from a Schopenhauerian strand of idealism and the complex relation of fascist politics to various forms of idealism.

66 The discourse on modernist mysticism is multifaceted and complex. Much has focused on individual figures, such as Luigi Pirandello, whose world view was branded a form of "atheist mysticism" by his contemporary, the philosopher Adriano Tilgher: Tilgher, *Studi sul teatro contemporaneo*. Much of the literature on the topic has referred to anglophone examples; see, for instance: Anderson, *H.D. and Modernist*; Childs, *T.S. Eliot*. On the topic of mysticism and its relation to Catholic modernism, see the volume edited by C.J.T. Talar, *Modernists and Mystics*.

67 I have in mind here Jürgen Habermas's argument that the transformation of the public sphere into a field of rational discursive exchange represents a step in a larger historical progress, what he terms modernity's rationalization of the lifeworld: Habermas, *The Structural Transformation*.

68 Brera, *Novecento all'Indice*.

69 See Jodock, *Catholicism*, for an excellent account of Catholic modernism and anti-modernist responses within the Church. See also O'Connell, *Critics on Trial*.

70 The metaphor has a long history of its own, appearing in Dante's *Paradiso* among other sources. On this metaphor for the union of empirical and transcendent truth, see Ernst, *Tommaso Campanella*; and Gatti, *Il gran libro del mondo*. On the way this naturalist element of Campanella's thought involves a rewriting of earlier idealist positions such as that of Plato's *Republic*, see Subialka, "Transforming Plato."

71 Wittman, "*Omnes velut aqua dilabimur*," 131, 134.

72 In Church history mystical experience and miracles occupy a space fraught with tension and risk, for the miracle as a material instantiation of transcendent reality has the dangerous potential to undermine doctrine with a voice that is hard to silence. The contentious history of the cult of saints illustrates the point nicely: as it consolidated power and extended its worldly reign, the Church sought to develop mechanisms to control local cults and centralize a process of canonization to control this challenge: Brown, *The Cult of Saints*. Likewise, claims of divine revelation asserted by mystics, particularly women, posed challenges to Church and patriarchal authority that needed to be managed: Jantzen, *Power, Gender*.

73 Cangiano, *La nascita*, 345.

74 Barzilai et al., *I processi al futurismo*, offer a first-hand account of the trials as seen by Marinetti's supporters, including Corra and Settimelli. Ialongo, "Marinetti and the *Mafarka* Trial," examines the trial of Marinetti's book, its relation to Notari's, and the efforts to combat Futurist ideology. Brera reveals the unexpected publicity arising from Church proceedings against D'Annunzio and others: Brera, *Novecento all'Indice*, 198.

75 Gregor, *Totalitarianism*, 142–69.

76 Emilio Gentile, *Il culto del Littorio*.

77 On the history of this conflict between Church and State and the resolution achieved in the "conciliazione," see John Pollard, *The Vatican*; and Nelis, Morelli, and Praet, *Catholicism and Fascism*.

78 This journal followed in the footsteps of a Sicilian predecessor, *La Balza futurista*, which published only three issues in 1915 before two of its founders, Guglielmo Jannelli and Vann'Antò (Giovanni Antonio di Giacomo) left for the front lines. Like Corra's *L'Italia futurista*, *La Balza futurista* exceeded the limits of "official" Futurism: Tommasello, "*La Balza futurista*," 235–9. In this respect the journal follows in the footsteps of Papini and Soffici's *Lacerba*, which launched an important critique of how Marinetti dominated Futurist thought in the February 1915 article "Futurismo e Marinettismo," signed by Papini, Palazzeschi, and Soffici. For them, the Florentine Futurists were the only *true* Futurists.

79 He is so little-known today that a recent article on Corra began with the words "Bruno Corra: chi era costui?" ("Bruno Corra: Who was he?"): Cigliana, "Diritto di uccidere," 85.

80 Verdone, "L'amicizia," 13.

81 Corra's collection of short stories about the bad results of miscegenation, *I matrimoni gialli* (1928), declares itself an attempt to create a "future dictionary entry" for his neologism: "Yellow marriage – a marriage between people of different races, more or less badly matched; a locution derived from others: the yellow press, meaning a hybrid press; yellow dogs, dogs of a bastard race." Corra's Orientalist fantasy is also evident in a novel from the same period, *Sanya, la moglie egiziana: Il romanzo dell'Oriente moderno* (1927). On the fascist racial imaginary and its views of hybridity, see Caponetto, *Fascist Hybridities*.

82 Occult Futurism included not only the Florentine circle but also a group in Milan, as well as interest in Turin and Rome. See, for example: D'Ambrosio, "Notes on 'Esoteric Futurism'"; Hanstein, "Edith von Haynau"; Chessa, *Luigi Russolo, Futurist*; Cigliana, *Futurismo esoterico*.

83 Corra, *Battaglie*, 79.

84 Corra, *Battaglie*, 81–2. My translation here is for the Italian term "gabinetto medianico," which is described in Fulvio Rendhell's guide to spiritualist magic as "consisting of a canopy attached to the back wall, surrounded by black curtains" (*Magia spiritica*, 32). The medium might be located in this space during a seance rather than being physically linked to the others, whose hands are clasped to form a "chain."

85 The manifesto opens with a condemnation of the scientific establishment, which the authors label German and accuse of a misleading penchant for precision and certainty: Corra, *Battaglie*, 71. The second numbered point in their manifesto is a call to upend established "conceptual schemas" ("schemi mentali") of scientific prejudice (76).

86 Simona Cigliana, *Futurismo esoterico*, illustrates the importance of esoteric spiritualism for the Futurists. Cigliana, "Spiritismo e parapsicologia," examines the same topic in relation to the broader culture responding to positivist materialism.
87 Corra, *Sam Dunn Is Dead*, 57.
88 There has been very little critical attention paid to this particular collection; one of the only sustained treatments is in a section of Simona Cigliana's article, "Diritto di uccidere" (87–9), which itself actually focuses on a different novel by Corra, *Why I Killed My Wife* (*Perché ho ucciso mia moglie*, 1918). The term "grottesco" becomes important again in the context of Italian modernism, where it is used by authors like Luigi Chiarelli (1880–1947) to describe his anti-bourgeois play, *The Mask and the Face* (*La maschera e il volto*, 1913, first staged in 1916) and thus inaugurates a new "movement" of the grotesque theatre, "il teatro grottesco." See Livio, *Il teatro in rivolta*; and Vena, "Introduction."
89 See Marinetti and Palazzeschi, *Carteggio*.
90 Sica, "Time and Space."
91 Corra, *Madrigali e grotteschi*, 21.
92 Corra, *Madrigali e grotteschi*, 24.
93 Marinetti, Settimelli and Corra, *Il teatro futurista sintetico*, 41.
94 Corra, *Madrigali e grotteschi*, 9.
95 Corra, *Madrigali e grotteschi*, 10.
96 Subialka, "The Seduction of Innocence," esp. 70–2.
97 Corra, *Madrigali e grotteschi*, 75–7.
98 Corra, *Sam Dunn Is Dead*, 17–18.
99 Corra, *Battaglie*, 3.

5. Occult Spiritualism and Modernist Idealism: Reanimating the Dead World

1 The bibliography on nineteenth-century spiritualism and the occult has expanded considerably in recent years, although already in the 1980s there was significant work being done: Oppenheim, *The Other World*; Owen, *The Darkened Rook*; Thurschwell, *Literature, Technology*; Luckhurst, *The Invention of Telepathy*; Owen, *The Place of Enchantment*; Warner, *Phantasmagoria*. The field has grown so large that it now requires an *Ashgate Research Companion to Nineteenth-Century Spiritualism and the Occult* (edited by Kontou and Willburn).

The texts cited above paint a clear and convincing picture of how spiritualism emerged in the period and became a major cultural force, yet they often tend to focus on the Anglo-American development of this "Victorian" mode of thought. It is true that Spiritism (a particular form of spiritualist belief) and its cognate movements can be traced to America, where in Hydesville, New York, Kate and Margaret Fox launched the century's fascination with mediums with their alleged communications with the dead via "rappings": Weisberg, *Talking to the Dead*. This fascination in turn dovetailed with the developing struggles for women's rights in America and abroad: Braude, *Radical Spirits*. Arthur Conan Doyle examined these origins and the subsequent development of the movement in his two-volume study on *The History of Spiritualism* (1926). This book was one of some twenty volumes on the subject that the author wrote, no doubt contributing in his own right to the continuing interest in spiritualism into the early twentieth century, especially when he went on tour across the anglophone world (the UK, Australia, New Zealand, the United States, and South Africa) to discuss spiritualism from 1918 through the mid-1920s. On American spiritualism's presence in art and the evolution of modern visualizations of creativity, see Colbert, *Haunted Visions*. Kerr, *Mediums, Spirit-Rappers*, examines the American scene in connection with radical politics and literature, while more recently Cox, *Body and Soul*, has reread those connections in light of current interest in affect theory. Tromp, *Altered States*, shows that the confluence of spiritualism with changing social and political views is likewise prominent in its British diffusion.

Notwithstanding the preponderance of anglophone scholarship, spiritualism's nineteenth-century spread was truly global. One intervention of my study is thus to demonstrate aspects of its transnational development that have not been fully examined. In the global anglophone context, McMullin, *Anatomy of a Séance*, examines networks of diffusion that spread spiritualism among Canada's elite; Gabay, *Messages from Beyond*, similarly looks at cultural forces that brought spiritualism into vogue in Australia. But the global reach of spiritualism is not limited to the anglophone world. For instance, significant scholarly work has examined its influence in Brazilian culture, with Hess's study, *Spirits and Scientists*, offering a fascinating view of how European spiritualism and Brazilian spiritualism relate, an argument developed further in his *Samba in the Night*, which (following Allan Kardec) examines European Spiritism's relations to Afro-Brazilian Spiritism.

2 Condé and Gossling, "The Devil in the Detail," iii.

3 Surette takes the approach of situating modernist occultism in the broad history of ideas, seeing British modernism's interest in the occult as a means of unearthing an "indiscretion" in modernist thought that had long been shunned by critics: Surette, *The Birth of Modernism*, 5. Surette demonstrates how "canonical" figures in the modernist genealogy (Nietzsche, Schopenhauer, even Freud) operated in relation to occult discourses in establishing a perennial tradition of secret wisdom. For

Surette, this establishes a sense of modernism in which modernity's self-understanding as a time separate from the classical past is actually transformed into a sense of belonging to a time outside of time, having "transcended history" (4).

4 Wilson, *Modernism and Magic*, 14.

5 Josephson-Storm, *The Myth of Disenchantment*, 69.

6 Josephson-Storm, *The Myth of Disenchantment*, 187.

7 Steinfeld, Review of "*Modernism and Magic*," 385.

8 I thus see a connection between what Kermode would call "traditionalist" modernist responses to crisis time and what Norman has convincingly argued is the useful "shock" of the ancient in an earlier moment of modernity's move toward self-awareness, the seventeenth-century *querelle des anciens et des modernes*: Kermode, *The Sense of an Ending*; Norman, *The Shock of the Ancient*.

9 Morselli, *Psicologia e "spiritismo,"* 86.

10 Morselli, *Il magnetismo animale*, 8.

11 Many spiritualists saw their movement as a direct response to positivist materialism. For example, in a lecture on "Materialism and Occultism" given on 10 October 1915, Rudolf Steiner argued that the mid-nineteenth century was in fact the apex of materialism in human history, the high-water mark of humanity turning away from spiritual knowledge: Steiner, *Spiritualism*, 144. He claims that those initiated into occult secrets then held an internal debate and decided to begin making part of their knowledge public to combat that materialism by reminding people that the world "is not devoid of the spiritual" (149). Such characterizations notwithstanding, the nineteenth-century rebirth of spiritualism was in important ways fuelled by scientific culture and methods: R. Moore, "Spiritualism and Science," 477.

12 Josephson-Storm, *The Myth of Disenchantment*, 1–3. Palladino's prominence in Italy is widely attested. See, for instance, the first-hand accounts of the prominent Neapolitan physicist Filippo Bottazzi's *Fenomeni medianici* (1909), translated as *Mediumistic Phenomena*.

13 See chapter 4 for my analysis of the "Manifesto of Futurist Science" and Corra's magical-occult vitalism.

14 I adapt here from the definition of "metapsichica" in Abbagnano's *Dizionario di filosofia*, 581.

15 The discourse on modern re-enchantment comes to a head in Landy and Saler's volume, *The Re-Enchantment of the World*, which argues forcefully against the narrative of modern disenchantment.

16 Kontou and Willburn, *The Ashgate Reseearch Companion*, explain this lexical and conceptual complexity further: "If spiritualism sought to make the spiritual world visible, scientifically proven and technologically

advanced, resulting in overcoming death, distances, and socio-economic, racial and gendered differences, the occult did not. Hidden and dark, instead of sunlight at daybreak, the occult signaled secret societies, magic, strange ancient languages and more than a touch of the Gothic ... Yet, ironically perhaps, the occult, being a broadly defined older term, could also encompass the term 'spiritualism' in both the nineteenth century and today. Especially early in the heyday of spiritualism, the 1850s and 1860s, someone opposed to spiritualist séances or premises might indeed term these practices and concepts as occult" (3).

17 I am grateful to Alessio Baldini for his valuable discussion about this section's argument and its relation to the anthropological / ethnographic examination of magical culture.
18 "The Nobel Prize in Literature 1926," online.
19 Deledda's ethnographic work has been the subject of only limited scholarly interest in comparison with her creative fiction. Fuller analyses her book in relation to the positivist discourse on Sardinia in the age of Lombroso: Fuller, "Regional Identity," 61–3. Likewise, Aste situates the work as part of an "ethnic" corpus: Aste, *Grazia Deledda*, 14–15. See also Gunzberg, "Ruralism." Unfortunately, even Deledda's creative fiction has been under-studied in comparison with that of her male contemporaries, despite her importance to the articulation of Italian modernity: see Heyer-Caput, *Grazia Deledda's Dance*.
20 Fuller, "Regional Identity," 58.
21 Heyer-Caput, *Grazia Deledda's Dance*, 28.
22 Deledda, *Tradizioni populari*, 13.
23 Deledda, *Tradizioni populari*, 14.
24 Cassano, *Il pensiero meridiano*, 8.
25 De Martino's *Sud e magia* (1960) was reissued by Feltrinelli in 2017 after being translated into English by Dorothy Louise Zinn as *Magic: A Theory from the South*. See Fabrizio Ferrari, *Ernesto De Martino on Religion*, on De Martino's importance for thinking about magic and religion in modernity.
26 Weber, *The Vocation Lectures*, 30.
27 Weber, *The Vocation Lectures*, 30. Weber's characterization was seminal, with figures like Habermas echoing but also reconfiguring that view: Habermas, *The Philosophical Discourse*. See also Cascardi, *The Subject of Modernity*, 16–23.
28 De Martino, *Sud e magia*.
29 As David Forgacs shows, De Martino's aim is also political: having recognized that the forces holding back southern Italy's development are not only economic / material but also discursive / imaginary, he aims to naturalize what others view as the "backwards" views of the south so as

to topple narratives that reinforce southern disadvantage: Forgacs, *Italy's Margins*, 143.

30 Deledda, *Tradizioni populari*, 127–37, 155–68.

31 Deledda, *Tradizioni populari*, 158–61.

32 Horkheimer and Adorno's *Dialectic of Enlightenment* famously critiqued the Enlightenment ideology that placed myth as its antithesis, showing how that ideology is itself mythical – responding to and countering the discourse on modern disenchantment already in 1944. Nevertheless, this progressivist narrative of positive science continues to have traction today: see, for example, Sagan, *The Demon-Haunted World*; and Krebs, *Scientific Development*, 12.

33 These examples summarize the section in Deledda, *Tradizioni populari*, 158–61.

34 An English translation of "The Sorcer" is published in Manley and Lewis's volume, *Sinister Stories*.

35 Gautier, "The Tales of Hoffmann," 142. Deledda's sense of a foreboding, fantastic fatalism likewise resonates with the style of Gautier's fantasy writing. See, for instance, *The Jinx*, which is also set in an exotic-magical-dangerous Italian locale, Naples.

36 Cigliana, "Introduzione," 26.

37 Cigliana, "Introduzione," 29.

38 Capuana, *Mondo occulto*, 165.

39 Capuana, *Novelle del mondo occulto*, 387–8.

40 Capuana, *Novelle del mondo occulto*, 379.

41 Capuana, *Mondo occulto*, 62–63.

42 Saint-Simon, *Opinions littéraires*, 341.

43 On Saint-Simon's role in the emergence of "avant-garde" as an artistic-political category: Egbert, "The Idea of Avant-Garde."

44 In Corra, *Battaglie*.

45 Capuana, *Mondo occulto*, 239–40.

46 Marinetti, *Teoria*, 299.

47 Capuana, *Mondo occulto*, 242.

48 Capuana, *Mondo occulto*, 240.

49 Capuana, *Mondo occulto*, 241.

50 Besant and Leadbeater, *Thought-Forms*. Pirandello had a copy of one of Leadbeater's other famous books, *The Astral Plane: Its Scenery, Inhabitants and Phenomena* (1895), in his personal library in French translation, *Le plan astral du Monde invisible, d'après la Théosophie*: Saponaro and Torsello, *La biblioteca*, 81. Olga Ragusa offers an account of Pirandello's readings in Theosophy: Ragusa, *Luigi Pirandello*, 22–30. On the topic of his relation to spiritualism, see Macchia, "Pirandello e gli <<spiriti>>"; Illiano, *Metapsichica e letteratura*; Costanzo, "Pirandello, Theosophy"; and Barbina, *La biblioteca*, 28, 153.

51 See Sinnett, *The Mahatma Letters*, xiii; and Besant, *The Ancient Wisdom*, 116. Leadbeater argued that the Masters are philosophically necessary – that is, there *must* be such people if Theosophical doctrines about reincarnation are true: Leadbeater, *The Masters and the Path*, 4–6. The quasi-hagiographical story of how Madame Blavatsky met one of these Masters, Morya, through a psychic connection during the Great Exhibition of 1851, is recounted in Abdill, *Masters of Wisdom*. Godwin shows that Blavatsky's Theosophy is in fact deeply indebted not just to an ancient tradition but to an ongoing one, specifically a series of speculative theories about the origins of religion and myth circulating in Enlightenment and post-Enlightenment culture: Godwin, *The Theosophical Enlightenment*, esp. 303–6.

52 Blavatsky's fantasy writing is a further testament to the close relationship between the modernist interest in repurposing nineteenth-century generic forms, such as the Gothic, and the spiritual beliefs that were fundamental to re-envisioning modern materialism. See Blavatsky, *Nightmare Tales* (1892).

53 Blavatsky, *The Key to Theosophy*, 3. In her magnum opus, *The Secret Doctrine* (1888), Blavatsky likewise describes their system as a synthesis of science, religion, and philosophy.

54 Blavatsky, *The Key to Theosophy*, 14.

55 On Pirandello's scepticism as part of a broad modern trajectory in Italy, see: De Liguori, *Il sentiero dei perplessi*. Andrea Bini, "L'umorismo di Pirandello," contends that despite his open scepticism, Pirandello is actually interested in recuperating subjective interiority. Petruzzi, "Nihilism, Errancy, and Truth," argues that Pirandello's gaze into the abyss should be read ontologically rather than as a sceptical emptying out of values and meaning.

56 Stocchi-Perucchio offers the most convincing sustained reading of *Il fu Mattia Pascal*, focusing on epistemological scepticism and lost identity: Stocchi-Perucchio, *Pirandello and the Vagaries*.

57 In this respect, then, I disagree with Cangiano's characterization of the supposedly hegemonic form of modernist thought he sees typified in Pirandellian "relativism," which he claims elevates sceptical nihilism to a kind of orienting first principle or essence to replace the lost "God" at the centre of Western metaphysics: Cangiano, *La nascita*, 25.

58 Bergson likewise examines the relation between "becoming" and "form" in similar terms, situating his notion in conversation with both ancient and post-Kantian idealist traditions: Bergson, *L'Évolution créatrice*, 323–56.

59 This is something like a sceptical or negative inflection of Bergson's understanding of human reason as an evolutionary development allowing us to navigate our external environment. See his section on the "Fonction primordial de l'intelligence": Bergson, *L'évolution créatrice*, 164–79.

60 Witt, *The Search for Modern Tragedy*, 91.
61 Witt, *The Search for Modern Tragedy*, 133.
62 Puchner, *The Drama of Ideas*, 103.
63 See, for example, Cerasi, *Quasi niente*; and Pomilio, *La formazione*.
64 On Pirandello and Nietzsche, see Witt, *The Search for Modern Tragedy*, 90; Cerasi, *Quasi niente*; and Bini, "Pirandello, Nietzsche."
65 Harrison, *Essayism*, sees the protagonist of *Henry IV* as renouncing actual life to live a coherently organized fiction (89) in an attempt to achieve a false experience of settled structure (118). This helps to explain the frightening consequences, in Pirandello's imaginary, of life giving way to an image, which is fixed and coherent in a way that life's essayistic becoming pointedly is not.
66 Bini, *Pirandello and His Muse*, 107. Seddio suggests that in Pirandello, logical reasoning strips the world bare to reveal human life in an undesirable, almost uninhabitable form, and feminity is posited as a resolution to that loss; however, his reading invokes the religious where Bini's does not: Seddio, *Le donne di Pirandello*, 295. Cf. Frassica, *Her Maestro's Echo*.
67 This element of self-destruction in Pirandello's novel can also be thought of as a form of Zen self-dissolution: Vettore, "Approximation to Nirvana."
68 Thomas Harrison sees Pirandello as an instance of the effort to achieve existential authenticity in the face of modern disillusionment: Harrison, "Michelstaedter and Existential Authenticity."
69 I thus disagree with Witt, *The Search for Modern Tragedy*, who sees aesthetic fascism as a key to understanding Pirandello's outlook. The aesthetic resonance with fascism is actually a subset of this larger mode of non-affirmative affirmation, one instance of a kind of "necessary illusion" but not the definitive such instance. Indeed, following Pirandello's logic, there can be no definitive instance, as the forms necessitated by life will surely change.
70 Caesar examines the role of the pre-existing character in detail, arguing that it is not specific to Pirandello but rather is shared by writers like Joseph Conrad: Caesar, *Characters and Authors*, 43–4. She holds that this view of characters is symptomatic of a broader modern crisis of authorial omniscience (33).
71 A more detailed examination of Pirandello's theory of the visual imagination and artistic creation is in Di Lieto, Sarti, and Subialka, *Scrittura d'immagini…*, 119–43.
72 Pirandello, *Maschere nude*, vol. 1, 37.
73 The play thus resembles Shakespeare's *The Tempest* and its themes of magical creation ultimately linked to artistic imagination.

74 Schopenhauer introduces this notion already in book II of *WWR* I, where he describes the levels of gradation of will's objectification in the world as Platonic Ideas (§25, 198).
75 *Verismo* is a much-discussed realist movement. As Baldini has argued, Verga's *verismo* might be seen as a pluralist alternative to the nationalism of his contemporaries who sought to pose and / or solve a "southern question" about how to integrate the south into Italy's industrializing modernity: Baldini, "The Liberal Imagination." The impact of the "southern question" on Italian literature and culture was profound: see Moe, *The View from Vesuvius*.
76 Luperini, *Luigi Pirandello e Il fu Mattia Pascal*, 89–94.
77 Nichols and O'Keefe-Bazzoni, *Pirandello and Film*; Càllari, *Pirandello e il cinema*; Lauretta, *Pirandello e il cinema*.
78 Pirandello had a copy of Schopenhauer's magnum opus in his library, the Italian translation published in 1914 (vol. 1) and 1916 (vol. 2) – potentially placing his acquisition of the text around the time he was contending with the First World War and the loss of his mother's life: Saponaro and Torsello, *La biblioteca*, 162. He likewise had a 1934 study of Schopenhauer by Pietro Mignosi, *Schopenhauer*, alongside a volume Mignosi wrote on *Il segreto di Pirandello*: Saponaro and Torsello, *La biblioteca…*, 100. The link between Pirandello and Schopenhauer has been discussed by Subialka, *The Aesthetics of Ambivalence*; Costa, "Pirandello and Philosophy," 11; Stella, *Forma e memoria*, 178; Adank, *Luigi Pirandello*, 66–9; and Tilgher, *La scena e la vita*, 141.
79 Schopenhauer, *WWR* II, 191.
80 Schopenhauer, *On the Will in Nature*, 3.
81 For Schopenhauer, "character" denotes a kind of individual essence, or individual will, which is determined and unchanging. See Janaway, "Necessity, Responsibility, and Character"; Janaway, "Introduction," 9; Zöller, "Schopenhauer on the Self," 28–30; and Atwell, *Schopenhauer on the Character of the World*.
82 Schopenhauer, *On the Will in Nature*, 102–28.
83 Schopenhauer, *On the Will in Nature*, 102–3.
84 Schopenhauer, *On the Will in Nature*, 106.
85 Schopenhauer, *On the Will in Nature*, 107.
86 Schopenhauer, *On the Will in Nature*, 111.
87 Schopenhauer, *On the Will in Nature*, 113.
88 Croce, "Il risveglio filosofico," 178.
89 Bobbio argues in *La filosofia del decadentismo* that irrationalism unites what he terms decadentism (which includes what we would now call modernism) and fascism. Griffin, *The Nature of Fascism*; and Braun, *Mario Sironi*, both highlight the irrationality of fascist myth. Antliff, "Fascism,

Modernism, Modernity," offers an excellent overview of the links between Italian Fascism and modernism.

90 Pirandello, *Maschere nude*, I, 116.

91 Eliot, *Selected Essays*, 13–22.

92 Smith, "Proper Frontiers." In a similar vein, Schwartz argues that Eliot's essay, like many of his early essays, seeks to problematize the limited one-sidedness of both "idealism" and "realism": Schwartz, "Eliot's Ghosts," 19.

93 Breton, *Manifestoes of Surrealism*, 32.

94 Breton, *Manifestoes of Surrealism*, 47.

95 On the Italian case of occult fascism, see in particular de Turris, *Esoterismo e fascismo*. Poggi demonstrates how "traditional" or pagan spiritualist beliefs play an important role in various political struggles, from Risorgimento Neopythagoreanism to Fascist Neopaganism in Evola's case: Poggi, *In Defiance of Painting*, 276. This connection aligns with what Emilio Gentile has analysed as the sacralization of politics in Italian Fascism in his *The Sacralization*.

96 Evola, *Saggi sull'Idealismo magico*.

97 Evola, *Teoria dell'Individuo assoluto*.

98 On Evola's journals and efforts to influence Mussolini, see: Furlong, *The Social and Political Thought*, 87–8; Iacovella, "Julius Evola"; and Del Ponte, "Quando il Gruppo di Ur."

99 Evola, *Saggi sull'Idealismo magico*, 110.

100 Indeed, Mussolini's cult and the various practices designed to excite and channel the energies of the masses resonate with the language of spiritualist vitalism in multiple respects, an intersection visible in the early crowd theory of thinkers like Gustave Le Bon, *Psychologie des foules* (1895). Adorno contends that the leader and the crowd are engaged in a mutual performance: Adorno, *The Culture Industry*, 152. Nye, "Two Paths," argues that theorists like Le Bon and Sorel provided a template for this fascist repurposing of the crowd (412). Tratner, *Modernism and Mass Politics*, contends that modernist form is in part a response to this mass psychology. Bragato, *Futurismo in nota*, points out the way that the language of magnetism and spiritualist ideas likewise shaped the Futurists' vision of mass communication in Marinetti's practice (13).

101 Jonathan Eburne, *Outsider Theory*, is discussed in more detail in the Introduction.

102 Evola, *Rivolta contro il mondo moderno*. This stance against modernity and in favour of a return to popular tradition has been a major factor in the enduring influence of Evola's thought on elements of the far right, in Italy and beyond. See, for example, Risé, whose reading of Evola hopefully proclaims how the "desiccating experience of modernity" ("esperienza disseccante della modernità") has run its course and that humanity will

look away from modernity toward a tradition that allows it to give itself a form again: Risé, "Julius Evola," 22.

103 Surette, *The Birth of Modernism.*

104 Emilio Gentile argues that Mussolini bridges fascist modernity with Roman antiquity in a way that harmonizes them through shared drives, such as athleticism and an orientation toward action: Gentile, "The Conquest of Modernity." See also Arthurs, *Excavating Modernity.*

105 There is a wide literature on primitivism in the modernist imaginary, particularly focusing on postcolonial readings of race and empire. See, for example: Hutchinson, *The Indian Craze;* McGarrity and Culleton, *Irish Modernism;* Flam and Deutch, *Primitivism;* Lemke, *Primitivist Modernism;* Barkan and Bush, *Prehistories of the Future;* Harrison, Frascina, and Gill, *Primitivism, Cubism, Abstraction;* and Goldwater, *Primitivism in Modern Art.* This impulse also involves recourse to earlier "primitive" models from within the Western tradition, looking at the Medieval as a pre-modern alternative: Saler, *The Avant-Garde,* 20. On modernist medievalism more generally, see Ullyot, *The Medieval Presence;* and Pike, *Passage through Hell.* Henrike Christiane Lange's forthcoming book, *Giotto's Triumph,* examines Giotto's art in a similar vein, as both modern rearticulation of the ancient and a point of reference for the primitivist impulse in nineteenth- and twentieth-century modernism.

6. Cinematic Idealism: Modernist Visions of Spiritual Vitality Mediated by the Machine

1 Natale, "A Short History of Superimposition," shows how the fake spirit photographs of the late nineteenth century directly influenced the development of new effects and techniques in early cinema.

2 Already in 1946, André Bazin was tracing the history of these techniques: translated in Bazin, *What Is Cinema?* There is now a wide-ranging bibliography examining how early film transformed visual culture, including via a "new spatiality" (Lant, "Haptical Cinema," 45) and in the enjoyment of "images lingering in uncertainty" (Wiegand, "The Unsettling of Vision," 34), as well as in relation to the "view aesthetic" (Gunning, "Before Documentary," 9), which can also be understood in relation to static images informing early film techniques (DeLassus, "Ruptured Perspectives"). For Arnheim, *Film as Art,* film, like photography, not only reproduces the world but also functions as art in the sense that it is the product of an artistic procedure of creating visual effects; thus it blends reality with artistic vision, exceeding the limits of mechanical reproduction (57). The formal innovations and interests of early cinema are in turn linked

to the developing high-art discourse of modernist art theory: Schweinitz, "Shared Affinities."

3 Visual culture, celebrity culture, literary culture, and the cinema overlap and sometimes butt heads during this rich period. See, for example: Quaresima and Vichi, *La decima musa*, and Welle, "The Beginnings of Film Stardom."

4 See Gunning, "The Cinema of Attraction," which is the starting point of a rich discourse on early film as attraction.

5 Perhaps the most recognizable crystallization of these fears is Charlie Chaplin's famous film about mechanization, *Modern Times* (1936), in which images of the machine and its inhuman rhythm dominate scene after scene, reducing the Tramp to a literal cog in a wheel. Chaplin's representation is an instance of an already decades-long discourse. In her reading of Pirandello's *Shoot!*, Eugenia Paulicelli connects the pessimistic view of the triumph of the machine from that novel to films like Chaplin's and Fritz Lang's *Metropolis* (1927) to characterize a "mechanization of life" that is also "part of the spectacle of cinema" (Paulicelli, *Italian Style*, 5).

6 Syrimis studies this metaphor at length in his rich book on Italian modernist cinema, *The Great Black Spider.*

7 The anxieties of modernists like Pirandello over the technological reduction of life to mere materiality prefigures what Giorgio Agamben would theorize as the biopolitics of bare life. Agamben argues that Hannah Arendt's description of the Nazi concentration camp misses the way in which it was the reduction of political subjects to mere biological existence, bare life, that "legitimated and necessitated total domination" (Agamben, *Homo Sacer*, 120). Totalitarian politics and its physical limit case, the concentration camp, are thus extensions of a conceptual shift eliminating the "sacred" from life. Pirandello's critique of cinematic materialism presciently envisions the ways in which that materialism reduces the value of life, as evidenced by the novel's gruesome ending in which an actress is brutally murdered by a man who is in turn devoured by a tiger; all while the cameraman continues to mechanically turn the crank, capturing it on film.

8 Levine, *Forms.*

9 Marcus, *The Tenth Muse.* McCabe contends that the new film methods of the early 1900s resonate with the poetics of modernist literary texts, including those by Williams, Stein, and HD: McCabe, *Cinematic Modernism.*

10 Jaffe, *Modernism and the Culture of Celebrity*, argues that in the modernist period the author emerges as a celebrity figure in conjunction with the new star system; Goldman, *Modernism Is the Literature of Celebrity*, adds to this an analysis of how the internal features of modernist texts replicate the logic of celebrity (self-)promotion, focusing exclusively on anglophone

modernists. Welle, "The Beginnings of Film Stardom," examines celebrity culture in the Italian context, linking emerging film culture to literary and journalistic spaces and institutions. Turconi and Bassotto, *Il cinema nelle riviste,* have assembled a bibliography of the various Italian periodicals on or about film up through the 1970s, showcasing the breadth of cinema's permeation.

11 W. Mitchell, *Picture Theory,* 11.

12 Both Abel, *French Film Theory,* and Aitken, *European Film Theory,* problematize overly neat periodizations of various avant-garde movements/groups.

13 One indicator of Papini's notoriety is his "canonization" in the series "Uomini del giorno" ("Men of the Day"), printed by the Milanese press Modernissima: Lazarillo, *Papini;* this series of celebrity biographies issued after the First World War placed Papini alongside Mussolini, D'Annunzio, Marinetti, and other prominent figures: Welle, "The Alcove of Celebrity," 97–8.

14 Adamson, *Avant-Garde Florence,* situates Papini's polemics in relation to his immediate cultural sphere (including local academic figures, an older generation espousing aestheticist views, socialist groups, and the liberal establishment under Giolitti).

15 Papini's connections to Florentine and Italian intellectual life and to figures such as Soffici and Prezzolini, among many others, are studied by Soldateschi, *Il tragico quotidiano*; Luti, *Papini, Soffici*; and Richter, *Papini e Soffici.*

16 Cangiano, *La nascita,* 23.

17 This characterization of Croce's initial response comes from Eugenio Garin. The philosopher then adds that in fact Papini and his circle drew on a much wider and more varied intellectual foundation than Bergsonian intuitionism: "from Kierkegaard to Dostoyevsky and Nietzsche, from Pascal to Bergson and Blondel, from James to Peirce and Dewey – and then from revolutionary syndicalism to nationalism (and perhaps racism), Buddhism, modernism, magic, theosophy, and all the most extravagant and absurd adventures [of the century]" (Garin, *History of Italian Philosophy,* 1031).

18 The sole year of the journal's publication has recently been reissued as a book, which includes a helpful introduction and a postscript situating its short-lived interests: Zarlenga and Lucchetta, *L'Anima.*

19 The recent publication of the volume edited by Casetti, Alovisio, and Mazzei, *Early Film Theories,* has taken an important step toward recognizing this overlooked moment of film theory, but there is still more work to be done (28).

20 Welle, "Early Cinema," 44.

21 As Welle, "Early Cinema," points out, however, the context around this early theorization is still one of encountering a perceived threat – state and Church authorities were concerned about the moral impacts of the cinema, and if Papini's article sidesteps some of the concerns about the threat to the system of arts, it is still situated in the broader context of another perceived threat (30).

22 It bears noting that Papini's essay begins by describing the cinema as a feature of the modern city, in a paragraph filled with italicized foreign words emphasizing the cosmopolitan nature of these modern spaces and the changing public who consume art within them.

23 Papini's account thus dovetails with the *fin-de-siècle* intellectual stance against the massification of society, which was often seen as a form of modern social degeneration. Translations of Papini's article are my own, though an English translation was published in Casetti, Alovisio, and Mazzei, *Early Film Theories*: Papini, "The Philosophy." This translation, while making the essay more available, misses important particularities of Papini's language (such as issues of gender in the passage quoted here, or the historical specificity of spirit photography, which it renders as "ghostly photographs" in a later passage); I have thus opted for my own renditions.

24 Gunning's notion of the cinema of attraction can be fruitfully compared to scholarship focusing on the documentary impulse in cinema and cinema's tension with that early function as a medium for disseminating news or information: see, for example, Gahéry, "De la presse illustrée."

25 Sherry, *Modernism…*, 42.

26 Here Papini uses a familiar metaphor from Plato onwards: artistic representation's "illusion" is conceived in terms of the play of shadows on the wall of the cave: Plato, *Republic* (514a–520a).

27 Shakespeare, *As You Like It*: "All the world's a stage, / And all the men and women merely players" (Act II, Scene 7). Calderón's *El gran teatro del mundo* (1634) is perhaps the most famous articulation of the wider metaphor here, though it pervades early-modern theatrical discourse spanning national/linguistic traditions. In the Italian context the metaphor took on hermetic meaning in the microcosmic architectural design of Giulio Camillo's Theatre of Memory, which he described in *L'idea del theatro* (1550); a similarly magical notion can be seen in the follower of Marilio Ficino's philosophy, the astronomer Giovanni Paolo Gallucci, who authored the *Theatrum mundi et temporis* (1588), which circulated widely and tied the metaphor to the creation of an astronomical atlas. Ezio Raimondi offers an overview of the role and development of the Baroque "theatre of the world," arguing that the equation of life to a stage opens the door toward the historical process of secularization: Raimondi, *Un teatro delle idee*, 145.

28 Here I have in mind Hans Ulrich Gumbrecht's *Production of Presence*: the technological materiality of cinema that Papini emphasizes repeatedly in his account is not incidental but rather the whole point. Cinema does not thematize but rather makes present a mode of representation based in reproduction that challenges our notions of what constitutes the real.
29 Here I have in mind Wittgenstein's distinction between saying and showing in the *Tractatus Logico-Philosophicus* (4.1212), which ultimately points us, as Adrian Moore argues, toward an ineffable insight that cannot be put into propositional content: Moore, "On Saying and Showing," 475. Stanley Cavell argues that film represents the world at a distance in a way that displaces the spectator and thus confirms our sense of estrangement from the world: Cavell, *The World Viewed*, 226. In this respect Cavell's argument resonates with Papini's theorization of film's existential significance.
30 Papini's stance on Schopenhauer is complicated. In *Il crepuscolo dei filosofi*, he argues that Schopenhauer is fundamentally significant because he articulates a world view that gives rise to two "heroic" figures of German thought, Nietzsche and Wagner, or what he terms philosophical and musical romanticism: Papini, *Il crepuscolo dei filosofi*, 94. It is thus telling that Papini's stance in his article on cinema echoes precisely the insights of those "romantic" approaches.
31 Fain argues that Papini's approach to cinema in this article reveals a pessimistic outlook on everyday life: Fain, *Giovanni Papini*, 92.
32 Chessa refers to this as a "synesthetical manifesto" and reads it in relation to a series of occult-inspired manifestos and writings by the Futurist Enrico Prampolini, whose journal *Noi* first published it. Prampolini had written an article in the *Gazzetta Ferrarese* (26 August 1913) on "Chromophony – The Color of Sounds" ("La cromofonia – Il colore dei suoni"), examining the theory that a sound can produce a light vibration that influences the atmosphere or aura of a body: Chessa, *Luigi Russolo*, 63.
33 No English translation of "La idealità del cinematografo" exists; translations here are my own.
34 Originally published as "Impressionismo scenico" and "Poetica del cinematografo," these pieces are both translated in Casetti, Alovisio, and Mazzei, *Early Film Theories*.
35 Luciani's views thus resonate with Bergsonian vitalism, so we might think that they prefigure to some extent the later film theory developed by Gilles Deleuze in *Cinema 1* and *Cinema 2*. Marrati, *Gilles Deleuze*, 2–3. Pursuing this comparison, while potentially quite interesting, goes beyond the scope of my argument here.
36 Luciani, "La idealità," 3.
37 Craig, "The Actor," begins with the familiar idealist/aestheticist claim that actors are not artists, as "accident is the enemy of the artist" (3). He

then goes on to propose a new model, one in which the actor ultimately approaches the ideal of a puppet, enabling the realization of a cohesive aesthetic production.

38 Luciani, "La idealità," 4.

39 It is no coincidence, I think, that Luciani's view of the actor so closely mirrors the negative assessments of Pirandello, who likens the actor to a translator and bemoans the distance that the actor/translator creates between the author's vision and what is realized on stage. Both participate in the age-old, Platonic anxiety about representation's inability to give access to the ideal form it means to represent. Pirandello's stance on translation and actors has been widely debated; see, for instance, the long conversation in volume 31 of *PSA*, the journal of the Pirandello Society of America: Sarti and Subialka, *Pirandello and Translation*.

40 Luciani, "La idealità," 4.

41 Luciani, "La idealità," 4.

42 Croce had already noted the centrality of music in Schopenhauer's aesthetics, comparing it to Schelling, who Croce argues "considered it [music] a representation of the very rhythm of the universe" (Croce, *Estetica*, 322).

43 Aitken, *European Film Theory*, notes that French modernist movements like Surrealism and Dada have received much more attention from film scholars despite having produced far fewer films (86).

44 Bordwell, *French Impressionist Cinema*, 1; Abel, *French Cinema*, 280.

45 Of course, grouping early French filmmakers and theorists into one "movement" has come under criticism. Thus, for example, in their introduction to his writings Keller and Paul argue that it is incorrect to consider Epstein an "Impressionist": *Jean Epstein*, 267–8.

46 Theories of the avant-garde that focus on political praxis, such as Peter Bürger's notion that the avant-garde is characterized by the rejection of bourgeois art institutions (Bürger, *Theory of the Avant-Garde*, 49), see the discourse of pure art as an instance of "previous" models of art rooted in notions of aesthetic autonomy. My suggestion here is that in order to understand the avant-garde as a political fact, these theories reduce away key elements of avant-garde notions of things such as media specificity and artistic purification. The counter-tradition of the avant-garde builds its own networks for production, diffusion, and reception and challenges the art institution, but it is not reducible to a specific model of political action as such – it remains, in some cases exceedingly so, steeped in romantic outlooks of elevated aesthetic experience. In this respect Poggioli's notion of the avant-garde "mystique of purity" seems to capture something essential that Bürger's more insistently Marxist narrative is missing: Poggioli, *The Theory of the Avant-Garde*, 200–1.

47 For Abel, Delluc's use of the term already implies an operation whereby we see the ordinary in a previously impossible way: Abel, *French Film Theory*, 110. *Photogénie* is not photographic – it does not simply reproduce; rather it is closer to painting and poetry, in that it creates along with its work of reproducing: Delluc, *Photogénie*, 13.

48 It is not the case that Delluc "invented" the word, but he was the first to repurpose the term from its "monotonous" mass-cultural meaning of a beauty being "photogenic" to a more complex, theoretical sense: Williams, *Republic of Images*, 97.

49 Paci, "The Attraction," suggests that Delluc's and Epstein's definitions are distinguished primarily in that for Delluc *photogénie* magnifies an existing beauty in the world whereas for Epstein "*photogénie* is created out of the encounter between the cinema and the world" (135).

50 "On Certain Characteristics of Photogénie" is translated in Keller and Paul, *Jean Epstein*; "Photogénie and the Imponderable" has not been translated; see Epstein, *Écrits*.

51 Keller and Paul, *Jean Epstein*, 300.

52 Keller and Paul, *Jean Epstein*, 300–2.

53 Epstein, *Écrits*, 346.

54 Keller and Paul, *Jean Epstein*, 301.

55 The Austro-Hungarian philosopher and writer Fritz Mauthner (1849–1923) is the key figure of *Sprachkritik*, having written a three-volume work on the critique of language that was published in 1901–3, *Beiträge zu einer Kritik der Sprache*. This strand of thought however resonates more broadly with those modernist writers and thinkers who were sceptical of linguistic meaning and its logical capabilities, from Hugo von Hofmannsthal to Luigi Pirandello. Ludwig Wittgenstein refers to Mauthner in his *Tractatus Logico-Philosophicus*, arguing that all philosophy must be critique of language yet differentiating his own project from Mauthner's by seeking to delineate the limits of linguistic philosophy while nevertheless pointing toward an alternative mode of showing what cannot be said. The connection between Pirandello's visual philosophy and this tradition of *Sprachkritik*, which also positions him in relation to figures like Carlo Michelstaedter, is examined in Di Lieto, Sarti, and Subialka, *Scrittura d'immagini…*, esp. 99–100.

56 Chapter 4 of my book examines *Lebensphilosophie* and the emergence of avant-garde vitalism in relation to modernist spiritualism, the focus of chapter 5.

57 Keller and Paul, *Jean Epstein*, 301.

58 Turvey, *Doubting Vision*, 22.

59 As Laurent Guido, "The Supremacy," succinctly puts it, "the notion of rhythm occupies a central position among the early attempts by

French critics and cinéastes to grasp the so-called 'specific language' of film" (143).

60 Keller and Paul, *Jean Epstein*, 332.
61 Keller and Paul, *Jean Epstein*, 332.
62 Keller and Paul, *Jean Epstein*, 333.
63 Keller and Paul, *Jean Epstein*, 333.
64 Keller and Paul, *Jean Epstein*, 301.
65 Keller and Paul, *Jean Epstein*, 356–9.
66 Quoted in Abel, *French Cinema*, 279.
67 For example, in the context of the visual arts see Greenberg, "Avant-Garde and Kitsch" and "Towards and Newer Laocoön"; and Fried, "Art and Objecthood." They suggest that modern art moves toward a self-referential focus on pictorial form and the materiality of representation, making the expression of its own medium the point of art, abstracted from representational content.
68 Aitken, *European Film*, 1.
69 Andrew, *Mists of Regret*, 28.
70 Papini was diffused by many contemporaries, such as Prezzolini, who authored studies of Papini's work during the period: for example, see Prezzolini, *Discorso*; and Fondi, *Un costruttore*. De Paulis-Dalembert, *Giovanni Papini*, examines the reception and influence of Papini more generally, including in France. Epstein's significance was likewise impactful in his immediate context as well as on the reception of the broader notion of *photogénie*: Keller, "Introduction," 26. Jane House and Antonio Attisani refer to Luciani as the most significant Italian theorist of early cinema, particularly in the context of the debate over the new medium's relation to theatre: House and Attisani, *Twentieth-Century Italian Drama*, 6.
71 Recent studies of note include Catanese, *Futurist Cinema*; Syrimis, *The Great Black Spider*; Lista, *Il cinema futurista*; Lista, *Cinema e fotografia futurista*; and Berghaus, *International Futurism*.
72 Verdone and Berghaus, "*Vita futurista*," argue that this notion of *cinepittura* represents the only truly "futurist" impulse in the Futurist cinema, in contrast to Bragaglia's less innovative experiments (398). They situate the Corradini brothers' experiments relative to the reception of visual Impressionism and spiritualism, connecting Futurist cinema to Kandinsky's theory of art.
73 Verdone, "Nascita della cinepittura," 387.
74 Rainey, Poggi, and Wittman, *Futurism*, 230. Bold in original.
75 Rainey, Poggi, and Wittman, *Futurism*, 231.
76 Rainey, Poggi, and Wittman, *Futurism*, 232. Bold in original.
77 Rainey, Poggi, and Wittman, *Futurism*, 233.

78 Leander Kaiser argues that Kandinsky is the primary force shaping the ideology of modernist painting, pairing him with Arnold Schönberg's reconfiguration of an abstracted modernist music: Kaiser, "Geist versus Intelligenz."

79 Harrison, *1910*, 4. Harrison examines Kandinsky as a key facet of the modernist/expressionist interest in the relation between intuition and formal expression.

80 Kandinsky, *On the Spiritual in Art*, 35. In this respect, Kandinsky is replicating the general argument of Saint-Simon's progressive vision for an avant-garde art at the head of social and political development: Saint-Simon, *Opinions*, 341.

81 Kandinsky, *On the Spiritual in Art*, 35.

82 Gori, *Studi di estetica*, 42–4.

83 Gori, *Studi di estetica*, 22.

84 Gori, *Studi di estetica*, 84.

85 Gori, *Studi di estetica*, 131.

86 Gori, *Studi di estetica*, 139.

87 See: Poggi, *Inventing Futurism*.

88 Pirandello, *Saggi, poesie, scritti varii*, 998; translated in Pirandello, "Will Talkies Abolish," 198–9. Pirandello's criticism in "Will Talkies Abolish the Theater?" ("Se il film parlante abolirà il teatro," 16 June 1929, *Corriere della sera*) and "Drama and Talkie Cinema" ("Il dramma e il cinematografo parlato," 7 July 1929, *La Nación*, Buenos Aires) insists that cinema should not have sound because dramatic realism leads to cinema being nothing but a poor copy of theatre. Pirandello's stance has been widely examined, for example, in Luzzi, "Sister Arguments"; Syrimis, *The Great Black Spider*; and Subialka, "The Meaning of Acting." As Dudley Andrew notes, there was a broad resistance in France to sound cinema among cultural figures, including directors and critics, who were concerned with maintaining the artistic quality of film: Andrew, *Mists*, 95. Pirandello's stance is thus consonant with a larger trend. Indeed, the battle over sound became a major flashpoint and is the starting point of Bazin's treatment of cinema's evolving language: Bazin, *What Is Cinema?*, 23–40.

89 "The Futurist Cinema" in Rainey, Poggi, and Wittman, *Futurism*, 230.

90 L'Herbier's film forges an important link between Pirandello's theoretical and creative production and the avant-garde aesthetics of French film at the time.

91 In 2014–15 British artist Anne-Marie Creamer created a film adaptation of Pirandello's unrealized project, *Treatment for Six Characters, an Unrealized Film by Luigi Pirandello*, in which she draws directly from the written treatment and visualizes Pirandello's creative endeavour almost entirely without actors, envisioning what she terms a "cinema of the mind"

(Creamer, online). Creamer's version is, as she termed it in an interview with Lesley Sullivan, "a kind of *mise en abyme*" (Creamer and Sullivan, "Pirandello's Unrealized Film," 103). The 41st International Conference on Pirandello Studies (December 2004) examined the question of Pirandello's relation to film by asking why filmmakers had never attempted an adaptation of his final, unfinished play, *The Mountain Giants* (*I giganti della montagna*, 1937); see Lauretta, *I giganti della montagna*. Milioto and Klem both responded to this call by envisioning proposals for such an adaptation, but unlike Creamer's film these remain only written scenarios for a project: Milioto, "*I giganti della montagna…*"; and Klem, "Progetto di un metafilm."

92 For Micheli, *Pirandello in cinema*, this is the contradiction between Pirandello's theoretical and practical stances on cinema (17). The most detailed accounts of Pirandello's thought and practice can be found in Càllari, *Pirandello e il cinema*, and Nichols and O'Keefe Bazzoni, *Pirandello and Film*. Interest in Pirandello and cinema is however widespread, as indicated by the number of conferences on the topic, leading to a series of collected volumes: Lauretta, *Quel che il cinema*; Lauretta, *Il cinema e Pirandello*; Lauretta, *Pirandello e il cinema*.

93 Pirandello, "Will Talkies Abolish the Theater?," 202.

94 The intermedial visuality of Pirandello's production is demonstrated in Sarti and Subialka, eds., *Pirandello's Visual Philosophy*; and Di Lieto, Sarti and Subialka, *Scrittura d'immagini*.

95 On the lasting impact of Schopenhauer's theory of music, which helped shape subsequent European theories and practice, see: Goehr, *The Quest for Voice*; and Goehr, "Schopenhauer and the Musicians." On Pirandello's "visible language of music," see Comuzio, "Il cinema."

96 Schopenhauer, *WWR* I, §52, 262–3.

97 For Schopenhauer, musical rhythm aligns with features of human striving and the inner movement of life, contributing to the sense that music offers a revelation of what cannot be said: Alperson, "Schopenhauer," 158.

98 Nichols and O'Keefe Bazzoni, *Pirandello and Film*, 144.

99 Harrison, "Regicide, Parricide," 208–9.

100 Claudia Sebastiana Nobili argues that Pirandello's outlook on cinema should be situated relative to the Futurists' as well as that of Epstein, with focus on how the cinema has the potential to serve as a mirror revealing oneself from various distorted angles: Nobili, *La materia del sogno*, 46 and 76–7.

101 Viva Paci claims that Pirandello's *Si gira…* already prefigures elements of *photogénie*, specifically the way in which the film lens penetrates reality and exposes something hidden within: Paci, "The Attraction," 127–32.

102 Schopenhauer, *WWR* I, §52, 257.

103 Dudley Andrew argues that while Impressionism, Surrealism, and German Expressionism all "aim for a cinema of the imagination" (*Mists of Regret*, 40), Surrealism actually prepares the ground for a new realist "optique" and thus fits unexpectedly with Bazin's rejection of art cinema's notion of purity (x).
104 Dalí, "Abstract," 65. As Hammond points out in his notes to this essay, Dalí's stance in this piece marks a direct repudiation of his own earlier writings on film: Dalí, "Abstract," 67.
105 Dalí, "Abstract," 63.
106 Breton, *Manifestoes*, 23, 29.
107 Breton's first "Manifesto of Surrealism" describes what it terms the "Secrets of the Magical Surrealist Art" (*Manifestoes*, 29). It likewise envisions surrealism as an "invisible ray" that revolutionizes the world, playing on popular images of parapsychological and spiritual-scientific interest, such as energy waves that are invisible yet have impact on the actual world: Breton, *Manifestoes*, 47.
108 Breton, *Manifestoes*, 51–109.
109 Valentin, "Introduction to Black-and-White Magic," 95.
110 Artaud, "Sorcery and Cinema," 103.
111 Artaud, "Sorcery and Cinema," 104.

Conclusion: Overdetermined Idealist Legacies

1 De Sanctis, "Schopenhauer e Leopardi," 232.
2 Re, "Gabriele D'Annunzio's Theater of Memory," 8–9.

Appendix. Schopenhauer and Leopardi: A Dialogue between A and D

1 The title page of the *Rivista contemporanea* lists the topics of interest to the journal in the following sequence: "PHILOSOPHY — HISTORY — SCIENCE — LITERATURE / POETRY — NOVELS — TRAVEL / CRITICISM — ARCHAEOLOGY — FINE ARTS" (*Rivista contemporantea*, Vol. 15).
2 This notion of brotherhood resonates with the case of D'Annunzio and Shimoi that I examine at the opening of the Introduction, highlighting another way in which idealism functions as a transnational paradigm drawing modern writers into literary-philosophical-political constellations of shared spiritual ambition.
3 My translation is based on the version collected in De Sanctis's *Saggi critici. Prima edizione milanese*, 4 vols., ed Paolo Arcari, vol. 1 (Milan: Treves, 1921), 227–70. Paolo Arcari's notes have been instructive.

4 [Cesare Cantù (1804–1895) was a cultural figure of the mid-nineteenth century. He taught in Como and was the author of numerous historical treatises as well as a historical commentary on Manzoni's *I promessi sposi*, with a Catholic and somewhat reactionary perspective. De Sanctis's essay on Cantù, "Una storia della letteratura italiana di Cesare Cantù," is collected in his *Saggi critici*, vol. 1, 271–87. In his *Prison Notebooks*, Gramsci recounts an entertaining story about an academic battle he witnessed at the university concerning De Sanctis's negative judgment of Cantù, which was a topic of debate among professors and students: *Prison Notebooks*, vol. 2, 14–15.

Giovanni Prati (1814–1884) was a poet in the Italian romantic tradition, who published numerous relatively well-known collections between 1843 and 1878. De Sanctis collected two essays on Prati in his *Saggi critici*: "*Satana e le Grazie*, leggenda di Giovanni Prati," vol. 1, 64–90; and "*L'Armando*," vol. 2, 110–34.]

5 An infamous cop in the Bourbon government. (De Sanctis's note.) [Campagna was well-known for enforcing the Bourbon monarchy's political repression of liberal political activists, including Luigi Settembrini, who mentions him by name in his *Ricordanze della mia vita* (vol. 2, lxxix–lxxx), to which De Sanctis had written a preface noting Settembrini's importance for the generations of 1848 and 1860 – the two key revolutionary moments in Naples and Italy. Campagna had a long career and was promoted to the rank of *commissario*, a chief of police with oversight of key areas, including the port. Throughout the dialogue there are references to Campagna's "scissors," an allusion to regulations under Ferdinand II prohibiting long beards, which were associated with liberal revolutionaries.]

6 [Annibale De Gasparis (1819–1892) was a prominent astronomer, a professor of astronomy at the University of Naples from 1853, who directed the Capodimonte observatory in Naples starting in 1864; he also became a senator of the newly unified kingdom in 1861 and was elected to the prominent Accademia dei Lincei, a Roman group devoted to the renewal of naturalism founded in 1603.]

7 [Carlo Maria Curci (1810–1891) was a prominent priest in Naples, ordained at the age of twenty-six, who was also an important cultural figure: he edited an edition of Vincenzo Gioberti's famous essay on the *Primato morale e civile degli italiani* before turning against Gioberti and launching attacks on his thought that were ultimately influential in convincing Pope Pius IX that Gioberti was problematic. Curci was exiled from Naples along with the Jesuit order in 1848–49, and travelled first to Malta and then to Paris: Curci, *Memorie*, 316–43. Pius IX later elevated Curci to make him one of the authors responsible for the periodical *Civiltà*

Cattolica, which grew its circulation during his tenure: see De Mattei, *Pius IX*, 43.]

8 ["Pangloss taught metaphysico-theologico-cosmo-codology. He could prove wonderfully that there is no effect without a cause and that, in this best of all possible worlds, His Lordship the Baron's castle was the most beautiful of castles and Madam the best of all possible baronesses": Voltaire, *Candide*, 4.]

9 Warden of the prison where the author was locked up. (De Sanctis's note.)

10 [The word "idea" is sometimes capitalized and sometimes in lowercase throughout the text. I have maintained those variations.]

11 [There is a pun in the Italian here – "accidenti," which translates as "damnit," is also the plural form of "accident," which is used earlier in the paragraph in its philosophical sense as a non-essential trait or a non-necessary predicate.]

12 *Die Welt als Wille und Vorstellung*. (De Sanctis's note.)

13 *Demofoonte*, Act III, Scene 2. (De Sanctis's note.) [The reference is to a well-known opera libretto by Pietro Metastasio (1698–1782), perhaps the most famous Italian author of the eighteenth century alongside Alfieri; it was first set to music by Antonio Caldara in 1733. The line quoted comes from Timante's speech at the beginning of the scene, though there are variations on the language here: Metastasio, *Opere*, vol. 2, 199.]

14 See the appendix to his "Sketch of a History of the Doctrine of the Ideal and the Real" in Frauenstädt's edition of *Parerga und Paralipomena* (Leipzig: Brockhaus, 1878), vol. 1, 22. (De Sanctis's citation.) [Schopenhauer's invective against Fichte and the other post-Kantian idealists is pointed to say the least: "Readers who are acquainted with what has passed for philosophy in Germany in the course of this [nineteenth] century, might perhaps wonder why they do not see mentioned in the interval between Kant and me either the idealism of Fichte, or the system of the absolute identity of the real and the ideal, as they quite properly appear to belong to our subject. But I have not been able to include them because Fichte, Schelling, and Hegel are in my opinion not philosophers; for they lack the first requirement of a philosopher, namely a seriousness and honesty of inquiry. They are merely sophists who wanted to appear to be rather than to be something. They sought not truth, but their own interest and advancement in the world. Appointments from governments, fees and royalties from students and publishers, and, as a means to this end, the greatest possible show and sensation in their sham philosophy – such were the guiding stars and inspiring genii of those disciples of wisdom. And so they have not passed the entrance examination and cannot be admitted into the venerable company of thinkers for the human race"

(Schopenhauer, *Parerga and Paralipomena*, vol. 1, 21). Schopenhauer goes on for several pages to level charges against Hegel in particular as a sham philosopher and charlatan, although he likewise continues to disparage the ways in which he perceives Fichte and Schelling as having created confusion in a dishonest way.]

15 *Parerga und Paralipomena*, vol. 1, 27. (De Sanctis's citation.) [This is a paraphrase rather than a quotation from Schopenhauer's "Appendix," but the tone is accurate enough: Schopenhauer, *Parerga and Paralipomena*, vol. 1, 25.]

16 Spinoza, *Ethics*, pt 2, Proposition 7. (De Sanctis's citation.)

17 Spinoza, *Ethics*, pt 3, Proposition 2. (De Sanctis's citation.)

18 [La Vicaria (the hall of justice) is another name for the Castel Capuano, a twelfth-century structure built at the juncture in Naples's city walls where the road leads to Capua, hence the name. Originally a royal palace, the Bourbons used its basement as a prison.]

19 "Some Further Elucidations of the Kantian Philosophy," in "Fragments for the History of Philosophy," §13, in *Parerga und Paralipomena*, vol. 1, 101. (De Sanctis's citation.)

20 *Parerga und Paralipomena*, vol. 1, 103. (De Sanctis's citation.)

21 *Letters to Goethe, Herder, Wieland, and Other Significant Contemporaries* (Darmstadt: 1835), 239. (De Sanctis's citation.) [De Sanctis has translated the German edition's title into Italian, and so I have translated it into English. The reference is to: Karl Wagner, ed., *Briefe*, 239.]

22 *Parerga und Paralipomena*, vol. 1, 104. (De Sanctis's citation.)

23 Chapter 27, "On Women and Other Things," and chapter 11, "On Politics," in *Parerga und Paralipomena*, vol. 2, 649, 256. (De Sanctis's citation.) [De Sanctis has translated the chapter titles into Italian, so I have rendered them in English here.]

24 [There is a pun in the Italian between will (*il volere*, which also means desire) and the phrase "ci volea molto a trovar questa," which plays on another meaning of the term. Throughout the dialogue, but particularly in this paragraph and those that follow, there is an ambiguity or multiplicity in the way that De Sanctis uses the verb *volere* ("to want," "to desire," "to will") and its cognate forms that cannot be captured in English. I use both "will" and "want" as it seems most appropriate given the context, but the word in Italian is the same.]

25 *Über den Willen in der Natur*, chapter on "Linguistics," in *Works*, Brasch edition, vol. 1, 634. (De Sanctis's citation.) [See Schopenhauer, *Werke*, vol. 1, 634. I have again rendered in English those parts of the title that De Sanctis translated into Italian.]

26 "Fragmente zur Geschichte der Philosophie," §2, *Parerga und Paralipomena*, vol. 1, 88. (De Sanctis's citation.)

27 [On Gioberti's philosophy and its relation to Pythagoreanism, see Copenhaver and Copenhaver, *From Kant to Croce*, 37.]
28 *Die Welt als Wille und Vorstellung*, vol. 1, Book II, §18 (Leipzig, 1873), 122. (De Sanctis's citation.)
29 On the subject of the intellect see his principal work, *Die Welt als Wille und Vorstellung*, vol. 2, ch. 15, 161 (De Sanctis's note and citation.)
30 *Die Welt als Wille und Vorstellung*, vol. 2, ch. 25, 367 (De Sanctis's citation.)
31 "Preface," *Über den Willen in der Natur*, ed. Brasch, vol. 1, 565 (De Sanctis's citation.)
32 On ideas, see his principal work, volume I, book three, pages 30–52, where you will find an exaggerated aesthetic theory. (De Sanctis' note.)
33 *Parerga und Paralipomena*, vol. 1, 18–43; vol. 2, ch. 5, 105. (De Sanctis's citation.)
34 *Parerga und Paralipomena*, vol. 2, ch. 5, 105 (De Sanctis's citation.)
35 [Again De Sanctis is playing on the ambiguity of meaning in Italian attached to *volere* and its cognate forms, which I translate as both "to will" and "to want" (and "to desire") here, according to the context.]
36 *Die Welt als Wille und Vorstellung*, vol. 1, Book IV. (De Sanctis's citation.)
37 ["Se la vita è sventura, / perché da noi si dura?" (Leopardi, *Canti*, "Canto notturno di un pastore errante dell'Asia," vv. 55–56), Translation by Jonathan Galassi, "Night Song of a Wandering Shepherd in Asia." De Sanctis cites pages from an edition of Leopardi's poems, but he does not specify the bibliographical details of that edition. I have thus chosen not to replicate those citations but rather to add citations to a recent edition instead.]
38 ["[…] Arcano è tutto, / Fuor che il nostro dolor. […]" (Leopardi, *Canti*, "Ultimo canto di Saffo," vv. 46–47), Translation by Jonathan Galassi, "Sapho's Last Song," v. 46.]
39 ["[…] il brutto / Poter che, ascoso, a comun danno impera" and "l'infinita vanità del tutto" (*Canti*, "A sé stesso," vv. 14–16). Translation by Jonathan Galassi, "To Himself," vv. 14–16.]
40 "Frammento apocrifo di Stratone da Lampsaco." (De Sanctis' citation.) ["Apocryphal Fragment of Strato of Lampsacus," in Leopardi, *The Moral Essays*, 174–8; see Leopardi *Operette morali*, 190–4.]
41 *Die beiden Grundprobleme der Ethik*, pt 2, §19, ed. Brasch, vol. 2, 377. (De Sanctis's citation.) [See Schopenhauer, *Werke*, vol. 2, 377.]
42 "La ginestra." (De Sanctis's citation.) ["Broom," in *Canti*, trans. Jonathan Galassi, 286–309.]
43 ["Lazzarone" is a term used to describe the poorest class of beggars who live on the streets of Naples, derived from the Spanish "lázaro."]
44 *Die Welt als Wille und Vorstellung*, vol. 1, §63, 419. (De Sanctis's citation.)

45 *Die Welt als Wille und Vorstellung,* vol. 2, §8; *Die beiden Grundprobleme der Ethik, Ethik,* pt 2, "Critical Appendix on the Kantian Philosophy," vol. 1, 610. (De Sanctis's citation.)
46 *Die beiden Grundprobleme der Ethik,* in *Werke,* vol. 2, 313; *Parerga und Paralipomena,* vol. 2, ch. 8. (De Sanctis', citation.)
47 *Parerga und Paralipomena,* vol. 2, ch. 9; *Die Welt als Wille und Vorstellung,* vol. 2, ch. 17. (De Sanctis's citation.)
48 [Saint Januarius (San Gennaro) is the patron saint of Naples, after whom the city's cathedral is unofficially named (its official name is the Cathedral of Santa Maria Assunta, but it houses the relics of Saint Januarius).]
49 The political part is taken nearly word for word from chapter 9 of *Parerga und Paralipomena,* vol. 2. (De Sanctis's note.)
50 *Parerga und Paralipomena,* vol. 2, 270. (De Sanctis's citation.)
51 *Parerga und Paralipomena,* vol. 2, 273. (De Sanctis's citation.)
52 *Parerga und Paralipomena,* vol. 2, 275. (De Sanctis's citation.)
53 *Parerga und Paralipomena,* vol. 2, 268. (De Sanctis's citation.)
54 *Parerga und Paralipomena,* vol. 2, ch. 29, "On Physiognomy," 677. (De Sanctis's citation.)
55 *Die Welt als Wille und Vorstellung,* vol. 2, ch. 38, 506. (De Sanctis's citation.)
56 *Die Welt als Wille und Vorstellung,* vol. 1, §51, 291. (De Sanctis's citation.)
57 [Pantalone (Pantaloon) and Colombina (Columbina) are "masks" or characters in the traditional Italian theatrical form of the *commedia dell'arte,* which uses stock characters who never change as the basis for its performances. Pantalone is a well-off merchant typifying avarice and ego, originating in the Venetian *commedia.* Colombina is a servant and the mistress of Harelquin, typifying the clever/tricky servant.]
58 *Die Welt als Wille und Vorstellung,* vol. 1, §62, 400. (De Sanctis's citation.)
59 [Daniello Bartoli (1608–1685) became the official historian of the Jesuit order, the Compagnia di Gesù, and wrote numerous volumes of history. He was admired by not only Leopardi but also by leading literary figures of the nineteenth century such as Niccolò Tommaseo and Giosuè Carducci.]
60 *Die Welt als Wille und Vorstellung,* vol. 1, §62, 414. (De Sanctis's citation.)
61 ["Chiudi alla luce omai / Questi occhi tristi, o dell'età reina" (Leopardi, *Canti,* "Amore e morte," vv. 106–7). Translation by Jonathan Galassi, "Love and Death," vv. 106–7.]
62 *Die Welt als Wille und Vorstellung,* vol. 1, §55, 347, 348. (De Sanctis's citation.)
63 [Piazza San Marco, St Mark's Square, is the main public square in Venice.]
64 *Parerga und Paralipomena,* vol. 1, 141; *Die Welt als Wille und Vorstellung,* vol. 2, ch. VI, 68, and ch. 7, 91. (De Sanctis's citation.)
65 *Parerga und Paralipomena,* vol. 2, §126, 269. (De Sanctis's citation.)
66 Rousseau, *Confessions,* bk 7. (De Sanctis's citation.)

Works Cited

Abbagnano, Nicola, and Giovanni Fornero. *Dizionario di filosofia*. Turin: UTET, 1998.

Abdill, Edward. *Masters of Wisdom: The Mahatmas, Their Letters, and the Path*. New York: Penguin, 2015.

Abel, Richard. *French Cinema: The First Wave, 1915–1929*. Princeton: Princeton University Press, 1984.

– *French Film Theory and Criticism: A History/Anthology, 1907–1939*. Vol. 1. Princeton: Princeton University Press, 1988.

Abelsen, Peter. "Schopenhauer and Buddhism." *Philosophy East and West* 43.2 (April 1993): 255–78.

Adamson, Walter L. *Avant-Garde Florence: From Modernism to Fascism*. Cambridge, MA: Harvard University Press, 1993.

– *Embattled Avant-Gardes: Modernism's Resistance to Commodity Culture in Europe*. Berkeley: University of California Press, 2007.

– "Modernism and Fascism: The Politics of Culture in Italy, 1903–1922." *American Historical Review* 95 (April 1990): 359–90.

Adank, Mathias. *Luigi Pirandello e i suoi rapporti con il mondo tedesco*. Arau, Druck: Druckerei Genossenschaft, 1948.

Adorno, Theodor. *The Culture Industry: Selected Essays on Mass Culture*, edited by J.M. Bernstein. London: Routledge, 1991.

Agamben, Giorgio. *Homo Sacer: Sovereign Power and Bare Life*, translated by Daniel Heller-Roazen. Stanford: Stanford University Press, 1998.

– *The Man without Content*, translated by Georgia Albert. Stanford: Stanford University Press, 1999.

Aitken, Ian. *European Film Theory and Criticism: A Critical Introduction*. Edinburgh: Edinburgh University Press, 2001.

Albert, Karl. *Lebensphilosophie: Von den Anfängen bei Nietzsche bis zu ihrer Kritik bei Lukács*. Freiburg: Verlag Karl Alber, 2018.

Alperson, Philip. "Schopenhauer and Musical Revelation." *Journal of Aesthetics and Art Criticism* 40.2 (Winter 1981): 155–66.

Amann, Elizabeth. *Dandyism in the Age of Revolution: The Art of the Cult.* Chicago: University of Chicago Press, 2015.

Amano, Ikuho. *Decadent Literature in Twentieth-Century Japan: Spectacles of Idle Labor.* New York: Palgrave Macmillan, 2013.

Ameriks, Karl, ed. *The Cambridge Companion to German Idealism.* Cambridge: Cambridge University Press, 2000.

Anderson, Elizabeth. *H.D. and Modernist Religious Imagination: Mysticism and Writing.* London: Bloomsbury, 2013.

Andrew, Dudley. *Mists of Regret.* Princeton: Princeton University Press, 1995.

Annavini, Silvia. "<<Un filo di fumo>>. Malattia, sigarette e letteratura in Italo Svevo e Fernando Pessoa." In *Italo Svevo and His Legacy for the Third Millennium*, vol. 2: *Contexts and Influences*, edited by Giuseppe Stellardi and Emanuela Tandello Cooper, 72–85. Leicester: Troubador, 2014.

Antliff, Mark. "Fascism, Modernism, Modernity." *Art Bulletin* 84.1 (March 2002): 148–69.

Antonucci, Giovanni. *Cronache del teatro futurista.* Roma: Edizioni Abete, 1975.

Appiah, Kwame Anthony. "Cosmopolitan Patriots." In *For Love of Country? Debating the Limits of Patriotism.* Edited by Joshua Cohen, 21–9. Boston: Beacon Press, 1996.

– *Cosmopolitanism: Ethics in a World of Strangers.* New York: W.W. Norton, 2006.

– *The Ethics of Identity.* Princeton: Princeton University Press, 2005.

Ardoin, Paul, S.E. Gontarski, and Laci Mattison, eds. *Understanding Bergson, Understanding Modernism.* London: Bloomsbury, 2013.

Arnheim, Rudolf. *Film as Art.* Berkeley: University of California Press, 1957.

Artaud, Antonin. "Sorcery and Cinema." In *The Shadow and Its Shadow: Surrealist Writings on the Cinema*, edited, translated, and introduced by Paul Hammond. 3rd ed., 103–5. San Francisco: City Lights Books, 2000.

"Arthur Schopenhauer." In *Nineteenth-Century Literature Criticism*, vol. 372, edited by Catherine C. DiMercurio., 121–307. Farmington Hills: Layman Poupard Publishing / Gale Cengage, 2019.

"Arthur Schopenhauer." *The Christian Examiner* 76 (Fifth Series, Vol. XIV; January, March, May, 1864). London: 46–80.

"Arthur Schopenhauer." *The Saturday Review*, 5 September 1863, 323–5.

Arthurs, Joshua. *Excavating Modernity: The Roman Past in Fascist Italy.* Ithaca: Cornell University Press, 2012.

Aste, Mario. *Grazia Deledda: Ethnic Novelist.* Potomac: Scripta Humanistica, 1990.

Atti del Reale Istituto d'Incoraggiamento di Napoli, vol. 9. Naples: 1896.

Atwell, John. *Schopenhauer on the Character of the World: The Metaphysics of Will.* Berkeley: University of California Press, 1995.

Aubert, Jacques. *The Aesthetics of James Joyce* [1973]. Baltimore: Johns Hopkins University Press, 1992.

Baioni, Massimo. "*La lotta politica in Italia* di Alfredo Oriani: Parabola di una fortuna." *Storiografia* 1 (1997): 177–94.

Baldi, Valentino. *Reale invisibile: Mimesi e interiorità nella narrativa di Pirandello e Gadda*. Venice: Marsilio, 2010.

Baldini, Alessio. "The Liberal Imagination of Giovanni Verga: *Verismo* as Moral Realism." *The Italianist* 37.3 (2017): 348–68.

Barbina, Alfredo. *La biblioteca di Luigi Pirandello*. Rome: Bulzoni, 1980.

Barcénas, Alejandro. "Modern Japanese Aesthetics and the Neo-Kantians." In *Frontiers of Japanese Philosophy 6: Confluences and Cross-Currents*, edited by Raquel Bouso and James W. Heisig, 13–21. Nagoya: Nanzan Institute for Religion and Culture, 2009.

Barkan, Elazar, and Ronald Bush, eds. *Prehistories of the Future: The Primitivist Project and the Culture of Modernism*. Stanford: Stanford University Press, 1995.

Barnaby, Paul. "*Superuomini e no*: Dannunzian Hypotexts in Capuana's *Rassegnazione*." *Forum Italicum* 51.2 (August 2017): 432–51.

Barzilai, Salvatore, Luigi Capuana, Innocenzo Cappa, F.T. Marinetti, Cesare Sarfatti, Renato Zavataro, Bruno Corra, and Emilio Settimelli. *I processi al futurismo per oltraggio al pudore*. Rocca San Casciano: L. Cappelli, 1918.

Basile, Jonathan. "Life/Force: Novelty and New Materialism in Jane Bennett's *Vibrant Matter*." *SubStance* 48.2 (2019): 3–22.

Baudelaire, Charles. *Les fleurs du mal. Précédées d'une notice par Théophile Gautier*. Paris: Calmann-Levy, 1869. Online: HathiTrust.

– *Les paradis artificiels*. Paris: Poulet-Malassis et De Broise, 1860.

– *Paris Spleen*, translated by Louise Varèse. New York: New Directions, 1970.

Bazin, André. *What Is Cinema?* 2 vols, edited and translated by Hugh Gray. Berkeley: University of California Press, 2005.

Beard, Michael. The Blind Owl *as a Western Novel*. Princeton: Princeton University Press, 1990.

Behler, Ernst. *German Romantic Literary Theory*. Cambridge: Cambridge University Press, 1993.

Beiner, Ronald. *Dangerous Minds: Nietzsche, Heidegger, and the Return of the Far Right*. Philadelphia: University of Pennsylvania Press, 2018.

Beiser, Frederick C. *After Hegel: German Philosophy 1840–1900*. Princeton: Princeton University Press, 2014.

– "The Enlightenment and Idealism." In *The Cambridge Companion to German Idealism*, edited by Karl Ameriks, 18–36. Cambridge: Cambridge University Press, 2000.

– *The Fate of Reason: German Philosophy from Kant to Fichte*. Cambridge, MA: Harvard University Press, 1987.

– *German Idealism: The Struggle against Subjectivism, 1781–1801*. Cambridge, MA: Harvard University Press, 2008.
– "Hegel's Historicism." In *The Cambridge Companion to Hegel*, edited by Frederick C. Beiser, 270–300. Cambridge: Cambridge University Press, 1993.
– "Romanticism and Idealism." In *The Relevance of Romanticism*, edited by Dalia Nassar, 30–43. Oxford: Oxford University Press, 2014.
Beja, Morris. *Epiphany in the Modern Novel*. London: Peter Owen, 1971.
Bellamy, Richard. "What Is Living and What Is Dead in Croce's Interpretation of Hegel." *Bulletin of the Hegel Society of Great Britain* 5.1 (1984): 5–14.
– "Croce, Hegel, and Gentile and the Doctrine of the Ethical State." *Rivista di Studi Crociani* 20 (1983): 263–81.
Benjamin, Walter. *The Arcades Project*. Ed. and trans. Howard Eiland. Cambridge, MA: Harvard University Press, 2003.
– "The Work of Art in the Age of Its Technological Reproducibility. Second Version." *Selected Writings*, vol. 3: *1935–1938*, edited by Howard Eiland and Michael W. Jennings, translated by Edmund Jephcott, Howard Eiland, et al., 101–33. Cambridge, MA: Harvard University Press, 2002.
Bennett, Jane. *Vibrant Matter: A Political Ecology of Things*. Durham: Duke University Press, 2010.
– "A Vitalist Stopover on the Way to a New Materialism." In *New Materialisms: Ontology, Agency, and Politics*, edited by Diana Coole and Samantha Frost, 47–69. Durham: Duke University Press, 2010.
Berghaus, Günter, ed. *International Futurism in Arts and Literature*. Berlin and New York: Walter de Gruyter, 2000.
– *Italian Futurist Theatre, 1909–1944*. Oxford: Oxford University Press, 1998.
Bergson, Henri. *Creative Evolution*. New York: Cosimo Books, 2005. (Reprint of translation by Arthur Mitchell, published by H. Holt and Company, 1911.)
– *The Creative Mind: An Introduction to Metaphysics*, translated by Mabelle L. Andison. Mineola: Dover, 2007.
– *Les deux sources de la morale et de la religion*. Paris: Presses Universitaires de France, 1932. Translated as *The Two Sources of Morality and Religion*, translated by R. Ashley Audra and Cloudesley Brereton. Notre Dame: University of Notre Dame Press, 1977.
– *L'évolution créatrice*. Paris: Felix Alcan, 1907. Online: HathiTrust.
– *An Introduction to Metaphysics*, translated by T.E. Hulme, introduction by Thomas A. Goudge. Indianapolis: Hackett, 1999.
Berman, Antoine. "Translating and the Trials of the Foreign," translated by Lawrence Venuti. In *The Translation Studies Reader*, edited by Lawrence Venuti, 284–97. London and New York: Routledge, 2000.
Berman, Jessica. *Modernist Commitments: Ethics, Politics, and Transnational Modernism*. New York: Columbia University Press, 2011.

Bernardini, Paolo L. "Introduction: A Culture of Death." In *Voglio morire! Suicide in Italian Literature, Culture, and Society 1789–1919*, edited by Paolo L. Bernardini and Anita Virga, 1–26. Newcastle upon Tyne: Cambridge Scholars, 2013.

Bernardini, Paolo L., and Anita Virga. *Voglio morire! Suicide in Italian Literature, Culture, and Society 1789–1919*. Newcastle upon Tyne: Cambridge Scholars, 2013.

Besant, Annie. *The Ancient Wisdom: An Outline of Theosophical Teachings*. Madras: Theosophical Publishing House, 1897. Online: HathiTrust.

Besant, Annie, and Charles W. Leadbeater. *Thought-Forms: A Record of Clairvoyant Investigation*. London: Theosophical Publishing Society, 1901.

Bettini, Filippo. *La critica e gli scapigliati*. Bologna: Cappelli, 1976.

Bini, Andrea. "L'umorismo di Pirandello tra *Opera Aperta* e la scoperta dell'*io*." *Forum Italicum* 52.1 (2018): 63–84.

Bini, Daniela. "Pirandello, Nietzsche, and the Good Mask." *PSA* 11 (1995): 5–16.

– *Pirandello and His Muse: The Plays for Marta Abba*. Gainesville: University Press of Florida, 1998.

Blavatsky, Helena Petrovna. *The Key to Theosophy; Being a Clear Exposition, in the Form of Question and Answer, of the Ethics, Science, and Philosophy, for the Study of which the Theosophical Society Has Been Founded, with a Copious Glossary of General Theosophical Terms*, 3rd ed. London: The Theosophical Publishing Society, 1893. Online: HathiTrust.

– *Nightmare Tales*. Theosophical University Press Online Edition. https://www.theosociety.org/pasadena/nightmar/night-hp.htm.

– *Nightmare Tales*. London: The Theosophical Publishing Society, 1892. Online: HathiTrust.

– *The Secret Doctrine: The Synthesis of Science, Religion, and Philosophy*. 2 vols. Point Loma: The Aryan Theosophical Press, 1925.

Blumenberg, Hans. *Work on Myth*, translated by Robert M. Wallace. Cambridge, MA: MIT Press, 1985.

Bobbio, Norberto. *La filosofia del decadentismo*. Turin: Chiantore, 1944. Translated by David Moore as *The Philosophy of Decadence*. Oxford: Blackwell, 1948.

Borchmeyer, Dieter. *Drama and the World of Richard Wagner*. Princeton: Princeton University Press, 2003.

Bordwell, David. *French Impressionist Cinema: Film Culture, Film Theory, and Film Style*. New York: Arno Press, 1980.

Borges, Jorge Luis. *Ficciones*, edited by Anthony Kerrigan. New York: Grove, 1962.

Bottazzi, Filippo. *Fenomeni medianici: Osservati in una serie di sedute fatte con Eusapia Palladino*. Naples: Francesco Perella, 1909. Translated by Irmeli

Routti and Antonio Giuditta as *Mediumistic Phenomena: Observed in a Series of Sessions with Eusapia Palladino*. Princeton: ICRL Press, 2011.

Bourget, Paul. *Essais de psychologie contemporaine*. Paris: A. Lemere, 1895. Online: HathiTrust.

Bowie, Andrew. "German Idealism and the Arts." In *The Cambridge Companion to German Idealism*, edited by Karl Ameriks, 239–57. Cambridge: Cambridge University Press, 2000.

Bragato, Stefano. *Futurismo in nota: Studi sui taccuini di Marinetti*. Florence: Franco Cesati Editore, 2018.

Braida, Antonella. "Salute o malattia? Il valore del commercio come <<farmaco>> nella *Coscienza di Zeno*." In *Italo Svevo and His Legacy for the Third Millennium*, vol. 1: *Philology and Interpretation*, edited by Giuseppe Stellardi and Emanuela Tandello Cooper, 180–94. Leicester: Troubador, 2014.

Braude, Ann. *Radical Spirits: Spiritualism and Women's Rights in Nineteenth-century America*, 2nd ed. Indianapolis: Indiana University Press, 2001.

Braun, Emily. *Mario Sironi and Italian Modernism: Art and Politics under Fascism*. Cambridge: Cambridge University Press, 2000.

Breazeale, Daniel, and Tom Rockmore, eds. *Fichte, German Idealism, and Early Romanticism*. Amsterdam: Rodopi, 2010.

Brera, Matteo. *Novecento all'Indice: Gabriele d'Annuzio, i libri proibiti e i rapporti stato-chiesa all'ombra del Concordato*. Rome: Edizioni di Storia e Letteratura, 2016.

Breton, André. *Manifestoes of Surrealism*, translated by Richard Seaver and Helen R. Lane. Ann Arbor: University of Michigan Press, 1974.

Brown, Peter. *The Cult of Saints: Its Rise and Function in Latin Christianity*. Chicago: University of Chicago Press, 1981.

Bubner, Rüdiger. *The Innovations of Idealism*, translated by Nicholas Walker. Cambridge: Cambridge University Press, 2003.

Buñuel, Luis, dir. *L'âge d'or*. Written by Luis Buñuel and Salvador Dalí. 1930. Film.

– *Un chien andalou*. Written by Luis Buñuel and Salvador Dalí. 1929. Film.

Burnett, Swan M. "Giuseppe Mazzini – Idealist: A Chapter in the Evolution of Social Science." *American Anthropologist* 2.3 (July–September 1900): 502–26.

Burnham, Helen. "Introduction: The Allure of Japan." In *Looking East: Western Artists and the Allure of Japan*, edited by Helen Burnham, 12–27. Boston: MFA, 2014.

Burrow, John W. *The Crisis of Reason: European Thought, 1848–1914*. New Haven: Yale University Press, 2002.

Bürger, Peter. *Theory of the Avant-Garde*, translated by Michael Shaw. Minneapolis: University of Minnesota Press, 1984.

Bush, Christopher. "Contexts for Modernism: Intellectual Currents in East Asia." In *The Modernist World*, edited by Stephen Ross and Allana C. Lindgren, 17–24. New York: Routledge, 2015.

Caesar, Ann Hallamore. *Characters and Authors in Luigi Pirandello*. Oxford: Clarendon Press, 1998.

Calderón de la Barca, Pedro. *El gran teatro del mundo*, edited by John Jay Allen and Domingo Ynduráin. Barcelona: Crítica, 1997.

Calinescu, Matei. *Five Faces of Modernity: Modernism, Avant-Garde, Decadence, Kitsch, Postmodernism*. Durham: Duke University Press, 1987.

Càllari, Francesco. *Pirandello e il cinema*. Venice: Marsilio, 1991.

Camillo, Giulio. *L'idea del theatro*, edited by L. Domenichi. Florence: Torrentino, 1550.

Cangiano, Mimmo. *La nascita del modernismo italiano: Filosofie della crisi, storia e letteratura. 1903–1922*. Macerata: Quodlibet, 2018.

– *The Wreckage of Philosophy: Carlo Michelstaedter and the Limits of Bourgeois Thought*. Toronto: University of Toronto Press, 2019.

Caponetto, Rosetta Giuliani. *Fascist Hybridities: Representations of Racial Mixing and Diaspora Cultures under Mussolini*. New York: Palgrave Macmillan, 2015.

Capuana, Luigi. *Mondo occulto*. Ed. Simona Cigliana. Catania: Edizioni del prisma, 1995.

– *Novelle del mondo occulto*, edited by Andrea Cedola. Bologna: Pendragon, 2007.

Carli, Mario. *Con D'Annunzio a Fiume*. Milan: AGA Editrice, 2013.

Cartwright, David E. *Historical Dictionary of Schopenhauer's Philosophy*, 2nd ed. Lanham: Rowman and Littlefield, 2016.

Cascardi, Anthony. *The Subject of Modernity*. Cambridge: Cambridge University Press, 1992.

Caselli, Mauro. "<<Bisogna isolare una cosa perché diventi una cosa sola>>. Saggio sull'ontologia di Svevo." In *Italo Svevo and His Legacy for the Third Millennium*, vol. 1: *Philology and Interpretation*, edited by Giuseppe Stellardi and Emanuela Tandello Cooper, 12–30. Leicester: Troubador, 2014.

Casetti, Francesco, Silvio Alovisio, and Luca Mazzei, eds. *Early Film Theories in Italy, 1896–1922*. Amsterdam: Amsterdam University Press, 2017.

Cassano, Franco. *Il pensiero meridiano*. Bari: Laterza, 2005.

Cassano, Franco, and Claudio Fogu. "Il pensiero meridiano oggi: Interviste e dialoghi con Franco Cassano." *California Italian Studies* 1.1 (2010): 1–14. Online.

Castellana, Riccardo. *Finzione e memoria: Pirandello modernista*. Naples: Liguori, 2018.

– *Parole, cose, persone: Il realismo modernista di Federigo Tozzi*. Pisa: F. Serra, 2009.

– "Realismo modernista: Un'idea del romanzo italiano (1915–1925)." *Italianistica: Rivista di letteratura italiana* 39.1 (January–April 2010): 23–45.

Catanese, Rossella. *Futurist Cinema: Studies on Italian Avant-garde Film*. Amsterdam: Amsterdam University Press, 2017.

Cavell, Stanley. *The World Viewed: Reflections on the Ontology of Film.* Expanded ed. Cambridge, MA: Harvard University Press, 1979.

Cavour, Gustavo Benso di. "Saggio sui principii della morale." *Il cimento* 1 (1852): 3–22, 129–52.

Cerasi, Enrico. *Quasi niente, una pietra: per una nuova interpretazione della filosofia pirandelliana.* Padova: Il Poligrafo, 1999.

Cerimonia, Daniela. *Leopardi and Shelley: Discovery, Translation, and Reception.* Cambridge: Legenda, 2015.

Chaplin, Charlie. *Modern Times.* United Artists, 1936. Film.

Chessa, Luciano. *Luigi Russolo, Futurist: Noise, Visual Arts, and the Occult.* Berkeley: University of California Press, 2012.

Chiarelli, Luigi. *La maschera e il volto.* Milan: Treves, 1920.

Childs, Donald J. *T.S. Eliot: Mystic, Son, and Lover.* London: Bloomsbury, 2013.

Cigliana, Simona. "Diritto di uccidere. Su un romanzo dimenticato di Bruno Corra e sull'ipotesi di un suicidio letterario." *Annali d'Italianistica* 27 (2009): 85–102.

– *Futurismo esoterico: contributi per una storia dell'irrazionalismo italiano tra Otto e Novecento.* Naples: Liguori, 2002.

– "Introduzione." *Mondo occulto* by Luigi Capuana, edited by Simona Cigliana, 9–53. Catania: Edizioni del prisma, 1995.

– "Spiritismo e parapsicologia nell'età positivistica." In *Storia d'Italia, Annali 25: Esoterismo,* edited by Gian Mario Cazzaniga, 521–46. Turin: Einaudi, 2010.

Ciracì, Fabio. *La filosofia italiana di fronte a Schopenhauer.* Lecce: Pensa Multimedia, 2017.

– "Mainländer all'Inferno." In Ciracì and Fazio, *Schopenhauer in Italia.*

Ciracì, Fabio, and Domenico M. Fazio, eds. *Schopenhauer in Italia: Atti del I Convegno Nazionale della Sezione Italiana della Schopenhauer-Gesellschaft, San Pietro Vernotico-Lecce, 20 E 21 Giugno 2013.* Lecce: Pensa multimedia, 2013.

Clifton, W. Scott. "Schopenhauer and Murdoch on the Ethical Value of the Loss of Self in Aesthetic Experience." *Journal of Aesthetic Education* 51.4 (Winter 2017): 5–25.

Colbert, Charles. *Haunted Visions: Spiritualism and American Art.* Philadelphia: University of Pennsylvania Press, 2011.

Collins, Randall. *The Sociology of Philosophies: A Global Theory of Intellectual Change.* Cambridge, MA: Harvard University Press, 1998.

Collodi, Carlo. *Le avventure di Pinocchio: Storia di un burattino,* edited by Carlo Fruttero, Daniela Marcheschi, and Enrico Mazzanti. Milan: Mondadori, 2009.

Comay, Rebecca. *Mourning Sickness: Hegel and the French Revolution.* Stanford: Stanford University Press, 2011.

Comuzio, Ermanno. "Il cinema: il linguaggio visible della musica." In *Il cinema e Pirandello*, edited by Enzo Lauretta, 43–61. Agrigento: Centro Nazionale di Studi Pirandelliani, 2003.

Conant, James. "Nietzsche's Perfectionism: A Reading of Schopenhauer as Educator." In *Nietzsche's Postmoralism: Essays on Nietzsche's Prelude to Philosophy's Future*, edited by Richard Schacht, 181–257. Cambridge: Cambridge University Press, 2000.

Condé, Alice and Jessica Gossling. "The Devil in the Detail: An Introduction to Decadent Occultism from the Editors." *Volupté: Interdisciplinary Journal of Decadence Studies*, 1.2 (2018): i–ix.

Contarini, Silvia. "<<Vedere l'infanzia>>: Autobiography and Freudian Rhetoric in *La coscienza di Zeno*." In *Italo Svevo and His Legacy for the Third Millennium*, vvol 1: *Philology and Interpretation*, edited by Giuseppe Stellardi and Emanuela Tandello Cooper, 195–212. Leicester: Troubador, 2014.

Coole, Diana, and Samantha Frost. "Introducing the New Materialisms." *New Materialisms: Ontology, Agency, and Politics*, edited by Diana Coole and Samantha Frost, 1–43. Durham: Duke University Press, 2010.

Copenhaver, Brian. *Magic in Western Culture from Antiquity to the Enlightenment*. Cambridge: Cambridge University Press, 2015.

Copenhaver, Brian, and Rebecca Copenhaver, eds. and trans. *From Kant to Croce: Modern Philosophy in Italy 1800–1950*. Toronto: University of Toronto Press, 2011.

Corra, Bruno [Bruno Ginanni Corradini]. *Per l'arte nuova della nuova Italia*. Milan: Studio Editoiale Lombardo, 1918.

–*Battaglie*. Milan: Facchi, 1920.

– *Madrigali e grotteschi*. Milan: Facchi editore, 1919.

– *I matrimoni gialli*. Milan: Edizioni "Alpes," 1928.

– *Perché ho ucciso mia moglie*. Milan: Facchi, 1918.

– *Sam Dunn è morto: racconto insolito*, edited by Mario Verdone. Turin: Einaudi, 1970.

– *Sam Dunn Is Dead*, translated by John Walker, illustrations by Rosa Rosà. London: Atlas Press, 2015.

– *Sanya, la moglie egiziana: Il romanzo dell'Oriente moderno*. Milan: Casa Editrice "Alpes," 1927.

Costa, Gustavo. "Pirandello and Philosophy." In *A Companion to Pirandello Studies*, edited by John Luis DiGaetani, 3–16. New York: Greenwood Press, 1991.

Costanzo, Samantha Burrier. "Pirandello, Theosophy, and the Tantalus Syndrome." *PSA* 23 (2010): 43–69.

Cox, Robert S. *Body and Soul: A Sympathetic History of American Spiritualism*. Charlottesville: University of Virginia Press, 2003.

Craig, Edward Gordon. "The Actor and the Über-Marionette." *The Mask* 1.2 (April 1908): 3–8.

Creamer, Anne-Marie. *Treatment for Six Characters, an Unrealised Film by Luigi Pirandello.* Film. 2015. http://amcreamer.net/treatment-for-six-characters.

Creamer, Anne-Marie and Lesley G. Sullivan. "Pirandello's Unrealized Film, *Treatment for Six Characters*: An Interview with Film Director and Artist Anne-Marie Creamer." *PSA* 27 (2014): 101–15.

Croce, Benedetto. "Alfredo Oriani." *La Critica* 7 (1909): 1–28.

– *Il carattere della filosofia moderna.* Bari: Laterza, 1941.

– *A Croce Reader: Aesthetics, Philosophy, History, and Literary* Criticism, edited and translated by Massimo Verdicchio. Toronto: University of Toronto Press, 2017.

– "De Sanctis e Schopenhauer. Nota letta all'Accademia Pontaniana nella tornata del 16 marzo 1902." Naples: Stab. Tipografico nella R. Università A. Tessitore e Figlio, 1902.

– *Estetica come scienza dell'espressione e linguistica generale. I. Teoria. II. Storia.* Milan: Remo Sandron, 1902.

– "Il risveglio filosofico e la cultura italiana." *La Critica* 6 (1908): 161–78. Digital edition from CSI Biblioteca di Filosofia, Università di Roma "La Sapienza," Fondazione "Biblioteca Benedetto Croce." Online.

– "An Unknown Page from the Last Months of the Life of Hegel." In *Philosophy, Poetry, History: An Anthology of Essays,* translated by Cecil Sprigge, 170–91. Oxford: Oxford University Press, 1966.

Croce, Elena, and Alda Croce. *Francesco De Sanctis.* Turin: UTET, 1974.

Cuoco, Vincenzo. *Platone in Italia,* edited by Antonio De Francesco and Annalisa Andreoni. Rome: Laterza, 2006.

– *Saggio storico sulla rivoluzione di Napoli,* edited by Antonio De Francesco. Manduria: Piero Lacaita, 1998.

Curci, Carlo Maria. *Memorie.* Florence: G. Barbèra, 1891.

Da, Nan Z. "The Computational Case against Computational Literary Studies." *Critical Inquiry* 45.3 (Spring 2019): 601–39.

Dale, Eric Michael. *Hegel, the End of History, and the Future.* Cambridge: Cambridge University Press, 2014.

Dalí, Salvador. "Abstract of a Critical History of the Cinema." In *The Shadow and Its Shadow: Surrealist Writings on the Cinema,* edited, translated, and introduced by Paul Hammond, 3rd ed., 63–7. San Francisco: City Lights Books, 2000.

D'Ambrosio, Matteo. "Notes on 'Esoteric Futurism': Marinetti and the Occultist Circle in Milan." *International Yearbook of Futurism Studies* 8 (2018): 294–324.

D'Annunzio, Gabriele. *Il caso Wagner,* edited by Paola Sorge. Bari: Laterza, 1996.

– *Il fuoco*, edited by Niva Lorenzini. Milan: Mondadori, 1996. Translated as *The Flame* by Susan Bassnett. London: Quartet Books, 1991.
– *L'innocente*. Milan: Rizzoli, 2012.
– *Notturno*, translated by Stephen Sartarelli. New Haven: Yale University Press, 2011.
– *Notturno*, edited by Giansiro Ferrata and Alfredo Gargiulo. Milan: Mondadori, 1983.
– *Pleasure*, translated by Lara Gochin Raffaelli. New York: Penguin, 2013.
– *Trionfo della morte*, edited by Maria Giulia Balducci. Milan: Mondadori, 1995.
– *Le vergini delle rocce*, edited by Giansiro Ferrata. Milan: Mondadori, 1986.
de Arcangelis, Alessandro. "Towards a New Philosophy of History: European Vichianism and Neapolitan Hegelianism (1804–48)." *Journal of Modern Italian Studies* 24.2 (2019): 226–43.
De Castris, Arcangelo Leone. *Il decadentismo italiano: Svevo, Pirandello, D'Annunzio*. Bari: Laterza, 1989.
"Degeneration and Pessimism." *The Edinburgh Review or Critical Journal*, 24 (July–October 1911): 138–64.
DeLassus, Leslie. "Ruptured Perspectives: The 'View,' Early Special Effects, and Film History." In *The Image in Early Cinema: Form and Material*, edited by Scott Curtis, Philippe Gauthier, Tom Gunning, and Joshua Yumibe, 120–31. Indianapolis: Indiana University Press, 2018.
Deledda, Grazia. *Cenere*. Rome: Ripamonti & Colombo, 1904. Translated as *Ashes* by Jan Kozma. Teaneck: Fairleigh Dickinson University Press, 2004.
– "Il mago." In *Racconti sardi*. Sassari: Dessì, 1894. Translated as "The Sorcerer" in *Ladies of Fantasy: Two Centuries of Sinister Stories by the Gentle Sex*, edited by Seon Manley and Gogo Lewis. New York: Lee and Shepard, 1975.
– *Tradizioni popolari di Nuoro*. Nuoro: Ilisso, 2010.
Deleuze, Gilles. *Cinema 1: The Movement-Image*, translated by Hugh Tomlinson and Barbara Habberjam. Minneapolis: University of Minnesota Press, 1986.
– *Cinema 2: The Time-Image*, translated by Hugh Tomlinson and Robert Galeta. Minneapolis: University of Minnesota Press, 1989.
De Liguori, Girolamo. *Il sentiero dei perplessi: Scetticismo, nichilismo, e critica della religione in Italia da Nietzsche a Pirandello*. Naples: Città del Sole, 1995.
De Lorenzo, Giuseppe. *Leopardi e Schopenhauer*. Naples: Riccardi, 1923.
Delluc, Louis. *Photogénie*. Paris: M. de Brunoff, 1920. Online: HathiTrust.
Del Ponte, Renato. "Quando il Gruppo di Ur cercò di influenzare il Fascismo." In *Esoterismo e fascismo: Storia, interpretazioni, documenti*, edited by Gianfranco de Turris., 147–52. Rome: Edizioni Mediterranee, 2006.
Delville, Michel. "Epiphanies and Prose Lyrics: James Joyce and the Poetics of the Fragment." In *Giacomo Joyce: Envoys of the Other*, edited by Louis Armand and Clare Wallace, 101–30. Prague: Litteraria Pragensia, 2006.

De Martino, Ernesto. *Sud e magia.* Milan: Feltrinelli, 1960. Translated as *Magic: A Theory from the South*, edited and translated by Dorothy Louise Zinne. Chicago: Hau Books, 2015.

De Mattei, Roberto. *Pius IX*, translated by John Laughland. Leominster: Gracewing, 2004.

De Michelis, Eurialo. "D'Annunzio e Huysmans." *Rassegna di cultura e vita scolastica* (July–August 1961).

– "D'Annunzio e i plagi." *Quaderni dannunziani* 20–1 (1965): 859–65.

De Paulis-Dalembert, Maria Pia. *Giovanni Papini: Culture et identité.* Toulouse: Presses Universitaires du Mirail, 2007.

De Quincey, Thomas. *Confessions of an English Opium-Eater.* London: 1821.

De Sanctis, Francesco. "Epistolario di Giacomo Leopardi." In *Saggi critici*, edited by Paolo Arcari, vol. 1, 204–10. Milan: Fratelli Treves, 1921.

– *Nuovi saggi critici*, 2nd ed. Naples: A. Morano, 1879.

– *Opere: La crisi del Romanticismo: scritti del carcere e primi saggi critici.* Turin: Einaudi, 1972.

–"La prima canzone di Giacomo Leopardi." In *Nuovi saggi critici*, 2nd ed., 105–26. Naples: A. Morano. 1879.

– *Saggi critici.* 4th ed. Naples: A. Morano. 1881.

– "Schopenhauer e Leopardi: dialogo tra A e D." In *Saggi critici*, edited by Paolo Arcari, vol. 1, 227–70. Milan: Fratelli Treves, 1921.

– *Schopenhauer e Leopardi e altri saggi leopardiani*, 6th ed. Como: Ibis, 2013.

De Turris, Gianfranco, ed. *Esoterismo e Fascismo: Storia, interpretazioni, documenti.* Rome: Edizioni Mediterranee, 2006.

Dienstag, Joshua. *Pessimism: Philosophy, Ethic, Spirit.* Princeton: Princeton University Press, 2009.

– "What Is Living and What Is Dead in the Interpretation of Hegel?" *Political Theory* 29.2 (April 2001): 262–75.

Diepeveen, Leonard. *The Difficulties of Modernism.* New York: Routledge, 2003.

Di Lieto, Carlo, Lisa Sarti, and Michael Subialka. *Scrittura d'immagini: Pirandello e la visualità tra arte, filosofia e psicanalisi.* Soveria Mannelli: Rubbettino, 2021.

Dilthey, Wilhelm. *Dilthey's Philosophy of Existence: Introduction to Weltanschauungslehre*, translated by William Kluback and Martin Weinbaum. Westport: Greenwood Press, 1978.

Di Nunzio, Novella. "La differenza tra il concetto di inettitudine e il concetto di senilità nell'opera di Italo Svevo." In *Italo Svevo and His Legacy for the Third Millennium*, vol. 1: *Philology and Interpretation*, edited by Giuseppe Stellardi and Emanuela Tandello Cooper, 74–86. Leicester: Troubador, 2014.

Donati, B. "L'insegnamento della filosofia del diritto e l'attività didattica di Bertrando Spaventa all Università di Modena nel 1859–60." *Rivista internazionale di filosofia del diritto* 18.6 (1938): 541–71.

Donnarumma, Raffaele. "Maschere della violenza. Teorie e pratiche dell'umorismo fra modernismo e avanguardia: Pirandello, Gadda, Palazzeschi." In *Modi di ridere: Forme spiritose e umoristiche della narrazione*, edited by Emanuele Zinato, 171–208. Pisa: Pacini, 2005.

Downes, Stephen. *Music and Decadence in European Modernism: The Case of Central and Eastern Europe.* Cambridge: Cambridge University Press, 2010.

Doyle, Arthur Conan. *The History of Spiritualism.* 2 Vols. 1926.

Drake, Richard. *Apostles and Agitators: Italy's Marxist Revolutionary Tradition.* Cambridge, MA: Harvard University Press, 2003.

Dunham, Jeremy, Iain Hamilton Grant, and Sean Watson. *Idealism: The History of a Philosophy*. New York: Routledge, 2011.

Eburne, Jonathan. *Outsider Theory: Intellectual Histories of Unorthodox Ideas.* Minneapolis: University of Minnesota Press, 2018.

Eco, Umberto. "Ur-Fascism." *New York Review of Books* 42.11 (22 June 1995). https://www.nybooks.com/articles/1995/06/22/ur-fascism.

Egbert, Donald D. "The Idea of Avant-Garde in Art and Politics." *Leonardo* 3.1 (1970): 75–86.

Eisenstadt, S.N. "Multiple Modernities." *Daedalus* 129.1 (Winter 2000): 1–29.

Eliot, Thomas Sterne. *The Poems of T.S. Eliot*, vol 1: *Collected and Uncollected Poems*, edited by Christopher Ricks and Jim McCue. New York: Farrar, Straus and Giroux, 2018.

– *Selected Essays.* New York: Harcourt, Brace and Company, 1932.

Epstein, Jean. *Écrits sur le cinéma, 1921–1953. Édition chronologique en deuz volumes.* 2 vols. Paris: Seghers, 1974.

Ernst, Germana. *Tommaso Campanella: Il libro e il corpo della natura.* Rome: Laterza, 2002.

"The Essays of Schopenhauer, the Expounder of Pessimism." *Self Culture: A Magazine of Knowledge with Departments Devoted to the Interests of....* edited by G. Mercer Adam, vol. 6 (Chicago: October 1897–March 1898), 335–7.

Even-Zohar, Itamar. "The Position of Translated Literature within the Literary Polysystem." *Poetics Today* 11 (1990): 45–51.

Evola, Julius. *Rivolta contro il mondo moderno*, edited by Gianfranco de Turris. Rome: Edizioni Mediterranee, 1998.

– *Saggi sull'Idealismo magico. Quarta edizione corretta e con Appendici*, edited by Gianfranco de Turris. Rome: Edizioni Mediterranee, 2006.

– *Teoria dell'Individuo assoluto*, edited by Gianfranco de Turris. Rome: Edizioni Mediterranee, 1998.

Fain, Francesco. *Giovanni Papini: Il Tutto, Il Nulla*. Florence Firenze Atheneum, 2011.

Faraone, Rosella. *Giovanni Gentile, "the Philosopher of Fascism": Cultural Leadership in Fascist and Anti-Semitic Italy.* New York: Edwin Mellen Press, 2017.

Fellmann, Ferdinand, ed. *Geschichte der Philosophie im 19. Jahrhundert: Positivismus, Linkshegelianismus, Existenzphilosophie, Neukantianismus, Lebensphilosophie*. Reibek bei Hamburg: Rowohlt Taschenbuch Verlag, 1996.

Ferrari, Fabrizio M. *Ernesto de Martino on Religion: The Crisis and the Presence*. London and New York: Routledge, 2012.

Ficino, Marsilio. *El libro dell'amore*, edited by Sandra Niccoli. Florence: Leo S. Olschki Editore, 1987.

Flam, Jack, and Elizabeth Deutch, eds. *Primitivism and Twentieth-Century Art: A Documentary History*. Berkeley: University of California Press, 2003.

Fogu, Claudio. *The Historic Imaginary: Politics of History in Fascist Italy*. Toronto: University of Toronto Press, 2003.

Fondi, Renato. *Un costruttore: Papini*. Florence: Vallecchi, 1922.

Forgacs, David. *Italy's Margins: Social Exclusion and Nation Formation since 1861*. Cambridge: Cambridge University Press, 2014.

Fourie, Elsje. "A Future for the Theory of Multiple Modernities: Insights from the New Modernization Theory." *Social Science Information* 51.1 (2012): 52–69.

François, Arnaud. 2007. "Life and Will in Nietzsche and Bergson." *SubStance*, #114, 36.3 (2007): 100–14.

Franklin, J. Jeffrey. *Spirit Matters: Occult Beliefs, Alternative Religions, and the Crisis of Faith in Victorian Britain*. Ithaca: Cornell University Press, 2018.

Frassica, Pietro. *Her Maestro's Echo: Pirandello and the Actress Who Conquered Broadway in One Evening*. Kibworth: Troubador, 2010.

Freud, Sigmund. *Civilization and Its Discontents*, edited and translated by James Strachey. New York: W.W. Norton, 1989.

– *The Future of an Illusion*, edited and translated by James Strachey. New York: W.W. Norton, 1989.

Fried, Michael. "Art and Objecthood." *ArtForum* 5 (June 1967): 12–23.

Friedman, Susan Stanford. "Planetarity: Musing Modernist Studies." *Modernism/Modernity* 17.3 (2010): 471–99.

– *Planetary Modernisms: Provocations on Modernity across Time*. New York: Columbia University Press, 2018.

Fukuyama, Francis. *The End of History and the Last Man*. New York: Free Press, 1992.

Fuller, Peter J. "Regional Identity in Sardinian Writing of the Twentieth Century: The Work of Grazia Deledda and Giuseppe Dessì." *The Italianist* 20.1 (2000): 58–97.

Furlong, Paul. *The Social and Political Thought of Julius Evola*. London: Routledge, 2011.

Gabay, Al. *Messages from Beyond: Spiritualism and Spiritualists in Melbourne's Golden Age, 1870–1890*. Carlton South: Melbourne University Press, 2001.

Gabriel, Markus, and Anders Moe Rasmussen, eds. *German Idealism Today*. Berln: De Gruyter, 2017.

Gahéry, Rodolphe. "De la presse illustrée à l'actualité filmée (1894–1910): l'émergence d'une nouvelle «culture visuelle de l'information»?" In *The Image in Early Cinema: Form and Material*, edited by Scott Curtis, Philippe Gauthier, Tom Gunning, and Joshua Yumibe, 69–77. Indianapolis: Indiana University Press, 2018.

Gaiger, Jason. "Lebensphilosophie." In *Routledge Encyclopedia of Philosophy*, edited by E. Craig. London: Routledge, 1998.

Galbo, Joseph. "A Decadence Baedeker: D'Annunzio's *The Triumph of Death*." *European Legacy* 22.1 (2017): 49–67.

Gallo, Fernanda. "The Rise of the Ethical State in Italy: Neapolitan Hegelians and Risorgimento Political Thought (1848–1871)." *Journal of Modern Italian Studies* 24.2 (2019): 244–65.

Gallo, Fernanda, and Axel Körner. "Challenging Intellectual Hierarchies. Hegel in Risorgimento Political Thought: An Introduction." *Journal of Modern Italian Studies* 24.2 (2019): 209–25.

Gallucci, Giovanni Paolo. *Theatrum mundi et temporis*. Venice: G.B. Somasco, 1588.

Garin, Eugenio. *History of Italian Philosophy*, vol. 1, edited and translated by Giorgio Pinton. Amsterdam: Rodopi, 2008.

Garrett, Brian. "Vitalism versus Emergent Materialism." In *Vitalism and the Scientific Image in Post-Enlightenment Life Science, 1800–2010*, edited by S. Normandin and C.T. Wolfe, 127–54. New York: Springer, 2013.

Gatti, Paolo. *Il gran libro del mondo nella filosofia di Tommaso Campanella*. Rome: Gregorian and Biblical Press, 2010.

Gautier, Théophile. *The Jinx*, translated by Andrew Brown. London: Hesperus, 2002.

– "The Tales of Hoffmann," translated by Anne E. Duggan. *Marvels and Tales* 23.1 (2009): 138–45.

Gay, Peter. *Modernism: The Lure of Heresy*. New York: W.W. Norton, 2008.

Gazzola, Giuseppe. *Montale the Modernist*. Florence: Olschki, 2016.

Genova, Pamela A. *Writing Japonisme: Aesthetic Translation in Nineteenth-Century French Prose*. Evanston: Northwestern University Press, 2016.

Gentile, Emilio. "The Conquest of Modernity: From Modernist Nationalism to Fascism," translated by Lawrence Rainey. *Modernism/Modernity* 1.3 (1994): 55–87.

– *Il culto del Littorio*. Bari: Laterza, 2001.

– *The Origins of Fascist Ideology, 1918–1925*, translated by Robert L. Miller. New York: Enigma, 2005.

– *The Sacralization of Politics in Fascist Italy*. Cambridge: Cambridge University Press, 1996.

– *The Struggle for Modernity: Nationalism, Futurism, and Fascism*. London: Praeger, 2003.

Gentile, Luigi. *Coscienza nazionale e pensiero europeo in Bertrando Spaventa.* Chieti: Nobus, 2000.

Gikandi, Simon. *Writing in Limbo: Modernism and Caribbean Literature.* Ithaca: Cornell University Press, 1992.

Gillespie, Gerald. "Epiphany: Notes on the Applicability of a Modernist Term." *Proust, Mann, Joyce in the Modernist Context*, 50-–67. Washington, D.C.: Catholic University of America Press, 2003.

Gioberti, Vincenzo. *Del primato morale e civile degli italiani*, edited by Ugo Redanò. Milan: Fratelli Bocca, 1938.

Gochin Raffaelli, Lara, and Michael Subialka. "Introduction: D'Annunzio's Beauty Reawakened." *Forum Italicum* 51.2 (August 2017): 311–34.

Godioli, Alberto. *Laughter from Realism to Modernism: Misfits and Humorists in Pirandello, Svevo, Palazzeschi, and Gadda.* Cambridge: Legenda, 2015.

Godwin, Joscelyn. *The Theosophical Enlightenment.* Albany: SUNY Press, 1994.

Goehr, Lydia. *The Quest for Voice: On Music, Politics, and the Limits of Philosophy.* Oxford: Oxford University Press, 1998.

– "Schopenhauer and the Musicians: An Inquiry into the Sounds of Silence and the Limits of Philosophizing about Music." In *Schopenhauer, Philosophy, and the Arts*, edited by Dale Jacquette, 200–28. Cambridge: Cambridge University Press, 1996.

GoGwilt, Christopher. *The Passage of Literature: Genealogies of Modernism in Conrad, Rhys, and Pramoedya.* Oxford: Oxford University Press, 2011.

Goldman, Jonathan. *Modernism Is the Literature of Celebrity.* Austin: University of Texas Press, 2011.

Goldstein, Amanda Jo. *Sweet Science: Romantic Materialism and the New Logics of Life.* Chicago: University of Chicago Press, 2017.

Goldwater, Robert. *Primitivism in Modern Art*, expanded ed. Cambridge, MA: Harvard University Press, 1986.

Goodrick-Clarke, Nicholas. *Black Sun: Aryan Cults, Esoteric Nazism, and the Politics of Identity.* New York: NYU Press, 2001.

Gordon, Robert S. "The Italian Futurist Theatre: A Reappraisal." *Modern Language Review* 85.2 (April 1990): 349–61.

Gori, Gino. *Studi di estetica dell'irrazionale.* Rome: Edizioni della Casa D'Arte Bragaglia, 1921.

Goya, Francisco. "El sueño de la razón produce monstrous." In *Los caprichos: aguafuertes satíricos*. Series 29, no. 1[–75]. Spain: S. y M. H. [?], 18--[?]. HathiTrust.

Gramsci, Antonio. *Prison Notebooks*, vol. 2, translated and edited by Joseph A. Buttigieg. New York: Columbia University Press, 1996.

Greenberg, Clement. "After Abstract Expressionism." *Art International* 6 (25 October 1962). Reprinted in *The Collected Essays and Criticism*, vol. 4:

Modernism with a Vengeance, 1957–1969, edited by John O'Brian, 121–34. Chicago: University of Chicago Press, 1993.

– "Avant-Garde and Kitsch." In *The Collected Essays and Criticism*, vol. 1: *Perceptions and Judgements, 1939–1944*, edited by John O'Brian, 5–22. Chicago: University of Chicago Press, 1986.

– "Towards a Newer Laocoön." *Partisan Review* 7.4 (July–August 1940), 296–310.

Gregor, Anthony James. *Giovanni Gentile: Philosopher of Fascism*. London and New York: Routledge, 2001.

– *Totalitarianism and Political Religion: An Intellectual History*. Stanford: Stanford University Press, 2012.

Griffin, Roger. *The Nature of Fascism*. London: Routledge, 1993.

Grosz, Elizabeth. *The Incorporeal: Ontology, Ethics, and the Limits of Materialism*. New York: Columbia University Press, 2018.

Guido, Laurent. "'The Supremacy of the Mathematical Poem': Jean Epstein's Conceptions of Rhythm." In *Jean Epstein: Critical Essays and New Translations*, edited by Sarah Keller and Jason N. Paul, 143–60. Amsterdam: Amsterdam University Press, 2012.

Gumbrecht, Hans Ulrich. *Production of Presence: What Meaning Cannot Convey*. Stanford: Stanford University Press, 2004.

Gumbrecht, Hans Ulrich, Friedrich Kittler, and Bernhard Siegert, eds. *Der Dichter als Kommandant: D'Annunzio erovert Fiume*. Munich: Wilhelm Fink Verlag, 1996.

Gunning, Tom. "The Cinema of Attraction: Early Film, Its Spectator, and the Avant-Garde." *Wide Angle* 8.3–4 (1986): 63–70.

– "Before Documentary: Early Nonfiction Film and the 'View' Aesthetic." In *Uncharted Territory: Essays on Early Nonfiction Film*, edited by Daan Hertogs and Nico De Klerk, 9–24. Amsterdam: Stichting Nederlands Filmmuseum, 1997.

Gunzberg, Lynn. "Ruralism, Folklore, and Grazia Deledda's Novels." *Modern Language Studies* 13.3 (1983): 112–22.

Gupta, R.K. "Freud and Schopenhauer." *Journal of the History of Ideas* 36.4 (October–December 1975): 721–8.

Habermas, Jürgen. *The Crisis of the European Union: A Response*, translated by Ciaran Cronin. Cambridge: Polity, 2012.

– "Hegel's Critique of the French Revolution," translated by John Viertel. In *Theory and Practice*, 121–41. Boston: Beacon Press, 1974.

– *The Philosophical Discourse of Modernity: Twelve Lectures*, translated by Frederick Lawrence. Cambridge: Polity Press, 1998.

– *The Structural Transformation of the Public Sphere: An Enquiry into a Category of Bourgeois Society*, translated by Thomas Burger and Frederick Lawrence. Cambridge, MA: MIT University Press, 1989.

– *The Theory of Communicative Action*, vol. 1: *Reason and the Rationalization of Society*, translated by T. McCarthy. Boston: Beacon Press, 1984.

Hammer, Espen, ed. *German Idealism: Contemporary Perspectives*. London and New York: Routledge, 2007.

Hammermeister, Kai. *The German Aesthetic Tradition*. Cambridge: Cambridge University Press, 2002.

Hampton, Alexander J.B. *Romanticism and the Re-Invention of Modern Religion: The Reconciliation of German Idealism and Platonic Realism*. Cambridge: Cambridge University Press, 2019.

Hanstein, Lisa. "Edyth von Haynau: A Viennese Aristocrat in the Futurist Circles of 1910." *International Yearbook of Futurist Studies* 5 (2015): 333–65.

Härmänmaa, Marja. "The Seduction of Thanatos: Gabriele D'Annunzio and the Decadent Death." In *Decadence, Degeneration, and the End: Studies in the European* Fin de Siècle, edited by Marja Härmänmaa and Christopher Nissen, 225–43. London: Palgrave Macmillan, 2014.

Harms, Friedrich. "Arthur Schopenhauer's Philosophy," translated by Ella S. Morgan. *The Journal of Speculative Philosophy* 9.2 (April 1875): 113–38.

Harrison, Charles, Francis Frascina, and Gill Perry. *Primitivism, Cubism, Abstraction: The Early Twentieth Century*. New Haven: Yale University Press, 1993.

Harrison, Thomas. *1910: The Emancipation of Dissonance*. Berkeley: University of California Press, 1996.

– *Essayism: Conrad, Musil, and Pirandello*. Baltimore: Johns Hopkins University Press, 1992.

– "Michelstaedter and Existential Authenticity Avant la Lettre: From Heidegger and Sartre to Simone Weil." In *Storia e Storiografia di Carlo Michelstaedter*, edited by Valerio Cappozzo, 25–46. University of Mississippi Romance Monographs, 2017.

– "Overcoming Aestheticism." In *Italian Modernism: Italian Culture between Decadentism and Avant-Garde*, edited by Luca Somigli and Mario Moroni, 167–90. Toronto: University of Toronto Press, 2004.

– "Regicide, Parricide, and Tyrannicide in *Il fu Mattia Pascal*: Stealing from the Father to Give to the Son." In *Luigi Pirandello: Conemporary Perspectives*, edited by Gian-Paolo Biasin and Manuela Gieri, 189–213. Toronto: University of Toronto Press, 1999.

Havard, Robert G. *From Romanticism to Surrealism: Seven Spanish Poets*. Cardiff: University of Wales Press, 1988.

Hayot, Eric, and Rebecca L. Walkowitz, eds. *A New Vocabulary for Global Modernism*. New York: Columbia University Press, 2016.

Hedayat, Sadegh. *The Blind Owl*, translated by D.P. Costello. New York: Grove, 2010.

– *Three Drops of Blood*, translated by Deborah Miller Mostaghel. Surrey: Alma, 2008.

Hegel, Georg Wilhelm Friedrich. *Filosofia della storia*, translated by Giovanni Battista Passerini, edited by Eduard Gans. Capolago: Elvetica, 1840.

– *Hegel's Aesthetics: Lectures on Fine Art*, translated by T.M. Knox. 2 vols. Oxford: Oxford University Press, 1975.

– *Lectures on the Philosophy of World History*, translated by H.B. Nisbet. Cambridge: Cambridge University Press, 1975.

– *Phenomenology of Spirit*, edited and translated by Terry Pinkard and Michael Baur. Cambridge: Cambridge University Press, 2018.

– *Political Writings*, edited by Laurence Dickey and H.B. Nisbet, translated by H.B. Nisbet. Cambridge: Cambridge University Press, 1999.

Gli hegeliani di Napoli e la costruzione dello stato unitario. Rome: Istituto poligrafico e zecca dello Stato, 1989.

Henry, Anne, ed. *Schopenhauer et la création littéraire en Europe.* Paris: Méridiens Klincksieck, 1989.

Hess, David J. *Samba in the Night: Spiritism in Brazil.* New York: Columbia University Press, 1994.

– *Spirits and Scientists: Ideology, Spiritism, and Brazilian Culture.* University Park: Pennsylvania State University Press, 1991.

Heyer-Caput, Margherita. *Grazia Deledda's Dance of Modernity*. Toronto: University of Toronto Press, 2008.

– "Leopardi tra Schopenhauer e Nietzsche." *Italian Culture* 9.1 (1991): 197–212.

Hofmann, Reto. *The Fascist Effect: Japan and Italy, 1915–1952*. Ithaca: Cornell University Press, 2015.

Hofmann, Werner, et al. *Goya, das Zeitalter der Revolutionen, 1789–1830.* Munich: Prestel, 1980.

Hoffmeister, Gerhart. "Hegel and Hegelianism in European Romanticism." In *Nonfictional Romantic Prose: Expanding Borders*, edited by Steven P. Sondrup and Virgil Nemoianu, 57–68. Amsterdam and Philadelphia: John Benjamins, 2004.

Hom, Stephanie Malia. "On the Origins of Making Italy: Massimo D'Azeglio and 'Fatta l'Italia, bisogna fare gli Italiani,'" *Italian Culture* 31.1 (2013): 1–16.

Honneth, Axel. "Atomism and Ethical Life: Hegel's Critique of the French Revolution," translated by Jeremy Gaines. *Philosophy and Social Criticism* 14.3–4 (July 1988): 359–68.

Horkheimer, Max, and Theodor Adorno. *Dialectic of Enlightenment: Philosophical Fragments*, edited by Gunzelin Schmid Noerr, translated by Edmund Jephcott. Stanford: Stanford University Press, 2002.

Houlgate, Stephen. *The Opening of Hegel's* Logic: *From Being to Infinity*. West Lafayette: Purdue University Press, 2006.

House, Jane, and Antonio Attisani, eds. *Twentieth-Century Italian Drama: The First Twenty Years.* New York: Columbia University Press, 1995.

House, John. "Impressionism and Japan." In Gregory Irvine, *Japonisme and the Rise of the Modern Art Movement: The Arts of the Meiji Period. The Khalili Collection*, 104–39. New York: Thames and Hudson, 2013.

Hu, Jane. "Epiphany." In *The Routledge Encyclopedia of Modernism*. Milton Park: Taylor and Francis, 2016. https://www.rem.routledge.com/articles/epiphany.

Hutchinson, Elizabeth. *The Indian Craze: Primitivism, Modernism, and Transculturation in American Art, 1890–1915*. Durham: Duke University Press, 2009.

Huysmans, Joris-Karl. *Against Nature*, edited by Nicholas White, translated by Margaret Mauldon. Oxford: Oxford University Press, 1998.

Iacovella, Angelo. "Julius Evola e Arturo Reghini, un sodalizio 'occulto.'" In *Esoterismo e fascismo: Storia, interpretazioni, documenti*, edited by Gianfranco de Turris, 155–61. Rome: Edizioni Mediterranee, 2006.

Ialongo, Ernest. "Marinetti and the *Mafarka* Trial: Rethinking the Early History of Futurism." *Mise en Abyme: International Journal of Comparative Literature* 2.2/3.1 (July–December 2015/January–June 2016): 5–23.

"Iconoclasm in German Philosophy." *The Westminster Review*, Vol. LIX (January and April, 1853): 202–12.

"Idealism, n." (2019). *OED Online*, Oxford University Press, December 2019, www.oed.com/view/Entry/90960.

Illiano, Antonio. *Metapsichica e letteratura in Pirandello*. Florence: Vallecchi, 1982.

"Introduzione." *Rivista contemporanea* 1 (1854): 1–4.

Invernizzi, Giuseppe. "Schopenhauer all'università di Torino nella seconda metà dell'Ottocento." In *Schopenhauer in Italia: Atti del I Convegno Nazionale della Sezione Italiana della Schopenhauer-Gesellschaft, San Pietro Vernotico-Lecce, 20 E 21 Giugno 2013*, edited by Fabio Ciracì and Domenico M. Fazio. Lecce: Pensa Multimedia, 2013.

Irvine, Gregory. *Japonisme and the Rise of the Modern Art Movement: The Arts of the Meiji Period. The Khalili Collection*. New York: Thames and Hudson, 2013.

Jacobitti, Edmund. "Labriola, Croce, and Italian Marxism (1895–1910)." *Journal of the History of Ideas* 36.2 (April–June 1975): 297–318.

Jacobs, Helmut C. *Die Rezeption und Deutung von Goyas Werk in der Lyrik: Edition der internationalen Bildgedichte*. Würzburg: Königshausen & Neumann, 2015.

– *El sueño de la razón: El Capricho 43 de Goya en el arte visual, la literatura y la música*. Frankfurt and Madrid: Vervuert and Iberoamericana, 2011.

Jacquette, Dale. "Schopenhauer on the Ethics of Suicide." *Continental Philosophy Review* 33.1 (2000): 43–58.

Jacquette, Dale, ed. *Schopenhauer, Philosophy and the Arts*. Cambridge: Cambridge University Press, 1996.

Jaffe, Aaron. *Modernism and the Culture of Celebrity.* Cambridge: Cambridge University Press, 2005.

Jaillant, Lise, and Alison E. Martin. "Introduction: Global Modernism." *Modernist Cultures* 13.1 (2018): 1–13.

Janaway, Christopher. "Introduction." In *The Cambridge Companion to Schopenhauer*, edited by Christopher Janaway, 1–17. Cambridge: Cambridge University Press, 1999.

– "Necessity, Responsibility, and Character: Schopenhauer on Freedom of the Will." *Kantian Review* 17.3 (2012): 431–57.

Jantzen, Grace M. *Power, Gender, and Christian Mysticism.* Cambridge: Cambridge University Press, 1995.

Jeffreys, Peter. *Reframing Decadence: C.P. Cavafy's Imaginary Portraits.* Ithaca: Cornell University Press, 2016.

Jodock, Darrell, ed. *Catholicism Contending with Modernity: Roman Catholic Modernism and Anti-Modernism in Historical Context.* Cambridge: Cambridge University Press, 2000.

Jones, Donna V. *The Racial Discourses of Life Philosophy: Négritude, Vitalism, and Modernity.* New York: Columbia University Press, 2010.

Josephson-Storm, Jason Ā. *The Myth of Disenchantment: Magic, Modernity, and the Birth of the Human Sciences.* Chicago: University of Chicago Press, 2017.

Joyce, James. *Epiphanies*, edited by O.A. Silverman. Buffalo: University of Buffalo Lockwood Memorial Library, 1956.

– *A Portrait of the Artist as a Young Man*, edited by R.B. Kershner, 2nd ed. Boston: Bedford / St Martin's Press, 2006.

– *Stephen Hero.* New York: New Directions, 1963.

– *Ulysses*, edited by Hans Walter Gabler, Wolfhard Steppe, and Claus Melchior. New York: Random House, 1986.

Kaiser, Leander. "Geist versus Intelligenz: Kandinsky als Ideologe der modernen Kunst." In *Von der Romantik zur ästhetischen Religion*, edited by Leander Kaiser and Michael Ley, 99–108. Munich: Wilhelm Fink Verlag, 2004.

Kandinsky, Wassily. *On the Spiritual in Art*, edited by Hilla Rebay. New York: Solomon R. Guggenheim Foundation, 1946.

Kant, Immaneul. *Critique of Pure Reason*, translated and edited by Paul Guyer and Allen W. Wood. Cambridge: Cambridge University Press, 1998.

– *Prolegomena to any Future Metaphysics*, translated and edited by Gary Hatfield. Cambridge: Cambridge University Press, 2004.

Keller, Sarah. "Introduction: Jean Epstein and the Revolt of Cinema." In *Jean Epstein: Critical Essays and New Translations*, edited by Sarah Keller and Jason N. Paul, 23–47. Amsterdam: Amsterdam University Press, 2012.

Keller, Sarah, and Jason N. Paul, eds. *Jean Epstein: Critical Essays and New Translations.* Amsterdam: Amsterdam University Press, 2012.

Kermode, Frank. *The Sense of an Ending: Studies in the Theory of Fiction with a New Epilogue.* Oxford: Oxford University Press, 2000.

Kerr, Howard. *Mediums, Spirit-Rappers, and Roaring Radicals: Spiritualism in American Literature, 1850–1900.* Urbana: University of Illinois Press, 1972.

Kierkegaard, Søren. *Either/Or.* 2 vols., edited and translated by Howard V. Hong and Edna H. Hong. Princeton: Princeton University Press, 1987.

Kim, Sharon. *Literary Epiphany in the Novel, 1850–1950: Constellations of the Soul.* New York: Palgrave Macmillan, 2012.

Klem, Lone. "Progetto di un metafilm: Proposta per una versione cinematografica di Luigi Pirandello *I giganti della montagna.*" In *I giganti della montagna: progetto per un film,* edited by Enzo Lauretta, 273–80. Agrigento: Centro Nazionale di Studi Pirandelliani.

Knipp, Kersten. *Die Kommune der Faschisten: Gabriele D'Annunzio, die Republik von Fiume und die Extreme des 20. Jahrhunderts.* Darmstadt: Theiss, 2018.

Kohn, Hans. "Romanticism and the Rise of German Nationalism." *Review of Politics* 4 (1950): 443–72.

Kontou, Tatiana, and Sarah Willburn, eds. *The Ashgate Research Companion to Nineteenth-Century Spiritualism and the Occult.* Farnham: Ashgate, 2012.

Koss, Juliet. *Modernism after Wagner.* Minneapolis: University of Minnesota Press, 2010.

Krebs, Robert E. *Scientific Development and Misconceptions through the Ages: A Reference Guide.* Westport: Greenwood, 1999.

Labriola, Antonio. "Contro il 'ritorno a Kant' propugnato da Eduardo Zeller." In *Scritti varii: editi e inediti di filosofia e politica,* edited by Benedetto Croce, 1–33. Bari: Laterza, 1906.

Landy, Joshua. *How to Do Things with Fictions.* Oxford: Oxford University Press, 2012.

Landy, Joshua, and Michael Saler, eds. *The Re-Enchantment of the World: Secular Magic in a Rational Age.* Stanford: Stanford University Press, 2009.

Lang, Fritz, dir. *Metropolis.* UFA. 1927. Film.

Lange, Henrike Christiane. *Giotto's Triumph: The Arena Chapel, the Roman Jubilee of 1300, and the Question of Modernity.* Cambridge: Cambridge University Press, forthcoming.

Lant, Antonia. "Haptical Cinema." *October* 74 (Autumn 1995): 45–73.

Lauretta, Enzo, ed. *Il cinema e Pirandello.* Agrigento: Centro Nazionale di Studi Pirandelliani, 2003.

– *I giganti della montagna: Progetto per un film.* Agrigento: Centro Nazionale di Studi Pirandelliani, 2004.

– *Pirandello e il cinema. Atti del convegno internazionale.* Agrigento: Centro Nazionale di Studi Pirandelliani, 1978.

– *Quel che il cinema deve a Pirandello.* Agrigento: Centro Nazionale di Studi Pirandelliani, 2011.

Lazarillo. *Papini*. Series "Uomini del giorno," 31. Milan: Modernissima, 1920.
Leadbeater, Charles. *The Astral Plane: Its Scenery, Inhabitants, and Phenomena.* London: Theosophical Publishing Society, 1895.
– *The Masters and the Path.* Madras: Theosophical Publishing House, 1925.
Lear, Jonathan. *Radical Hope: Ethics in the Face of Cultural Devastation.* Cambridge, MA: Harvard University Press, 2006.
Le Bon, Gustave. *Psychologie des foules.* Paris: 1895.
Lemke, Sieglinde. *Primitivist Modernism: Black Culture and the Origins of Transatlantic Modernism.* Oxford: Oxford University Press, 1998.
Leopardi, Giacomo. *Canti*, translated and edited by Jonathan Galassi. New York: Farrar, Straus and Giroux, 2011.
– *The Moral Essays (Operette Morali)*, translated by Patrick Creagh. New York: Columbia University Press, 1983.
– *Operette morali*, edited by Antonio Prete. 11th ed. Milan: Feltrinelli, 2012.
– *Scritti vari inediti di Giacomo Leopardi dalle carte napoletane, seconda impressione.* Florence: Le Monnier, 1910. Online: HathiTrust.
– *Zibaldone*, translated by Michael Caeser, Franco D'Intino, and Kathleen Baldwin. New York: Farrar, Straus and Giroux, 2013.
Levine, Caroline. *Forms: Whole, Rhythm, Hierarchy, Network.* Ithaca: Cornell University Press, 2015.
Lewis, Pericles. "Introduction." In *The Cambridge Companion to European Modernism*, edited by Pericles Lewis, 1–9. Cambridge: Cambridge University Press, 2011.
– *Modernism, Nationalism, and the Novel.* Cambridge: Cambridge University Press, 2004.
L'Herbier, Marcel. *Feu Mathias Pascal.* Films Armor. 1925. Film.
Lincicome, Mark E. *Principle, Praxis, and the Politics of Educational Reform in Meiji Japan*. Honolulu: University of Hawai'i Press, 1995.
Lista, Giovanni. *Cinema e fotografia futurista.* Milano: Skira, 2001.
– *Il cinema futurista.* Genoa: Le mani, 2010.
Livio, Gigi. *Il teatro in rivolta: Futurismo, grottesco, Pirandello e pirandellismo.* Milan: Mursia, 1976.
Lougee, Robert. "German Romanticism and Political Thought." *Review of Politics* 21.4 (October 1959): 631–45.
Luciani, Sebastiano Arturo. "La idealità del cinematografo." *In penombra* 2.1 (January 1919): 3–4.
– "Impressionismo scenico." *Apollon* 1.3 (1 April 1916): 3–4. Translated by Siobhan Quinlan as "Scenic Impressionism" in *Early Film Theories in Italy, 1896–1922*, edited by Francesco Casetti, Silvio Alovisio, and Luca Mazzei, 321–4. Amsterdam: Amsterdam University Press, 2017.
– "Poetica del cinematografo." *Apollon* 1.4 (1 May 1916): 1–2. Translated by Siobhan Quinlan as "The Poetics of Cinema" in *Early Film Theories in Italy,*

1896–1922, edited by Francesco Casetti, Silvio Alovisio, and Luca Mazzei, 329–32. Amsterdam: Amsterdam University Press, 2017.

Luckhurst, Roger. *The Invention of Telepathy*. Oxford: Oxford University Press, 2002.

Lukács, Georg. *The Destruction of Reason,* translated by Trans. Peter Palmer. Atlantic Highlands: Humanities Press, 1980.

– *The Young Hegel: Studies in the Relations between Dialectics and Economics,* translated by Rodney Livingstone. Cambridge, MA: MIT Press, 1975.

Luperini, Romano. *Gli esordi del Novecento e l'esperienza della Voce.* Rome: Laterza, 1990.

– *Luigi Pirandello e Il fu Mattia Pascal*. Turin: Loescher, 1990.

– *Pirandello*. Rome: Laterza, 1999.

Luperini, Romano, and Massimiliano Tortora, eds. *Sul modernismo italiano*. Naples: Liguori, 2012.

Luti, Giorgio. *Papini, Soffici e la cultura toscana del primo Novecento*. Arezzo: Helicon, 2008.

Luzzi, Joseph. "Sister Arguments: Pirandello's 'Shoot!' and the Birth of Film." *PSA: The Journal of the Pirandello Society of America* 26 (2013): 51–69.

Macchia, Giovanni. "Pirandello e gli <<spiriti>>." *Corriere della Sera,* 18 July 1972.

Magee, Bryan. "Misunderstanding Schopenhauer." The 1989 Bithell Memorial Lecture. Institute of Germanic Studies, University of London, 1989, 1–18.

–"Schopenhauer and Wagner: Part Two." *The Opera Quarterly* 1.4 (Winter 1983): 50–73.

Magee, Glenn Alexander. *Hegel and the Hermetic Tradition.* Ithaca: Cornell University Press, 2001.

Mao, Douglas, and Rebecca L. Walkowitz. "The New Modernist Studies." *PMLA* 123.3 (2008): 737–48.

Maraldo, John C. "The Japanese Encounter with and Appropriation of Western Philosophy." In *The Oxford Handbook of Japanese Philosophy,* edited by Bret W. Davis, 333–63. Oxford: Oxford Unviersity Pres, 2020.

Marcus, Laura. *The Tenth Muse: Writing about Cinema in the Modernist Period.* Oxford: Oxford University Press, 2007.

Marcuse, Herbert. *Reason and Revolution: Hegel and the Rise of Social Theory,* 2nd ed. London and New York: Routledge, 2000.

Marinetti, Filippo Tommaso. *Futurismo e fascismo*. Foligno: Franco Campitelli Editore, 1924.

– *Mafarka il futurista: Romanzo africano*. Milan: Sonzogno, 1920. Translated by Carol Diethe and Steve Cox as *Mafarka the Futurist: An African Novel.* London: Middlesex University Press, 1997.

– *F.T. Marinetti: Critical Writings,* edited by Günter Berghaus, translated by Doug Thompson. New York: Farrar, Straus and Giroux, 2006.

– *Teoria e invenzione futurista*, editedby Luciano De Maria. Milan: Mondadori, 1968.

Marinetti, Filippo Tommaso, and Aldo Palazzeschi. *Carteggio*, edited by Paolo Prestigiacomo. Milan: Mondadori, 1978.

Marinetti, Filippo Tommaso, Emilio Settimelli, and Bruno Corra. *Il teatro futurista sintetico*. Piacenza: G. Costantino, 1921.

Marrati, Paola. *Gilles Deleuze: Cinema and Philosophy*, translated by Alisa Hartz. Baltimore: Johns Hopkins University Press, 2008.

Marx, Karl, and Friedrich Engels. *The Communist Manifesto*, edited by Friedrich L. Bender. New York: W.W. Norton, 1988.

Mauthner, Fritz. *Beiträge zu einer Kritik der Sprache*. 3 vols. 1901–1902. http://www.literature.at/alo?objid=926

McCabe, Susan. *Cinematic Modernism: Modernist Poetry and Film*. Cambridge: Cambridge University Press, 2005.

McGarrity, Maria, and Claire A. Culleton, eds. *Irish Modernism and the Global Primitive*. New York: Palgrave Macmillan, 2009.

McMullin, Stanley Edward. *Anatomy of a Seance: A History of Spirit Communication in Central Canada*. Montreal and Kingston: McGill–Queen's University Press, 2004.

Metastasio, Pietro. *Opere*, edited by A. Buttura. 3 vols. Paris: Baudry, 1863.

Michaelis, Meir. "Italy's Mediterranean Strategy, 1935–1939." In *Britain and the Middle East in the 1930s: Studies in Military and Strategic History*, edited by Michael J. Cohen and Martin Kolinsky, 41–60. London: Palgrave Macmillan, 1992.

Micheli, Sergio. *Pirandello in cinema: Da <<Acciaio>> a <<Káos>>*. Rome: Bulzoni, 1989.

Mignosi, Pietro. *Schopenhauer*. Brescia: Morcelliana, 1934.

– *Il segreto di Pirandello*. Palermo: La Tradizione Editrice, 1935.

Milioto, Stefano. "*I giganti della montagna*: progetto per un film." In *I giganti della montagna: Progetto per un film*, edited by Enzo Lauretta, 287–302. Agrigento: Centro Nazionale di Studi Pirandelliani, 2004.

Minghelli, Giuliana. *In the Shadow of the Mammoth: Italo Svevo and the Emergence of Modernism*. Toronto: Unviersity of Toronto Press, 2002.

Mirabile, Andrea. *Multimedia Archaeologies: Gabriele D'Annunzio, Belle Époque Paris, and the Total Artwork*. Amsterdam: Rodopi, 2014.

Mitchell, Robert. *Experimental Life: Vitalism in Romantic Science and Literature*. Baltimore: Johns Hopkins University Press, 2013.

Mitchell, W.J.T. *Picture Theory: Essays on Verbal and Visual Representation*. Chicago: University of Chicago Press, 1994.

Moe, Nelson J. *The View from Vesuvius: Italian Culture and the Southern Question*. Berkeley: University of California Press, 2002.

Moevs, Christian. *The Metaphysics of Dante's* Comedy. Oxford: Oxford University Press, 2005.

Moggach, Douglas. "Italian Receptions of Hegel: Epilogue." *Journal of Modern Italian Studies* 24.2 (2019): 324–7.

Mondini, Marco. *Fiume 1919: Una Guerra civile italiana.* Rome: Salerno Editrice, 2019.

Moneta, Marco. *L'Officina delle aporie: Leopardi e la riflessione sul male negli anni dello* Zibaldone. Milan: FrancoAngeli, 2006.

Montale, Eugenio. *Collected Poems 1920–1954*. Revised Bilingual Edition. Translated by Jonathan Galassi. New York: Farrar, Straus and Giroux, 2000.

Montesquieu. *The Spirit of the Laws*, edited and translated by Anne M. Cohler, Basia C. Miller, and Harold S. Stone. Cambridge: Cambridge University Press, 1989.

Moore, Adrian. "On Saying and Showing." *Philosophy* 62.242 (October 1987): 473–97.

Moore, R. Laurence. "Spiritualism and Science: Reflections on the First Decade of the Spirit Rappings." *American Quarterly* 24.4 (October 1972): 474–500.

Morel, Michel. "The Modernists' Commitment to the Instant Moment." In *Autonomy and Commitment in Twentieth Century British Literature*, edited by Christine Reynier and Jean-Michel Ganteau, 125–33. Montpellier: PULM, 2010.

Morrow, John. "Romanticism and Political Thought in the Early Nineteenth Century." In *The Cambridge History of Nineteenth-Century Political Thought*, edited by Gareth Stedman Jones and Gregory Claeys, 39–76. Cambridge: Cambridge University Press, 2011.

Morselli, Enrico. *Il magnetismo animale: La fascinazione e gli stati ipnotici.* Turin: Roux e Favale, 1886.

– *Psicologia e "spiritismo": Impressioni e note critiche sui fenomeni medianici di Eusapia Paladino.* Turin: Fratelli Boca, 1908. Online: HathiTrust.

Moses, Omri. *Out of Character: Modernism, Vitalism, Psychic Life.* Stanford: Stanford University Press, 2014.

Mosher, Michael. "The Particulars of a Universal Politics: Hegel's Adaptation of Montesquieu's Typology." *American Political Science Review* (1984): 179–88.

Moss, M.E. *Mussolini's Fascist Philosopher: Giovanni Gentile Reconsidered.* New York: Peter Lang, 2004.

Nalbantian, Suzanne. *Seeds of Decadence in the Late-Nineteenth Century Novel.* London: Palgrave Macmillan, 1988.

Natale, Simone. "A Short History of Superimposition: From Spirit Photography to Early Cinema." *Early Popular Visual Culture* 10.2 (2012): 125–45.

Negri, Antonio. *Flower of the Desert: Giacomo Leopardi's Poetic Ontology*, translated by Timothy S. Murphy. Albany: SUNY Press, 2015.

Nelis, Jan, Anne Morelli, and Danny Praet, eds. *Catholicism and Fascism in Europe 1918–1945.* Hildesheim: Georg Olms Verlag, 2015.

Nichols, Nina Davinci, and Jana O'Keefe Bazzoni. *Pirandello and Film*. Lincoln: University of Nebraska Press, 1995.

Nietzsche, Friedrich. *The Anti-Christ, Ecce Homo, Twilight of the Idols, and Other Writings*, edited by Aaron Ridley and Judith Norman, translated by Judith Norman. Cambridge: Cambridge University Press, 2005.

– *Beyond Good and Evil: Prelude to a Philosophy of the Future*, edited by Rolf-Peter Horstmann and Judith Norman, translated by Judith Norman. Cambridge: Cambridge University Press, 2002.

– *The Birth of Tragedy and The Case of Wagner*, translated by Walter Kaufmann. New York: Random House, 1967.

– *The Birth of Tragedy and Other Writings*, edited by Raymond Geuss and Ronald Speirs, translated by Ronald Speirs. Cambridge: Cambridge University Press, 1999.

– *On the Genealogy of Morality*, edited by Keith Ansell-Pearson, translated by Carol Diethe. Cambridge and New York: Cambridge University Press, 2007.

– *Thus Spoke Zarathustra*, edited by Adrian Del Caro and Robert B. Pippin. Cambridge: Cambridge University Press, 2006.

– *Untimely Meditations*, edited by Daniel Breazeale, translated by R.J. Hollingdale. Cambridge: Cambridge University Press. 1997.

"The Nobel Prize in Literature 1926." NobelPrize.org. Nobel Media AB 2019. 4 May 2019. https://www.nobelprize.org/prizes/literature/1926/summary.

Nobili, Claudia Sebastiana. *La materia del sogno: Pirandello tra racconto e visione*. Pisa: Giardini, 2007.

Norman, Larry. *The Shock of the Ancient: Literature and History in Early Modern France*. Chicago: University of Chicago Press, 2011.

Notari, Umberto. *Quelle signore*. Milan: Otto/Novecento, 2008.

Nussbaum, Martha. *The Cosmopolitan Tradition: A Noble but Flawed Ideal*. Cambridge, MA: Harvard University Press, 2019.

– "Reply." In *For Love of Country? Debating the Limits of Patriotism*, edited by Joshua Cohen, 131–44. Boston: Beacon Press, 1996.

– "The Transfigurations of Intoxication: Nietzsche, Schopenhauer, and Dionysus." *Arion: A Journal of Humanities and the Classics* 1.2 (Spring 1991): 75–111.

– *Upheavals of Thought: The Intelligence of Emotions*. Cambridge: Cambridge University Press, 2003.

Nye, Robert A. "Two Paths to a Psychology of Social Action: Gustave LeBon and Georges Sorel." *Journal of Modern History*,45.3 (September 1973): 411–38.

O'Brien, Dennis. *Hegel on Reason and History: A Contemporary Interpretation*. Chicago: University of Chicago Press, 1975.

O'Connell, Marvin R. *Critics on Trial: An Introduction to the Catholic Modernist Crisis*. Washington, D.C.: Catholic University of America Press, 1994.

Oldrini, Guido. *Gli Hegeliani di Napoli*. Milan: Feltrinelli, 1964.
– *Il primo Hegelismo italiano*. Florence: Vallecchi, 1969.
Omuka, Toshiharu. "Futurism in Japan, 1909–1920." In *International Futurism in Arts and Literature*, edited by Günter Berghaus, 244–70. Berlin and New York: De Gruyter, 2000.
Oppenheim, Janet. *The Other World: Spiritualism and Psychical Research 1850–1914*. Cambridge: Cambridge University Press, 1985.
Oriani, Alfredo. *Fino a Dogali*. Bologna: A. Gherardi, 1912. Online: HathiTrust.
– *La rivolta ideale*. Bologna: A. Gherardi, 1912. Online: HathiTrust.
Orr, Leonard. "Modernism and the Issue of Periodization." *CLCWeb: Comparative Literature and Culture* 7.1 (March 2005). https://doi.org/10.7771/1481-4374.1254.
Owen, Alex. *The Darkened Rook: Women, Power, and Spiritualism in Late Victorian England*. London: Virago, 1989.
– *The Place of Enchantment: British Occultism and the Culture of the Modern*. Chicago: University of Chicago Press, 2004.
Paci, Viva. "The Attraction of the Intelligent Eye: Obsessions with the Vision Machine in Early Film Theories." In *The Cinema of Attractions Reloaded*, edited by Wanda Strauven, 121–37. Amsterdam: Amsterdam University Press, 2006.
Packham, Catherine. *Eighteenth-Century Vitalism: Bodies, Culture, Politics*. London: Palgrave Macmillan, 2012.
Palazzeschi, Aldo, Giovanni Papini, and Ardegno Soffici. "Futurismo e Marinettismo." *Lacerba* (February 1915). Reprinted in *Manifesti, proclami, interventi e documenti teorici del futurismo, 1909–1944*, edited by Luciano Caruso. Florence: SPES, 1990.
Papini, Giovanni. *Il crepuscolo dei filosofi* [1905], 4th ed. Florence: Vallecchi, 1921. Online: HathiTrust.
– "Filosofia del cinematografo." *La stampa* 41 (18 May 1907): 1–2.
– "The Philosophy of Cinematograph." Translated by National Cinema Museum of Turin. In *Early Film Theories in Italy, 1896–1922*, edited by Francesco Casetti with Silvio Alovisio and Luca Mazzei, 47–50. Amsterdam: Amsterdam University Press, 2017.
– "Schopenhauer in Italia." *La cultura contemporanea* 2.8 (16 April 1910): 128–32.
Paulicelli, Eugenia. *Italian Style: Fashion and Film from Early Cinema to the Digital Age*. London: Bloomsbury, 2016.
Perloff, Marjorie. *The Futurist Moment: Avant-Garde, Avant Guerre, and the Language of Rupture*, 2nd ed. with new preface. Chicago: University of Chicago Press, 2003.
Petruzzi, Anthony. "Nihilism, Errancy, and Truth in Pirandello's *Così è (se vi pare)*." *Italica*, 83.3–4 (Fall–Winter 2006): 433–67.
Piccone, Paul. "From Spaventa to Gramsci." *Telos* 31 (March 1977): 35–65.

Piga, Francesco. *Il mito del superuomo in Nietzsche e D'Annunzio*. Florence: Vallecchi, 1979.

Pike, David L. *Passage through Hell: Modernist Descents, Medieval Underworlds*. Ithaca: Cornell University Press, 1997.

Pinkard, Terry P. *German Philosophy 1760–1860: The Legacy of Idealism*. Cambridge: Cambridge University Press, 2002.

Pippin, Robert. *Hegel's Practical Philosophy: Rational Agency as Ethical Life*. Cambridge: Cambridge University Press, 2008.

– *Idealism as Modernism: Hegelian Variations*. Cambridge: Cambridge University Press, 1997.

Pirandello, Luigi. *As You Desire Me. A Drama in Three Acts*, translated by Marta Abba. New York: S. French, 1948.

– "Cronache stravaganti. Un fantasma." *Gazzetta del Popolo* (24 December 1905).

– "Il dramma e il cinematografo parlato." *La Nación*, Buenos Aires (7 July 1929).

– *Henry IV*. In *Naked Masks: Five Plays*, translated by Eric Bentley. New York: Meridian, 1990.

– *On Humor*, translated by Antonio Illiano and Daniel P. Testa. Chapel Hill: University of North Carolina Press, 1974.

– *The Late Mattia Pascal*, translated by William Weaver. New York: NYRB, 2007.

– *Maschere nude*. 2 vols., edited by Manlio Lo Vecchio-Musti. Milan: Mondadori, 1958.

– *One, No One, and One Hundred Thousand*, translated by William Weaver. Sacramento: SPURL Editions, 2018.

– *Saggi, poesie, scritti varii*, edited by Manlio Lo Vecchio-Musti. Milan: Mondadori, 1960.

– *Shoot!: The Notebooks of Serafino Gubbio, Cinematograph Operator*, translated by Charles Kenneth Scott Moncrieff. Chicago: University of Chicago Press, 2005.

– *Six Characters in Search of an Author*. In *Naked Masks: Five Plays*, translated by Eric Bentley. New York: Meridian, 1990.

– "Will Talkies Abolish the Theater?," translated by Nina daVinci Nichols. In *Pirandello and Film*, edited by Nina daVinci Nichols and Jana O'Keefe Bazzoni, 195–202. Lincoln: University of Nebraska Press, 1995.

Pius X. *Pascendi Dominici Gregis*. The Holy See. (8 September 1907).

Plato. *Republic*, translated by G.M.A. Grube and C.D.C. Reeve. Indianapolis: Hackett, 1992.

– *Timaeus*, translated and edited by Peter Kalkavage. Indianapolis: Hackett, 2016.

Poggi, Christine. *In Defiance of Painting: Cubism, Futurism, and the Invention of the Collage*. New Haven: Yale University Press, 1992.

– *Inventing Futurism: The Art and Politics of Artificial Optimism*. Princeton: Princeton University Press, 2009.

Poggioli, Renato. *The Theory of the Avant-Garde*, translated by Gerald Fitzgerald. Cambridge, MA: Harvard University Press, 1968.

Pollard, Charles. *New World Modernisms: T.S. Eliot, Derek Walcott, and Kamau Brathwaite*. Charlottesville: University of Virginia Press, 2004.

Pollard, John F. *The Vatican and Italian Fascism, 1929–1932: A Study in Conflict*. Cambridge: Cambridge University Press, 1985.

Pomilio, Mario. *La formazione critico-estetica di Pirandello*. L'Aquila: M. Ferri, 1980.

Potolsky, Matthew. *The Decadent Republic of Letters: Taste, Politics, and Cosmopolitan Community from Baudelaire to Beardsley*. Philadelphia: University of Pennsylvania Press, 2013.

Prezzolini, Giuseppe. *Discorso su Giovanni Papini*. Firenze: Libreria della Voce, 1915.

Puchner, Martin. *The Drama of Ideas: Platonic Provocations in Theater and Philosophy*. Oxford: Oxford University Press, 2010.

Quaresima, Leonardo, and Laura Vichi, eds. *La decima musa: Il cinema e le altre arti/The Tenth Muse: Cinema and the Other Arts*. Proceedings of the Sixth DOMITOR Conference, Udine/Gemona del Friuli, 21–25 March 2000. Udine: Università degli Studi di Udine, 2001.

Rabaté, Jean-Michel. *James Joyce*. Paris: Hachette, 1993.

Rabiner, Emily. "Dannunzian Aesthetics and the Necrophilic Imagination in *Le vergini delle rocce*." *Forum Italicum* 51.2 (August 2017): 488–504.

Ragusa, Olga. *Luigi Pirandello: An Approach to his Theatre*. Edinburgh: Edinburgh University Press, 1980.

Raimondi, Ezio. *Un teatro delle idee: Ragione e immaginazione dal Rinascimento al Romanticismo*, edited by Davide Monda. Milan: Rizzoli, 2011.

Rainey, Lawrence. "F.T. Marinetti, Wyndham Lewis, and Tristan Tzara." In *The Cambridge Histry of Modernism*, edited by Vincent Sherry, 663–81. Cambridge: Cambridge University Press, 2016.

Rainey, Lawrence, Christine Poggi, and Laura Wittman, eds. *Futurism: An Anthology*. New Haven: Yale University Press, 2009.

Ram, Harsha. "Futurist Geographies: Uneven Modernities and the Struggle for Aesthetic Autonomy: Paris, Italy, Russia, 1909–1914." In *The Oxford Handbook of Global Modernisms*, edited by Mark Wollaeger and Marr Eatough, 3113–40. Oxford: Oxford University Press, 2012.

Ramazani, Jahan. *A Transnational Poetics*. Chicago: University of Chicago Press, 2009.

Ranciére, Jacques. *Aisthesis: Scenes from the Aesthetic Regime of Art*, translated by Zakir Paul. London and New York: Verso, 2013.

Re, Lucia. "D'Annunzio, Duse, Wilde, Bernhardt: Il rapporto autore/attrice fra decadentismo e modernità." *MLN* 117.1 (January 2002): 115–52.

– "Gabriele D'Annunzio's Theater of Memory: Il Vittoriale degli Italiani / Il teatro della memoria di Gabriele D'Annunzio: Il Vittoriale degli Italiani." *Journal of Decorative and Propaganda Arts* 3 (Winter 1987): 6–51.

– "Italians and the Invention of Race: The Poetics and Politics of Difference in the Struggle over Libya, 1890–1913." *California Italian Studies* 1.1 (2010): 1–58.

– "Mater-Materia: Maternal Power and the Futurist Avant-Garde." In *The Great Mother: Women, Maternity, and Power in Art and Visual Culture, 1900–2015*, edited by Massimiliano Gioni, 48–73. Milan: Skira, 2015.

– "Women, Sexuality, Politics, and the Body in the Futurist Avant-Garde during the Great War." In *The Avant-garde Body in Spain and Italy*, edited by Maria Truglio and Nicolás Fernández-Medina, 174–209. New York: Routledge, 2016.

Recchia, Stefano, and Nadia Urbinati, "Introduction: Giuseppe Mazzini's International Political Thought." In *A Cosmopolitanism of Nations: Giuseppe Mazzini's Writings on Democracy, Nation Building, and International Relations*, edited by Stefano Recchia and Nadia Urbinati, translated by Stefano Recchia, 1–30. Princeton: Princeton University Press, 2009.

Reed, Christopher. *Bachelor Japanists: Japanese Aesthetics and Western Masculinities*. New York: Columbia University Press, 2017.

Rekret, Paul. "A Critique of New Materialism: Ethics and Ontology." *Subjectivity* 9.3 (2016): 225–45.

Rendhell, Fulvio. *Magia spiritica: Lo Spiritismo alla luce della Scienza Magica. Esperienze, fenomeni, teoria e pratica*. Rome: Hermes Edizioni, 1997.

Rennie, Nicholas. *Speculating on the Moment: The Poetics of Time and Recurrence in Goethe, Leopardi, and Nietzsche*. Göttingen: Wallstein Verlag, 2005.

Richter, Mario. *Papini e Soffici: Mezzo secolo di vita italiana, 1903–1956*. Florence: Le lettere, 2005.

Riding, Laura, and Robert Graves. *A Survey of Modernist Poetry; and, a Pamphlet against Anthologies*, edited by Charles Mundye and Patrick McGuinness. Manchester: Carcanet, 2002.

Risé, Claudio. "Julius Evola, o la vittoria della Rivolta." In *Rivolta contro il mondo moderno* by Julius Evola, edited by Gianfranco de Turris, 17–22. Rome: Edizioni Mediterranee, 1998.

Ritter, Joachim. *Hegel und die französischen Revolution*. Frankfurt: Suhrkamp, 1965.

Rizi, Fabio Fernando. *Benedetto Croce and Italian Fascism*. Toronto: University of Toronto Press, 2003.

Robbins, Bruce, and Paulo Lemos Horta. "Introduction." In *Cosmopolitanisms*, edited by Bruce Robbins and Paulo Lemos Horta, 1–20. New York: NYU Press, 2017.

Rockmore, Tom. *Before and After Hegel: A Historical Introduction to Hegel's Thought*. Berkeley: University of California Press, 1993.

Romer, Stephen. "Introduction." In *French Decadent Tales*, edited and translated by Stephen Romer. Oxford: Oxford University Press, 2013.

Rosada, Bruno. "Il contingentismo di Montale." *Studi Novecenteschi* 10:25–6 (June–December 1983): 5–56.

Rosengarten, Frank. *Giacomo Leopardi's Search for a Common Life through Poetry: A Different Nobility, A Different Love*. Teaneck: Fairleigh Dickinson University Press, 2012.

Ross, Stephen, and Allana C. Lindgren, eds. *The Modernist World*. New York: Routledge, 2015.

Rubini, Rocco. *The Other Renaissance: Italian Humanism between Hegel and Heidegger*. Chicago: University of Chicago Press, 2014.

– "(Re-)Experiencing the Renaissance: Introduction." In *The Renaissance from an Italian Perspective*, edited by Rocco Rubini, 7–20. Ravenna: Longo, 2014.

Ryan, Christopher. "Schopenhauer on Idealism, Indian and European." *Philosophy East and West* 65.1 (January 2015): 18–35.

Ryōsuke, Ōhashi, and Akitomi Katsuya. "The Kyoto School: Transformations over Three Generations," translated by Bret W. Davis. In *The Oxford Handbook of Japanese Philosophy*, edited by Bret W. Davis, 367–87. Oxford: Oxford University Press, 2020.

Sagan, Carl. *The Demon-Haunted World: Science as a Candle in the Dark*. New York: Random House, 1996.

Saint-Simon, Henri de. *Opinions littéraires, philosophiques et industrielles*. Paris: Galerie de Bossange Père, 1825. Online: HathiTrust.

Saler, Michael, ed. *The Avant-Garde in Interwar England: "Medieval Modernism" and the London Underground*. Oxford: Oxford University Press, 1999.

– *The Fin-De-Siècle World*. London and New York: Routledge, 2015.

Salierno, Vito. *Nino Daniele: Un "legionario" comunista con d'Annunzio a Fiume*. Lanciano: Carabba, 2013.

Salinari, Carlo. *Miti e coscienza del decadentismo italiano: D'Annunzio, Pascoli, Fogazzaro e Pirandello*. Milan: Feltrinelli, 1960.

Santi, Mara. "Ineptitude as Cultural Senility in Italo Svevo's Second Novel." In *Italo Svevo and His Legacy for the Third Millennium*, vol. 1: *Philology and Interpretation*, edited by Giuseppe Stellardi and Emanuela Tandello Cooper, 62–73. Leicester: Troubador, 2014.

Saponaro, Dina and Lucia Torsello, eds. *La biblioteca di Luigi Pirandello: Catologo alfabetico per autore*. http://www.studiodiluigipirandello.it/wp-content/uploads/2017/04/biblioteca_pirandello.pdf.

Sarti, Lisa, and Michael Subialka, eds. *Pirandello and Translation*. *PSA*, 31, Special Issue (2018).

– *Pirandello's Visual Philosophy: Imagination and Thought across Media*. Teaneck: Fairleigh Dickinson University Press, 2017.

Scappettone, Jennifer. *Killing the Moonlight: Modernism in Venice*. New York: Columbia University Press, 2016.

Schelling, Friedrich Wilhelm Joseph. *Ideas for a Philosophy of Nature*, translated by Errol E. Harris and Peter Heath. Cambridge: Cambridge University Press, 1988.

Schiermeier, Kris. "Imitation or Innovation? Van Gogh's Japonaiserie and Japanese Art of the Meiji Period." In Gregory Irvine, *Japonisme and the Rise of the Modern Art Movement: The Arts of the Meiji Period. The Khalili Collection*, 140–65. New York: Thames and Hudson, 2013.

Schneider, Jane, ed. *Italy's Southern Question: Orientalism in One Country*. Oxford and New York: Berg, 1998.

Schopenhauer, Arthur. *Parerga and Paralipomena*. 2 vols., translated by E.F.J. Payne. Oxford: Oxford University Press, 1974.

– *Parerga und Paralipomena: Kleine philosophische Schriften*. 2 vols., edited by Julius Frauenstädt. Leipzig: F.A. Brockhaus, 1878. Online: HathiTrust.

– *Schopenhauer-Briefe, Sammlung meist ungedruckter oder schwer zugänglicher Briefe von an und über Schopenhauer*, edited by Ludwig Schemann. Leipzig: Brockhaus, 1893.

– *Studies in Pessimism*, translated and edited by T. Bailey Saunders. London: Swan Sonnenschein & Co., 1891.

– *Die Welt als Wille und Vorstellung*. 2 vols., edited by Julius Frauenstädt. Leipzig: F.A. Brockhaus, 1873. Online. HathiTrust.

– *Werke*, edited by Moritz Brasch. Leipzig: G. Fock, 1891.

– *On the Will in Nature: A Discussion of the Corroborations from the Empirical Sciences that the Author's Philosophy Has Received Since Its First Appearance*, translated by E.F.J. Payne,edited by David E. Cartwright. New York and Oxford: Berg, 1992.

– *The World as Will and Representation*, vol. 1., translated and edited by Judith Norman, Alistair Welchman, and Christopher Janaway. Cambridge: Cambridge University Press, 2011.

– *The World as Will and Representation*. 2 vols., translated by E.F.J. Payne. New York: Dover, 1968.

Schwartz, Sanford. "Eliot's Ghosts: Tradition and Its Transformations." In *A Companion to T.S. Eliot*, edited by David E. Chinitz, 15–26. London: Blackwell, 2009.

Schweinitz, Jörg. "Shared Affinities and 'Kunstwollen': Stylistics of the Cinematic Image in the 1910s and Art Theory at the Turn of the Century in Germany." In *The Image in Early Cinema: Form and Material*, edited by Scott Curtis, Philippe Gauthier, Tom Gunning, and Joshua Yumibe, 153–63. Indianapolis: Indiana University Press, 2018.

Seddio, Pietro. *Le donne di Pirandello: Mondo femminile e teatro.* Acireale-Roma: Bonanno, 2008.

Segala, Marco. "Sulle traduzioni italiane di Schopenhauer." In Fabio Ciracì and Domenico M. Fazio, eds., *Schopenhauer in Italia: Atti del I Convegno Nazionale della Sezione Italiana della Schopenhauer-Gesellschaft, San Pietro Vernotico-Lecce, 20 E 21 Giugno 2013*, 157–73. Lecce: Pensa multimedia, 2013.

Settembrini, Luigi. *I neoplatonici.* Ed. Raffaelle Cantarella. Milan: Rizzoli, 1977.

– *Ricordanze della mia vita.* Preface by Francesco De Sanctis. 2 vols. 2nd ed. Naples: Antonio Morano, 1879–80.

Shakespeare, William. *As You Like It*, edited by Juliet Dusinberre. 3rd ed. London: Bloomsbury Arden Shakespeare, 2006.

– *The Tempest*, edited by Virginia Mason Vaughan and Alden T. Vaughan. London: Bloomsbury Arden Shakespeare, 2011.

Shapshay, Sandra. "Poetic Intuition and the Bounds of Sense: Metaphor and Metonymy in Schopenhauer's Philosophy." *European Journal of Philosophy* 16.2 (2008): 211–29.

Sherry, Vincent. "Introduction: A History of 'Modernism.'" In *The Cambridge History of Modernism*, edited by Vincent Sherry, 1–25. Cambridge: Cambridge University Press, 2016.

– *Modernism and the Reinvention of Decadence.* Cambridge: Cambridge University Press, 2014.

Shimoi, Harukichi. *La guerra italiana.* Naples: Libreria della Diana, 1919.

Sica, Beatrice. "Time and Space in the Writings of Marinetti, Palazzeschi, the Group of *L'Italia futurista*, and Other Futurist Writers." In *The History of Futurism: The Precursors, Protagonists, and Legacies*, edited by Geert Buelens, Harald Hendrix, and Monica Jansen, 155–78. Lanham: Lexington Books, 2012.

Simek, Nicole. "Baudelaire and the Problematic of the Reader in *Les fleurs du mal*." *Pacific Coast Philology* 37 (2002): 43–57.

Sinnett, A.P. *The Mahatma Letters to A.P. Sinnett from the Mahatmas M. & K.H.*, edited by A. Trevor Barker. Facsimile ed. Pasadena: Theosophical University Press, 1992.

Smith, Stan. "Proper Frontiers: Transgression and the Individual Talent." In *T.S. Eliot and the Concept of Tradition*, edited by Giovanni Cianci and Jason Harding, 26–40. Cambridge: Cambridge University Press, 2007.

Smith, Steven. "Hegel and the French Revolution: An Epitaph for Republicanism." *Social Research* 56.1 (Spring 1989): 233–61.

Snyder, Louis. *Roots of German Nationalism.* Bloomington: Indiana University Press, 1978.

Soldateschi, Jole. *Il tragico quotidiano: Papini, Palazzeschi, Cassola, Bianciardi.* Florence: M. Pagliai, 2010.

Somigli, Luca. "Italy." In *The Cambridge Companion to European Modernism*, edited by Pericles Lewis, 75–93. Cambridge: Cambridge University Press, 2011.

Somigli, Luca, and Mario Moroni. "Introduction." In *Italian Modernism: Italian Culture between Decadentism and Avant-Garde*, 3–33. Toronto: University of Toronto Press, 2004.

Somigli, Luca, and Mario Moroni, eds. *Italian Modernism: Italian Culture between Decadentism and Avant-Garde*. Toronto: University of Toronto Press, 2004.

Spackman, Barbara. *Decadent Genealogies: The Rhetoric of Sickness from Baudelaire to D'Annunzio*. Ithaca: Cornell University Press, 1989.

– "Mafarka and Son: Marinetti's Homophobic Economics." *Modernism/Modernity* 1.3 (1994): 89–107.

Spaventa, Bertrando. "Italian Philosophy in Relation to European Philosophy," translated by Michael Subialka. In *The Renaissance from an Italian Perspective: An Anthology of Essays 1860–1968*, edited by Rocco Rubini, 45–110. Ravenna: Longo, 2014.

– *Opere*, edited by Giovanni Gentile, with I. Cubeddu and S. Giannantoni. 3 vols. Florence: Sansoni, 1972.

– "Studii sulla filosofia di Hegel." *Rivista italiano*, 1850. Republished in *Unificazione nazionale ed egemonia culturale*, edited by G. Vacca. Bari: Laterza, 1967.

– *Unificazione nazionale ed egemonia culturale*, edited by G. Vacca. Bari: Laterza, 1967.

Spaventa, Silvio. *Dal 1848 al 1861: Lettere, scritti, documenti*, edited by Benedetto Croce. Naples: Libreria Editrice Italiana, 1898. Online: HathiTrust.

Spinoza, Baruch. *Ethics*. In *The Collected Writings of Spinoza*, vol. 1, translated by Edwin Curley. Princeton: Princeton University Press, 1985.

Steiner, George. *Nostalgia for the Absolute*. Toronto: House of Anansi Press, 1974.

Steiner, Rudolf. *Spiritualism, Madame Blavatsky, and Theosophy: An Eyewitness View of Occult History*, edited by Christopher Bamford. Great Barrington: Anthroposophic Press, 2001.

Steinfield, Thomas. Review of "*Modernism and Magic: Experiments with Spiritualism, Theosophy and the Occult*, by Leigh Wilson." *Modernism/Modernity* 21.1 (January 2014): 382–5.

Stella, Vittorio. *Forma e memoria: Croce, Venturi, Pirandello, Borgese*. Roma: Ianua, 1985.

Stern, Fritz Richard. *The Politics of Cultural Despair: A Study in the Rise of the Germanic Ideology*. Berkeley: University of California Press, 1961.

Stewart-Steinberg, Suzanne. *The Pinocchio Effect: On Making Italians, 1860–1920*. Chicago: University of Chicago Press, 2007.

Stocchi-Perucchio, Donatella. *Pirandello and the Vagaries of Knowledge: A Reading of* Il fu Mattia Pascal. Saratoga: ANMA Libri, 1991.

"Studies in Pessimism." Review in *The Spectator*, 14 February 1891, 251.

Subialka, Michael. *The Aesthetics of Ambivalence: Pirandello, Schopenhauer, and the Transformation of the European Social Imaginary*. PhD diss., University of Chicago, 2012.

–"The Meaning of Acting in the Age of Cinema: Benjamin, Pirandello, and the Italian Diva from Stage to Screen." *Comparative Literature* 68.3 (Fall 2016): 312–31.

–"Modernism at War: Pirandello and the Crisis of (German) Cultural Identity." *Annali d'Italianistica* 34 (2015): 75–97.

– "The Seduction of Innocence: Erotic Aesthetics from Kierkegaard to Decadentism." In *Innocence Uncovered: Literary and Theological Perspectives*, edited by Beth Dodd and Carl E. Findley, 58–75. London and New York: Routledge, 2017.

–"Transforming Plato: Tommaso Campanella's *La città del sole*, the *Republic*, and Socrates as Natural Philosopher." *Bruniana & Campanelliana* 17.2 (2011): 417–34.

Surette, Leon. *The Birth of Modernism: Ezra Poud, T.S. Eliot, W.B. Yeats, and the Occult*. Montreal and Kingston: McGill–Queen's University Press, 1993.

Svevo, Italo. *Zeno's Conscience*, translated by William Weaver. New York: Penguin, 2001.

Syrimis, Michael. *The Great Black Spider on Its Knock-Kneed Tripod: Reflections of Cinema in Early Twentieth-Century Italy*. Toronto: University of Toronto Press, 2012.

Takashi, Iida. "How Western Philosophy Was Received in Japan Compared to Western Music." *Tetsugaku* 1 (2017): 24–42.

Talar, C.J.T., ed. *Modernists and Mystics*. Washington, D.C.: Catholic University of America Press, 2009.

Tansman, Alan. *The Aesthetics of Japanese Fascism*. Berkeley: University of California Press, 2009.

Taylor, Charles. *Hegel*. Cambridge: Cambridge University Press, 1975.

– *Modern Social Imaginaries*. Durham: Duke University Press, 2004.

– *A Secular Age*. Cambridge, MA: Harvard University Press, 2007.

– *Sources of the Self: The Making of the Modern Identity*. Cambridge: Cambridge University Press, 1992.

Terrile, Cristina. "La parola all'ombra dell'idea. Narrazione e sentimento nell'opera di Svevo." In *Italo Svevo and His Legacy for the Third Millennium*, vol. 1: *Philology and Interpretation*, edited by Giuseppe Stellardi and Emanuela Tandello Cooper, 31–47. Leicester: Troubador, 2014.

Tessari, Roberto. *Pascoli, D'Annunzio, Fogazzaro e il decadentismo italiano: Irrazionalismo e crisi dell'ideologia borghese tra '800 e '900*. Turin: Paravia, 1976.

Thurschwell, Pamela. *Literature, Technology and Magical Thinking, 1880–1920.* Cambridge: Cambridge University Press, 2001.

Tilgher, Adriano. *La scena e la vita: Nuovi studi sul teatro contemporaneo.* Rome: Libreria di Scienze e Lettere, 1925.

– *Studi sul teatro contemporaneo, preceduti da un saggio su L'arte come originalità e i problemi dell'arte. 3ª edizione aggiornata e accresciuta* [1922], 3rd ed. Rome: Libreria di Scienze e Lettere, 1928.

Tommasello, Dario. "*La Balza futurista* e le avanguardie in Sicilia tra liberty e paroliberismo." *Rivista di letteratura italiana* 23.1–2, vol. 2 (2005): 235–40.

Tortora, Massimiliano. "Verifica dei valori: Pirandello nel canone del modernismo europeo." In *Pirandello oggi: Intertestualità, riscrittura, ricezione,* edited by Anna Frabetti, 267–86. Pesaro: Metauro, 2017.

Toulmin, Stephen. *Cosmopolis: The Hidden Agenda of Modernity.* Chicago: University of Chicago Press, 1990.

Tratner, Michael. *Modernism and Mass Politics: Joyce, Woolf, Eliot, Yeats.* Stanford: Stanford University Press, 1995.

Tromp, Marlene. *Altered States: Sex, Nation, Drugs, and Self-Transformation in Victorian Spiritualism.* Albany: SUNY Press, 2006.

Turconi, Davide, and Camillo Bassotto, eds. *Il cinema nelle riviste italiane dalle origini ad oggi.* Venice: Edizioni Mostracinema, 1973.

Turoff, Barbara. "Il Giappone di Gabriele D'Annunzio: dall'estetismo al militarismo." *Rivista di Studi Italiani* 22.2 (2005): 35–57.

Turvey, Malcolm. *Doubting Vision: Film and the Revelationist Tradition.* Oxford: Oxford University Press, 2008.

Ullyot, Jonathan. *The Medieval Presence in Modernist Literature: The Quest to Fail.* Cambridge: Cambridge University Press, 2015.

Valentin, Albert. "Introduction to Black-and-White Magic." In *The Shadow and Its Shadow: Surrealist Writings on the Cinema,* edited, translated, and introduced by Paul Hammond, 3rd ed., 95–8. San Francisco: City Lights Books, 2000.

Van Gogh and Japan. Van Gogh Museum, Amsterdam; Hokkaidō Shimbun Press, Sapporo; Mercatorfonds, Brussels; Yale University Press, 2018.

Vandenabeele, Bart. "Schopenhauer on Sense Perception and Aesthetic Cognition." *Journal of Aesthetic Education* 45.1 (Spring 2011): 37–57.

Vasalou, Sophia. *Schopenhauer and the Aesthetic Standpoint: Philosophy as a Practice of the Sublime.* Cambridge: Cambridge University Press, 2013.

Vena, Michael. "Introduction." In *Italian Grotesque Theater,* translated by Michael Vena. Teaneck: Fairleigh Dickinson University Press, 2001.

Venuti, Lawrence. *The Translator's Invisibility: A History of Translation,* 2nd ed. London and New York: Routledge, 2008.

Verdicchio, Massimo. "Introduction." In *A Croce Reader: Aesthetics, Philosophy, History, and Literary Criticism,* edited and translated by Massimo Verdicchio, ix–xlvi. Toronto: University of Toronto Press, 2017.

Verdone, Mario. "L'amicizia con Arnaldo Ginna." In *Armonie e disarmonie degli stati d'animo: Ginna futurista* by Arnaldo Ginna, edited by Lucia Collarile, Micol Forti, and Mariastella Margozzi, 13–14. Rome: Gangemi, 2009.

– "Nascita della cinepittura." In *La decima musa: Il cinema e le altre arti/The Tenth Muse: Cinema and Other Arts*, edited by Leonardo Quaresima and Laura Vichi, 385–8. Udine: Forum, 2000.

Verdone, Mario, and Günter Berghaus. "*Vita futurista* and Early Futurist Cinema." In *International Futurism in Arts and Literature*, edited by Günter Berghaus, 398–421. Berlin and New York: Walter de Gruyter, 2000.

Vettore, Enrico. "Approximation to Nirvana: From Intellectual Speculation to Zen Non-Philosophy in Pirandello's *Uno nessuno e centomila*." *PSA* 29 (2016): 13–29.

Virkar-Yates, Aakanksha. "Absolute Music and the Death of Desire: Beethoven, Schopenhauer, Wagner, and Eliot's *Four Quartets*." *Journal of Modern Literature* 40.2 (2017): 79–93.

– "*Erhebung*, Schopenhauer, and T.S. Eliot's Burnt Norton." *Notes and Queries* 61.1 (March 2014): 126–7.

Vogel-Walter, Bettina. *D'Annunzio – Abenteurer und charismatischer Führer: Propaganda und religiöser Nationalismus in Italien von 1914 bis 1921*. Frankfurt: Peter Lang, 2004.

Voltaire. *Candide and Other Stories*, translated by Roger Pearson. Oxford: Oxford University Press, 2006.

Wagner, Karl, ed. *Briefe an Johann Heinrich Merck von Goethe, Herder, Wieland und andern bedeutenden Zeitgenossen. Mit Mercks biographischer Skizze*. Darmstadt: J.P. Diehl, 1835. Online. HathiTrust.

Wagner, Peter. *Progress: A Reconstruction*. Cambridge: Polity Press, 2016.

Walker, D.P. *Spiritual and Demonic Magic: From Ficino to Campanella*. University Park: Pennsylvania State University Press, 2000.

Warner, Marina. *Phantasmagoria: Spirit Visions, Metaphors, and Media into the Twenty-First Century*. Oxford: Oxford University Press, 2006.

Weber, Max. *The Vocation Lectures: "Science as a Vocation" and "Politics as a Vocation,"* edited by David Owen and Tracy B. Strong, translated by Rodney Livingstone. Indianapolis: Hackett, 2004.

Weir, David. *Decadence and the Making of Modernism*. Amherst: University of Massachusetts Press, 1995.

Weisberg, Barbara. *Talking to the Dead: Kate and Maggie Fox and the Rise of Spiritualism*. New York: HarperCollins, 2004.

Welch, Rhiannon Noel. *Vital Subjects: Race and Biopolitics in Italy, 1860–1920*. Liverpool: Liverpool University Press, 2016.

Wellbery, David. "Emancipation from the Will." In *Debates in Nineteenth-Century European Philosophy: Essential Readings and Contemporary Responses*, edited by Kristin Gjesdal, 148–56. New York: Routledge, 2016.

– "Schopenhauer." *The Routledge Companion to Nineteenth Century Philosophy*, edited by Dean Moyar, 327–46. New York: Routledge, 2010.

– *Schopenhauers Bedeutung für die moderne Literatur*. Munich: Siemens Stiftung, 1998.

Welle, John. "The Alcove of Celebrity: Notes on Marinetti and Commercial Literature." *L'Anello che non tiene* 22 (Spring–Fall 2010): 97–106.

– "The Beginnings of Film Stardom and the Print Media of Divismo." In *The Italian Cinema Book*, edited by Peter Bondanella, 17–23. London: British Film Institute, 2014.

– "Early Cinema, *Dante's Inferno* of 1911, and the Origins of Italian Film Culture." In *Dante, Cinema, and Television*, edited by Amilcare A. Iannucci, 21–50. Toronto: University of Toronto Press, 2004.

West, Rebecca. "Diventare un aggettivo. La modulazione dell'autorità femminile nella poesia italiana del Novecento delle donne e sulle donne." In *Verso una storia di genere della letteratura italiana. Percorsi critici e gender studies*, edited by Virginia Cox and Chiara Ferrari, 243–65. Bologna: Il Mulino, 2011.

– *Montale: Poet on the Edge*. Cambridge, MA: Harvard University Press, 1981.

Wiegand, Daniel. "The Unsettling of Vision: Tableaux Vivants, Early Cinema, and Optical Illusions." In *The Image in Early Cinema: Form and Material*, edited by Scott Curtis, Philippe Gauthier, Tom Gunning, and Joshua Yumibe, 26–35. Indianapolis: Indiana University Press, 2018.

Wilde, Oscar. *The Picture of Dorian Gray*, edited by Joseph Bristow. Oxford: Oxford University Press, 2006.

Wildt, Andreas. "Hegels Kritik des Jakobinismus." In *Aktualität und Folgen der Philosophie Hegels*, edited by Oskar Negt. Frankfurt: Suhrkamp, 1971.

Williams, Alan. *Republic of Images: A History of French Filmmaking*. Cambridge, MA: Harvard University Press, 1992.

Wilson, Leigh. *Modernism and Magic: Experiments with Spiritualism, Theosophy, and the Occult*. Edinburgh: Edinburgh University Press, 2013.

Witt, Mary Ann Frese. *The Search for Modern Tragedy: Aesthetic Fascism in Italy and France*. Ithaca: Cornell University Press, 2001.

Wittgenstein, Ludwig. *Tractatus Logico-Philosophicus*, translated by D.F. Pears and B.F. McGuiness. London: Routledge, 1961.

Wittman, Laura. "*Omnes velut aqua dilabimur*: Antonio Fogazzaro, *The Saint*, and Catholic Modernism." In *Italian Modernism: Italian Culture between Decadentism and Avant-Garde*, edited by Luca Somigli and Mario Moroni, 130–66. Toronto: University of Toronto Press, 2004.

– *The Tomb of the Unknown Soldier, Modern Mourning, and the Reinvention of the Mystical Body*. Toronto: University of Toronto Press, 2011.

Wollaeger, Mark. "Introduction." In *The Oxford Handbook of Global Modernisms*, edited by Mark Wollaeger and Matt Eatough, 3–18. Oxford: Oxford University Press, 2012.

Wood, Jessica. "The Art of Dying in *Trionfo della morte.*" *Forum Italicum* 51.2 (August 2017): 469–87.

Woodhouse, John. *Gabriele D'Annunzio: Defiant Archangel*. Oxford: Oxford University Press, 1998.

Woolf, Virginia. *Moments of Being*, edited by Hermione Lee and Jeanne Schulkind. London: Pimlico, 2002.

– *A Writer's Diary*, edited by Leonard Woolf. New York and London: Harcourt, 1982.

Wu, Chingshin. "Transcending the Boundaries of the 'isms': Pursuing Modernity through the Machine in 1920s and 1930s Japanese Avant-Garde Art." In *Rethinking Japanese Modernism*, edited by Roy Starrs, 339–61. Leiden: Brill, 2012.

Young, Julian. "Death and Transfiguration: Kant, Schopenhauer, and Heidegger on the Sublime." *Inquiry* 48.2 (2005): 131–44.

– "Schopenhauer, Nietzsche, Death, and Salvation." *European Journal of Philosophy* 16.2 (2008): 311–24.

Yourcenar, Marguerite. *Mishima: A Vision of the Void*, translated by Alberto Manguel. Chicago: University of Chicago Press, 2001.

Zarlenga, Achille, and Giulio Lucchetta, eds. *L'Anima: saggi e giudizi, 1911*. Lanciano: Rocco Carabba, 2017.

Ziolkowski, Saskia Elizabeth. *Kafka's Italian Progeny*. Toronto: University of Toronto Press, 2020.

Zöller, Günter. "Schopenhauer on the Self." In *The Cambridge Companion to Schopenhauer*, edited by Christopher Janaway, 18–43. Cambridge: Cambridge University Press, 1999.

Zumbini, Bonaventura. *Studi sul Leopardi*, vols. 1–2, 2nd ed. Florence: G. Barbèra, 1909.

Index

Page numbers in *italics* refer to figures.

www.ingramcontent.com/pod-product-compliance
Lightning Source LLC
LaVergne TN
LVHW090146080826
844660LV00013B/697/J